David Baker

A LEGACY IN MUSIC

David Baker

MONIKA HERZIG

With contributions by
NATHAN DAVIS, JB DYAS,
JOHN EDWARD HASSE,
WILLARD JENKINS, LISSA MAY,
BRENT WALLARAB, and
DAVID WARD-STEINMAN

Foreword by QUINCY JONES

INDIANA UNIVERSITY PRESS   Bloomington & Indianapolis

This book is a publication of

INDIANA UNIVERSITY PRESS
601 North Morton Street
Bloomington, IN 47404-3797 USA

iupress.indiana.edu

Telephone orders 800-842-6796
Fax orders 812-855-7931

*Manufactured in the
United States of America*

Library of Congress
Cataloging-in-Publication Data

Herzig, Monika, [date]
  David Baker : a legacy in music /
Monika Herzig, with contributions
by Nathan Davis ... [et al.] ;
foreword by Quincy Jones.
    p. cm.
  Includes bibliographical
references and index.
  ISBN 978-0-253-35657-4 (cloth : alk.
paper) – ISBN 978-0-253-00524-3
(e-book) 1. Baker, David, 1931–
2. Composers – United
States – Biography. 3. Jazz
musicians – United States – Biography.
I. Davis, Nathan, 1973– II. Title.
  ML410.B17426K47 2011
  781.65092 – DC23
  [B]
                                  2011023574

1 2 3 4 5   16 15 14 13 12 11

To David Baker, composer, teacher, performer, conductor, leader, mentor, and friend – whose work, leadership, and friendship have touched generations of musicians and audiences around the globe.

From that first meeting I had a reaction, which I think is a pretty common reaction, that this is just a great guy, a great human being, a great musician, a great music teacher, and a great soul.

Dana Gioia, former chairman of the National Endowment for the Arts, about his work with David Baker

Contents

·   FOREWORD   *Quincy Jones*   xiii

·   PREFACE   xv

·   ACKNOWLEDGMENTS   xix

1   Indiana Avenue and Crispus Attucks High School
    Lissa May   1

2   A Star Is Born   *Monika Herzig*   16

3   New Beginnings   *Monika Herzig & Nathan Davis*   46

4   Defining Jazz Education   *JB Dyas*   65

·   ILLUSTRATIONS   121

5   21st Century Bebop   *Monika Herzig & Brent Wallarab*   139

6   The Composer   *David Ward-Steinman*   173

7   David Baker and the Smithsonian: A Personal Perspective
    John Edward Hasse   230

8   Social Engagement   *Willard Jenkins*   288

9   Coda   *Monika Herzig*   303

· APPENDIXES 327

· BIBLIOGRAPHY OF WRITTEN WORKS
BY DAVID BAKER 371

· DISCOGRAPHY 381

· SELECTED LIST OF BOOKS, ARTICLES, AND OTHER
PUBLICATIONS ABOUT DAVID BAKER 395

· ABOUT THE CONTRIBUTORS 398

· CD TRACK LISTING 401

· INDEX 403

Foreword

David and I were both born less than eighteen months apart during America's Great Depression – David in Indianapolis, and myself less than two hundred miles away on the South Side of Chicago. We both fell in love with music at an early age, and decided to make it our lives. For more than fifty years now I have considered David my brother, and to say that we have a connection is an understatement.

In 1960, I invited him to join my big band for a tour of Europe. We were both still in our twenties, and David could really play. But beside being a trombonist, he could also write. Nadia Boulanger, my foremost music teacher, told me that your music can never be any more or less than you are as a human being and that it takes a special kind of person to write good music. Well, David had it, and his tune "Screamin' Mee-mies" was part of our nightly repertoire. The reviews of our tour in the Swiss newspapers noted our impromptu jam sessions during the train rides and never failed to point out our inadequate skiing skills. We have been in close touch ever since and have collaborated on many projects.

As my success grew scoring films, arranging, and producing, I tempted David to come and join me in Hollywood. But his dedication to teaching, and to the program he built at Indiana University, was stronger than the promise of riches and fame. I'm sure there have been many similar temptations over the years – promising more financial rewards, more artistic freedom, more public visibility – but he always chose his teaching and his students as his principal calling. In a society that most commonly rewards glamorous careers with a focus on highly visible personalities, the choice to dedicate one's life to helping others achieve their aspirations is a mark of a truly selfless and kind person.

Just recently, I invited him to help me develop a national music curriculum as part of the Quincy Jones Musiq Consortium. Once again, I have been witnessing David's selfless dedication to sharing his music and to education.

David, never forget – as George Burns used to point out – that when you get "over the hill" that's when you really start to pick up some speed! Happy eightieth birthday, my brother! I could not be more excited to endorse this wonderful and long overdue tribute to your life and work. I love you, my brother.

Quincy Jones

November 2010

Preface

In August 1991, my soon-to-be-husband Peter Kienle and I arrived in Bloomington, Indiana, with my letter of admission to the doctoral program in Music Education and a mutual determination to pursue our careers as jazz musicians. After I had completed a master's degree at the University of Alabama in May 1991, we decided to keep learning as much as possible about the music that had captured our attention and led us to move to the country where jazz was born. The decision to apply for doctoral studies in music at Indiana University was guided by David Baker's reputation as a musician and jazz educator. Growing up in the small town of Albstadt, in southern Germany, we used David Baker's publications as learning tools; in the early 1980s, we even had the opportunity to participate in a series of Jamey Aebersold Summer Jazz Workshops that were held just thirty minutes away from our hometown. The ABCs of jazz education – Jamey Aebersold, David Baker, and Jerry Coker – brought along a host of stellar artists for a week of jazz education and concerts. During my first weeks at Indiana University, it became clear to me that many of my fellow students had similar experiences and decided to come to Bloomington to study with the man whose work and pedagogy had touched them in their remote locations around the world. Furthermore, we also realized that the same level of energy, quality, and enthusiasm that David Baker shared with us in ensemble, improvisation, arranging, composition, pedagogy, and history classes was expected from us in return. Every class was extremely demanding, and quite often students ended up taking classes multiple times before completing all coursework; some even changed career paths. I remember many hours of desperately trying to live up to such high expectations, but also the gratifying feeling of mastering skills and materials that once seemed beyond reach. The jazz students at Indiana University form a culturally diverse, highly motivated, and accomplished community – one which not only excels thanks to the quality of instruction they receive as well as inspiration from their teachers and peers, but which continues to share their skills and pedagogical insights around the globe.

When I travel around the world as a performer, I am constantly reminded of David Baker's legacy as I meet former students, students of his students, students of his books, admirers of his music and work, and even second- and third-generation students whose parents and grandparents have been influenced and inspired by Baker's work. During recording sessions for *Imagine: Indiana in Music and Words,* as David Baker read a tribute poem to the Hampton family, I mentioned my observations to Norbert Krapf, former Indiana poet laureate, and he inquired whether anyone was documenting Baker's work. I replied that I assumed surely such a work was in progress. Later I mentioned Norbert's inquiry to David and he replied that this is a common assumption, but no one had actually taken on the task of writing such a book. As a jazz performer and composer, his former student, and now his colleague at Indiana University – and with my husband Peter as his music copyist – I saw an opportunity to pay tribute to one of the most influential figures in the jazz community and to express my gratitude for the gracious mentorship that shaped my career. It also became very clear that such a project needed collaborators and experts in different areas, owing to the breadth and depth of David's work. This is not a biography but an analysis of and testament to the work of one of our most prolific composers – a stellar musician, pioneering educator, effective activist, and selfless person.

The first chapter chronicles the special circumstances of the Indiana Avenue district of Indianapolis, which produced a host of legendary jazz musicians. Lissa May is a music educator who herself grew up in Indianapolis and who has done extensive research on Crispus Attucks High School, where David Baker and his peers got their early schooling. She is also a colleague at the Indiana University Jacobs School of Music. Chapter 2 is an account of Baker's early career as a trombonist and member of the George Russell Sextet. His virtuosity is showcased in "Sandu" performed with his group at the Topper in Indianapolis in 1959, which is released for the first time on the accompanying CD. The chapter also includes an analysis of one of his best-known jazz compositions, "Kentucky Oysters," and a transcription of his trombone solo as recorded on George Russell's Riverside release *Stratusphunk,* also included in this book's accompanying CD. The turning point in Baker's career is covered in chapter 3. A tragic accident triggers the end of his trombone career, but Baker takes the opportunity to focus on composition and development of his concept of jazz pedagogy. Nathan Davis recalls the early resistance to teaching jazz – from both the academy and the jazz community – and the trademarks of a master teacher. One of David's closest friends is JB Dyas, currently vice president of education for the Thelonious Monk Institute. His analysis of David's approach to pedagogy in chapter 4 is a thorough account of his demanding, yet nurturing method. Fellow arranger and Indiana University colleague Brent Wallarab chronicles David's trademarks as a jazz composer and arranger in chapter 5. The recording of "Dance of the Jitterbugs," as performed by the Buselli-Wallarab Jazz Orchestra, showcases this masterful composition and arrangement, which stretches the limits of traditional form and arranging techniques. Fellow composer David Ward-Steinman exemplifies the variety and characteristics of Baker's large body of work – often categorized as Third Stream owing to his modern combination of jazz and classical genres – in chapter 6. A variety of examples is included on the CD. John Hasse, curator of American Music at the Smithsonian Institution, provides a detailed history of the Smithsonian Jazz Masterworks Orchestra and Baker's contributions as musical director in chapter 7. (John and David have collaborated on a variety of preservation projects – most recently the newly revised *Jazz: The Smithsonian Anthology.*) As noted by Dana Gioia, former chairman of the National Endowment for the Arts, David Baker has played a crucial role as an advocate for jazz and black musicians. In chapter 8, fellow advocate and writer Willard Jenkins gives us insights on Baker's service as panelist for the National Endowment for the Arts, as co-founder of the National Jazz Service Organization, as former president of the International Association for Jazz Education, and more. Like a good musical composition, this book has a coda: a final recap (or rekaB) of the current state and future of jazz education as well as a variety of personal testimonials collected in interviews. David's wife, Lida, in particular, summarized her early impressions of him succinctly: "He is just a really nice guy."

The long and meticulous listings of Baker's work, compiled by Lida Baker, are proof of his immense creative drive and output. In addition, a series of radio programs created by David Brent Johnson, producer for Indiana University's public radio station WFIU, will be aired in fall 2011, and an interactive web forum linked to the WFIU website (indiana publicmedia.org/radio) will feature complete interview files for this project, additional music selections and educational materials, as well as a blog with news from the Indiana University Jazz Studies department, and more.

Completing this project has been immensely rewarding and a wonderful learning experience. My hope is that this book and the online forum ensure access to the work of this master teacher and master musician in even the remotest areas of the world, where it may inspire others' lives and careers as it has mine.

Acknowledgments

This book was the collaborative effort of many contributors, teachers, colleagues, and friends of David Baker. I'd like to consider myself a team leader rather than an author, and would like to express my deepest appreciation to all the team members.

This project was inspired by a suggestion from Norbert Krapf. The proposal stage was completed with the help of Gwyn Richards, Jane Behnken, and JB Dyas. Chapter contributions come from some of the closest friends and most prominent leaders in their respective fields. Many thanks to Nathan Davis, JB Dyas, John Hasse, Willard Jenkins, Lissa May, Brent Wallarab, and David Ward-Steinman for sharing their knowledge and expertise so generously. In addition, Quincy Jones's testimony to the friendship and respect that he has shared with David Baker for more than five decades sets the grateful tone expressed throughout this book by writers and interviewees. It was an honor to conduct interviews with a large number of Baker's friends, family members, and colleagues; and their willingness to share their knowledge and memories is much appreciated. The interviewees include Jamey Aebersold, April Baker, Jeannie Baker, Lida Baker, Jim Beard, Randy Brecker, Wayne Brown, Tillman Buggs, Mark Buselli, Gary Campbell, John Clayton, Jerry Coker, Nathan Davis, Reginald DuValle, Jr., Mari Evans, Edythe Fitzhugh, Luke Gillespie, Dana Gioia, Tom Gullion, Dan Haerle, Pat Harbison, John Hasse, Ken Kimery, Willis Kirk, David Lahm, Janet Lawson, James Moody, Shawn Pelton, Mary Jo Papich, Larry Ridley, Randy Salman, Duncan Schiedt, A. B. Spellman, Tom Walsh, and Joe Wilder. We were especially fortunate to capture the memories of Reginald DuValle, Jr. and James Moody before they passed on in 2010. May they rest in peace.

Photographs came from the collections of the Smithsonian Institution, Duncan Schiedt, Jamey Aebersold, and David Baker. Additional thanks go to John Abbott for allowing us to use his photo of the Living Jazz Legends in 2007 at the Kennedy Center, as well as the White House Photo Office for the 1998 photos with President and Mrs. Bill Clinton.

The accompanying CD has been edited and mastered under the supervision of Konrad Strauss, director of the Recording Arts program at Indiana University, with assistance by Wayne Jackson and Mark Hood. Several tracks have been previously released on a variety of recordings and are compiled here with the permission of Liscio Recordings, Albany Records, Laurel Records, Concord Music Group, Acme Records, and the Louisville Orchestra.

Additional thanks go to Michael Rushton, David Audretsch, Matthew Auer, Christina Kuzmych, and Randy Rogers for their letters of recommendations and networking in support of the project. Much appreciation goes to Jane Behnken, Sarah Swanson-Wyatt, and the staff at Indiana University Press. Their enthusiasm, patience, and coaching has reached far beyond any duties as publishers.

This project would not have been possible without the help of Lida Baker, who provided the listings of David's work, accomplishments, and honors that she meticulously assembled over many decades. In addition, she spent countless hours with me editing text; researching facts; pulling out recordings, photos, books, and articles from their extensive personal library; and reminiscing with David about their journey together. And of course, I owe immense gratitude to David Baker himself, who never complained about honoring another interview request or answering another telephone query, and who shared his precious time and memories so graciously.

My deepest gratitude goes to my husband, Peter Kienle, and my daughters, Jasmin and Melody Herzig, who came along on many interview trips and patiently took charge of home duties at other times. I also thank my mother, siblings, nieces, and nephews in Germany, who provided office space, nutrition, lodging, babysitting, and moral support throughout the writing process in summer 2010.

This project has been supported by grants from Indiana University and the National Endowment for the Arts, as well as generous financial contributions by David Pfenninger and Cleve Wilhoit.

David Baker

1

Indiana Avenue and Crispus Attucks High School

LISSA MAY

THE STORY OF DAVID Baker's life began in 1931 in Indianapolis, Indiana. At that time, nearly 45,000 African Americans lived in the city of approximately 365,000 people.[1] Neighborhoods, parks, businesses, and schools were segregated, yet African American children – for the most part – were insulated from the harsh political and racial tensions that marked the times. The eastside neighborhood of Baker's childhood was a close-knit community in which black children had little contact with white people. A sense of innocence prevailed, with little notion that there was any other way of life. It was a time of strong extended families and neighbors who shared the responsibility of raising children. There was a spirit of hope, optimism, and pride among African Americans, despite the racial indignities of everyday life. As in many communities across the United States in the 1930s and '40s, life revolved around the local business district, neighborhood schools, and churches.

Indiana Avenue was the business and social thoroughfare of the African American community in Indianapolis, and it offered a vast range of enterprises – from barber shops, beauty salons, and restaurants to bars, pool halls, and nightclubs. In 1927, the Madame Walker Theatre opened its doors and became a mecca for blacks who were not allowed in the same theaters as whites, or – if admitted – were forced to sit in the balcony. The theatre was the realization of a longtime dream of African American businesswoman Madame C. J. Walker, who built a fortune in the early 1900s marketing hair care and beauty products to African American women.[2] When she died in 1919, she was the wealthiest black woman in America. Sunday afternoons at "The Madame Walker" were legendary. The Walker Building was an elegant place where African Americans, dressed in their finest clothes, were treated like royalty. After a leisurely Sunday lunch, families often went upstairs to enjoy a movie in the beautiful theater with African-type décor, where patrons were not relegated to the balcony because of skin color.

Lining Indiana Avenue at any given time during the 1930s and '40s were fifteen to twenty clubs that featured jazz six nights a week. The Sunset Terrace and the Cotton Club often showcased artists of international renown such as Count Basie, Dizzy Gillespie, or Charlie Parker. After-hours clubs provided the opportunity for local musicians to meet after their regular playing engagements to listen to and play with one another. Perhaps the most famous of these was the Missile Room, where the Wes Montgomery Trio was the house band. The trio featured Wes Montgomery on guitar, Melvin Rhyne on organ, and Paul Parker on drums.[3] Indianapolis, which was a hub for car and train travel, was host to countless traveling musicians, many of whom ended their evenings at one of these clubs. Talented locals and visiting celebrities engaged in many a late-night battle at Henri's, where the sign over the door read, "Through these portals pass the world's finest musicians."[4]

The public schools in Indianapolis, like those in many large city school districts across America in the first half of the twentieth century, were very strong and provided children an excellent education. De facto segregation in Indianapolis assured that elementary schools were mostly segregated: however, before 1927 there was not a separate high school for blacks. Members of the Ku Klux Klan dominated the school board and police force in Indianapolis, as well as much of the Indiana state government. Under their leadership, support for a "separate but equal" high school for blacks grew. Despite strong opposition from black organizations such as the Indianapolis branch of the NAACP and the black press, the Indianapolis School Board voted to construct a separate high school for African Americans.[5] Just four years before David Baker's birth, the all-black Crispus Attucks High School opened its doors amidst considerable controversy. It soon became a cultural center and a source of great pride for the African American community. Indianapolis poet Mari Evans writes,

> The neighborhood was sustaining. Children were protected and insulated by classrooms manned by Black teachers who cared passionately about their charges' futures, who saw promise in them, loved them, chastised them promptly, and encouraged them to be more than even they envisioned. Those schools were places where Black children understood above all else they were loved, and being cared for with love.[6]

In the mid-1920s, prior to the opening of Crispus Attucks High School, approximately 800 black students were enrolled at three Indianapolis high schools: Shortridge, Emmerich Manual, and Arsenal Technical. Although Attucks had been designed to accommodate 1,000 students, more than 1,350 students arrived on opening day.[7] Influenced by the progressive education movement and a greater emphasis on secondary education, African American families increasingly valued formal education and personal intellectual development. Many black children who had earlier withdrawn from other high schools, as well as those who had not attended high school at all, enrolled at Attucks now that there was a high school where blacks were supported and embraced. Norman Merrifield, who graduated from Arsenal Technical High School in 1923, recalls that before Attucks opened, "Negro students were not encouraged to complete high school and get diplomas."[8] Ironically, Crispus Attucks High School, a byproduct of the segregationist philosophy of the Klan, provided unprecedented opportunities for African American students and became a beacon of excellence and a source of great pride.

On December 21, 1931, David Nathaniel Baker, Jr., was born to working-class parents in the center of this culturally rich environment, which was nurturing and at the same time riddled with contradictions. His father, who moved to Indianapolis from Kansas City, Missouri, in 1928, held a degree in carpentry from Hampton Institute in Hampton, Virginia. Despite his training and credentials, he wasn't able to work as a carpenter because of the Indianapolis labor union's racially closed policies. Ultimately, as many blacks did at the time, he went to work in public service. David's mother died when he was four, and his father remarried. David's immediate family included his younger sister, Shirley; his half-sister, Cleela; and stepbrother, Archie. Although there is no evidence of significant musical background in David's family, his father played the alto saxophone while at the Hampton Institute and "messed around" playing boogie-woogie on the piano when David was a child. Unsubstantiated family lore holds that while in Kansas City, his father played violin in an orchestra with Ben Webster.[9]

David's formative years were filled with all types of music. Attracted to the family's player piano, he spent countless hours pumping the pedals to operate the piano rolls and watching the various configurations of keys. According to his stepmother, "Boys didn't take piano," yet he listened with interest as his sister practiced for lessons she was forced to take. When David was a child, his grandmother enlisted his help winding the Victrola at his aunt's teenage parties. There he was exposed to the dance music of the time such as Peggy Lee's rendition of "Why Don't You Do Right," and Al Hibbler's "Don't Get Around Much Anymore." His father frequently listened to the radio, and favored the music of Louis Armstrong, which David recalls having little interest in at the time, since he much preferred Grand Ole Opry stars Gene Autry and Minnie Pearl. "In the Mood" and "Tuxedo Junction" wafted from the jukebox at the skating rink, and Saturdays at his cousin Walt's barbershop were filled with the bebop tunes of Jay McShann and, later, Charlie Parker and Dizzy Gillespie.[10]

As a youngster, Baker benefited from a caring school environment and exceptional teachers. His earliest musical experiences were in Mrs. Kirk's grade-school choir at Francis Parker Elementary School, the neighborhood school just a block from Baker's house. In addition to music classes once or twice a week, the choir performed at special events such as the annual May Day Celebration. George Bright, Indianapolis saxophonist and contemporary of Baker's, recalls Clara Reese Kirk was a "really fine teacher who had a box of 78s [records] in her cloakroom, was 'hip' to Stan Kenton, and really knew what was going on."[11]

In seventh grade at Public School 26, David had his first, albeit brief, introduction to the trombone, which his parents rented from the school. After just two weeks, his band teacher sent the fifty-cent rental fee home with a note saying he had no talent. Fortunately he was still singing in Mrs. Kirk's choir and the following year, a new band teacher at the school started him on the Eb tuba, which he played throughout eighth grade. He even practiced on the streetcar on his way home, much to the dismay of other passengers.[12]

Crispus Attucks High School had been open for nineteen years when David began his freshman year. A tradition of excellence had been established in many areas, not the least of which was music. When the school opened in 1927, excellent teachers, all with master's degrees and some with doctorates, were recruited from traditionally black colleges in the South and from segregated high schools in other states. Although the faculty was among the finest in the country, the school often had to settle for secondhand equipment from one of the other high schools in the city.[13] In 1932 Attucks's founding principal, Matthius Nolcox, was replaced by Russell Lane, who had ascended the ranks of the original Attucks faculty. Lane faced a myriad of challenges as he accepted the leadership position at the end of the Great Depression, as sentiments about the school remained mixed among whites and blacks alike. Lane met the situation head on, and strove to expand the curriculum, maintain the best possible faculty, and to inspire and motivate students. He set high standards, encouraging students to do their best and instilling in them a strong work ethic and pride in their accomplishments. The image of him standing in the street in front of the school before the morning bell, shepherding students into the building, is indelibly etched in the memories of many Attucks graduates.[14] Lane and the Crispus Attucks faculty believed that the students could be anything they wanted to be. They expected and accepted only the best, encouraging students to refrain from behavior that would promote the stereotypical image of African Americans held by many whites at the time. Crispus Attucks High School symbolized the paradox of segregation. Founded as a result of Ku Klux Klan efforts to keep black children separate, and provided with secondhand resources, it was "programmed to fail, but excelled instead."[15]

The attitude of excellence that permeated the school was exemplified by the music department. Instrumental teachers LaVerne Newsome, Norman Merrifield, and Russell W. Brown were outstanding musicians, trained at some of the finest music schools in the country. LaVerne Newsome, a graduate of Northwestern University, taught orchestra, string classes, and music appreciation, and was known for his dedication to his students. Merrifield, chairman of the Attucks music department, was a pianist, choral director, band director, composer, and arranger. He held bachelor and master's degrees in music education from Northwestern University. The music department thrived under his leadership, embodying the values of post-Reconstruction black American life, which blended African heritage with European art music. The curriculum included offerings in music theory, music appreciation, and humanities – as well as band, choir, and orchestra. A dedicated teacher, Merrifield sought meaningful musical experiences for his students and presented music as a creative art. An exhibit at the Crispus Attucks Museum displays a letter Merrifield wrote to W. C. Handy, in which he asked the composer to communicate with emerging Attucks musicians. Handy's reply, an autographed copy of a portion of his "St. Louis Blues" manuscript, includes an inspirational note from the composer.[16] Baker, who studied music theory with Merrifield, remembers him as a perfectionist who, on one occasion, had Baker redo a chorale harmonization assignment several times. The third time the paper was returned, Merrifield's comments read, "Even in baseball, three strikes are out."[17]

It was as a freshman at Crispus Attucks High School that David Baker first met band director Russell W. Brown, who would become a major influence in David's life. Baker entered his freshman year at Attucks with a strong desire to continue to play in band: however, no instrument was available. David recounts, "Mr. Brown saw that I could sing the parts. And I had made myself a mock tuba out of a cigar box, and I put some cylinders on it. He saw that I was playing the right fingerings. A sousaphone came open, and he put me in the band playing the sousaphone."[18]

David soon returned to his first instrument, and his destiny as a trombone player was set by his junior year in high school; however, he continued to play sousaphone in the Crispus Attucks Marching Band. The marching band was an ROTC (Reserve Officer Training Corps) unit, as were most high school marching bands at the time. The captain of the band, Tillman Buggs, a trombone player who was a year older than David, was responsible for conducting military inspections to ensure that buttons were polished and shoes were shined. David and "Terrible T" – as Tillman was fondly referred to – became fast friends, establishing a bond that was to last a lifetime.[19]

Russell Brown, a role model and father figure to Baker, influenced the musical development of scores of students – including a long list of jazz musicians of regional and national fame, such as Otis "Killer" Ray Appleton, George Bright, Tillman Buggs, Reginald DuValle, Alonzo "Pookie" Johnson, Virgil Jones, Jimmy Spaulding, Melvin Rhyne, Russell Webster, and David Young. Trained as a classical violinist, Brown held a Bachelor of Arts degree from Temple University and a Master of Science in Education from the University of Pennsylvania, the institution that later granted him an honorary doctorate. His former students speak of "Mr. Brown" with the utmost respect, citing high expectations, a love of music and learning, and open trusting relationships with students among his most impressive characteristics. Indianapolis saxophonist Pookie Johnson, one of Brown's first students at Attucks, called him a "fabulous teacher" who was "with the kids."[20]

Mr. Brown could play any instrument and taught private lessons to many of his students. He charged twenty-five cents per lesson unless a kid couldn't afford it, in which case the lessons were free. Although he usually taught private lessons at the school or at the YMCA, sometimes lessons took place at the local barbershop, where there were billiard tables. According to Baker, "Mr. Brown would give you a lesson in between shooting pool."[21] Tillman Buggs captures the essence of this great man in these words: "Mr. Brown was a special gentleman, really special, because he cared about people – his students. That's what set him aside from all other teachers. Everybody else taught the subject matter and whatnot, but he had a good relationship with all of his students. The clock didn't mean anything. If school were out at 3:30, it didn't make any difference, he continued to teach and we had all kind of things goin'."[22]

One of those "things" was a jazz band called the Rhythm Rockets. Although jazz was not typically taught in most schools in the 1940s, Russell Brown was sympathetic to the students' desire to learn the music. To teach the students to count, Brown had them practice from *The Jay Arnold Swing Method,* which Baker recalls as "some sad stuff." He bought stock arrangements of popular tunes like "Jumpin' at the Woodside," and in Baker's words, "we butchered them. . . . Mr. Brown would be sittin' over there playing ragtime [on piano], and we would be trying to play our bebop against it. I recently reminded Tillman that we played 'The Man I Love' . . . on blues changes!"[23]

When Baker entered Crispus Attucks in 1946, J. J. Johnson, a 1941 Attucks graduate, had just debuted a recording with his quintet, Jay Jay Johnson and the Beboppers. Johnson, who joined the Benny Carter Orchestra at age eighteen after filling in for a couple of sets at the Sunset Terrace, was rapidly gaining national fame.[24] Tillman Buggs remembers walking down the hall at Attucks where pictures of graduates were displayed, pointing to Johnson's, and commenting with reverence, "There he is!"[25] In addition to Johnson's success, which was an inspiration to the younger generation of musicians at Attucks, other Indianapolis musicians just a few years older than David and his friends were gaining local, regional, and national attention. Jimmy Coe, a saxophonist and 1938 Attucks graduate, caught Jay McShann's attention as a player, arranger, and composer during one of McShann's appearances in Indianapolis. Coe was recruited to take Charlie Parker's seat on the McShann Band and went to New York to play at the Apollo Theater.[26] Pookie Johnson, a very talented tenor player who attended Attucks in the early 1940s, returned to Indianapolis after a stint in the service and was playing the clubs. In the late 1940s, he joined the Montgomery-Johnson Quintet, with Wes, Buddy, and Monk Montgomery; and Sonny Johnson on drums. The quintet remained together for several years, playing the Turf Bar on Sixteenth Street and touring in the Midwest and South. Pookie remembers David and his high school friends coming by and standing against the back wall of the Turf Bar to listen to the quintet.[27]

This cadre of incredible Indianapolis musicians inspired David's generation, giving them a feeling of being part of something greater than themselves, a sense of continuity with the past, and of a road set before them. There was some interaction among the various generations of Attucks graduates, but there were also more subtle reminders of the legacy of those who traveled the same path just a few years earlier. Most of the young musicians in Indianapolis who aspired to play jazz sooner or later played in the YMCA band. The Senate Avenue YMCA, which opened in 1913, hosted a variety of neighborhood programs, clubs, training events, and recreational activities – including a jazz band.[28] According to Baker, the YMCA band was "like a Shrine band, where the guys walk around with the epaulets on their shoulders and the whole thing and get to travel."[29] For David, Tillman, and others, it was a great thrill to sit in that band and realize that they were playing dog-eared music with names of the people they idolized written on the top: J. J. Johnson, Jimmy Coe, Roger Jones, and others. These "older" musicians were the pros who served as role models for David's generation; their success set a high standard for those who followed and also made it realistic for the high school kids to believe that they, too, could "make it" as jazz musicians.

David associated with a close group of friends who shared a similar passion for music in general, and bebop in particular. The desire to make music was the driving force in their lives, and they grew up listening to amazing musical models not only in Indianapolis, but also on records and the radio. They were regulars at the Lyric Record Shop, at the corner of Ohio and Illinois streets, where they spent a lot of time in the listening booth checking out the latest record releases such as Charlie Parker on Dial Records's yellow label and Gene Ammons on the purple label of Capitol Records.[30] They seldom had money to buy anything, even at twenty-five cents a record. They also were avid listeners to "Easy Gwyn," who hosted jazz programming on WIBC, the local radio station, and *Randy's Record Shop,* a radio show aired from Gallatin, Tennessee, which featured 1940s artists such as Ray Charles and Nat "King" Cole.[31]

Many after-school hours were spent learning to play bebop in various settings. There was a great personal investment in the music, so finding people to play with wasn't difficult. David and trumpet player friend Nelson Alvarez learned to play bebop tunes like "Groovin' High" from a published book of Dizzy Gillespie solos.[32] Jam sessions took place on a regular basis. A particular Tuesday night session was especially memorable for Tillman Buggs: "I can remember the guys comin' by, playin' at my house and going around, you know. And I remember Slide [Hampton] playin' 'Body and Soul', and when he got to that bridge where it goes to D, he played 'Over the Rainbow', and I said, 'Wow!' We were just trying to learn how to grab the changes and there's Slide . . ."[33]

The Hamptons' house was another popular hangout. The Hamptons – who moved to Indianapolis from Middletown, Ohio, in 1935 – had a family band led by Deacon Hampton, patriarch of the family of twelve children. Locksley "Slide" Hampton, the youngest, recalls being given a trombone to learn to play: "See, our training was coming from our father, and he hadn't had any formal training and my mother also, who had probably studied some on the piano. As the kids were born, he would give them an instrument and teach them as much about it as he knew. And so we were mostly self-taught. They gave me the trombone left handed and I played it that way. It's the only thing I do with my left hand."[34]

All the Hampton kids played in the band, and Deacon filled out the instrumentation with young musicians from the neighborhood. They played the music of famous bands such as those led by Count Basie, Duke Ellington, Dizzy Gillespie, and Stan Kenton by learning the parts from records, and using their own notation system of writing letter names, fingerings, and slide positions in "double Q" school notebooks. They later learned to read music so that non-family members could be more easily integrated into the band. David Baker remembers rehearsals at the house with a big washtub filled with Kool-Aid and a fifty-pound block of ice to dip into between tunes.[35] Tillman recalls the Hamptons as "the most amazing band, the most amazing people" and describes a rehearsal: "You go in the house, they'd have the saxophone section in the living room, trombones right behind them, and then right at the archway you'd have the trumpet section. And then the rhythm section would be in the back and you could hear them two, three blocks down the street."[36] When the Hamptons invited Baker to join the band he began playing bass trombone, an alternative much more acceptable to him than being relegated to third trombone.[37]

As high schoolers, David and his friends often tried to bluff their way into the Indiana Avenue clubs, wearing berets and glasses and even drawing on fake mustaches. When the disguises didn't work, they would stand outside the Sunset Terrace or the Cotton Club to listen to such luminaries as Coltrane, J. J., and Basie – as well as local heroes and role models Jimmy Coe, Pookie Johnson, and the Montgomery brothers. Other times, they got into the clubs and became a part of the hotbed of musical exchange that took place among musicians young and old, famous and soon to be famous. Although the youngsters admitted that they had "no business there," the older musicians were generally tolerant of these emerging players who went from session to session trying to figure out what was going on with the music.[38]

Many of the developing jazz musicians in Indianapolis in the 1930s and '40s had the good fortune to experience the best of both worlds: learning to read music and play their instruments in the formal musical setting of Crispus Attucks's music department, and immersion in the informal music learning process prevalent throughout the neighborhood and at the clubs. At school, Mr. Brown chastised his young charges to "count" as they worked through *The Jay Arnold Swing Method;* by night the word on the street was, "Just keep listening; you'll hear it."[39] The standards were extremely high in both worlds. Trumpet player Maceo Hampton was known for his incredible ears, and easily transcribed Dizzy Gillespie solos note for note; and the Montgomery brothers, who didn't read music at all, were legendary for their ability to play anything they heard.[40]

By his senior year in high school, David was playing and touring with the Hampton Band and went on a ten-day tour with a band led by Mr. Hibbert. It was a great thing to be called to sub in one of the professional bands; it was a chance to get a start. Baker's first real professional experience was with the Eldridge Morrison Big Band, the band that J. J. Johnson and Jimmy Coe had played in. As David and his friends matured as jazz musicians, more and more of them got opportunities to play and some began to gain wider attention. Baker recalls the pride they all felt when bass player Leroy Vinnegar, who was a few years older than David, left for Los Angeles.[41]

David grew up in a time and place that was characterized by strong, close-knit, nurturing families who valued education and instilled a strong work ethic in their children. Jimmy Coe credits his own success to the model his father's work ethic and will to survive during the Depression provided.[42] According to Norman Merrifield, born and raised in Indianapolis in the early twentieth century, "We had fine mamas and papas who kept us straight."[43] This was certainly still true of David's generation. No stranger to hard work, Baker had a job during high school at LaRue's Supper Club, where he was able to practice trombone on his break between lunch and dinner shifts. Occasionally he was allowed to sit in with the house band led by Denny Dutton, and recalls playing "Lullaby of the Leaves" with the band.[44] Other jobs included caddying at the Douglass Park Golf Course and setting pins at the neighborhood bowling alley. Juggling work, school, and the pursuit of bebop left little time for sleep. Still, David excelled. Known even then for his intellectual prowess, he was one of three Crispus Attucks students to make it to advanced French, during which he often fell asleep. Dr. Morton-Finney, who was one of the incredibly caring Attucks teachers, would wake David, asking, "Don't you ever sleep at home?" Thirty years later, Dr. Morton-Finney ran into David and commented, "I know who you are, boy. Do you ever sleep at home now?"[45] His friends from high school speak of his incredible drive, work ethic, and tenacity. Buggs offers, "He's the kind of guy, if he wants to do it, he's gonna do it. I remember when he couldn't swim. We were down at I U [Indiana University] and after about four or five days David was swimming, because he has that perseverance; he knows how to stay with it."[46]

The 1949 Crispus Attucks yearbook pictures seniors and lists their career ambitions. Not surprisingly, with role models like LaVerne Newsome, Norman Merrifield, and Russell Brown, David listed "music teacher" as his future career. At that time, David wasn't thinking seriously about a career as a jazz musician; he and his friends had devoted much of their young lives to music and were aware that professional opportunities existed for them to play jazz.[47]

Malcolm Gladwell writes about the path to success, noting that although talent and intelligence are important, extraordinary opportunity is often the determining factor for those who achieve great things.[48] Imagine being sixteen years old at the apex of bebop – right in the eye of the storm – and learning the fundamentals of playing an instrument under the tutelage of Russell Brown, an incredible musician and teacher who devoted every day of his life to kids and music. Imagine hanging out after school at the Lyric Record Shop with buddies Tillman Buggs and George Bright, checking out the latest Dizzy Gillespie record or local hero J. J. Johnson's newest release. Then imagine heading to Slide Hampton's house after school to transcribe and rehearse the newest Stan Kenton hit – and then on to "The Avenue" to listen to Charlie Parker in the alley behind the Sunset Terrace, or to the Missile Room, hoping to sneak in and jam with visiting luminary Cannonball Adderley and the Montgomery Brothers Trio. All the while, David followed in the footsteps of childhood heroes who were discovered on Indiana Avenue and rocketed to national fame.

The first eighteen years of David Baker's life set the stage for his remarkable career as a jazz musician and educator. In the words of Mari Evans, "creativity is the reaction of the human spirit to the variety of its experiences."[49] Baker's autobiographic big band tunes of the 1970s pay tribute to the environment that shaped him ("25th and Martindale"), honor his influential peers ("Terrible T"), and memorialize the business where he spent countless Saturdays listening to bebop ("Walt's Barbershop"). Baker takes little credit for his success, stressing that he is a product of his experiences and circumstances, but lifelong friends point to his exceptional talent, work ethic, and dedication. Combining all of these, David has drawn inspiration from a life rich with experiences and applied his keen intellect and musical talent to help make the world a better place.

NOTES

1. Bodenhamer and Barrows, eds., The Encyclopedia of Indianapolis, 7.

2. Madame C. J. Walker built a fortune in the early 1900s marketing hair care and beauty products to African American women. She moved her company from Denver, Colorado, to Indianapolis in 1910 and left her legacy on Indiana Avenue, where the Madame Walker Theatre became a landmark. See "Madam C. J. Walker."

3. Baker, "Indianapolis, Indiana," 19–23.

4. George Bright, interview by Lissa F. May, August 13, 2003, tape recording, collection of author.

5. Bodenhamer and Barrows, The Encyclopedia of Indianapolis, 81.

6. Evans, "Ethos and Creativity," 34.

7. Warren, Crispus Attucks High School, 34.

8. Norman Merrifield, interview by Flora Bell Wilson, January 9, 1980, Indianapolis, Ind., tape recordings, Indiana Historical Society Library Indianapolis. Merrifield would later become music

department chairman at Crispus Attucks
High School.

9. David Baker, interview by Lissa F.
May, May 26, 2010, Bloomington, Ind.,
tape recording in possession of author.

10. David Baker, interview by Lida
Baker, June 19–21, 2000, transcript,
Smithsonian Jazz Oral History Project,
www.smithsonianjazz.org/oral_
histories/pdf/joh_DavidNBaker_
transcript.pdf.

11. Bright, interview.

12. Baker, interview, May 26, 2010.

13. Warren, Crispus Attucks High
School, 32.

14. Mickey, "Russell Adrian Lane,"
112–30.

15. Baker, interview, May 26, 2010.

16. Gilbert Taylor, interview by Lissa
F. May, November 4, 2003, Indianapolis,
Ind., tape recordings in possession of
author.

17. Baker, interview, May 26, 2010.

18. Ibid.

19. Ibid.

20. Alonzo "Pookie" Johnson, interview by Lissa F. May, August 22, 2003,
Indianapolis, Ind., tape recordings in possession of author.

21. Russell Brown retired from teaching in 1973 after twenty-seven years of
service at Crispus Attucks High School.
He died in 1992, at age eighty-four, while
shaving. He was getting ready to teach
a bassoon lesson. Baker, interview, June
19–21, 2010.

22. Tillman Buggs, interview by Lissa
F. May, August 19, 2003.

23. Baker, interview, May 26, 2010.

24. Berrett and Bourgois, The Musical
World of J. J. Johnson, 23.

25. Buggs, interview.

26. Jimmy Coe, interview by Lissa F.
May, August 27, 2003, Indianapolis, Ind.,
tape recordings in possession of author.

27. Johnson, interview.

28. Warren, The Senate Avenue YMCA,
79, 123.

29. Baker, interview, June 19–21, 2000.

30. Baker, interview, May 26, 2010.

31. Baker, interview, June 19–21, 2000.

32. Ibid.

33. Buggs, interview.

34. Slide Hampton, interview by Bob
Bernotas, 1994 (revised 2000), Online
Trombone Journal, www.trombone.org/
articles/library/slidehampton-int.asp.

35. Baker, interview, June 19–21, 2000.

36. Buggs, interview.

37. Baker, interview, May 26, 2010.

38. Bright, interview.

39. Baker, interview, June 19–21, 2000.

40. Buggs, interview.

41. Baker, interview, June 19–21, 2000.

42. Coe, interview.

43. Merrifield, interview.

44. Baker, interview, June 19–21, 2000.

45. Ibid.

46. Buggs, interview.

47. Baker, interview, May 26, 2010.

48. Gladwell, Outliers, 175–76.

49. Evans, "Ethos and Creativity," 29.

REFERENCES

Baker, David N. "Indianapolis, Indiana."
In Lost Jazz Shrines, edited by Willard
Jenkins, 29–33. N.p.: The Lost Jazz
Shrines Project, 1998.

Berrett, Joshua, and Bourgois, Louis G.,
III. The Musical World of J. J. Johnson.
Lanham, Md., and London: Scarecrow
Press, 2002.

Bodenhamer, David J., and Barrows, Rob-
ert G. The Encyclopedia of Indianapolis.
Bloomington: Indiana University
Press, 1994.

Evans, Mari. "Ethos and Creativity." In *Where We Live: Essays about Indiana,* edited by David Hoppe, 28–44. Bloomington: Indiana University Press, 1989.

Gladwell, Malcolm. *Outliers: The Story of Success.* New York: Little, Brown and, Company: 2008.

"Madam C. J. Walker." *Indianapolis Star Library FactFiles,* January 22, 2001. http://www2.indystar.com/library/factfiles/history/black_history/walker_madame.html.

Mickey, Rose Cheatham. "Russell Adrian Lane: Biography of an Urban Negro School Administrator." ED.D. diss., the University of Akron, 1983. ATT 8315524.

Warren, Stanley. Crispus Attucks High School: "Hail to the Green, Hail to the Gold." Virginia Beach, Va.: Donning, 1998.

———. *The Senate Avenue YMCA: For African American Men and Boys, Indianapolis, Indiana, 1913–1959.* Virginia Beach, Va.: Donning, 2005.

2

A Star Is Born

MONIKA HERZIG

WHILE JAZZ SINGER Janet Lawson was on tour in Latvia in the 1990s, she was given a book to read by a friend. It was *A Woman in Amber,* a memoir about the destruction of Agate Nesaule's home in Latvia during World War II and her subsequent immigration to Indianapolis. While reminiscing with her mother about washing dishes and working in the cannery in order to support their graduate studies at Indiana University, they mention a busboy named David at LaRue's Supper Club, who was so crazy about music. During the early 1950s attitudes toward the black and immigrant populations were similar, and Nesaule was expected to be grateful for any job and assumed to have little potential for higher achievements. Despite such humiliating conditions, Nesaule and busboy David excelled in their academic careers, encouraging each other in the kitchen at LaRue's in 1950. She recalls, "He had to hear every day about Negroes and natural rhythm, and they laughed that a black man talked about music theory and wanted to be a professor."[1]

Baker confirmed his early determination and the decision to become a professional musician in high school by exploring every opportunity to learn and perform together with his buddy Slide Hampton, but was most surprised to find out when he was given a copy of Nesaule's book that even as a young busboy his dedication had been already such an inspiration.[2] Bandleader Denny Dutton occasionally asked the busboy at LaRue's to sit in with the band on "Lullaby of the Leaves," and after Baker got off work at midnight, he was a regular at after-hour jam sessions that lasted until 3:00 AM. Classes would start at 8:00 AM, though, and French teacher Dr. Morton-Finney had to ask young David, "Mr. Baker, don't you ever sleep at home?" whenever he drifted off during class.[3]

This chapter documents David Baker's early professional life from high school graduation in 1949 until he became a fulltime faculty member at Indiana University in 1966. His dream of becoming a professional musician came true, but fate had several unexpected and tragic detours in store. Most notable were his developing artistry on the trombone that earned him *DownBeat Magazine*'s New Star Award in 1962, shared with his friend and fellow trombonist Slide Hampton; as well as the need to start over on a new instrument as a result of an injury to the jaw. A devastating prospect then, it turned out to be a crucial element in the development of one of the leading composers and pedagogues of our time. David acknowledges this fateful turning point himself:

> I think God works his wonders in mysterious ways because if I had stayed in New York, I probably wouldn't have turned to teaching and all the other things I do, like composing; but because of that accident, it forced me into areas I would have never considered.[4]

COLLEGE EDUCATION

Baker's college career started in 1949 in Indianapolis, Indiana, at the Arthur Jordan Conservatory of Music (then affiliated with Butler University), where he spent a year studying mainly baritone horn. Even though

the school was still segregated, the conservatory accepted a certain number of black students. Some of Baker's colleagues then included Oliver
Bell, Jimmy Coe, Trili Stewart, and Reginald DuValle, Jr. David got to
play in the concert band on the baritone horn, and practiced all day and
still worked as a busboy at LaRue's. He started taking trombone lessons
from Thomas Beversdorf at Indiana University–Bloomington, which
turned out to be an important connection after he was expelled from
Arthur Jordan Conservatory:

> They [Jordan Conservatory] had a big jazz band which was really quite good. I
> never got to play in that band, but I did make contacts and good friends while I
> was there, even though I was ultimately asked to leave, because I danced with
> a white girl at the Christmas dance. They let me know they were very unhappy
> with that. I didn't have enough sense to take low, so I got kicked out of Butler.[5]

Luckily one of his previous high school teachers, Dr. Roscoe Polin, also
president of the National Association of Negro Musicians at the time, in-
tervened, and brought him to Indiana University, where he continued his
studies on trombone with Dr. Beversdorf. Even though David still performed on baritone horn and tenor tuba, he switched to trombone as his
primary instrument at this point and performed on bass trombone in the
Indianapolis Philharmonic as well as the Indiana University orchestra.

When David Baker arrived at Indiana University in 1950, the campus
was still completely segregated. Black students were not allowed to live
in the dormitories, had separate eating facilities in the student union,
couldn't go to any restaurants, and could not even get a haircut in town.
David also remembers instances of segregation when touring as the only
black member of the Indiana University Orchestra:

> I was in the orchestra, and we went [by bus] to play at Carnegie Hall. I can re-
> member them calling ahead for all the stops that we were going to make, because
> we had a hundred-piece orchestra and another maybe 150 people who were in
> the choir – because we did *The Dream of Gerontius* or one of those big works,
> Brahms's *Requiem* or something. We went in one restaurant en route there, and
> they refused to serve me. [The conductor] Dr. Ernst Hoffman said: "If you're not
> going to serve him, you're not going to serve anybody." They were left with all
> those meals, and we got back on the bus.[6]

Baker pursued bachelor and master degrees in music education at
Indiana University, with an eye to becoming a classical bass trombon-

ist. Unfortunately, such goals seemed futile after his audition for the Indianapolis Symphony Orchestra, when he realized that the chances for finding employment would be slim because of his race:

> I remember [conductor] Fabien Sevitzky telling me after I had auditioned that I was probably the best bass trombonist that they were going to hear, and certainly the best one that they had heard up to that time, but I realized that this was an exercise in futility, that in fact no board of trustees – any more than they're going to do that now, if they can avoid it – is going to hire a black in a symphony orchestra.[7]

In the jazz scene, things seemed to be much more integrated; Baker realized that he probably could make it as a jazz player, and refocused his attention towards learning jazz. There were jam sessions around campus almost daily, and there were great players among the students as well as visitors from surrounding cities. Some of Baker's fellow students at that time included Jerry Coker, Al Kiger, Joe Hunt, David Young, Al Cobine, Max Hartstein, and Al Plank. Since there was no formal jazz instruction offered by the music school, jazz musicians learned by playing as much as possible in sessions, with dance bands, and touring with some of the prominent jazz orchestras. With this new goal in mind, David immersed himself completely in the jazz tradition, learning from live sessions and recordings alike. According to fellow student Jerry Coker,

> We noticed immediately that he knew all the solos and all our favorite records and things and he knew what all the personnel was, what the name of this was, what label it was on. This was back in the days of 78 rpms, which were a lot harder to keep up with because there were no liner notes and just a little bit of music. It wasn't like a CD with seventy or seventy-five minutes of music on it, they were just two-sided discs. But he knew them, and he knew them better than anybody I knew at the time. He could remember all the heads and he could sing them.[8]

Saxophonist Jerry Coker and David Baker were invited to join Fred Dale, who had put together an all-star band after moving to Bloomington. In 1953 Dale entered a tape of the band in the first collegiate contest held by *Metronome Magazine,* and they shared first prize with a group from Westlake College in Los Angeles. Thanks to their high quality and Dale's good business sense, the group worked frequently, including summer engagements at Lake Hamilton resort near Fort Wayne. But these activities were strictly extracurricular. Classical music was the core of the college curriculum and even playing jazz in the practice room could result in losing practice room privileges:

> I can never forget practicing one day in my room, and I was practicing learning "Straight No Chaser." Ernst Hoffman, who comes definitely out of the Nikisch-Furtwangler school of conducting – he was not going to make a big stink about me. He hears me practicing, and I see him look in the glass window. He walks away. He comes back. I'm still trying to learn "Straight No Chaser," because it is so oblique to try to learn it. He comes back. And this happens several times. Finally, when he couldn't take it any more – I'm going [Baker sings the melody], he walks in and he says, "Mr. bass trombone player, if you *must* practice it, the melody goes [Baker sings the famous French horn melody from Richard Strauss's composition *Till Eulenspiegel*]."[9]

After graduating with a Master's degree in music education from Indiana University in 1954, Baker moved back to Indianapolis and continued to play jazz. Quite frequently he could be seen with Wes Montgomery or some of his own groups, including the Modern Jazz Septet. He joined Jack Mason's group for a six-week engagement in Traverse City, Michigan:

> This one was a group that had Oliver Bell, a wonderful trumpet player. It had David Young on tenor saxophone, Bill Boyd on baritone saxophone. It had a guy named Gene Hudson on drums, a lady named Toni Zale, who was the niece of the boxer Tony Zale, on bass. Jack Mason was the leader of the group. [It] had Jim Houston, who would form a lot later his own publishing company, playing baritone [saxophone]. We went up there, and we played at Traverse City for, I think, six weeks. It rained every night. We were playing on a minesweeper that was converted. So they went broke, and we finished up there.[10]

In 1955, David decided to move to Los Angeles and follow in the footsteps of some of his former bandmates who seemed to find success on the West Coast, such as Buddy Parker and Leroy Vinnegar. Things got off to a slow start, and David often had to decide between spending money on a streetcar to go practice at the Musicians' Union facilities or buy a meal:

> I went down to a pancake place, and they thought I was a junkie, because I hadn't had anything in my stomach, and I just simply fainted. So I'm laid out there, and they figure I must be a junkie because I got an instrument.[11]

A call from Lincoln University in Jefferson City, Missouri, asking him to fill in for a year for trombone teacher Marshall Penn seemed to be the right thing at the right time, and Baker left Los Angeles behind to start his first teaching position. His luggage was delayed, and his arrival just after a snowstorm in pink pants and without a coat caused quite some amusement among the students. The traditionally black college had opened its doors to a diverse student population, and many veterans returned to school on the GI Bill. Julius Hemphill was one of those students, and the appearance of Baker in his pink pants must have been quite memorable – Hemphill mentions the occasion in the liner notes of two of his recordings.

Knowing that the job at Lincoln would last for only one year, David kept practicing and performing extensively. The university environment inspired him to return to Indiana University to pursue a doctoral degree. Additional inspiration came from Eugenia Marie Jones, a fine opera singer at Lincoln University who asked David for lessons in vocal jazz. Soon she became Mrs. David Baker, despite strong resistance from her family and even the law – interracial marriage was still illegal in most states. The couple eloped to Chicago so they could marry legally; as a consequence, Baker had to leave Lincoln University immediately, and Eugenia Baker was disowned by her parents:

> So we went across the state line to Chicago and got married, and when we came back, the vigilantes were looking for us. I'm serious: the vigilantes. It was very tense. We'd given a ride up there to one of my colleagues, and he cut the thing [the marriage notice] out of the paper when it was in there the next day, that we got married, so he could bring it back and scream on us. And he did.[12]

The birth of their daughter April in 1958 did calm the waters, and both families became very close. Eugenia "Jeannie" Baker worked full time while David pursued graduate studies at Indiana University, started teaching private lessons at their home in Indianapolis, formed several small groups and a big band, and took care of their daughter during the day. April Baker recalled Sundays being teaching days. There was no formal studio space in the duplex owned by Baker's grandmother and shared with his sister Shirley's family at 1237 Burdsal Parkway; lessons took place in the living room, and instrument cases were stored in April's bedroom. Local players as well as Indiana University students from Bloomington drove up for their weekly lessons, including Jamey Aebersold, Randy Brecker, Gary Campbell, and many more. Randy Brecker recalls,

April Baker at age three.
Courtesy of David Baker.

It was a fascinating time for me because he helped codify stuff that I had learned but I didn't know the terminology and I didn't know how to apply certain scales to chords. So it was a very fertile learning period for me.[13]

Jamey Aebersold confirms Brecker's comments about Baker's ability to codify the new and still evolving language of jazz improvisation. Aebersold's first lesson turned out to be a major turning point in his career, as he was finally able to grasp intellectually what he had been hearing and searching for as a student of jazz:

I took lessons from David. I can't remember how long. And I remember the first one. He was on the piano and he asked me what to play. I'm pretty sure it was "I'll Remember April." We played the whole tune and then he stops and I improvise. I don't know if he let me play or he stopped me but he pointed out that the second scale was G Dorian minor. And I can remember I was thinking – I didn't know anything about Dorian but I remember thinking standing there in his living room up there on Burdsal Parkway, "I thought this was going to be fun." So then he played the scale and I played the scale. As soon as I played the scale I could tell that one note difference between pure minor and Dorian minor. It was just perfect. And then my next thought was, "Why hadn't someone told me this before now?" 'Cause that's what they were playing on the records. I could tell that sound. And that was the beginning, and we kind of just went on from there. And he'd give me assignments and stuff. And I can remember the day also – I don't know if I was married or if I was dating my wife – but I can remember driving back to Bloomington and telling her, "When I get back, I'll go over to the music building and I'm going to take 'Stella by Starlight' and I'm going to learn every scale and every arpeggio because I'm tired of playing through that tune and being lost here and being lost there and not knowing the scale that goes over that $G7^{\flat9\sharp5}$, you know, whatever." I said, "I'm going to start doing this." So that's when I started to think differently.[14]

Of course, not all students were that serious and determined. Daughter April Baker remembered a trumpet player who really didn't show much improvement and motivation for practice. One week he forgot to pack up his trumpet after the lesson and left with an empty case. At the beginning of the next week's lesson, David asked him about his progress, and he claimed to have had several good practice sessions before David handed him the trumpet he hadn't played for a week.

There is a strong consensus among his early students that David Baker was the center of a dynamic jazz scene in Indianapolis through teaching, performing, and just bringing likeminded people together.

Even though his pedagogy was highly structured and his method intellectually precise, David was able to individualize materials and instructional approaches for each student by quickly analyzing their level,
needs, and learning style – the hallmarks of a master teacher. Saxophonist and educator Gary Campbell started lessons with David when he was
sixteen and continued until he graduated from Indiana University. He
describes Baker's pedagogy thus:

> And so in that respect, David did start me with the whole organization of, and
> priorities, well these are the raw materials that the music is constructed of and so
> you have to master this, you know, to a pretty good degree, along with learning
> repertoire all the time, and memorizing everything and all of that. And this
> was good, too, because this was before *The Real Book* and all that business. So
> if you wanted to learn a tune, I mean, sometimes David ran out a tune for me if
> I wanted to know it or if it was my lesson for that week. He'd say, "OK. 'What Is
> This Thing Called Love?'" He'd write out the title and write out the changes,
> teach me the melody by playing it on the piano, and I would copy it and then
> learn the melody and then we would play some exercises that we were learning it
> to and every week we would do another one. And so it's basically, he taught me
> how to teach myself and that's what you have to do.[15]

David Baker's performance career was in full swing after returning
to Indianapolis. Besides a regular gig at the Topper on Thirty-fourth
Street and appearances at the abundance of jazz clubs around Indiana
Avenue, David also toured with the Hampton Band, Maynard Ferguson's
group, and Stan Kenton's band. The newly formed Indianapolis Jazz Club
started a Sunday night series at 1444 North Pennsylvania Avenue and
featured some of the most popular Indianapolis musicians. Founding
member Ted Watts put together an extensive report about the series and
describes the successful collaboration of David with guitar legend Wes
Montgomery thus:

> During the Indianapolis 500 race weekend in 1959, we put together the super
> crowd pleaser: a concert featuring both Wes Montgomery and Dave Baker. By
> this, our sixth concert, we knew that this is what our audience wanted – both
> jazz fans and jazz musicians, and almost everyone. Dave Baker was and still is an
> intellectual, cerebral musician. Wes on the other hand, was largely a self-taught,
> natural musician, who actually could not read music, or perhaps it would be
> more accurate to say, could not read Dave's intricate scores. Although Wes could
> pick up instantly when he heard it, the process slowed down Dave's rehearsals,
> but it did not prevent them from making great jazz together.[16]

David Baker and Wes Montgomery "back to back": a photo intended for a
poster for a concert that went on, but without Wes, who suddenly departed
for New York and his recording debut (summer 1959). © *Duncan Schiedt.*

The year 1959 turned out to be a landmark in Baker's as well as Wes
Montgomery's career. Cannonball Adderley heard Wes perform during
a jam session at the Missile Room on Indiana Avenue and immediately
called producer Orrin Keepnews at Riverside Records and persuaded

The rehearsal: David Baker (trombone), David Young (tenor saxophone),
Larry Ridley (bass), Wes Montgomery (guitar), Melvin Rhyne (piano),
and Sonny Johnson (drums) (summer 1959). © *Duncan Schiedt.*

him to sign Montgomery.[17] Baker's big band won first prize at the Notre
Dame Jazz Festival that year and attracted the attention of French horn-
ist, historian, and composer Gunther Schuller. While visiting Indianapolis, Schuller got to hear Baker's big band as well as Montgomery's
trio and was so impressed that he authored an article entitled "Indiana
Renaissance" for *Jazz Review* magazine, in which he raved about the two
musicians:

> I heard there [Indianapolis] two groups – one an 18-piece band, the other a trio
> consisting of guitar, organ, and drums – which were of such superior quality that
> it seemed hard to believe that none of the musicians, jazz writers, critics, and
> assorted cognoscenti in New York knew of them, had ever written about them in
> the various jazz journals.[18]

In addition, he invited David and his small group on scholarship to a
new summer jazz program, the Lenox School of Jazz – held very close

to Tanglewood, the summer home of the Boston Symphony Orchestra. They were determined to make their way up to Massachusetts and
change the world of jazz forever:

> We [David Baker, Al Kiger, Larry Ridley] left from that gig in Newport
> [Kentucky] to drive up to Lenox, because we were invited there that year. I just
> remember it took us forever, because we were driving a raggedy-ass car that
> Kiger had. We'd have to stop and get gas and oil at so many places. So we got to
> Lenox late. We were coming up there as the fair-haired boys. We were going to
> be the heroes, Gunther had raved about us. We could all play. We figured, boy,
> when we get there, we're going to turn that place inside out.[19]

In fact, bassist Larry Ridley recalls further details about the challenging
travel from Indiana to Massachusetts:

> Al Kiger had this 1950 Ford and we drove from Bloomington to Lenox,
> Massachusetts. And as we were going on the [Pennsylvania] Turnpike going
> cross country, suddenly something happened to the car and we got stuck in Erie,
> Pennsylvania, and we had to get the car fixed and we had to stay over. After we
> got everything straight and we were driving, we came to one of these rest stops
> on the Turnpike. David was in the back napping and I was in the front passenger
> seat. I got out when we stopped to get gas and I told Alan, "I'm going to the men's
> room, I'll be right back." So Al fills up the tank and he takes off. And I come out
> and they're gone. So there we are on the Pennsylvania Turnpike and you know,
> that's a very boring Turnpike because it's going straight for miles and miles.
> And so I was mad. You could have cooked a chicken or anything else on my
> body because I can't begin to tell you how hot I was. I was so angry. I was calling
> him everything but a child of God. . . . So this truck driver asked me, "What's
> happening?" and I said "This M.F. trumpet player left me here at this rest stop
> and I don't know why he took off and just left me." So this guy said "Well, come
> on and get in. There is only one way they can go." As we passed the different rest
> stops I would look for the car and we finally caught up with them. I said, "Kiger,
> why did you leave me like this?" So David told me later what he said. David says,
> "Yeah, Larry, I was asleep in the back seat and I woke up. And we would just
> drive along and Kiger's just talking and talking. And I said to him, 'Kiger, where
> is Larry?' He says 'Oh, he's sitting over there. We're talking, we're carrying on
> this conversation right now.'"[20]

THE LENOX SCHOOL OF JAZZ

An outgrowth of a lecture series and roundtable discussions founded in
1950 by Dr. Marshall Stearns, a professor of English at Hunter College,
the Lenox School of Jazz under the direction of John Lewis brought

David Baker at the Lenox School of Jazz in 1959. *Courtesy of David Baker.*

together the world's greatest jazz musicians in unprecedented numbers
with a select group of students for three weeks of classes in composition,
history, small-ensemble playing, and private lessons on a primary as well
as secondary instrument. The all-star faculty list is mind boggling:

> Dizzy Gillespie, trumpet, 1957
> Ralph Pena, bass in residence, 1957 (Jimmy Giuffre 3)

Chuck Israels, guest bass, 1957

Oscar Peterson, piano, 1957–58 (Oscar Peterson Trio)

Ray Brown, bass, 1957–58 (Oscar Peterson Trio)

Herb Ellis, guitar, 1957–58 (Oscar Peterson Trio)

Milt Jackson, vibraphone, 1957–60 (MJQ)

Percy Heath, bass in residence, 1957–58, bass, 1959–60 (MJQ)

Connie Kay, drums in residence, 1957–59, drums, 1960 (MJQ)

Jim Hall, guitar, 1957–59 (Jimmy Giuffre 3)

Jimmy Giuffre, composition, woodwinds, 1957–59 (Jimmy Giuffre 3)

John Lewis, director: composition, piano, 1957–60 (MJQ)

Bill Russo, composition, 1957–59

Max Roach, percussion, 1957–59 (Max Roach Quintet)

Marshall Stearns, history, 1957–59

Lee Konitz-saxophone, 1958

George Coleman, saxophone in residence, 1958 (Max Roach Quintet)

Art Davis, bass in residence, 1958 (Max Roach Quintet)

Ray Draper, tuba in residence, 1958 (Max Roach Quintet)

Booker Little, trumpet in residence, 1958 (Max Roach Quintet)

Bob Brookmeyer, trombone, 1958–59 (Jimmy Giuffre 3)

Kenny Dorham, trumpet, 1958–59

George Russell, composition, 1958–60

Bill Evans, piano, 1959

Herb Pomeroy, ensemble, 1959–60, trumpet, 1960

Gunther Schuller, history, analysis, composition, 1959–60

J. J. Johnson, trombone, 1960

Earl Zindars, drums in residence, 1960

Susan Freeman, bass in residence, 1960

George Russell, sextet in residence, 1960

John Garvey, strings, 1960

Ed Summerlin, saxophone, 1960

Freddie Hubbard, guest trumpet, 1960

Don Heckman, guest saxophone, 1960[21]

From 1957 to 1960, beginning in mid-August, jazz students traveled
to the Music Inn in Lenox, Massachusetts. Stephanie and Philip Barber
fell in love with the area during a weekend outing from New York City

and bought several buildings on the property of a magnificent mansion known as Wheatleigh; they established the Music Inn in 1950 as a retreat offering a variety of music programs. Gradually, the programs and popularity of the Music Inn grew and the Barbers decided to incorporate the Lenox School of Jazz as a nonprofit organization in 1957; John Lewis was named executive director.[22]

The Berklee School of Music had been founded in 1945, but the principle of teaching jazz as an art form by gathering such large numbers of prominent performers and scholars was unheard of. The competition for scholarships was fierce and a maximum of forty-five students from all over the world were accepted on the basis of taped auditions. Many of the invited faculty had never taught before, and the structure of the curriculum was quite experimental.[23] As a result, lectures might take detours into lengthy theory discussions; the new ideas of free spirit Ornette Coleman, who arrived as a student in 1959, caused a split in two camps holding opposing views on the value of the avant-garde. David recalls,

> When I look back now, it must have been like Paris was at the time of *Le Sacre du Printemps*. I remember George Russell saying to me, "You wait 'till Ornette gets to the Five Spot. He's going to upset New York." Of course, I couldn't imagine this; but I'll be damned if people didn't line up and take sides. I mean, there was no middle ground: you either thought that Ornette was valid or that he wasn't.[24]

Bassist and fellow Lenox student Larry Ridley confirmed the impact that Coleman's participation had in 1959, the year that produced the first important bossa nova records, early liturgical jazz, the emergence of free jazz, modal music, the Brandeis Jazz Festival with Third Stream, and the beginning of the National Stage Band camps under Stan Kenton.[25] Interestingly, this was also the year that Buddy Holly died, Barbie made her debut, Perry Como and Ella Fitzgerald won the first Grammy Awards, Elvis Presley had his first UK hit, and 1959 became generally associated with the birth of rock 'n' roll. Larry Ridley remembers,

> At that time, when Ornette came, that's when Ornette first came east and he just upset everybody. And Ornette used to say, "Just play what you hear and what you feel." And he gave me this music to read with no bar lines. I'm saying, "Wait a minute, Ornette, what's happening here? There are no bar lines." And he says, "Oh, just play it."[26]

William Russo, a composer and arranger and an alumnus of the Stan Kenton Orchestra, set the basic philosophy of the camp by learning through immersion with his initial announcement to the first class of students in 1957, during which he proclaimed, "Ladies and gentlemen, I'm going to drown you."[27] Even though other instructors were critical of this potentially overwhelming strategy, many students cite this method as the highlight of their stay. It certainly left a deep impression on student David Baker, and the "dump truck method" has become a trademark of his teaching. Saxophonist and IU colleague Tom Walsh explains,

> It's like, back up the truck. Dump everything on the student. And then the students have to dig their way out. He just throws everything at you, you know. And so what I did was I recorded the classes and I wrote out everything that he said. I still have that notebook. And this was when I was in high school. And then when I needed something to practice, I went to that notebook and I said, "Oh yeah, I should practice the bebop scales like this," you know. And so I think what's effective about his approach is that he challenges people. And there's no spoon feeding.[28]

Composer and pianist George Russell also broke new ground at the camp by teaching music theory based on his Lydian Chromatic Concept, originally self-published as a pamphlet in 1953. It was an attempt to reorganize tonal relationships while abandoning the traditional major/minor system and setting the path for Miles Davis's modal improvisations on the seminal album *Kind of Blue*. The recording was released in 1959 on Columbia Records and was a landmark for modal jazz – further pursued by John Coltrane, who performed on the original recording, and Eric Dolphy. Russell followed the natural overtone series and thereby created a root scale from C to C including an F♯ instead of the customary F in a major scale, resulting in the Greek Lydian mode. A detailed biography of Russell's life and the development of his concept can be found in Duncan Heining's *George Russell: The Story of an American Composer*. Russell's ideas became an essential ingredient in Baker's compositions, and the personal relationship established at the Lenox School was to be a turning point in David Baker's career:

> And I fought tooth-and-nail, man: I was the thorn in George's side. I was Mr. Inquisitive: "Tell me why: I want to know. Don't tell me it's *a priori*. I want to know why." And he presented me with cogent arguments that allowed me to shape a philosophy that encompasses the Lydian Concept but is not exclusively that – even though I suppose George would say that if I were to look at it; I probably could confirm that everything that happened in music has been embraced by the Concept. And that's no different from Scriabin and others who thought the "chord of nature" encompassed everything. I can only say that for me it

works. Only when I started playing with George and began to write pieces did I actually begin to use the Lydian Concept. I probably had used that material; but until George presented it, I had never thought to put a label on it that would have enabled me to use it consistently.[29]

In a 1964 interview with Don DeMichael for *DownBeat Magazine,* David confirmed that Russell's Lydian Chromatic Concept was influential to his musical career. Besides formulating into theory the predominantly orally transmitted principles of jazz thus far, it helped Baker realize that the language of jazz could easily be communicated to other players through written materials and instruction. In the interview, he pointed out,

> I consider George one of the really giant jazz minds today – if only because of his book [*The Lydian Chromatic Concept of Tonal Organization for Improvisation*]. It marked the turning point in my musical life. I think ultimately it will do that for other young players, because it opens doors nobody knows about or is commonly practicing. I've tried to put it into my own book, *Practical Applications of the Lydian Concept,* which hasn't been published yet. It's a book that shows how to use George's book.[30]

The Lenox School of Jazz held classes and rehearsals all day and concerts and jam sessions all night, and became the prototype for most jazz camps. The direct continuations were Stan Kenton's National Stage Band Camps, and one of the longest running series since 1972, the Jamey Aebersold Summer Jazz Workshops. Baker has taught theory, improvisation, and combos at the Aebersold Summer Camps every summer since its inception, passing on the concepts, immersion learning, and networking opportunities that he experienced during the summers at the Lenox School of Jazz. David remembers,

> So it was all these people and all these great, great teachers. We met all day and sessioned every night. Then the final night we played, and they covered it in the magazines, and they made some acetates from it. I guess now there's a commercial recording of it. So the School of Jazz was probably the prototype for what a school of jazz could be.[31]

Baker returned to Lenox the following summer, but not as a student. His Indianapolis group, under the leadership of George Russell – with David Young (saxophone), Al Kiger (trumpet), Chuck Israels (bass), and Joe Hunt (drums) – had become the George Russell Sextet.

THE GEORGE RUSSELL SEXTET

Born in Cincinnati, Ohio, on June 23, 1923, George Russell started out
as a drummer and soon entered the New York jazz scene.[32] Bouts of
tuberculosis kept him for extended periods in hospitals, where he developed much of the framework for his Lydian Chromatic Concept. The
1953 pamphlet grew into the quintessential jazz theory approach and
became the inspiration for Miles Davis's foray into modal jazz, as well as
codified the chord/scale relationships commonly used for jazz improvisation. After Max Roach replaced him in Benny Carter's band, Russell
gave up drumming and focused solely on composition. After launching
his career as a composer and bandleader with the 1956 album *The Jazz
Workshop*,[33] Russell was looking for a group willing to learn and perform
his intricate compositions, as well as an opportunity to play piano. During the Lenox Summer Workshop, Russell noted Baker's curiosity and
interest in composition as well as the high level of knowledge and skill
of his Indianapolis colleagues Larry Ridley and Al Kiger. He asked them
to be in his band, and they welcomed the opportunity:

> That first year was a revelation for me, because I really did start to learn and
> understand what George was talking about. So when George – at the end of the
> six weeks, George called me and Kiger and Joe Hunt and David Young in and
> talked to us and said he was getting ready to form a sextet. Would we like to be
> a part of his sextet? But he had first said he was going to do a recording and said
> we could come up and do the recording with him. He did a recording called *Jazz
> in the Space Age*. That was with me and David Young and Al Kiger, because he
> was using the drummer who used to play with Milt Hinton ... Osie Johnson on
> drums. Bill Evans and Paul Bley were the two piano players, even though neither
> one of them had big reputations at the time.[34]

Baker's group had a nightly gig at the Topper in Indianapolis, and
Russell decided to come out and rehearse with them daily as well as
join them on piano for their gigs. The group slowly but surely adapted
to Russell's new concept and ideas, and Baker describes the process as
an expansion of using colors, meaning different types of scales that have
distinctive sounds:

> It's hard to verbalize a concept that's so vague as playing freedom, so at first
> George had to use artificial methods to show us. He would say, "Here are the
> changes, but instead of playing in this key, move it around to another key, even

while the changes are going on at the same level." Then, instead of using chords or some kind of pre-existent idea that we might have had about what we were going to play, he had us use the tune itself-thematic development-what Sonny Rollins and Monk have been doing a long time. Then, it grew into taking any idea to its logical conclusion, irrespective of what's going on in the tune, chords, key or anything. . . . But though there would be a general chord scheme, we would use the Lydian concept, which would have, say, nine scales. So we could color using this or that scale, each of which has its own implied dictatorial way of playing. But even at that, with nine choices you have considerably more freedom than if you ran the four or five notes in a chord.[35]

The group then went on to record several albums for Riverside and Decca (see discography)[36] as well as appearing at major venues around the country, most notably an extended engagement at New York's Five Spot:[37]

I remember opening night in the Five Spot. George [Russell] had written all of this music and we hadn't perfected it, but we had it under control. I remember looking out and there was J. J. Johnson sitting at one table, John Coltrane with one leg against the wall was eating a box of Sunkist raisins, Miles Davis was there, you name it, not because of us but because of George Russell. We were so busy trying to play this difficult music that we couldn't really think about who was watching us, but we also had the advantage of them not knowing exactly what we were trying to do![38]

Thelonious Monk was playing with his group around the corner from the Five Spot at the Jazz Gallery. Baker and his colleagues often went around the corner after their gigs to hear them, but Monk's group hadn't come over to the Five Spot yet. Baker recalls this humorous encounter with Thelonious Monk:

So one night I looked up when I'd finished playing a solo and I opened my eyes and Monk is standing 20 feet from me with his hat on and his arms crossed and when I came off stage he said, "You do look a little like me." Somebody had told him that we looked alike. This was 1959. I didn't see Monk again until 1964. I was with Jamey Aebersold and we were in Cincinnati and we were down in the ballpark in the warm-up rooms. I hear a gasp and I look around and there's Monk and he walked up to me and said, "But you're uglier than I am." And I thought, "This is so out. This conversation started five years ago."[39]

Several of David Baker's compositions were included on George Russell's recordings, such as "Kentucky Oysters," "War Gewesen," "Honesty," "Lunacy," and "121 Bank Street." The success with the group and the recognition of Baker's artistry culminated in the New Star Award from

Newspaper article on 1960 tour with the Quincy Jones Big Band.
Courtesy of David Baker.

DownBeat Magazine in 1962, shared with his childhood friend and fellow trombonist Slide Hampton. Another lifelong friendship evolved during this period as Baker was a member of Quincy Jones's big band during their European tour in 1960. In fact, exactly fifty years after making music together, Baker initiated the awarding of an honorary doctorate by the Indiana University Jacobs School of Music to Quincy Jones, where Jones also addressed the class of 2010 with a most memorable commencement speech. This specific tour in 1960 ended Jones's extended stay in Paris where he studied with Nadia Boulanger, leaving the bandleader deeply in debt and ready to accept a job offer from Mercury Records as musical director. Baker brought along the arrangement of his tune "Screamin' Meemies" for the tour, and it became part of the nightly performance repertoire. He shares some tour memories:

> You couldn't take the money out of the country. So you could buy anything you wanted to, but you were not allowed to take any money out of the country. This was still a rough time. And so consequently you could make enough money to do what you needed to do but any exchange of that money stayed in wherever we were. And so we were, as Quincy said, broker than the Ten Commandments.[40]

Baker shared a newspaper article from Switzerland, where the reporter noted that the band started an impromptu jam session on the train to the delight of the fellow passengers. An invitation to a skiing trip in the Alps didn't work out very well though, since the musicians were not dressed for the occasion and had never skied in their lives.

TROMBONE ARTISTRY AND JAZZ COMPOSITION

David Baker's composition "Kentucky Oysters" was first recorded on the 1960 Riverside recording *Stratusphunk* by the George Russell Sextet. It featured George Russell as leader and on piano, David Baker on trombone, David Young on saxophone, Al Kiger on trumpet, Chuck Israels on bass, and Joe Hunt on drums; and was produced by legendary jazz producer Orrin Keepnews. The album has recently been reissued in CD format.

The tune is notated in $\frac{3}{4}$ meter, resulting in a blues of twenty-four-bars length. It certainly has a $\frac{6}{8}$ gospel feel to it and if notated in $\frac{6}{8}$ meter

"Kentucky Oysters" by David Baker.

Blues Motif.

or even $\frac{6}{4}$ meter, the regular twelve-bar-blues form would be restored. But either way, it clearly is a triple meter variation on the blues, incorporating the gospel feel of the black churches, and has been referred to as twenty-first-century soul music. In the liner notes to the album, Russell refers to it as a "good old funky down-home blues in $\frac{3}{4}$."

The melody is based on a simple blues riff, using mainly notes 6, 1, and 3 of the blues scale and rocking back and forth between those notes in very fast eighth-note motion.

Traditionally, the melody of a blues is divided into three equal phrases, with the first two using similar melodic and lyric materials and the third one providing contrast. Similarly, the first two phrases of "Kentucky Oysters" are based on the principal motif and incorporate similar rhythmic structures. The third phrase establishes contrast, by departing from the blues scale with triadic quarter-note sequences outlining the V–IV–I chord structure.

In the spirit of Russell's theoretical concept based on the Lydian scale and explorations into contemporary techniques – the trademarks of the group – "Kentucky Oysters" is clearly rooted in the gospel and blues tradition with added technical and compositional challenges. Most notable is the overall speed of the recording, requiring advanced technical facility on each instrument and double tonguing on the horns during the sixteenth-note sequences. Further intellectual twists are the subdivisions of the first phrase into two similar four-bar phrases, while the second phrase is extended into one eight-bar phrase – displacing the sixteenth-note motif of bar 3 into the seventh bar of the second phrase with reverse movement. Similar games of the intellect are often found in Baker's compositions and are also a trademark of his style of communication. Fellow jazz studies faculty member at Indiana University Tom Walsh points out Baker's frequent word plays:

> That curiosity and kind of active mind, it extends to just the way he likes to engage in word play. Puns are a big part of that. And, just all the, you know, storytelling and jokes and all that.[41]

On the initial recording, the group introduced the tune with an eight-bar intro based on the last eight bars of the form. After the customary repeat of the melody, David Young takes a saxophone solo followed by Baker's trombone solo. The most noticeable turn of events when Baker enters is his consistent improvisation in $\frac{4}{4}$ time against the triple meter of the rhythm section. Throughout all of his six choruses, his lines are in solid $\frac{4}{4}$, making his quarter notes the same length as the dotted quarter notes of the rhythm section. Such a polyrhythmic twist is a trademark of his performances, and colleague and 21st Century Bebop Band member Luke Gillespie shares these memories:

> I remember when Geoff Keezer was here a few years ago. I cannot remember what we were talking about, metric modulation and playing against the meter or whatever. He pointed out just what I was about to say. He said, "Yeah, you know, like the way David Baker plays on that George Russell album [*Stratusphunk*], [the tune] "Kentucky Oysters." There it is, a blues tune, but it was in three. Then David comes on with his solo and he plays completely in two and nobody goes there. They all stay home! In fact, to this day, every time I've played a gig with David, all the 21st Century Bebop [Band] gigs wherever they have been, in a concert setting, concert hall, or Bear's Place or anywhere, when it is time for his solo on a tune in three – he will do it only once a gig – he plays in

two. That is his signature. . . . I remember the first time I heard him do that, the bass player, the drummer, all three of us – I forgot who was on the gig – we were all students, we all thought oh, we hear what he did so we're gonna go with him. So we all started playing in two and David, after a few bars, he turned around to say, "Stay home, stay home. Don't go with me. Stay home!" So we go, "OK, oh, all right." We go back into three and that was what he wanted and unless somebody is asking you to do that, you don't necessarily go there. I learned a lot just about performance etiquette on the bandstand from David that way. Don't always go with the soloist as a basic admonition, as in don't always mutate [with] the soloist. Of course, have a conversation with the soloist. Let the soloist dictate what the mood is going to be and what the rhythmic groove is going to be and follow. But you don't always repeat and imitate. There is a fine line between repeating and trying to go with the soloist. He made us reflect and try to really get inside the music more on the bandstand that way.[42]

Another interesting rhythmic and textural twist is the placements of the solo breaks throughout his solo. Traditionally, such breaks would be placed during the first four bars of a solo chorus or possibly for a complete chorus. At the beginning of the third chorus, the band drops out for eight bars, then accompanies for twenty-four bars, repeating this pattern two more times. As a result, the consecutive breaks fall in the middle of the fourth chorus and at the end of the fifth chorus – establishing an asymmetric pattern against the blues form. Similarly, Baker patterns his melodic material for the breaks in a contrasting manner with two descending lines on the blues scale for the first break.

For the second break, placed in the middle of a chorus, he refers back to the descending augmented triad sequence used at the same spot during the previous chorus, moving back up using the F-major scale.

At the end of the fifth chorus, Baker built the tension into his last chorus through repetition of the high F with rhythmic variations.

Break fill 1.

Break fill 2.

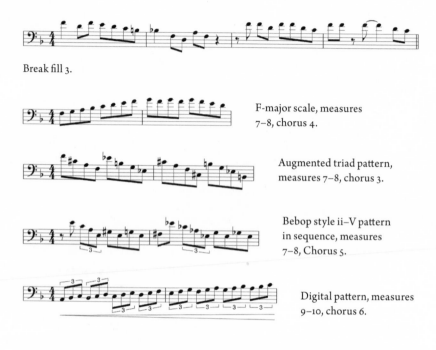

Break fill 3.

F-major scale, measures
7–8, chorus 4.

Augmented triad pattern,
measures 7–8, chorus 3.

Bebop style ii–V pattern
in sequence, measures
7–8, Chorus 5.

Digital pattern, measures
9–10, chorus 6.

In terms of melodic material, Baker employs several techniques that later appear in his instructional methods and classroom teaching. In chapter 11 of *Jazz Improvisation,* he offers the suggestion of employing a variety of scales to improvise over a blues progression.[43] Besides the common blues scale, he also uses the F-major scale.

Another component of his teaching is the use of patterns and sequences throughout the solo: augmented triad patterns, Bebop style ii–V patterns in sequence, and digital patterns (see examples above).

It is very important to note that all the theoretical and practical elements found throughout this analysis of Baker's solo appear throughout his instructional materials. For instance, *Jazz Improvisation* offers suggestions on using different melodic ideas to build tension during a blues improvisation, as well as ideas for creating sequential patterns, and the need to practice such ideas in all twelve keys. He makes a point of practicing and performing such principles himself, and Luke Gillespie confirms the inspiration of hearing a teacher practice what he teaches to his students:

> I remember hearing him in 1979 in his studio as an undergrad. I heard him practicing these bebop tunes and bebop scales working things out in twelve keys on

the cello. I remember he was practicing just like a student, just like he was asking us to do and had to do it all over again.[44]

In terms of trombone technique, the influence of J. J. Johnson can be heard in his clear execution of fast lines and melodies. The instrument doesn't lend itself naturally to playing quickly changing notes over a large range, as the combination of placing the slide at the right spot and articulating through the mouthpiece requires much coordination and practice. Even the fast triplet sequence at the end of the sixth chorus leading up to an exciting finale of the solo was executed clearly and crisply.

Fellow trombonist, arranger, and composer Brent Wallarab adds the following comments on the special features of David Baker's trombone technique:

> I would say without question that David was the most contemporary trombonist of his generation, displaying concepts that were as advanced as any musician playing at the time. In his playing, one can hear a deep exploration of harmonic and time concepts. His technique utilized the now common approach called "doodle-tonguing." It is a multiple-tongue technique, which allows trombonists to articulate very rapidly, always the most challenging hurdle to overcome. Without keys or valves, which on saxophones and trumpets permit natural quick articulation with the use of less tongue, the trombone has no mechanical device for articulation. It must all come from techniques developed especially for the trombone. David was an innovator in several of these techniques including doodle-tongue, against-the-grain playing, and fretting.
>
> The doodle-tongue technique incorporates a dual-action articulation. Most wind players single tongue, which uses a single stroke of the tip of the tongue toward the front roof of the mouth (ta). To play rapidly, brass musicians developed the double-tongue technique which alternates a glottal (ka) articulation with a tongue stroke. The effect is ta-ka-ta-ka-ta-ka. More effective in classical playing, the ta-ka style double tongue is too harsh and "straight" to sound natural in jazz. David (along with a few others of his generation) modified it to a softer, more swinging technique utilizing a "dl" articulation combined with the single stroke tongue similar to saying duh-dl-duh-dl-duh-dl. David, being one of the initial developers of this technique, was able to play at extremely fast tempos with incredible accuracy. It is now a very common technique among modern trombonists.
>
> Against-the-grain playing is when the trombonist manipulates the embouchure (placement and tension on the mouthpiece) to play higher, while the slide moves down the horn. This allows the embouchure to articulate across the overtones of the horn without using any tongue at all. The initial concept seems counterintuitive. Typically, when a trombonist plays a single sustained note and moves the slide down the horn, the effect is a descending smear. Makes sense: the slide goes down so the note goes down. But when this technique is used, the

Complete trombone solo on "Kentucky Oysters," as recorded on
Stratusphunk by the George Russell Sextet, Chorus 1–3.

slide goes down, the air is sustained, but the player "lips" the note up, creating an
against-the-grain effect.

Fretting is very similar to the technique guitarists use. A trombonist can work
out a melodic idea (or lick) using a combination of slide positions. The player
can then transpose the slide combinations in any direction, thereby transposing
the entire lick to a new key. The trombone is the only wind instrument that can
utilize this technique.

"Kentucky Oysters"(continued), Chorus 4–6.

In addition to David's advanced harmonic/time concepts and innovative techniques, David's trombone playing was also characterized by a very recognizable tone quality (warm, intimate, and burry in a very pleasant way) and an impeccable sense of time. David's time feel was as solid and spot on as the best drummers of the era. He was a controlled player in every sense.[45]

NOTES

1. Nesaule, *A Woman in Amber*, 215.
2. David Baker, interview by Lida Baker, June 19–21, 2000, transcript, Smithsonian Jazz Oral History Project, www.smithsonianjazz.org/oral_histories/pdf/joh_DavidNBaker_transcript.pdf.
3. Ibid.
4. David Brent Johnson, "The Basics of David Baker," August 28, 2007, indianapublicmedia.org/nightlights/the-basics-of-david-baker-a-conversation/.
5. Baker, interview, June 19–21, 2000.
6. Ibid.
7. Ibid.
8. Jerry Coker, interview by Monika Herzig, July 7, 2009.
9. Baker, interview, June 19–21, 2000.
10. Ibid.
11. Ibid.
12. Ibid.
13. Randy Brecker, interview by Monika Herzig, January 11, 2010.
14. Jamey Aebersold, interview by Monika Herzig, August 22, 2009.
15. Gary Campbell, interview by Monika Herzig, July 7, 2009.
16. Ted Watts (founding member of the Indianapolis Jazz Club), unpublished article on the Gallery series at 1444 North Pennsylvania Avenue in Indianapolis from December 1958 to March 1961.
17. Duncan Schiedt, personal communication. Schiedt witnessed the phone call but had run out of batteries for his camera that night and wasn't able to take pictures.
18. Schuller, "Indiana Renaissance," 48.
19. Baker, interview, June 19–21, 2000.
20. Larry Ridley, interview by Monika Herzig, January 11, 2010.
21. Michael Fitzgerald, "Lenox School of Jazz," November 1, 1993, www.jazzdiscography.com/Lenox/lenhome.htm.
22. Yudkin, *The Lenox School of Jazz*, 54.
23. Further details in Fitzgerald, "Lenox School of Jazz."
24. Brubeck, "David Baker and the Lenox School of Jazz," 44.
25. Baker mentions this list of "firsts" in Brubeck, "David Baker and the Lenox School of Jazz," 53.
26. Ridley, interview.
27. Fitzgerald, "Lenox School of Jazz."
28. Tom Walsh, interview by Monika Herzig, May 4, 2010.
29. Brubeck, "David Baker and the Lenox School of Jazz," 51.
30. DeMichael, "Vortex," 15–18.
31. Baker, interview, June 19–21, 2000.
32. Detailed info in Ratliff, "George Russell."
33. George Russell Smalltet, *The Jazz Workshop*, RCA Victor LPM-1372, featuring Art Farmer (tp), Hal McKusick (fl, as), Bill Evans (p), Barry Galbraith (g), Milt Hinton (b), Teddy Kotick (b), George Russell (chromatic d -1), Osie Johnson (woodblocks -1, d -2/5), and Paul Motian (d).
34. Baker, interview, June 19–21, 2000.
35. DeMichael, "Vortex," 17.
36. Most notably *The George Russell Sextet at the Five Spot* and *The George Russell Sextet in Kansas City* for Decca; and *The Stratus Seekers* and, with Eric Dolphy, *Ezz-thetics* for Riverside.
37. George Russell Sextet at the Five Spot, Decca, recorded September 20, 1960.
38. Johnson, "The Basics of David Baker."
39. Johnson, "The Basics of David Baker."
40. David Baker, interview by Monika Herzig, May 25, 2010.
41. Walsh, interview.

42. Luke Gillespie, interview by Monika Herzig, May 6, 2010.
43. Baker, *Jazz Improvisation*, 66ff.

44. Gillespie, interview.
45. Brent Wallarab, e-mail message to
Monika Herzig, July 2010.

REFERENCES

Baker, David. *Jazz Improvisation: A Comprehensive Method for All Musicians.* 2nd ed. Van Nuys, Calif.: Alfred Publishing, 1983.

Brubeck, Darius. "David Baker and the Lenox School of Jazz." *Jazz Education Journal* 35, no. 2 (September/October 2002): p. 42–55.

DeMichael, Don. "Vortex: The Dave Baker Story." *DownBeat*, nos. 31/32 (December 17, 1964): 15–18.

Heining, Duncan. *George Russell: The Story of an American Composer.* Lanham, Md.: Scarecrow Press, 2010.

Nesaule, Agate. *A Woman in Amber.* New York: Soho Press, 1995.

Ratliff, Ben. "George Russell, Composer Whose Theories Sent Jazz in a New Direction, Dies at 86." *New York Times*, July 29, 2009.

Russell, George. *The Lydian Chromatic Concept of Tonal Organization for Improvisation, volume 1.* 4th ed. N.p.: Beekman, 2001.

Schuller, Gunther. "Indiana Renaissance." *Jazz Review* 2, no. 8 (September 1959): 48–50.

Yudkin, Jeremy. *The Lenox School of Jazz.* South Egremont, Mass.: Farshaw, 2006.

3

New Beginnings

MONIKA HERZIG AND NATHAN DAVIS

WITH A TRAGIC revelation at the height of Baker's career as a jazz trombonist and a young generation fighting for peace and civil rights, the 1960s started with fateful changes for America's social environment as well as for David Baker's career. The status of jazz as an art form and its inclusion in academia experienced a particularly remarkable surge during this period. A change of status for jazz came originally from abroad when many jazz performers moved to Paris and other European cities after World War I to escape the prejudice and discrimination they experienced in their home country. In fact, saxophonist and educator Nathan Davis, director of jazz studies at the University of Pittsburgh, had found a new home in Paris prior to returning to Pittsburgh on the recommendation of David Baker:

He [Robert Snow, chair of the Pittsburgh music department] contacted David Baker, and David Baker said, "I know a guy, you know, if you could get him to come back, but he's never gonna come back, 'cause he's said it in interviews and magazines. . . ." I was kinda, you know, I was working as a jazz musician, you know, I had a little rep, so I was doing fine, and I had done a lot of interviews, and I had always said that I wasn't gonna come back.[1]

Even though jazz is often referred to as "America's Classical Music" as its African roots evolved as a result of the uniquely American melting pot, its acceptance as a subject for education was slow, because its chief practitioners – especially during its first half century – were Afro-American innovators. In its infancy, jazz was blamed for the outrageous behavior and deteriorating morals of America's youth due to early associations with pure entertainment, sensual behavior, and poverty. The National Music Chairman of the Federation of Women's Clubs expressed then-current feelings about jazz in 1921 when she called it barbaric and claimed "it has a demoralizing effect upon the human brain [that] has been demonstrated by many scientists."[2]

As a result of the civil rights movement and an increased interest in black traditions during the 1960s, college-level jazz instruction experienced a surge in popularity. *DownBeat Magazine*'s "Guide to College Jazz Programs 1965–1969" reported an increase from 29 to 165 colleges offering jazz courses. All the while, the acceptance of jazz in academia was an uphill battle. This chapter documents Baker's pioneering work in jazz education during the 1960s, and culminates with Nathan Davis's piece on effective jazz education. Baker was outspoken about the ambivalence toward jazz studies as a component of the traditional music curriculum during this time. His knowledge of jazz as well as classical music styles, his pedagogical vision and wealth of materials, and most of all his willingness to bring factions together have played a major role in making America's "classical music" a legitimate course of study. In a 1973 article for *Black World,* he pinpointed the racial dilemma for the reluctant acceptance of jazz:

First, jazz is a Black music. The Black man gave this music – the language, the vocabulary, the essence – to the world, and every advancement and major innovation of this music has come from him. . . . Because jazz had its origins in a tradition outside the perimeters of Western art music, its lack of acceptance was virtually assured.[3]

REINVENTION

At the height of his career as a performer, Baker had to deal with the consequences of a tragic injury sustained in a car accident that required him to give up playing the trombone and effectively reinvent his musical career. On the drive back to Indianapolis with drummer Ray Church-man after their last night with Fred Dale's group at Lake Hamilton Resort in Hamilton, Indiana, in summer 1953, Baker was asleep in the front seat. The impact of a head-on collision with another vehicle ejected him through the windshield into a cornfield, as seat belts were not a common security measure at the time. Baker suffered life-threatening injuries, including a partially severed left arm, and awoke after a week-long coma in a hospital in Huntington, Indiana. Although he recovered the use of his arm, he began having problems with speech and embouchure several years later. Doctors informed him that he had been playing trombone with a dislocated jaw for seven years, and that the injured side had atrophied as the healthy side enlarged to compensate. Throughout the late 1950s until the end of 1960, Baker underwent multiple operations, wore acrylic braces to keep his jaw in place, and even had his jaws wired shut for weeks:

> So I'm in a hospital – in Passavant Hospital in Chicago. I spent off and on the better part of a year going back and forth, either as an inpatient or outpatient. There were some moments where I really – because I couldn't play. I had no instrument that I could play. I did write my first book – a set of exercises based on the Lydian concept, on George's stuff. Toward – I don't know – after about five or six months, I suppose, they suggested – the doctor who was treating me . . . Well, first of all, they wanted to go through – when nothing else was working, they had injected what they call sclerosing fluid. What that does is, it's an acid, and it scars the tissue. Then, when the tissue heals, it pulls it back into place. [My] face [was] swollen up as big as a basketball, almost, and the pain was just incredible. I stayed there. It didn't work. They were going to talk about severing the buccinator muscles, which are the muscles which open and close your mouth, and then see if they could retrain other muscles to do the job. Fortunately, the doctor that I was with said, "No. We're not going to do anything that is irreversible."[4]

Some have speculated about possible mis- or undertreatment following the accident because of Baker's race. The lingering question is whether a correct diagnosis at the time of the accident could have prevented the loss of Baker's ability to play trombone. It also remains unclear whether, even with a proper diagnosis, the injury could have been treated sufficiently to sustain the extensive embouchure demands of daily practice and performance of a professional brass player. Fellow Fred Dale band member Jerry Coker offers these recollections and thoughts:

> When we finished our last gig there [at Lake Hamilton in 1953] and when he was on his way back there to Indianapolis, that's when he had the accident. Two or three other members of the band were with him. They tried to take him to the nearest hospital. They were on the outskirts of Indianapolis. I wasn't there but they told me all about it. They tried to take him to the nearest hospital, but they wouldn't admit him because he was black. You gotta remember the year. This is like mid '50s, and things were very different then. Musicians like Al Kiger sometimes went up to Indianapolis with David and they would pull into a restaurant and jump out of the car to go eat. And David would still be sitting in the car and they'd ask, "What are you doing, aren't you hungry?" and he said, "They won't serve me, baby." So you have to remember, those times were very different. At any rate, the hospital wouldn't admit him, so they had to drive for about forty-five minutes to go to the other side of town to go to a hospital that did serve black people, probably a black hospital, period. When he got there, because he was black and underpaid, so to speak, the treatment they gave him – all they did was x-ray his shoulder area and found a broken collarbone. But they didn't know there was anything wrong with the jaw because they didn't want to spend the money on the x-ray. They didn't want to charge him for it. In other words, they were giving him a cheap examination for his benefit because he was black. They can't afford that kind of money, you know what I mean. Even a black doctor would probably try to protect a patient from being overcharged. White people don't care. They go in to have all these tests and x-rays and stuff and they figure, "Oh, it must be needed." It's hard to imagine what it was like for people who were disadvantaged. David wasn't disadvantaged, but he was black. That's all it took for them to do less than what they could have.[5]

In 1962 Baker received the New Star Award from *DownBeat Magazine,* shared with fellow Indiana Avenue alumnus Slide Hampton. The newest Riverside releases *Ezz-thetics* and *The Stratus Seekers* with the George Russell Sextet also garnered much positive attention and the world was taking note of this remarkable young trombonist as a member of Russell's sextet as well as a leader by himself. Unfortunately that same year it became clear that his trombone career was effectively over. In an interview with Tim Schneckloth for *DownBeat Magazine* in 1977, Baker describes this revelation:

We're talking about nightmare city . . . The year I had to give up trombone was the year we had a clean sweep from Indianapolis – J. J. had won the Established Talent award in the *DownBeat* Critics Poll, and Slide and I had tied for the New Star award. I was over at the *DownBeat* office with Don DeMichael and I had just come from the doctor, and he had told me, it was the end of a career for me. So it was kind of like a double trauma.[6]

The prospect of starting from scratch on a new instrument at the age of thirty-one was devastating and frustrating, as it would take years to achieve anything close to his facility on the trombone. Ericsson confirmed in a review of performance-related research that extended practice on an instrument over at least a ten-year period is a prerequisite for mastery.[7] Nevertheless, Baker attempted the task while simultaneously shifting his focus to composition and education:

I started thinking I have to have another instrument, so I decided I was going to play piano. Jeannie was working at Cadillac – Hoosier Cadillac in Indianapolis. I started practicing piano eight hours a day. I practiced eight hours a day. It only took me about six months to figure out that piano wasn't the instrument that I needed to play. So then I bought a bass, and I started to play the bass. That came pretty quick. Mr. Brown, my band teacher from Crispus Attucks High School said, "Bass is not challenging you enough." He went out and bought a $15 cello and put it back together from a pawn shop and gave me the cello. [Laughs] Whew! And I've never forgiven him, even though I love him, even for that.[8]

Baker acknowledged the support during this difficult period of family, friends, and fellow musicians who included the beginning cellist in the fertile Indianapolis jazz scene. Most of all, his superb work ethic and discipline enabled him to make the cello his performance tool and simultaneously hone his skills as a major composer:

It's a challenging thing on every level. But it was a time that so much was going on in Indianapolis at the time, even though I was a beginning cellist, everybody – Elvin [Jones] was coming out there, hanging out, during the summer, playing. Chuck Carter was there. Kiger was there. Willis Kirk, the drummer the other night, was there. David Lahm had moved to Indianapolis. Paul Plummer and all the guys that had been a part of the different versions of the George Russell group were there. And so all of those cats were coming out and we were having jam sessions. Man, we were having jam sessions and playing all the time, so I was growing by leaps and bounds. Cello is not a user-friendly instrument, for one thing. It was kicking my butt nine ways to Sunday, but I was playing with everybody, so it was easy to really begin to grow.[9]

Losing the ability to play an instrument as a medium of expression is similar to the loss of language – in the case of a vocalist, losing the voice means losing speech and the language of music. Grammy-nominated vocalist Janet Lawson unfortunately had this experience and testifies that Baker's mentorship in overcoming such obstacles helped her work through a similarly difficult period:

> This is why I connected with him, losing my voice nominated for a Grammy for my first album with my quintet and hearing and feeling my voice dwindle and dwindle and then getting that Lyme disease and Bell's palsy. And what do I do? I couldn't sing, I couldn't talk; I'm finally able to talk again. And so I have been drawing on the spirit of this man who I have gotten to know and call a dear friend. I'm drawing on that. Every time we talk he says, "You're in our prayers. You're going to get better." His spirit is indomitable, just indomitable.[10]

By 1964, Baker was back performing in the Indianapolis clubs with his groups. Given the unusual frontline of two horns and cello, the group played mostly David's compositions and arrangements. David Lahm, pianist and son of lyricist Dorothy Fields, decided to move to Indianapolis in 1964 to learn from Baker, whom he had admired as a trombonist at the Lenox School of Jazz. He recalls some audience resistance to the new sound:

> So I finish school, do my six months in the army, I get to Indiana and get myself an apartment and during that time I discover that David is no longer playing the trombone. He had this atrophy attack him and so now he's playing the cello. So this was not what I was expecting. But he had this group together and he was going to open this new jazz club in Indianapolis around Thirtieth Street. There was another club across the street from it where Pookie Johnson was playing. So he put together this group: Willis Kirk was playing drums and Al Reeve was playing bass, I'm playing piano, and David is playing the cello; he was the leader. And we were playing a bunch of his tunes and we played the club for six nights a week. And people came and they were scratching their heads – you guys are playing jazz on the cello?[11]

Throughout this traumatic period, Baker started writing music and sharpening his compositional tools. The smaller jazz pieces grew into larger works exploring extended classical forms. He wrote what he considered his first really serious composition – a cantata for string orchestra, jazz band, and solo singers with twelve movements based on Psalm 22 – to commemorate the death of his father in 1964. Psalm 22 includes King David's lamentation invoked by Jesus at the crucifixion, "My God, my God, why hast thou forsaken me?" – a thought that might have crossed Baker's mind during this period.

THE RISE OF JAZZ IN ACADEMIA

Hints started coming in from Indiana University that Dean Wilfred C. Bain was considering starting a jazz program. In 1947, during his previous appointment as head of the music department at what is now known as the University of North Texas, Bain had initiated the first bachelor's degree program in jazz studies. Under the direction of Edwin "Buddy" Baker, jazz ensembles were set up for credit at Indiana University in 1960. Roger Pemberton taught one of the ensembles as well as jazz arranging until 1964, when saxophonist Jerry Coker assumed responsibilities for jazz classes and ensembles.[12] In 1966 Jerry Coker was hired full time to create a jazz program at the University of Miami, and Bain asked him for recommendations to help him start a similar program at Indiana University. Jerry Coker recalls his conversations supporting David Baker's appointment:

> He [Bain] called me in and asked me, "Do you have any idea who could replace you?" "Yeah," I said, "my recommendation is David Baker." "Ah," he said and let it go. About two months passed and he called me in and he said, "Do you have any idea who could replace you?" And I said, "You just asked me that a couple of months ago – David Baker, it shouldn't be anybody else. He belongs here, he would pull all of the factions of the music department together in some quite extravagant presentations like choirs and singers and narrators." You know how he is, he builds huge things. And he thought about it for a second and he said, "You know, we had a black percussion instructor here." And I said, "Yes, I know, he was here when I was a student." He was talking about Dick Johnson. And I said, "What does he have to do with it?" And Dean Bain said, "Well, we tried that and he just didn't fit in." I had no idea that he had any kind of feelings like that. And I said, "Nevertheless, that's my only recommendation." And he said, "OK, tell him to come in." [imitates annoyed voice] in that kind of tone of voice because he was ticked, because I didn't give him any other suggestions. And it evidently worked out fine.[13]

Coker's predictions about pulling all factions together and creating extravagant presentations proved to be prophetic in many regards. A year earlier, David Baker had published an extensive article in *DownBeat*

Magazine documenting his vision for an ideal teacher of jazz as well as components of a jazz curriculum.[14] He argued for hiring as teachers competent professionals who had the skills and background to share their expertise with the students, rather than the currently available and socially acceptable weak section player. "Why the almost systematic exclusion of qualified Negro jazzmen from collegiate and clinic jazz programs?" he asked, referring to the stereotypes of the black jazz musician as drunk, irresponsible, generally inarticulate, and undesirable junkies – and the resulting play-it-safe policy by which the student suffers. Furthermore, Baker suggested the components of an effective jazz curriculum as courses in theory; history; style analysis of the works of great jazz composers, arrangers, and players; as well as improvisation. He even proposed a conference for jazz teachers, potential jazz teachers, and jazz names as a means for improving the quality of teaching through exchange of ideas and strategies. Arguments for the need of a jazz curriculum included diminishing performance and jam opportunities, diversification of jazz styles, and increased availability of learning resources. Baker documented in considerable detail the ideal jazz program, as exemplified by this excerpt:

> The student must be made aware of the importance of pacing himself, of working toward specific climaxes in a solo. He must be taught the concepts of tension and relaxation, of understatement and subtlety, of mixing the novel and the old to heighten musical interest. He must be constantly reminded of the value of economizing, getting the most from the material available to him. A student needs to know from what sources he may get material on which to improvise. He should know that often the tune itself (melody, rhythm, etc.) can be his best source of solo material.[15]

With such a detailed outline on the drawing board, despite resistance from some colleagues, the bachelor's degree in jazz studies was approved in 1968:

> I remember a man who unfortunately is dead now, because he was a good man, but he was pretty staunch in his belief that – he told me that, "as long as I'm here, jazz band will never be a major ensemble." Two weeks later, on a Thursday morning, it passed as a major ensemble.[16]

At the zenith of the civil rights movement, students were ready and eager to learn about Afro-American history and traditions. When Baker

put together new courses on jazz history and jazz analysis, their popularity was overwhelming:

> One year I taught a course over in the business building, because there were so
> many students, probably 500 students in the class, as well as the fact that it was
> then sent out over T V to other branches of our campus.[17]

Soon courses in jazz arranging, improvisation, and ensemble playing completed the degree program. Of course, the new demand was
not confined to Indiana. College jazz programs blossomed nationwide
and created a huge demand for instructional materials and jazz arrangements. In fact, during the last forty years, jazz education programs have
been incorporated into the course offerings of most colleges around the
country. Porter reports that the jazz program established in 1947 at the
University of North Texas (then North Texas State College) was the
first, followed by that established at the Berklee College of Music in
Boston. Some of today's leading jazz programs are at Indiana University, the University of Miami, Eastman School of Music, the New England Conservatory of Music, New York University, and the University
of Northern Colorado.[18] The 2008 Annual Jazz Education Guide in *Jazz
Times* magazine lists 361 colleges and 564 high schools in the United
States offering jazz programs.[19] In comparison, 189 colleges and 50 high
school programs were listed in the 1997 Annual Jazz Education Guide.[20]
Presently, the jazz ensemble has become a regular institution at nearly
all colleges and high schools.

The extravagant productions foreseen by Jerry Coker during his
communications with Wilfred C. Bain also became reality. In his history
interview for the Smithsonian Institution's Jazz Oral History Project,
Baker remembered his experiments with avant-garde music and large
productions during his first years at Indiana University:

> You couldn't get in a concert, whenever we played. And what we were playing
> was really out. I would have orchestras with people positioned all around the
> room, playing. I did a history of Louis Armstrong. It was an hour-long work. It
> started with trumpet sections [in] all four corners of the auditorium, and guys
> walking through, recreating the music of New Orleans. It was theater music.[21]

Many years of playing, jamming, teaching, and developing ideas together proved to be the building blocks for a series of influential method

books and a groundbreaking concept of music minus one recordings for three Indiana University alumni – Jamey Aebersold, David Baker, and Jerry Coker, often referred to as the A B C s of jazz education.[22] Jerry Coker's *Improvising Jazz* was released in 1964 and according to Tanner's 1971 survey report "Jazz Goes to College," quickly became the most widely used textbook for improvisation classes.[23] In 1969, the first edition of David Baker's *Jazz Improvisation* followed (with a revised edition in 1983) as the first one in a long series of instructional method books.[24] Fellow educator and trombonist Tillman Buggs remembers the novelty of the idea of writing a book:

> David at that time once told me, I remember, we used to play duets early in the morning. I think he was on cello back then. This was after he played trombone, you know. He says, "Man, I'm going to write a book." And I didn't challenge it, but in my mind I just said: "Yeah, yeah. Yeah, David, I know you're going to write a book." Of course, you look at the catalog now, and the rest is history. I mean, a book, *a* book?[25]

Beginning in 1965, one of Baker's former students and fellow jazz educator Jamey Aebersold transformed the principle of music minus one recording into a series of play-along records featuring the standard repertoire of jazz played by a group of outstanding performers. The opportunity to take the rhythm section along into the practice room and work up performance skills made learning jazz accessible to a much larger population and transformed practice techniques for aspiring as well as accomplished musicians alike. The series has grown to date to 127 volumes of play-along albums. David recalled,

> J. J. Johnson would tell me, when he was just coming back from Hollywood and getting himself back into playing all the time, he said he would practice and practice and practice, and then, two weeks before time for the gig to start, he would get the Aebersold things out, go back in his workroom, and turn the thing up as loud as possible and play as loud as possible all day long with the records, and he would be in shape, when he would get ready to go. So Jamey has changed the way people think about how to learn.[26]

The same core group of Indiana performer-educators became instrumental in the formation of a series of summer jazz camps in the mold of the Lenox School of Jazz and the Stan Kenton National Stage Band

Camps. Most notable is the Jamey Aebersold Summer Jazz Workshop, featuring week-long sessions and over sixty faculty members – Aebersold, Baker, and Coker among them – since its inception in 1973. The first camp was an extension of a big band camp in Bloomington, Illinois, with special combo instruction; its curriculum – based on theory, master classes, and combo playing – is still in place. Aebersold believes that the success of their methods, materials, and camps was based on their genuine love of and dedication to teaching:

> I think David's approach to being all encompassing – you want the information, I'll give you the information – that's the way he's always been. And I think it helped change jazz education. Well, jazz education hadn't really started; but these other people had the knowledge, but I certainly never asked them questions and I don't believe anybody else did either. . . . They didn't sit down and talk about scales and chords and soloing and stuff like that, but David [Baker] did and Jerry [Coker] and other people and there was a sharing going on. I think it was great because if that hadn't happened I don't know what would have happened to jazz education.[27]

Even Baker's early vision of a conference bringing together jazz teachers, students, and professionals proved prophetic: the National Association of Jazz Educators was established in the late 1960s. The group evolved into the International Association for Jazz Education (IAJE) and presented thirty-five international conferences presenting several days of clinics, discussions, concerts, and exhibits from 1975–2008.

This love for teaching, fueled by sincere dedication, was acknowledged by the jazz community in 2000, when Baker received the American Jazz Masters Award from the National Endowment for the Arts during a ceremony at the International Association for Jazz Education conference in New York. Over seven thousand audience members offered a standing ovation. Indiana University colleague Luke Gillespie witnessed the event and offers the following report:

> A good portion of the audience was either his students, or [people who had] studied with one of his students, or who studied from his books. That is quite a few people. Almost everybody was touched by him in some way. In the middle of his acceptance speech, he said something that brought a standing ovation. There

The "ABCs" of jazz education – (from left) Jerry Coker, Jamey Aebersold, and David Baker – in Denmark, 1983. *Courtesy of Jamey Aebersold.*

were two times that brought a standing ovation; one was he said he wanted to thank his wife, Lida, for putting up with him, the beautiful calligraphy she has done over the years and so forth. Everybody acknowledged that with a huge ovation. And he also said something that struck a chord with any educator and that is, he said, "I also want to thank everyone for this award because" – he didn't name all the past recipients – "but I am honored to be the first teacher-performer to accept this award." And everyone else was either a performer, or they were performer-teacher on the side, or most performers will go get a teaching gig whatever. He was a performer obviously from the beginning but was a teacher from the beginning.[28]

THE MASTER TEACHER

Nathan Davis

When I was first approached about contributing an essay on David Baker, I was more than thrilled to attempt such a prestigious task, simply because I consider David Baker to be the best jazz teacher that I have ever known (please notice that I have intentionally omitted the term jazz educator because the term is too often used to describe high school band directors who teach and direct "stage bands" at local high school music festivals). David Baker, in my estimation, is much more. Baker is one of those rare "music philosophers" who is able to transfer the inner wisdom of artistry into a sophisticated teachable format so that everyone willing to learn has the tools. I certainly don't mean to put down high school band directors with this statement. On the contrary, I am simply reinforcing that David Baker is one of those gifted and experienced music teachers who can successfully facilitate music learning regardless of the age or status of the pupil in such a way that the student is immediately able to process the information into a practical learning tool. In order to fully understand the nature of my respect for David Baker as a true Master Teacher, I feel that it is first necessary to take this opportunity to revert back to the first time I actually began to correspond with David.

Paris in the 1960s and the Paris American Academy of Music

In the wake of the civil rights movement in the 1960s and an expanding interest in black culture, many schools, universities, colleges, and conservatories found themselves caught off guard and unprepared to teach courses in the area of jazz and African American music. During that period, saxophonist Joe Henderson and I had made a pact that we would both stick together and stay in Europe (Paris) to study composition with French composer and theorist Nadia Boulanger and play at the famous Paris Blue Note jazz club with American "expatriate" jazz drummer Kenny Clarke, pianist Bud Powell and a host of other expatriate American musicians who had found a jazz home away from America. This is important in order to understand how and why, in 1969, I ended up accepting the job offer to create a jazz program at the University of Pittsburgh. Although I never did get the chance to study with Nadia Boulanger, instead I had the great fortune to study composition with André Hodeir (André Hodeir was considered one of France's leading "new music" jazz and classical composers, and scholar-historians of the 1960s) in Paris. However, I did end up working seven nights a week with Kenny Clarke at the Blue Note and occasionally playing with Bud Powell, Johnny Griffin, the Modern Jazz Quartet, and just about every prominent jazz musician (Donald Byrd, Eric Dolphy, Sonny Stitt, Ornette Coleman, Dizzy Gillespie, and more) who stopped by the Blue Note to sit in or work with the great Kenny Clarke.

It was here, while working at the Blue Note, that I first became aware of the importance of David Baker as a pivotal figure in the world of jazz academia. Everyone that I talked to knew about David Baker and respected his work as an emerging jazz artist and educator. It was purely by accident that one morning I walked past the Schola Cantorum located at rue St. Jacques and decided to enter. The Schola Cantorum was one of the most prestigious music conservatories in Paris and served as the summer home of the Paris American Academy of Music under the direction of Richard Roy, a Pittsburgh native. The Paris American Academy was primarily a summer program that attracted students from around the world, especially American college students and university teachers trying to get summer credit for their studies, and young British rock bands looking to increase their knowledge of jazz as they heard its influences in the music of popular rock groups such as Blood, Sweat & Tears and Chicago. Based on this information, I approached director Richard Roy about teaching courses in jazz history, improvisation, arranging, and composition. As I prepared for teaching such classes, a number of musicians – both French and American – recommended that I read and study the works of David Baker.

Over the course of the next four years (1965–69), I taught and performed at the Paris American Academy. Richard Roy and I gained a certain personal and professional respect for each other and our particular interest in music; he was primarily interested in French romantic composers and I was interested in jazz and African American music, classical and ethnic music. However, it was in 1969 that Richard Roy informed me that Robert Snow, the chairman of the music department at the University of Pittsburgh, had contacted him at the suggestion of David Baker, to see if I would be interested in returning to the United States to create a jazz program at the University of Pittsburgh. Needless to say, I was not interested in leaving Kenny Clarke, Bud Powell, Johnny Griffin, and the Paris music scene, even though by that time Donald Byrd had already returned to teach at Howard [University] and was constantly encouraging me to come back. But it was David Baker, who had toured with Quincy Jones's big band as an emerging new trombone star, and a member of the great George Russell's group, who encouraged me to be a part of a new movement in jazz: jazz education. I figured that if this great innovator had that much faith in me and believed that I could make a contribution to jazz education that I would give it a shot. I should note that I had made a commitment to my German-born wife, Ursula, that I would stay only three years and then we would return to Europe. In addition, most of the musicians that I was working with in Paris considered accepting such a position as "selling out."

Kenny Clarke was one of the few jazz musicians who actually supported my plans. Comments such as "you can't teach jazz," "don't give away the secrets," "you can't teach feeling," "don't sell out," and so on, were devastating and almost convinced me to decline the offer. I am sure that back in the States, Baker received the same negative comments about his pedagogical commitment. With the firm recommendation of David Baker and the verbal blessings of Kenny Clarke, Donald Byrd, and Dizzy Gillespie, I finally agreed to ask Richard Roy to negotiate for me a three-year agreement with the University of Pittsburgh to create a jazz studies program that would "simulate, to the best of my ability, the

David Baker in the classroom in the '70s. *Courtesy of David Baker.*

professional world of jazz." Once the university officials agreed to these terms, I immediately contacted David Baker for his advice concerning the inner workings of the academy. To this day, as we celebrate my forty-second year as director of jazz studies at the University of Pittsburgh, I have not stopped asking David Baker questions about how, why, and what to do to improve our program at the University of Pittsburgh. At Indiana University, David Baker eventually was appointed to the rank of distinguished professor in recognition of his dedication, academic achievements, and exceptional contributions to the university and to the field. Without doubt, David Baker "wrote the book" on curriculum programs for jazz in academia. More importantly, he was also one of the outstanding performers of our time and the combination of his experience in the field with his genuine interest in pedagogy, is what I consider the ingredients of a master teacher.

David Baker, the Master Teacher

What is the definition of a master teacher and why do I consider David Baker such a teacher? First of all, I have seen the immense impact and effectiveness with students during countless observations of Baker's lecture demonstrations on improvisation, composition, jazz history, and much more during the University of Pittsburgh's annual Seminar on Jazz and in similar master classes at Florida Memorial University, Ravinia's Steans Institute, and too many others to list. Perhaps the thing that impressed me most was the fact that he approached the subject of improvisation from a historical-cultural perspective. The students were first guided through a series of historical scenarios designed to provide a firm foundation for understanding the different jazz styles. Once the students appeared to intellectually embrace the historical importance of the period, David then began to lay out the theoretical principles associated with a particular style. Finally, only after the students seemed to be comfortable with the historical, cultural and theoretical aspects of the periods and styles did he introduce the principal patterns that form the language for a particular style. Unfortunately, I have often observed other jazz teachers focus prominently on memorizing the more popular lines of the current jazz stars and poll winners and students mainly copying one or two of their favorite performers. As a result, those young improvisers might blindly string together groups of uninspiring notes that have little or no relationship to any particular style. In contrast, David Baker's historical approach ensures that the student improviser at least has the background to make a sincere musical statement grounded in "historical substance" and associated with the period in question. Naturally, this is where Baker's firsthand experiences as a member in the big bands of Quincy Jones, Stan Kenton, and Maynard Ferguson; the more experimental groups such as the George Russell Sextet; and during countless performances and jam sessions with his Indiana Avenue peers Freddie Hubbard, Slide Hampton, Ted Dunbar, J. J. Johnson, and the Montgomery brothers fuel his vast practical knowledge.

In addition to providing such invaluable resources, Baker has the very special gift of putting students at ease thanks to his friendly self-confidence and gift in communicating – thereby creating the kind of atmosphere conducive to learning. I can't emphasize enough my passionate belief in David Baker as a model master teacher of jazz. We took on an immense responsibility when we decided to pass on the history and provide guidance for the future of jazz as we became the first generation of practicing jazz musicians to introduce jazz degree programs in academia. The promise I had made to Kenny Clarke was "to tell the truth." Presently, jazz has become accessible to students all over the world and thanks to master teachers such as David Baker, Billy Taylor, Donald Byrd, Jerry Coker, and others who excelled as performers, but also were able to formulate the essence of this music and to provide the historical framework, has become recognized as a valid and influential art form.

NOTES

1. Nathan Davis, interview by Monika Herzig, June 16, 2009.

2. Faulkner, "Does Jazz Put the Sin in Syncopation?" 16, 34.

3. Baker, "The Battle for Legitimacy: Jazz versus Academia," 20.

4. David Baker, interview by Lida Baker, June 19–21, 2000, transcript, Smithsonian Jazz Oral History Project, www.smithsonianjazz.org/oral_ histories/pdf/joh_DavidNBaker_ transcript.pdf.

5. Jerry Coker, interview by Monika Herzig, July 7, 2009.

6. Schneckloth, "Guardians of the Musical Future," 16.

7. Ericsson, "Deliberate Practice and the Acquisition of Expert Performance," 366. Ericsson confirms that it takes a minimum of ten thousand hours of practice to master a skill.

8. Baker, interview, June 19–21, 2000.

9. Ibid.

10. Janet Lawson, interview by Monika Herzig, January 11, 2010.

11. David Lahm, interview by Monika Herzig, March 23, 2010.

12. "A Brief History of the Jacobs School of Music Jazz Department: Genesis and Evolution," Indiana University Jacobs School of Music website, April 11, 2011, www.music.indiana.edu/ departments/academic/jazz/history .shtml.

13. Coker, interview.

14. Baker, "The Academy's Neglected Stepchild."

15. Ibid., 32.

16. Baker, interview, June 19–21, 2000.

17. Ibid.

18. Porter, "Jazz in American Education Today," 136.

19. *JazzTimes* 2008/2009 Annual Jazz Education Guide.

20. *JazzTimes* 1997/1998 Annual Jazz Education Guide.

21. Baker, interview, June 19–21, 2000.

22. Adler, "The Good Book," 44.

23. Tanner, "Jazz Goes to College," 88.

24. See chapter 4 for more detailed discussion of his method books.

25. Tillman Buggs, interview by Monika Herzig, May 16, 2009.

26. Baker, interview, June 19–21, 2000.

27. Jamey Aebersold, interview by Monika Herzig, August 22, 2009.

28. Luke Gillespie, interview by Monika Herzig, May 6, 2010.

REFERENCES

Adler, David. The Good Book. Annual Jazz Education Guide. *Jazz Times* 2004/2005 Annual Jazz Education Guide, 43–46.

Baker, David. "The Battle for Legitimacy: 'Jazz' Versus Academia." *Black World* 23, no. 1 (November 1973): 20–27.

———. "Jazz: The Academy's Neglected Stepchild." *DownBeat* 32, no. 20 (September 22, 1965): 29–32.

———. *Jazz Improvisation; A Complete Method for All Musicians.* 2nd ed. Van Nuys, Calif.: Alfred Publishing, 1983.

Coker, Jerry. *Improvising Jazz.* New York: Simon and Schuster, 1964.

Ericsson, K. A. "Deliberate Practice and the Acquisition of Expert Performance: An Overview." *Psychological Review* 100, no. 3 (1993): 363–406.

Faulkner, Ann Shaw. "Does Jazz Put the Sin in Syncopation?" *Ladies' Home Journal* 38, no. 8 (August 1921): 16–34.

JazzTimes 1997/1998 Annual Jazz Education Guide.

JazzTimes 2008/2009 Annual Jazz Education Guide.

Porter, L. "Jazz in American Education Today." *College Music Symposium* (1989): 4–9.

Schneckloth, Tim. "Guardians of the Musical Future." *DownBeat* 44, no. 20 (December 1, 1977): 16–17.

Tanner, Paul. "Jazz Goes to College: Part 2." *Music Educators Journal* 57, no. 8 (April 1971): 49–93.

4

Defining Jazz
Education

JB DYAS

I HAVE KNOWN DAVID Baker
for twenty-five years, actually longer if you count the decade or so I
knew him through his jazz improvisation books before ever meeting him in person. Back then, in
the 1970s, his and a few others'
were the only books available de-
mystifying the secrets of how to
play this music. Before that, it was
basically "you either had it or you
didn't," meaning you either had
the talent to learn strictly by ear
from the records of the jazz masters, or you were out of luck. Virtually no comprehensive systematic method existed. Until David
Baker.

David is an eminent per-
former, composer, arranger,
bandleader, and conductor – but
I believe he has made his greatest contributions as a pedagogue.
In the same way saxophone great
Charlie Parker revolutionized the
music of jazz, setting its lingua

franca for all generations to come, David has set the standard for its teaching and learning. His methods have been, and will continue to be, the point of departure for today's jazz educators who follow the path he has efficaciously forged, continuing and building upon his jazz pedagogical legacy.

I know from whence I speak. Over the past twenty-plus years I have studied with David privately, performed and recorded with his big band and sextet, and completed my PHD in music education with a double minor in jazz studies under his guidance at Indiana University, where he has served as chairman of the jazz department since 1966. In addition to having taken virtually every jazz course David teaches at Indiana University, I also have attended his Advanced Jazz Improvisation classes numerous times at the Jamey Aebersold Summer Jazz Workshop, where I have been a faculty member since 1986. And I have logged countless wonderful hours traveling and hanging out with him, talking about the teaching of jazz and everything else under the sun.

Over the past couple of decades I have witnessed David work in every imaginable didactic situation from explaining jazz to beginners in language they understand, to serving as a jazz master-in-residence at the Thelonious Monk Institute of Jazz (where I currently serve as vice president of education and curriculum development) teaching our Monk Fellowship recipients – some of the most advanced graduate students in the world. And I have seen him communicate and relate to a wide variety of peers in language *they* understand – from the street, where jazz slang abounds, to higher academia, where you'd best walk in with a dictionary to understand the sophisticated discourse. It's uncanny how he belongs and is at ease in both situations, handling them and everything in between with aplomb, warmth, genuine interest, and a marvelous sense of humor.

Additionally, I have worked out of most of David's jazz pedagogical books and read dozens of his magazine articles. Now totaling over sixty texts and four hundred articles on jazz improvisation, composition and arranging, ear training, and related topics, David's published methods remain among the best of the countless jazz education materials flooding the market today. Indeed, many jazz education authors have acknowledged and paid respect to David for getting the whole modern approach of studying jazz started – either directly in their forewords or, frankly, indirectly in their obviously transparent reworkings of his concepts and methods (it has been said that imitation is the sincerest form of flattery).

I also recently had the opportunity to walk a block in David's pedagogical shoes at Indiana University, where I taught his full load of classes and directed his band while he was away for two weeks. Not only did I have a ball working with everyone from the hundred-plus non-music majors in his Jazz History class to the talented graduate students in his top big band and combo, I had the rare opportunity to experience Indiana University life from his perspective, which gave me further insight into what it means to be David Baker, jazz pedagogue. And, thanks to David's gifted wife, Lida – who has been his primary advisor, editor, and everything else over the past three decades – I have also been privy to all of David's course syllabi, handouts, tests, and the like.

Based on these personal experiences, including using David's methods with my own students over the years, as well as conducting formal interviews and having informal conversations with numerous David Baker students, alumni, and colleagues (many of whom are well known in the jazz world today in no small way due to his tutelage), I offer the following account of David's teaching. The sections treat his Indiana University jazz courses, clinics, private teaching and more, reflecting his pedagogical philosophy, approaches, methodologies, and personality. All is intended to serve as a point of departure (as David likes to say) with the hope of inspiring more effective teaching and learning regardless of subject matter, jazz or otherwise.

EAR TRAINING

For most jazz students, getting all the way through David's ear-training course and book, that is, thoroughly perfecting all the skills he recommends and for which he provides exercises, is nearly impossible. However, those who have the talent and diligence to persevere are likely to come away with what all great jazz players possess, namely, the ability to truly play what they hear in their mind's ear immediately. They also know what they are hearing when listening to others play.

David often speaks and writes about the three levels upon which jazz improvisation takes place.[1] At the lowest level, the improviser plays only that which he or she has played before, for example, memorized scales, patterns, clichés, and licks – perhaps rearranged cleverly and transposed appropriately to fit the chords of the moment. The majority of beginning and mediocre jazz musicians play at this level. At stage two, players – in addition to calling upon their repository of memorized improvisatory repertoire (which virtually all jazz musicians have, although some might not care to admit it) – strive to integrate phrases they have never played before. This would be the common practice of most professional and advanced student jazz musicians. At the highest level, the best jazz musicians execute what they truly hear in their mind on the spur of the moment – based on what they are thinking and feeling, and what those around them are playing.

Of course, to reach this ultimate stage of improvisational skill, one needs to be able to genuinely play what one hears, not hear what one plays (and there is a huge difference). Throughout my career, I have often had students who had made a somewhat quixotic assessment of their improvisatory abilities, trying to convince me that they really played what they heard. I tested them by playing a phrase for them to immediately duplicate on their horn. If they could do this, then I was convinced. Few could. Most were hearing what they played, and not the other way around.

To help his students reach the point of truly being able to play what they hear in their mind's ear (or anywhere else), David has devised a comprehensive method for ear training for the jazz musician. He begins with interval singing and recognition – having his students name intervals, then sing them; and play a note instrumentally, then name any other note and sing it. Next he has his students play a note then arbitrarily list eight to ten intervals and subsequently sing them from one note to the next, each interval measured from the last one. When finished, the students check their last note for accuracy by playing it on their instruments and seeing (hearing) if it matches the last note they just sang. While those with perfect pitch might experience little difficulty, it never ceases to amaze me how far away from the correct last pitch the rest of us sometimes find ourselves, even those who are accomplished musicians.

Students also work on interval recognition by pairing up with another student – one plays intervals on his or her instrument and the other names them, and then they reverse roles. This exercise can also be accomplished solo by recording a hundred or so two-interval sets played at random, pausing, then naming each interval between sets while recording. During playback, the student identifies each interval during the pauses and finds out a second later if he or she was correct. This method is especially efficient because it can be done anywhere (and often) with an iPod and a pair of headphones. There are also ear-training software programs available that include interval recognition exercises.[2]

Next, students practice singing triads of all qualities (major, minor, augmented, and diminished), seventh chords (major, dominant, minor, half diminished, diminished, and augmented), and various ninth, eleventh, thirteenth, and altered chords (such as $C7^{\flat 9\sharp 5}$). This exercise is then made more difficult by having to sing them in all inversions. For instance, David will give a student a particular note – say, a G. He or she will then have to sing the rest of an E♭ major triad in which G is the third, a C triad in which G is the fifth, an A7 chord in which G is the seventh, an F9 chord in which G is the ninth, and so on. All chords in all inversions are sung ascending and descending. The students also have to identify all of the above, including the particular inversions, when someone else plays them.

While getting a handle on chords, the students move on to scales in a similar fashion. They must recognize by ear any of the scales typically used in jazz (e.g., major, Dorian, Lydian, Mixolydian, Locrian, melodic minor, Lydian augmented, Lydian dominant, Locrian ♯2, super Locrian, whole tone, diminished, pentatonic, and blues) and be able to sing them – along with their diatonic triads and seventh, ninth, eleventh, and thirteenth chords – starting on any degree of the scale, ascending and descending. This activity "separates the men from the boys," and the "women from the girls," in a hurry; attrition sets in big time. But for the survivors, the best is yet to come.

Whether in class or in a private lesson with David, or with the CD recording that accompanies his *A New Approach to Ear Training for Jazz Musicians*, the student hears a chord being played for a measure (at a medium tempo), then strives to play the appropriate related scale ascending and descending in eighth notes for two measures by himself or herself, then repeats the scale for another two measures playing in unison – ideally – with the correct version of the scale which is played by David (in

class or on the recording). Thus, each chord-and-scale sequence takes
five measures: one measure to hear the chord, two measures to play the
related scale alone, and two measures to check accuracy by playing the
scale again in unison with David (or with a fellow "study buddy"). In the
first exercise, the chord roots proceed around the circle of fourths (C,
F, B♭, E♭, and so on) with each chord quality changing at random; there
are no breaks between the five-measure sequences, and a metronome
clicks continuously in the background. In the second and third sets, the
chord progressions ascend and descend in half steps, respectively, and
are made more challenging because the student hears the chord for only
two beats instead of four. Again, information regarding the root movement between chords is known, but no information as to each chord's
quality is provided; the onus is on the student to immediately recognize
the chord quality by ear.

The fourth set requires the student to play the appropriate scale upon
hearing the chord as before, but this time from C to C on all chords. For
instance, if an A♭7 is sounded, the student would play C, D♭, E♭, F, G♭, A♭,
B♭, C (an A♭ Mixolydian scale from C to C), ascending and descending.
The next chord might be A7 alt, in which case the student would need to
identify immediately by ear that C is the ♯9 and play C, D♭, E♭, F, G, A,
B♭, C (an A super-Locrian scale from C to C). And now, making it ever
so much more difficult, the root movement from one chord to another
is random (unlike sets 1–3, in which you knew that the chord roots pro-
gressed by fourths or half steps ahead of time) as well as the qualities.
David continues along these lines with different starting notes, different
meters, and shorter periods of hearing the chord, having his students
alternate between ascending and descending the scales.

At this point in the class, all one sees are tumbleweeds rolling along
in the soft sounds of the prairie wind. Only the Michael and Randy
Breckers of the world remain.[3] For them, the fun is just beginning. Next
David provides call-and-response exercises in which he, beginning with
just the first five notes of the C Dorian scale (C, D, E♭, F, G), improvises a
two-bar phrase which the students must duplicate exactly, all at a steady
medium tempo totaling four measures per phrase group. This exercise
progresses to using all the notes in the scale, all the different quality
scales, different meters, faster tempos, and all keys.

David concludes his exercises by having his students improvise using notes from the appropriate scales as implied by the various chords
he plays for four measures apiece; that is, the student hears the chord on
the first beat then improvises for the remaining three and three-quarters
bars. David shows some mercy in the beginning by at least telling his
students beforehand the root movement from chord to chord (for example, around the cycle of fourths), however, he does not tell them the
chord qualities; they could be anything: minor, dominant 7 altered, Lydian dominant, diminished – anything. And finally – showing no mercy
whatsoever – David does this exercise again, but provides no information
ahead of time regarding the root movement either, that is, chords of any
quality and in any key are played at random. If you can make it through
this last one, you're ready for New York.

Throughout the course are jazz theory tutelage and transcription
projects. David does not teach a jazz theory course, nor has he written a
jazz theory book *per se,* as he feels all necessary jazz theoretical concepts
are covered in his other courses and books – namely, improvisation, arranging, composition, and, of course, ear training.[4] He provides instruction in theory as the need arises. It goes without saying that just by getting through his ear training course, students will have a comprehensive
grasp of chords and scales and their relationships – aurally and literally.

A recurring theme in all of David's courses is transcription; he believes it is the bedrock of the study of jazz.[5] This is manifested in his ear-
training course by his insistence that his students transcribe solos from,
and play along with, recordings of the jazz masters – paying careful attention to nuance (articulation, inflection, swing, and style) as well as the
notes and rhythms, as this teaches the *language* of jazz. He begins by having his students transcribe walking (quarter-note) bass lines from simple
blues, utilizing recognition of what is known or expected, probabilities,
logic, and the process of elimination, along with the ear. He then has his
students transcribe more complex bass lines, heads, and, finally, solos.
He has his students listen to each phrase, sing it, play it on their instruments, and write it down – in that order (writing it down being the least
important). David also stresses to his students the importance of using
their entire fund of theoretical knowledge, as well as reason and logic,
throughout the transcription process, analyzing what they've heard as

they go. He also suggests that his students slow the recording down for fast difficult-to-hear phrases, using a Superscope or similar digital recording/playback device or computer program that slows the tempo without changing the pitch.[6]

David concludes his ear-training course with the reminder that, in reality, the students have just begun their quests to develop their ears; what he has presented is merely a point of departure. Indeed, training one's ear is a multi-year (if not a lifetime) process for the jazz musician, and he urges his students to continue creating ever more challenging exercises along the same lines as those described above.

IMPROVISATION

Of all David's various pedagogical methods, it is perhaps that of teaching jazz improvisation for which he is best known. He was among the first to codify the teaching of this music, and his first book on the subject was published in the 1960s.[7] Unlike today, when there is a plethora of jazz educational teaching and learning materials available, David's early jazz publications were proverbial diamonds in the rough, helping students unlock the seemingly mysterious door of *learning* how to improvise. Before David and a few others, in order to play jazz you either had it or you didn't.

According to composer and jazz historian Gunther Schuller, "Mr. Baker's experience, both as a player and a teacher, and his long list of creative and educational accomplishments on behalf of jazz, [made] him an ideal 'interpreter' of the musical, technical problems the young jazz improviser faces and how most effectively to solve them."[8] Today, having revised his method continuously for over fifty years, David is still helping students solve their jazz problems, providing new and innovative ways to learn how to play this music.

In his early days as a teacher, David's approach was based on teaching theory before practice, that is, he would provide his students tutelage in jazz theory and nomenclature before discussing how to apply it. "I learned the lesson the hard way because when I started getting paid to go out and teach," David confesses, "I made the mistake for the first couple of years, or maybe longer, of teaching [students] theory before teaching them the application. I would get out there and I would say, 'All right. This goes with this chord. That goes with that chord. Here's a turn-around. Blah blah.' *Now* it would never occur to me to do that. We start playing [tunes] right away. We play and then we talk about what you do when you get there. But I'm sure [in the beginning] I had [my students] doing a lot of dumb stuff by having them learn the theory before they learned the music that they would do it on."[9]

David compares learning how to improvise to learning a language, that is, how playing jazz is like speaking, and learning theory is like learning grammar. He says, "It seems to me that a lot of [beginning jazz players and teachers mistakenly] start with a book; they start with theory. But you know, and I'm sure I reasoned this out, it would be insane to teach somebody how to speak English by starting them in a book. . . . You learn to speak the language [by ear], *then* you go back and learn why you do this. You say, 'Well, now you need a verb,' and so forth.'" He says of his beginning to teach improvisation, "I was going at it backwards because I didn't have any models; I didn't have anybody telling me how to do this and so for a long time I think I must have stalled [my students] by having them learn II–Vs in all keys and play turnarounds in all keys and *then* teach them how to put them on something. But then at some point I began to talk about, 'Why don't we start with a tune?'"[10]

Since then, David's method of teaching jazz improvisation has been more repertoire based than theory based; that is, it is centered around tunes, not abstract concepts. Theoretical understanding needed to improvise on any particular composition that he is discussing is provided as needed, not beforehand. This is not to say that his improvisation classes are not heavy on theory; they are. Indeed, virtually all of David's improvisation books include thorough explanations of jazz theory and nomenclature. Some even contain page after page of patterns, clichés, licks, turnarounds, and other common formulae.[11] However, his methodology for teaching improvisation does not begin nor end there, rather, it is incorporated as the necessity arises.

David's beginning jazz improvisation class at Indiana University begins with a list of twenty tunes his students are required to memorize and improvise on as the semester unfolds. They are not easy, nor do they necessarily proceed from less to more difficult. For example, on the second or third day of class he has his students learn Charlie Parker's "Con-firmation," an up-tempo bebop composition with fast harmonic rhythm (mostly two chords per bar) – a tune that challenges many a pro. When queried as to why he does not begin with more simple vehicles, such as modal tunes in which the harmonic rhythm is very slow (for example, one chord per eight measures) or a simple blues tune, as do many impro-visation teachers and books, David explains, "I don't tell [my students] that anything's difficult; I say we learn these tunes because they're fun ones to learn. So we start with 'Groovin' High,' 'Half Nelson,' and then we go to 'Confirmation' and the next one is probably 'Little Willie Leaps.' . . . The only thing I will make a concession on is the tempo."[12]

Besides not wanting his students to take on the mindset that a tune is difficult, David also believes that if he were to start with simple modal or blues tunes that they would get stuck there, and be less able to de-velop the skills of thinking while playing, thinking ahead, keeping their place, and being fluid. "If you start with modal tunes," David espouses, "it immediately lowers your guard." For him, "having kids starting here [with compositions that have many chords], by the end of the semester they can play on all of these tunes. If I started with modal music, they'd fall in love with [such modal classics as] 'So What,' they'd fall in love with 'Maiden Voyage,' they'd fall in love with 'Impressions.'" Putting it figuratively, David says, "It's a bitch getting them to move off the dime because once you've got that, all they want to do is worry about if they go to the bridge too early or too late. This way [working on tunes with swift harmonic rhythm first], they don't have to worry about [keeping their place] because it's going to be so articulated they don't have any choice [but to keep their place]. . . . There are so many [harmonic landmarks] along the way."[13]

For each tune, David has his students play the root movement of the chord progression, the melody, and generic bebop-sounding pat-terns that fit the chord changes. He is very systematic in his approach, methodically introducing nomenclature, foundation exercises, scales, patterns, and the like along with tunes in which to incorporate them. He also covers common tune types including modal and blues tunes (later in the semester), "I Got Rhythm" tunes and other contrafacts,[14] and more.

Throughout the course, David insists his students do as much as possible by ear, utilizing the intellect only as needed. For instance, when teaching the head for "Over the Rainbow," David points out that in the A section all the notes are diatonic and the three large interval leaps are 1–8, 1–6, and 6–4 (in the key of C this would be C–C, C–A, and A–F, respectively). That is the intellectual part; the rest should be played by ear. Along these lines, he assigns tunes and exercises from his how-to-learn-tunes book, which includes information regarding common harmonic formulae, tune types, form, and tune categories, as well as a systematic methodology for learning, memorizing, and retaining compositions.[15] He also systematically assigns scales, arpeggios, patterns, and theory from his book *Jazz Improvisation.*

As he does in all of his courses, David stresses the necessity of transcribing the masters. Every semester he assigns a transcription project in which his students each select a particular recording of a tune (with David's approval), transcribe the solo or a portion thereof (for example, three choruses), and play it along with the recording, paying close attention to articulation and other nuances to get it to sound as much like the original as possible. Along with other assignments during the semester, the transcription is performed by appointment for one of David's associate instructors (graduate assistants) who checks off that the assignment was completed, one of the requisites for receiving an A in the class.

Jazz Improvisation II is similar in structure, but focused on *contemporary* language, as detailed in his *Modern Concepts in Jazz Improvisation.* Whereas Jazz Improvisation I is virtually all bebop based, as the study of bebop teaches the common language of jazz and, frankly, how music works (chord/scale relationships, form, harmonic progression theory, and so on), Jazz Improvisation II is designed to acquaint the student with more modern playing – that is, post-bop. David discusses such contemporary improvisational techniques as bitonals, chromaticism, manipulation of pentatonics, and quartal playing.[16] He also spends a significant amount of time on Coltrane substitutions, utilizing his now infamous "Coltrane Matrix," a chord substitution chart that supplies his students with a virtually infinite number of combinational possibilities for improvising on such rites of passage as Coltrane's "Giant Steps" and "Countdown," as well as a plethora of other post-bop compositions.

David also provides his students with numerous II–V, turnaround, and other common formulaic patterns (to be memorized in all keys) derived from contemporary language as improvised by such artists as

Coltrane, Woody Shaw, Michael Brecker, Chick Corea, Herbie Hancock, and other post-bop masters. Included are patterns built on symmetrical scales (such as whole tone and diminished), permutations of pentatonic scales, triads to be superimposed over a variety of chord qualities and keys, fourths, and more.

Jazz Improvisation I is more repertoire driven than theory driven; Jazz Improvisation II reverses this emphasis. For instance, David begins by using a simple modal tune such as Coltrane's "Impressions" as the vehicle on which his students improvise utilizing whatever technique is under discussion – such as playing a chorus or two using strictly pentatonic scales, or fourths, or diminished scales, or what have you. The goal is to get the particular sound of each concept ingrained in his students' ears and under their fingers. It is not until near the end of the course that the students are allowed to truly improvise freely, using any or all of the techniques learned in class or anywhere else.

As the course progresses, so does the difficulty of tunes[17] the students have to play utilizing their newfound modern concepts. These include such compositions as Hancock's "Dolphin Dance," Wayne Shorter's "Nefertiti" and "Children of the Night," Cedar Walton's "Bolivia," Benny Golson's "Stablemates," Joe Henderson's "Isotope," and Eddie Harris's "Freedom Jazz Dance," as well as such Baker originals as "An Evening Thought" and "The Harlem Pipes." David also teaches his students how to convert any jazz standard into a modern vehicle by reharmonizing it using bitonals and other contemporary devices, exemplifying "Birdsong"[18] (David's bitonally reharmonized contrafact based on "Half Nelson," which his students learn in Jazz Improvisation I) among other Baker modern reharmonizations of common jazz repertoire.[19]

Throughout the course, David continually emphasizes the necessity of playing cleanly, with rhythmic precision – and always with flair, confidence, and imagination. He stresses that when improvising in the modern vein his students use bebop mannerisms sparingly (if at all),[20] strive for maximum contrasts (loud vs. soft, high vs. low, long vs. short phrases, and so on), and for the most part play straight eighth notes when soloing, even when the rhythm section is swinging – all characteristic of modern playing. He also provides numerous practice strategies, reminding his students not to allow themselves to neglect new material or approaches because they might feel awkward or uncomfortable at first.[21] Rather, they should reserve judgment regarding the new concepts' permanency in their playing until they have experienced and experimented with the new sounds over time.

Helping his students become more at ease with modern jazz language, David again stresses the importance of transcribing the masters and has his students do so in this class as well, but this time focusing on musicians who exemplify this newer style. He insists that besides learning solos note for note in order to become ever more familiar with contemporary playing and its nuances, his students use phrases in the solos they transcribe as catalysts for discovering new ideas. "I suggest [for instance] that they transcribe a Woody [Shaw] solo and the cats come in and they're so proud to play that Woody solo," David enthuses. "When Woody goes [David sings a phrase of the solo] and they say, 'Oh yeah, that sounds really hip,' and I say 'All right, but instead of starting that [line] on C playing it over a C-major chord, start it on F♯ so they have a B major playing over the top of the C,' and they say 'Oh yeah, that's hip'; then they wear it out [laughs]."[22]

The course ends with four days of in-class concerts in which all students participate in a twenty-minute set – improvising in the modern realm and showing what they have accomplished thus far in their jazz journey. David assumes that any student who passes both his Jazz Improvisation I and II courses will have the wherewithal to play on any tune type – traditional, bebop, or modern. "I expect them to be able to play anything," David says. "These are people who would be in my bands and I would pull anything I wanted to pull and expect them to be able to play it; I wouldn't even ask them if they could play it. It doesn't matter; I would expect them to be able to play anything that I would call. I tell them, 'Your whole rationale for being here is to take our jobs away from us; please just don't do it too soon.'"[23]

TUNE LEARNING

If you were to ask fifty professional jazz musicians the best way to learn how to play jazz, you would likely come away with fifty different answers: go to school/don't go to school, use play-along recordings/don't use play-along recordings, go to New York and hang/stay home and practice – the contradictions go on and on. However, although they might disagree on just about everything else, I have found there are two areas in which just about everyone is in accord. Whether their specialty is traditional, bebop, contemporary, all of the above, or anything in between, in my experience most great jazz players advocate that in order to learn how to play this music you must listen to it copiously, and memorize a whole lot of tunes – at least a couple hundred.[24] That's why it never ceases to amaze me that so few university jazz programs across the country offer a course in tune learning. Indiana University is one of the few.

Recognizing the fact that there are so many students who might be able to burn on "Giant Steps" but don't know enough tunes to get through a club date, David implemented a course called "Tune Learning for the Jazz Musician" at Indiana University in 2009. However, simply acquiring a working repertoire is not the end-all of this class. Rather, it is the tune learning *process* that is most important. Perhaps more than any other area of study, it is learning tunes that teaches you how music works – such as how chords progress and, especially, what makes a good melody. Such knowledge is essential for the jazz musician.[25]

On the first day of class, David collects from each student a list of tunes that he or she already knows – that is, is able to convincingly play the head and changes by heart. He then instructs them to memorize and retain one new song of their own choosing every day for the remainder of the semester. Rather than providing them a "must know" tune list, David urges his students to select tunes they like and are most likely to play professionally in the near future. In the beginning, however, he just wants them to learn a tune a day, regardless of what it is, so they get in the habit of learning something new *daily*. "I say it can be anything, even something silly like 'The [Theme from the] Flintstones,'" David explains. "I don't care what it is; I want a tune a day."[26]

Of course, he makes suggestions along the way, and even has his students learn particular tunes during class, but contends that the concepts learned in this course are applicable to any tune. By the end of the term, everyone is expected to be able to perform all the tunes on their respective lists – old and new – from memory. David's course content and instructional methodology provide them the means to do just that, in addition to a strategy for continuing to learn new tunes and remember them throughout their careers.

In order to quickly memorize multiple tunes and retain them for the long run, *organization* is key. As the course unfolds, David teaches numerous ways to categorize the tunes his students are learning, such as by common melodic beginnings, tune types, chord progressions, forms, and more as detailed in his text on tune learning.[27] He likes to start by categorizing standards that begin with the same interval, such as an ascending half step ("Bye, Bye, Blackbird," "I Remember You," and "What's New") and descending half step ("Sophisticated Lady," "Stella by Starlight," and "Solar"). Following suit, he covers all the intervals within an octave, providing numerous examples of tunes that begin with each.

During the first couple of weeks, David covers the blues, dividing them into three types: riff blues, through-composed blues, and altered blues, and suggests the class memorize a few representatives of each.[28] He then moves on to two types of rhythm changes tunes: conventional and altered,[29] again urging his students to learn as many as they can. And besides large harmonic schemes like blues and rhythm changes, David also has his students learn shorter common chord sequences like I–II7–ii–V7–I, found in so many standards' A sections ("Girl from Ipanema" and "Take the 'A' Train"). Learning common B sections like ii–V7–I in IV, followed by ii–V7 in V, followed by ii–V7 in I ("Honeysuckle Rose" and "Satin Doll") is a staple of this class as well.

Throughout the course, standards get put into two groups: traditional ("Autumn Leaves" and "All the Things You Are") and jazz ("Confirmation" and "Half Nelson"). They are then placed into narrower categories as the semester moves along, such as tunes that feature melodies that are predominantly chordal ("Without a Song" and "I Can't Get Started"), scalar ("Blue Bossa" and "Bluesette"), or chromatic ("Sophisticated Lady" and "Hot House"). Another classifying element is harmonic rhythm, that is, fast ("Giant Steps" and "Moment's Notice"), moderate ("Groovin' High" and "Night and Day"), and slow ("Impressions" and "Maiden Voyage"). And tunes are categorized according to various rhythmic characteristics as well, such as melodies that are highly syncopated ("Evidence" and "Moose the Mooch") and tunes that are usually performed in a particular dance style (for example, bossa nova or samba). As the students learn more tunes, they are able to place each one in a greater number of categories which, in turn, gives them more ways to look at them. While seeing (understanding) what the tunes are comprised of, they not only learn more about the inner workings of music, they acquire more mnemonics, ever increasing their ability to retain their repertoire.

In addition to organization, David's primary staple for this class is "ear-learning," that is, learning tunes mostly by ear but using intellect and theory knowledge in places where the ear might fail, such as large interval leaps, accidentals, key changes, and the like. He advocates that the more you know or suspect, the "better you hear." For instance, before teaching the A section of "Over the Rainbow," David points out that the melody is diatonic and that the leaps are 1–8, 1–6, and 6–4 (C–C, C–A, and A–F, respectively, in the key of C), which the students play before attempting the tune. This makes playing the song by ear and transposing it to other keys a snap. Other examples include "Sugar," which is simply comprised of a minor pentatonic scale with no leaps, "Blue Bossa" which is merely made up of two major scales a whole step apart, and "Satin Doll," but a series of simple sequences. Literally in minutes, the students have learned three tunes in all keys and are excited about learning more!

David uses similar strategies for teaching tunes' root movements and chord qualities, again reinforcing common combinations. Most standards actually use only a few different chord sequences, thus, the more tunes learned, the easier hearing and remembering the changes become as the same progressions occur again and again. Through tune learning, how chords progress becomes evident and – eventually – second nature.[30]

Keeping it light but intense as is his modus operandi, David likes to play educative in-class games with his students. One of his favorites is "follow the leader," in which, while everybody is standing, one student starts by playing a phrase from a standard. The next student must determine what the last interval played was and begin another tune with that same interval. This continues around the room; each person sits down only when he or she fails to come up with a new tune that begins with the correct interval. Last person standing gets a prize!

Also per his M.O., David insists that his students listen to recordings of the tunes they are learning. In some cases, he has them learn all the parts – introductions, hits, contrapuntal and harmony parts, backgrounds, vamps, interludes, endings – from the definitive version. He regularly points out that listening to jazz and being in the know are vital to becoming a respected jazz musician. Nothing causes you to lose credibility faster than being the only one on the bandstand who doesn't know what the others know.[31]

Grades are determined on the basis of playing and listening quizzes throughout the semester, as well as a final exam. Students are "kept honest" by having to periodically perform tunes selected from their respective lists. They also must recognize tunes discussed in class by hearing their melodies or chord progressions only. To test the latter, David uses Jamey Aebersold play-along recordings, as they are comprised solely of piano, bass, and drums accompaniment – that is, no melodies. For the final assessment, each member of the class must play a ten-to-fifteen-minute private performance exam for David, in which he selects tunes from the student's repertoire list. The percentage of tunes played correctly, and how well they are played, determine the lion's share of the final grade.

But being able to perform all the tunes on your list gives you far more than just another A on your transcript. Indeed, the knowledge gained is invaluable. Upon successful completion of this course, you will not only thoroughly know the root movement, chord qualities, and head of one hundred tunes (and have a strategy to keep learning more), you will have begun to internalize their definitive recordings, one of the most important aspects of becoming a good jazz player.[32] And you will *know* how chords progress, understand substitutions, have dozens of quotable phrases for improvisation, have further developed your ear and time feel, have credibility, and be employable.[33]

JAZZ HISTORY

Each year David teaches four separate jazz history courses, two general and two specific. History of Jazz and Contemporary Jazz and Soul

Music are electives designed for non-music majors. The Bebop Era and Duke Ellington, on the other hand, are highly specific courses designed with the music major, and particularly the jazz studies major, in mind. Two additional history courses, taught by one of David's colleagues, also are offered at Indiana University. One is Pre-Jazz to Bebop, a historical and musical analysis of the core repertoire, seminal performers, musical characteristics, and important recordings of the major jazz styles from the music's inception to 1945. The other is Jazz since Bebop, its post-bebop counterpart (covering 1955 to the present).[34]

When I attended Indiana University in the 1990s, the history of-ferings for the jazz major were a bit different. Instead of the threefold Pre-Jazz to Bebop–Bebop Era–Jazz since Bebop sequence that exists now, I took Bebop Era and Chamber Jazz: Literature and Performance (an analysis of seminal small groups throughout jazz history). Also of-fered at that time was History of the Big Band, the chamber jazz course's big band counterpart. Today, the subject matter of those original small group and big band jazz history courses are covered chronologically (rather than categorized by ensemble size) in a "pre-bebop–bebop–post-bebop" course trilogy.

The most significant difference between then and now is that The Be-bop Era and Chamber Jazz were combination history *and* performance classes when I took them. While learning about the history of bebop, all members of the class had to memorize, perform, and improvise on tunes that were representative of the artists being discussed. I still remember staying up all night trying to get Charlie Parker's "Dexterity" and "Moose the Mooch" – or whatever the two particular bebop heads assigned for the week were – under my fingers before class the next day. Much to Da-vid's chagrin, the courses have been more compartmentalized and now his Bebop Era is strictly a history class – that is, there is no performance component. "I made the change [of making Bebop Era strictly a history course] reluctantly, because I thought that we were onto something that really gave people an insight into the music when you have to perform it," David explains. "But what happened is that the class began to become popular, and all of a sudden I had [students] from American Studies, Ethnomusicology, [and other departments] who signed up to take the course, and there was no way that I could then deal in an equitable way as far as grading [was concerned] because they didn't know how to play an instrument at all; but they were interested in the history of the music."[35]

Not wanting to close the door to anyone capable of understanding the music's history but not able to perform it, and still wanting to keep the standard high for the jazz major by providing insights into the music that only performing it can provide, David wishes he had the time to offer two sections of the course. "I really felt, particularly for my jazz majors, that [by deleting the performance component] something was very much lost," David laments. "There was nobody else, that I know of, who was teaching a history course that was half performance and half factual data from history itself. I really regret it. If I had the option, I think I would probably now reinstate a dual version of the course: offer one semester of the course for everybody who wanted to take it without regard to their background; and then I would offer one that was strictly aimed at jazz majors."[36]

As is often the case in academia, compromises have to be made.[37] Given David's already inordinate workload, not to mention university scheduling problems and the like, only one section of Bebop Era is currently offered, one semester per year; it is open to all, without prerequisite. Still, the class remains a requirement for every undergraduate and graduate jazz major at Indiana University, as, according to David, "it is the foundational course for anyone who is going to study jazz mainly because it's [about] the common practice period; it is the lingua franca of this music."[38]

The course begins with the reasons for the demise of the preceding swing era – political, socioeconomic, and musical. This is followed by weekly lectures and discussions, including listening to recordings and watching videos of particular seminal artists or instruments. For instance, one week apiece is spent on Charlie Parker, Dizzy Gillespie, and Thelonious Monk. Subsequent weekly topics include "Fats Navarro and the Trumpet Players," "Bud Powell and the Pianists," and "Kenny Clarke, Max Roach, and the Drummers."[39]

Besides playing recordings and showing videos of the artists being examined – all the while highlighting particular points of interest – David adds personal anecdotes. Not only was he part of the scene during that era, he was a friend and musical colleague of many of the artists he covers. He frequently provides firsthand knowledge not available anywhere else, as well as information regarding contemporaneous political, socioeconomic, and racial issues that affected the music. I'll never forget David's discussion of the racial inequities that he and his African American friends and colleagues had to endure; it still makes me shudder.

Throughout the course, students are required to listen to numerous recordings on reserve at the university's music library and take periodic listening quizzes in which they must recognize players, groups, and tunes – including a list of thirty-four bebop heads provided in David's accompanying course packet, one of the texts for this course.[40] This book also contains organized lists of players (by instrument), composers and arrangers, and additional important bebop compositions. Most importantly, it includes David's account and analysis of the era, replete with history, artist biographies, tune analyses, and multiple references borrowed from his unpublished jazz history book.

Readings from the course's other text, *Bebop: The Music and the Players,* are assigned periodically. This book suits the general reader as well as the specialist since it is easily understood by the musical novice *and* it includes numerous notated musical examples with analysis for the musically literate. Rounding out the assignments are two required essays: one on the reasons for the demise of the big band, and the other on why bebop lost its place of preeminence in the music. Finally, there are four periodic tests and a final exam comprised of questions based on class lectures and discussions, assigned readings, and recordings.

"This is the one class that is sacrosanct," David insists, "as [it covers jazz's] common practice period. . . . I want [my students] to know the artists but the primary goal is to place this information in the context of the bigger scheme of things, understanding *why* [the music] evolved the way it did, *how* it evolved the way it did, *who* are the people who were responsible for it, and *what* is the residue that is left – the footprint that is left when we move to the next generation. . . . Dr. Martin Luther King said it better than anybody else. He said facts in and of themselves have no meaning; facts are only meaningful when they're connected to other facts."[41]

David's other specialized history course is Duke Ellington, an in-depth study of the life, times, and music of one whom David considers perhaps America's most important composer, jazz or otherwise. He was able to convince a relatively conservative Indiana University School of Music curriculum committee to accept this class as an accredited music history course because Ellington "was a major figure, somebody who transformed the aesthetic. . . . He was the one [jazz] person that was respected across the board."[42] Indeed, Ellington transcends any one particular style or genre; his prolific writing and over fifty years of band leading and piano playing encompass popular, classical, and sacred music, as well as jazz. He is the proverbial "Mount Olympus" of jazz composers, as David likes to say.[43]

As in David's Bebop Era course, classroom activities include lectures and discussions as well as listening to recordings, watching videos, and analyzing music. Class topic sequencing is mostly chronologically based, starting with Ellington's birth in 1899 and continuing to the lasting effects of his work today, years after his death in 1974. The syllabus is loosely aligned with the text for this course, *Beyond Category: The Life and Genius of Duke Ellington* by John Hasse, a former student who took many of David's classes.[44]

David expounds on Ellington's life as an innovative pianist, bandleader, and composer, paying greatest attention to his most important compositions and recordings across all genres. Eight compact discs containing over one hundred tracks of selected works in roughly chronological order are on reserve in the Indiana University music library, and are required listening for every member of the class. David also covers Ellington's pivotal sidemen (such as Johnny Hodges, Ben Webster, and Jimmy Blanton), vocalists, small groups, influences, and nonmusical writings. Additionally, he spends a significant amount of time discussing Ellington's relationship with and the music of Billy Strayhorn, his musical partner during most of his career.

Students are required to take four examinations throughout the semester as well as write a fifteen-page term paper on an Ellington topic of their choosing. Themes may include such subject matter as comparisons of Ellington's three Sacred Concerts or pieces recorded multiple times, analyses of major works, biographical and musical sketches of important sidemen, or any number of other areas of interest that the students may have and of which David approves. Upon completion of the project, the students are then required to give a twenty-minute presentation on the material to the class as well as provide a copy for each member, everyone expeditiously teaching and learning from one another.

By course's end, David expects all his students to know Ellington's background and "what it was that caused him to write this kind of music, how he came up with the concept of writing for people instead of for publishers," David explains. "I want [my students] to take from the class why he is singularly important; I want them to know his masterpieces ... why his music is more important than, say, the music of Count Basie – even though in 1938 and 1939 Ellington and Basie were roughly on par."[45]

Summing up, David would like his students to be sufficiently versed in Ellington to have a solid grasp of the man and his music as a point of departure for the further study of his and others' music, and to contextualize as they go. He insists that his students know "why Ellington did what he did [and] who the important people in his pantheon of greats" were. He also feels "they should know when there's something that is so unusual, [for instance], the fact that Ellington had [some of the same] people with him for forty years," evidencing the integral role of *community* in jazz and in Ellington's genius in particular. "No other jazz band leader ever had that [kind of loyalty]," David points out. "Most orchestras don't have that. Why? What is it about Ellington's music that made [his sidemen] want to do this?" Most importantly, David wants his students to be keenly aware of the important pieces and periods in Ellington's life, so that they "can put them beside what else was happening in the country at the time. . . . He was so conscious of philosophy and of purpose that he would write about the times. Ellington was commenting on the times all the time."[46]

As much as David enjoys teaching courses for his serious jazz majors, I think his greatest love is spreading the "gospel" of jazz to the general university population in his History of Jazz and Contemporary Jazz and Soul Music classes. It is not unusual for him to have well over one hundred students in his lecture hall, everyone from education and biology majors to football and basketball players. "I'm sure many of them sign up to take the class thinking it's going to be an easy A," David jokes. "They learn real quick that ain't the case."[47]

Earning an A might be somewhat difficult, but a B can certainly be achieved simply by attending class, paying attention, and keeping up with assigned outside class reading and listening. Given the heterogeneous background of the students, the courses' requirements are not nearly as demanding as those designed for David's jazz majors. Their purpose is not to create connoisseurs, but rather to acquaint a broader population with America's indigenous art form, providing students from all backgrounds a basic understanding of and appreciation for jazz and related music. The best-case scenario is that the students leave the classes as well-educated listeners and, hopefully, patrons of the music for the rest of their lives.

David prefers that students take Contemporary Jazz and Soul Music before taking History of Jazz because, although they can be taken independently, those who have completed the former are much better equipped to study the latter. "It's a much better preparation," David says, referring to completing the course that includes rhythm 'n' blues and soul music before enrolling in the jazz history course. "I think that if you're listening to Cannonball [Adderley] or you're listening to [John] Coltrane or you're listening to Charlie Parker, and you haven't heard Louis Jordan, Earl Bostic, and those guys,[48] then you're being deprived of the groundwork that made it possible for them to do what they did. . . . It's a very artificial thing to disconnect them."[49] To encourage this sequencing, David teaches the contemporary jazz and soul course in the fall and the jazz history course the subsequent spring.

Contemporary Jazz and Soul Music covers primarily the work of African American artists because, obviously, they were the primary inventors and innovators of this music, but also because this was the principal motivation for the adoption of the original version of this course in the 1960s. When David first proposed that a class such as this be included in the Indiana University curriculum at that time, there were virtually no courses other than Jazz History dealing with the African American aesthetic in music or otherwise. "I felt it was inappropriate for a student to come here, whether it was in music or whatever, and the only course they could take that had anything to do with the Negro in America and black music was jazz," David remembers. "I really felt they needed to have a much broader spectrum than just jazz."[50] Although jazz is still a major component, the course also includes gospel music, blues, boogie-woogie, rhythm 'n' blues, soul, and funk – right up to contemporary R & B, hip-hop, and other urban music styles popular today. And although David does not require his jazz majors to take the subsequent general jazz history course – they receive that information in much greater detail in the specific history courses described above – he does insist they take Contemporary Jazz and Soul Music, since "this is the only place they're going to get that."[51]

Meeting three days per week, the course begins with a synopsis of traditional African music, the foremost root of all the musical styles to follow. David then proceeds with the aforementioned styles roughly in chronological order, finishing the non-jazz genres at mid-semester. The second half of the course is a survey of the evolution of jazz from its origins to the present. Since this takes place in the last seven weeks, no one style can be covered in depth. However, by providing a brief overview of jazz's integral eras – early jazz, swing, bebop, cool, hard bop, free, fusion, and contemporary – the students are much better primed to take History of Jazz, in which there is more specificity (jazz being the sole topic for the entire semester). For instance, whereas David only has time to talk about the music of Louis Armstrong for one class session in the first course, he spends three sessions on the topic in the second.[52]

History of Jazz begins with the music's precursors (such as traditional African music, blues, ragtime, and brass bands) and continues chronologically, style by style and era by era, all the way up to the fusion sounds of the 1970s and 1980s by course's end. Highlighted are the seminal performers, composers, and recordings of each era along with the political, socioeconomic, and racial environments in which they evolved. Of particular importance is the work of Jelly Roll Morton, Louis Armstrong, Duke Ellington, Coleman Hawkins, Lester Young, Charlie Parker, Dizzy Gillespie, Miles Davis, John Coltrane, Ornette Coleman, and Herbie Hancock. David also spends time discussing various big bands, jazz vocalists, and important small groups, as well as focusing a lecture or two on styles not usually found in most mainstream jazz history courses – such as ethnic jazz, liturgical jazz, and Third Stream.[53]

David's teaching methodology for both general history courses includes lecturing, playing recordings, showing videos, and – as only someone who has "been there and done that" can do – relating personal stories. "When I cover bebop I can now show a video of Dexter [Gordon] playing 'Fried Bananas' or whatever," David enthuses. "And then I can give them personal experiences, 'cause like the last tour and the last recording Dexter made was with me when I wrote *Ellingtones* and did the tour of Japan with him. So I try to keep it anecdotal when it's possible because basically these are things they can't ask somebody else because the other people are dead; unless they can channel them somewhere."[54]

David's marvelous sense of humor permeates all his classes. Although it is very natural for him, he strategically uses it to add levity when things are seeming too serious and, perhaps, to reduce the sting when telling his students such things as that on reserve in the music library are twenty-three CDs containing over three hundred tracks they need to listen to throughout the semester (this is the case in both his general history courses).[55] His humor, personal charm, and genuineness are inseparable from the rest of his persona, inside and outside the classroom.

The classes are too large to assign essays (as they would take an inordinate amount of time to assess), so all grades are determined by attendance, weekly short-answer or computer-graded multiple-choice quizzes, and midterm and final exams. Students are tested on factual information as well as aural identification of formative players and styles. Questions are based on the lectures, recordings listened to in class, and assigned readings from the respective comprehensive course packets. Each of these two books contains over three hundred pages of highly readable discourse from David's unpublished jazz history book as well as numerous summary lists of style characteristics, important firsts, players categorized by instrument or era, recordings, compositions, and the like.[56]

Although challenging to the uninitiated, the courses are a complete joy for many. Imagine going to class three days per week and listening to recordings and watching videos of some of the greatest and most innovative musicians who ever lived, all the while being guided by a compelling expert whose own passion for the music abounds. While learning about America's music and how it came about, the students can acquire an aesthetic that has the potential to enrich the rest of their lives. "The whole thing is to civilize them," David proclaims. "Anytime in education, we're educating from many, many points, but the two main points are first of all to make [the students] marketable, [and] secondly, [to] civilize them. ... What I want them to take [from the class] is how what I've given them fits into the context of American civilization, of world civilization."[57]

JAZZ STYLES AND ANALYSIS

Whereas David's jazz history courses provide an overview of the rich heritage of jazz, and enable students to see (hear) the evolution of the general techniques and performance practices of the past and how they relate to those of the present, Jazz Styles and Analysis provides an opportunity to explore the music with far more specificity. In this course, the students not only analyze in great detail what they hear with regard to harmonic theory, melodic development, tone production, rhythmic concepts, and the like; but they transcribe, memorize, and perform solos of the masters note for note. Needless to say, this class is for serious jazz majors only.

The experience is intended to further the students' ability to know what they are hearing, and become ever more expert on the language of jazz. David insists that they always assess what they're hearing, make educated value judgments, and – most important – use the newfound information and inspiration in the development of their own improvised solos. He also contends that Jazz Styles and Analysis is far more than a one-semester course; it is a lifestyle.[58] The best jazz musicians are forever listening, transcribing, analyzing, emulating, and emendating, all the while using these experiences to inform and inspire their own unique voices.

Again, David has walked the talk. Not only has he continually listened, transcribed, analyzed, emulated, and emendated throughout his career himself, he has written eight illuminating style and analysis books on the playing of jazz greats Cannonball Adderley, Clifford Brown, John Coltrane, Miles Davis, J. J. Johnson, Fats Navarro, Charlie Parker, and Sonny Rollins.[59] Each volume begins with an introduction comprised of basic jazz theory instruction regarding chord and scale relationships as well as how to transcribe solos from recordings. This is followed by a biographical sketch, selected discography, list of original compositions, and primary influences of the respective artist.

The second section focuses on the artist's preferences and tendencies, including preferred tune types,[60] tempos, keys, and scales, as well as his solos' most prevalent melodic, harmonic, and rhythmic characteristics. The remainder and crux of the book is comprised of a number of transcriptions of the artist's quintessential solos featuring David's in-depth analyses, including the referencing of dramatic devices,[61] tessitura, prevailing jazz scales, recurrent melodic and rhythmic patterns, developmental techniques,[62] and performance practices[63] evident in the solo at hand. Each transcription is followed by a page or two of isolated melodic patterns and phrases built on common harmonic formulae (for example, II–V–I) drawn from the solo itself. Students are then able to use these jazz licks as points of reference, practice them in all keys, and utilize them in their own improvisations, expanding their jazz vocabulary from real-life literature.

As go the books, so goes the course. That is, students are required to transcribe solos of their choosing (with David's approval) and analyze them in the same manner as David has in his books. He provides them with blank transcription analysis sheets (similar to the ones found in each volume) that they fill out, indicating their recognition of the improvisational techniques found in the solos and whatever else becomes evident during the transcription process.

Lecture topics include aural recognition of scales, chords, instrumentation, form, harmonic formulae, and the like, as well as aural identification of important bands and soloists. David also spends a considerable amount of time examining the archetypal characteristics of jazz's primary eras – including early jazz, swing, bebop, hard bop, cool, free, and fusion. Additionally, he spends at least one class period apiece on jazz's pivotal players categorized by instrument – that is, the most influential trumpeters, saxophonists, trombonists, pianists, bassists, drummers, guitarists, and vibraphonists.

The course is rounded out with listening to definitive recordings, watching jazz videos, and reading jazz history, all with David's expert guidance. The two assigned texts are *The Jazz Book* by Joachim Berendt and *How to Listen to Jazz* by Jerry Coker.[64] Also required is David's substantial course packet that is replete with summaries of the most significant jazz bands and their leaders, pivotal small groups and their personnel, consequential recordings categorized by instrument, important firsts, and the like.[65] The packet also includes a host of style guide sheets – that is, crib sheets of the "least you need to know" about each style and era in jazz history, as well as about important figures such as John Coltrane and Miles Davis. Numerous excerpts from David's unpublished jazz history book also are found throughout. This source alone is worth the price of admission.

Grades are determined by the students' ability to recognize important names, soloists, and combos via aural and written examination. A great deal of weight is also placed on how well the selected solo is transcribed, analyzed, and performed. All in all, an A in this class means you're well on your way to truly understanding the art form.

JAZZ ARRANGING

Since few publications were available on arranging in general, and virtually none on jazz arranging for small groups, when David began to teach this subject in the 1960s, he did what he always does: write a book on the subject. "It was very, very difficult when I had to learn how to teach arranging because there were no books out there that I really felt comfortable with," David recalls. "When I first started trying to do this, the two books that were most available were the book by Glenn Miller and a book by Van Alexander,[66] and both these books were written in the '40s." They were not only dated but dealt more with big band swing writing and film scoring, respectively, than with *jazz* arranging. So, by necessity, David envisioned and then wrote *Arranging and Composing for the Small Ensemble: Jazz, R&B, Jazz-Rock.*[67]

The title of the book is a bit of a misnomer because it includes information suitable for writing for everything from a trio to a big band. David's original title was *Arranging and Composing for the Jazz Orchestra* but, as he explains, "Chuck Suber and *DownBeat* [the original publisher] decided they would sell more if it were *Arranging and Composing for the Small Ensemble* because there was no book like that.[68] But it also gave a very distorted illusion of what I wrote."[69] In any event, the book became the main text for David's arranging classes, which cover everything from writing for small groups to planning and producing a full big band arrangement.

David's systematic approach starts with an overview of some basic jazz theory and nomenclature, characteristics of the instruments in the orchestral families (brass, woodwinds, strings, and percussion), and instrumental ranges, tessituras, and transpositions. This is immediately followed by instruction on writing an arrangement for just a rhythm section, that is, piano, bass, and drums. He has his students transcribe a tune from recordings of the trios of Oscar Peterson, Ahmad Jamal, McCoy Tyner, Nat King Cole,[70] or other three-piece group in which there is an obvious arrangement,[71] for example, Cole's version of "Sweet Lorraine." His students then analyze their transcriptions and are assigned to select another tune and write an arrangement in the same style as the one they have transcribed. David follows suit on the next assignment by having them repeat the exercise, this time for a quartet (rhythm section plus one horn, guitar, or vibes) in the style of the 1950s quartets led by the likes of Clifford Brown, Sonny Stitt, Sonny Rollins, J. J. Johnson, and Wes Montgomery, as well as the Modern Jazz Quartet.

Moving on to two-horn writing (plus rhythm section), David teaches various two-part voicing techniques such as unison, parallel, polyphonic, and scalar writing, providing numerous examples of each. Then, following his established M.O., his students listen to, transcribe recordings from, and write arrangements in the style of such 1950s and 1960s quintets as those led by J. J. Johnson, Horace Silver, Art Blakey, Cannonball Adderley, Miles Davis, Max Roach and Clifford Brown, as well as the two-horn, pianoless quartet fronted by Chet Baker and Gerry Mulligan. All arrangements are played and evaluated in class, giving students the opportunity to hear their work, make corrections, and listen to their edited versions in subsequent sessions.

When the class gets to three-part writing (plus rhythm section), David is in full gear. "Once we get to three horns," David exuberates, "the world is your palace, because once you've got three horns you've got all the ingredients that you need."[72] Using the 1950s and 1960s sextets of Davis, Johnson, Blakey, George Russell (of which David was a member), and Art Farmer and Benny Golson as exemplars, David covers a wide variety of three-part voicing and scoring techniques, providing numerous examples, suggestions, and guidelines. A sextet assignment ensues, all arrangements are played in class, and Arranging I comes to a close.

Arranging II covers writing for four, five, six horns, and more, taking the students right up to the final project – writing a big band arrangement to be played by one of the university jazz ensembles in concert. However, this is certainly not the primary objective of the two arranging courses. Although it might appear that way, "The ultimate goal is not writing for the big band," David insists. "It never was. It is the progression that takes place."[73] Each individual assignment is an entity unto itself as well as part of an accumulation of knowledge for larger, more involved projects.

As he does in all his classes, David provides his students theory tutelage *as it is needed,* not beforehand. "You do it when it's practical. You get it when you need it," David explains. "Why would you do something before you ever know how you're going to use it, or that you need it? You know, you tell a cat in the boxing ring, 'I'm going to show you how to block a right hook. Why? Because you're going to get knocked on your ass if I don't show you.' So I tell them *when* they need it, not when it is still speculative, not when 'there might come a day.'"[74]

At the center of David's methodology is his pedagogical philosophy that the best learning of jazz skills, or anything else, is experiential, that is, he has his students transcribe both what they like and don't like, see what it is, then do it that way or not. "It's always based on experiential knowledge," David asserts. "If you want to write for a vocalist, you buy some Nancy Wilson records, you buy Billie Holiday, you find Doris Day, whoever. And then you write a piece in that style because basically that's really how you learn. You learn by imitating. We learn to walk, we learn how to talk by imitating."[75] So, of course, why not jazz?

"What I do in the arranging course," David continues, "is at the same time that I'm teaching about orchestration I say that any time you hear a sound you like, make a recording of it, write it down, 'cause that's a sound you might want to use. You hear a sound that you like and [for instance] it's that close writing that you hear of Benny Golson or one of those guys, I say write it down. If they can't figure it out, I say, 'Here's what they're doing.' Now when you want that sound, look in your notebook. 'Ah, here's that sound.' And you put it together."[76]

By the end of the second semester, all students are expected to know all instrument ranges, tessituras, and transpositions cold, be able to read a score, and have the skills to write for any size jazz group – with everything crystal clear, including tempos, dynamics, grooves, and the like. David sums it up: "You hear me say all the time, 'Where's the dynamic marking and what is the tempo indication? Don't tell me it's half fast or that it's slow; give me a metronomic marking that's verifiable.' So I try to get them first of all to think in terms of the most practical things." David wants to ensure that "the transpositions are correct" and his students are always as explicit as possible. He says, "When you say 'mute,' what does that mean? Do you want a hat, a cup mute, a straight mute, a pixie mute? And you tell me it's Latin. What do you mean it's Latin? Is it a tango? A mambo? A samba? What is it?" By taking things this way, David says that "I'm asking them to give me every bit of information that makes it possible for them to communicate with the band so that if I'm not there or you're not there, the piece can be played."[77]

Most importantly, David wants his students to forevermore be self sufficient, having the ability to find out for themselves whatever they need to know. "The main thing is to make it possible for them to write any style, anything that they want to do, [by telling] them where to go [for the information]," David contends. "Samuel Johnson, the great English philosopher, said there are two kinds of knowledge: you either know something or you know where to find out about it. That's what Google did, gave us all that at our fingertips."[78]

David strongly advocates that having the skills to find out what one needs to know, where to go for answers, is far more efficient, practical, and sane than trying to continually store information – much of which may never be used – in your brain. "I think it's unfair to ask people to pay a toll in a coin they don't possess," David philosophizes. "I can't tell them to go into a [jazz] club now and get this [as did many of the great jazz arrangers in the past] 'cause there ain't no clubs, you know, figuratively speaking. So I tell [my students] they have to listen to records; that's where we find out so much of what we need to know. . . . I can always go to the Rimsky-Korsakov book on orchestration[79] if I need to find out what a bass clarinet is supposed to sound like."[80]

JAZZ COMPOSITION

Like all David's skill-development courses, Jazz Composition incorporates imagination and craft; listening, analyzing, and emulating; and trial, error, and emendation. His goal is to have his students compose a variety of music, being as creative as possible but always cognizant of the "rules" (which he eventually allows them to break, provided they have a good reason).

To establish the "rules concept," David begins his one-semester composition class in a somewhat unorthodox way – by having his students write tone rows using the twelve-tone technique, a method devised by twentieth-century composer Arnold Schoenberg. In addition to numerous other rules, all twelve notes in the chromatic scale must be written as often as any other, avoiding any semblance of being in a particular key. "Even though I don't ever expect them to use the twelve-tone technique [in their professional lives] probably," David explains, "I make them write tone rows because they are so hard to write. I give them the rules and have them start working [on] *craft* because [twelve-tone music] is not something that you can hear immediately."[81] "Baptism by immersion," is how Estelle Jorgensen, an Indiana University colleague, describes David's teaching technique in general.[82]

David continues with the "rules" concept by having his students write rule-guided melodic fragments, the best of which they will subsequently incorporate into their first compositional assignment, an original pop tune. These rules include such limitations as each fragment cannot be more than ten notes, must stay within an octave, cannot include any tritones or outline any triads or have any more than four notes in a row that are scalar, and the like.[83] Observing the rules helps the students write their tune's melodic "hook," the part of the tune that "grabs" the listener and makes the song memorable. Simultaneously, the class looks at and analyzes existing hooks that have stood the test of time – for instance, the first phrase of "Over the Rainbow."

While continuing to compose melodic fragments on a daily basis – descriptively labeled, categorized, and put in a notebook for future use[84] – the students are assigned to write contrafacts, that is, new melodies based on the chord changes of standards. This way, they learn by example how chords move and what makes a good chord progression. Then David has his students reverse the process – that is, to write chord progressions for melodies they have composed, utilizing what they now know about how chords progress.[85] He also has them write three blues tunes (traditional, riff-based, and altered),[86] a modal tune, and a melody and chord progression for a given set of lyrics.

All the while, David covers such motivic development techniques as repetition, sequence, inversion, rhythmic augmentation and diminution, interval expansion and contraction, providing numerous examples of each technique from the standard jazz repertoire. For instance, interval expansion is found in "Blue Room" and "Invitation," and interval contraction is found in "All of Me" and "Easy Living"; scale-based tunes include "Blue Bossa" and "Blue Moon," and chord-based tunes include "Afternoon in Paris" and "Groovin' High." Learning by imitation and emulation is central to David's teaching.

Jorgensen points out that imitation and example are nothing new in the instruction of music, particularly the teaching and learning of composition. For centuries it was not unusual for composers-in-training in the Western classical music tradition to copy the scores of earlier masters.[87] Moreover, imitation, David insists, must be coupled with creative thinking. He warns that poor writing can often be attributed to laziness – that is, laziness of imagination. "That's lazy," David recalls telling a now-famous composer and arranger. "I said, 'You've got more tunes that have fade-aways [as endings] than anybody'; and he said, 'Oh, I like that.' I said, 'No you don't; you're too lazy to figure out something else to do to finish the tune.' That's lack of imagination. In the arranging class and in the composition class, [the objective] is to maximize the imagination."[88]

The class is rounded out with readings from the two texts for the course: David's *Arranging and Composing for the Small Ensemble* and *How to Learn Tunes*. Both books contain numerous examples of much of what is being taught as well as myriad suggestions for further listening and references for finding additional information. For their final project, the students are assigned to write, realize, and perform for the class an original composition in any style.[89] It does not necessarily have to be a jazz piece. "When we get to the last [assignment], I say, 'This is *your* project,'" David clarifies. "I say, 'I want a four-minute piece, or a five-minute piece, and it can be anything you want it to be.' It can be a string quartet, anything; one cat last semester wrote a theme and variations for several snare drums and it was a great piece."[90]

Although imitation might be key to the process, it is imagination that is paramount to the goal of this class and everything jazz. "[The final project] forces [my students] to use their imagination," David asserts. "In everything that I teach, imagination becomes the big point of departure, because the world works because of the imagination. I can teach you to do most anything if I define every parameter, but then what are you going to write? You've got more restrictions in a jazz context [than anywhere else] and it is your job to destroy every one of those restrictions, one at a time or all at the same time, and still have it be coherent."[91]

JAZZ ENSEMBLE

There is very little difference, if any, between the way David directs the top student big band at Indiana University and the way he directs the Smithsonian Jazz Masterworks Orchestra, one of the top professional big bands in the world.[92] Whether you're an advanced student or seasoned professional, David expects you to be able to function as the latter. This includes showing up prepared and on time, having your instrument and all your doubles in perfect working order,[93] and having all necessary appurtenances at the ready.[94] He also expects everyone in his band to play in tune, blend, solo, and be able to read whatever is put in front of them, regardless of style – swing, bop, rock, funk, Latin, ballad – the full gamut.

David prides himself on providing his students with experience performing virtually all styles of big band jazz, from traditional to contemporary. Most every concert will include at least one or two repertory pieces, that is, classics from the bands of such luminaries as Count Basie, Duke Ellington, Gil Evans, Dizzy Gillespie, Thad Jones, Charles Mingus, and Oliver Nelson. It will also inevitably include a contemporary work or two from the likes of such modern writers as John Clayton, Bob Curnow, Bill Holman, Chuck Owen, and a plethora of others. He also likes to program pieces composed or arranged by his good friends Quincy Jones and Slide Hampton, as well as those penned by former students such as Brent Wallarab, Mark Buselli, Luke Gillespie, and Tom Walsh. And if a current student has written a chart that meets David's high standards, it, too, will find its way onto the program. Finally, no David Baker concert would be complete without the inclusion of at least one David Baker tune, arrangement, concerto, or suite.

In addition to conducting two jazz ensemble concerts per semester, David puts on one of Indiana University's most popular annual programs: "Big Band Extravaganza: When Swing Was King." David and one of his colleagues – each in front of his own nineteen-piece student band on the same stage – present an evening of swing music, primarily from the 1930s and 1940s. This experience provides students the opportunity to prepare and authentically perform the music of such swing era icons as Basie, Jimmy and Tommy Dorsey, Ellington, Benny Goodman, Woody Herman, and Glenn Miller. Such hits as Miller's "In the Mood" and Goodman's "Sing, Sing, Sing" always bring the house down.

The band is comprised of five saxes, five trumpets, four trombones, tuba, and four rhythm. David usually carries two pianists, bassists, drummers, and guitarists in the band who switch off, each playing half the tunes. In so doing, he not only gives twice as many rhythm section players an opportunity to play and grow by being in the top band, he also affords them the opportunity to learn from one another, for this is the jazz way. And although he generally lets them decide among themselves who is going to play which tunes, he fully expects each of them to be able to play everything.

Besides standard big band instrumentation, David often adds a jazz violinist, cellist, or other nontraditional jazz instrumentalist if he or she is truly exceptional, and writes additional parts as the need arises. He also occasionally augments the band with a string section, French horns, and other orchestral instruments for pieces that require them. These musicians are commonly "borrowed" from one of the school's classical orchestras and are only too delighted to have the opportunity to work with someone so eminent in his field and to perform with this elite ensemble.

David also has an affinity for vocalists, and if one is enrolled who is truly up to the challenge, he or she will be featured on a tune or two as well.

When you attend a concert, you'll notice that David's setup is different from the conventional big band setup. Whereas most jazz ensembles arrange themselves with the baritone saxophonist and bass trombonist (and tuba if there is one) on stage left,[95] David has them seated on the other side, that is, immediately to the right of the rhythm section as you're looking at the band. He does this to allow the low-range horn players to sit close to the bassist and pianist, so that when playing unison lines with them, they can really hear one another, and are better able to match pitch, articulation, and groove. All the jazz ensembles at Indiana University follow suit, respectfully taking David's lead.

David treats his students like pros; thus, his rehearsal technique does not include a lot of stops and starts. Rather, he likes to play for the band the original recording of the piece about to be rehearsed (if available), and provide his students with insight into the style, tempo, and feel. He then has the ensemble read the chart down without stopping, giving them true sight-reading experience. He'll then go back and work on any trouble spots, difficult sections, and the like – as well as, perhaps, give them one more pass on the ending. At this point, he'll run the arrangement through from beginning to end, with obvious improvement heard by all.

David expects his students to mark any areas they need to practice, do so, and return to the next rehearsal a couple of days later with their parts completely under their fingers. And if the reeds or brass need a sectional, he expects them to get together on their own and take care of business. He also trusts that all those soloing will practice improvising on the changes of the tunes on which they are featured, and better solos will ensue the next time he hears them play.

Since everyone who makes the top band is already an accomplished musician, grades are not determined by how one plays but rather on professionalism. If you're always on time, bring the required equipment and music, have your parts down solid, dress appropriately for the gigs,[96] don't noodle on your instrument between tunes, have no unexcused absences, and comport yourself with a good attitude, you'll get an A and an experience of a lifetime.

PEDAGOGY OF JAZZ

I cannot think of anyone better equipped to teach Jazz Pedagogy than David Baker. He has taught jazz at all levels, neophytes to professionals, for over fifty years; written more than sixty books and four hundred articles on the subject; and experienced every facet of the art form as composer, arranger, performer, and bandleader.[97] This one-semester course is required for all jazz and music education majors at Indiana University, as well as anyone else possessing the good sense to realize that having jazz teaching skills can enhance one's career, regardless of music specialty.

The class is no substitute for experience – that is, actually play-ing, writing, studying, and critically listening to jazz for a number of years – but it does provide all students regardless of background with the basics of directing a jazz band and teaching improvisation, jazz educa-tion's two most prominent staples. Additionally, the course deals with teaching other jazz courses, such as Jazz History, Arranging, and Styles and Analysis, as well as private lessons. It also covers such practical mat-ters as organization, jazz band auditions, student concert programming, course syllabi preparation, lesson planning, testing, and the first week at a new job. If they do not have them already, students must acquire at least some minimal jazz skills, such as being able to voice piano chords and comp on simple tunes.[98] Most importantly, David directs his students to be self-sufficient, that is, to know how and where to find what they need to know long after the last day of class.

On the first day, David begins by dispelling typical jazz myths, the foremost being that jazz cannot be taught, a misconception often used by jazz professionals who do not know how to teach, and an excuse by music teachers who do not teach their students how to improvise. As David puts it, the adage "You either got it or you ain't" no longer flies. Other philosophical issues discussed early on include questions relating to teaching: what can and cannot be taught, why teaching should not be a "backup plan," and the idea that "the person who has all the skills and no knowledge is as bad off as the cat who has all the knowledge and no skills."[99] He also provides a brief overview of the history of jazz educa-tion from its origins, when jazz was strictly taught and learned aurally, to the present day, when it is an important and often eminent component of programs in the country's most distinguished conservatories and university schools of music.

Over the next few weeks, David covers the teaching of improvisation, including in jazz theory and nomenclature, functional piano, bass line construction, and guitar voicings. This is followed by a couple of weeks devoted to teaching arranging and composition, and three more dedicated to teaching jazz history and styles and analysis, which take the class just past mid-semester. Besides learning how these subjects can be taught, all students are required to observe a meeting of each jazz course currently in session at Indiana University (taught by David and other Indiana University jazz faculty) as well as several non-jazz courses of their choosing. They then must write a detailed critique of each visitation, to be turned in as part of their final grade.[100] "They have to have twelve or thirteen [classroom] visitations [throughout the semester]," David explains. "And I give them a list of fifteen things that they have to report on: demeanor, dress and carriage, communication, effectiveness, what [the teachers] say, [and so on]; and they have to bring me detailed [descriptions]."[101]

In addition to classes, David requires his students to visit jazz ensemble rehearsals, both at the university and in area high schools. "They have to observe each of the jazz bands: the four [university] jazz bands here [at Indiana University] and the two bands from North [Bloomington North High School] and South [Bloomington South High School]," David explains. "So they have to go and observe those, and talk about the rehearsal technique of whomever the band director is; talk about how effective they are, where they are in the evolution of this particular [upcoming] concert – is it the beginning, middle, or end of preparation? How successful are they, why are they successful, do they talk too much?" And the students are not required to observe only jazz, or even music, classes. "They can observe a history class or a math class or a class in calculus or pre-med or whatever," David clarifies. "Each time, they're trying to discern what makes a good teacher or what makes a bad teacher, or a capable teacher or one not so capable."[102]

David instructs his students to be as candid and honest as possible when critiquing the teachers they observe, assuring them that all their writing will be confidential; he alone will read their reports. However, he does admit to sometimes passing on their constructive criticism anonymously to his jazz faculty in an effort to bring attention to possible flaws in, and perhaps improve, their teaching methods.[103] David welcomes criticisms of, and is forever updating, his own teaching strategies as well.

The final third of the course is devoted to big band and combo directing, the crux of what most jazz educators will do in their careers. David covers everything from proper band setup and fingerings for all instruments to choosing appropriate repertoire and rehearsal techniques. This includes score reading, working with each member of the rhythm section, and planning and presenting a concert. He also spends time on directing a combo, using Jamey Aebersold's *Combo Rehearsal Guidelines* as the main source of tutelage.

During the final two weeks of the semester, after David's premier university jazz band has presented its final concert, selected jazz pedagogy students have the opportunity to spend a half hour directing this ensemble while their classmates and instructor observe. David will sometimes covertly instruct the band to do such things as ignore the key signature or turn the beat around to see how the student director handles the situation. "I'll give an eye signal or a hand signal [inconspicuously] to the band, letting them know that whenever a flat appears in their music not to play it. When the student [director] doesn't notice it's happening, I'll say, 'Didn't you notice a discrepancy there? Does that sound right to you?'" Wanting them to be able to hear the difference and react accordingly, David is continually challenging his students. "You've got to keep coming up with ways [for them] to use their minds so they don't get too comfortable," he asserts. "Once they get comfortable, you've lost them."[104] A bit devious, perhaps, but effective.

The activities are rounded out with readings from the two required texts: David's *Jazz Pedagogy: A Comprehensive Method of Jazz Education for Teacher and Student* and his 180-page course packet.[105] Both books contain a wealth of historical, philosophical, and practical information on the teaching of jazz. They include instructive content in all topics covered in class and, what David insists is the most paramount, references for a multitude of other sources. Along these lines, he also provides each of his students with a copy of the latest Jamey Aebersold jazz catalog[106] listing brief descriptions of hundreds of pedagogical books, play-along recordings, combo arrangements, and videos from numerous publishers. He also distributes the latest JW Pepper jazz ensemble catalog,[107] which includes descriptions of myriad charts categorized by style and level of difficulty.

It is unfortunate that more music teachers have not had the advantage of taking a class such as this. As I travel around the United States presenting jazz clinics in high schools from Anchorage to Miami, I find too many band directors who are trained as music educators but are ill prepared to run their jazz ensembles and teach improvisation. It is not unusual to visit band rooms in which the jazz groups do not even have the slightest idea of how to properly set up. When I work with ensembles under the direction of Baker alumni, however, I find that business is invariably taken care of. These teachers are typically well versed in the teaching of jazz or are astute as to how and where to find whatever information they need.

JAMEY AEBERSOLD SUMMER JAZZ WORKSHOPS

Internationally renowned jazz pedagogue and publisher Jamey Aebersold has been, and continues to be, a huge part of David Baker's life. Best known for his jazz play-along series and annual Summer Jazz Workshops (SJW), Aebersold was actually a student of David's in the 1960s.[108] Since then, David has published several books with Jamey Aebersold Jazz, written and recorded two play-alongs,[109] and has been a mainstay at the Aebersold SJW ever since its beginnings in the early 1970s. "We started the combo camps in 1972 or 3 and [David] was there," recalls Aebersold. "The first official combo camp was the week after a big band camp because I recall some of the big band faculty wishing us good luck with our [combo camp] venture."[110]

For nearly forty years, David has spent at least two weeks every summer teaching jazz students of all ages from all over the world in various venues at the preeminent weeklong workshops.[111] His duties have remained much the same during his entire tenure: teach the Advanced Theory class, direct the top combo, and present daily master classes for the string students. It's not unusual for his five-day theory class to have between fifty and one hundred relatively advanced students, all striving to play David's "active-learning" exercises in unison.[112] And the members of his top combo might range in age from fifteen to seventy-five, but at the end of the week when you hear their final performance, they sound of like mind and spirit (and if they were to make a recording, you'd want to buy it!).

A member of the Aebersold camp faculty myself since 1986, I took advantage of sitting in on David's Advanced Theory class every summer for two decades (until five years ago when I began teaching another theory class during the same time slot). The class title is Advanced Theory, but it is rather an advanced improvisation class, as David's teaching approach is to teach theory in conjunction with its practical application. Instrument in hand, I had the incredible opportunity to participate as a student and watch the class evolve over twenty consecutive years! What most struck me was that David always displayed the uncanny ability to immediately adapt his content and methodology to the particular class at hand, presenting new and different material from time to time, while still making sure particular fundamentals were covered every year like clockwork. More importantly, I witnessed his students (including myself) make tangible improvement right before my eyes.

David's foremost staple for this class is bebop language. He begins with the bebop dominant scale, having the students play it in the keys of F, Bb, and C (I, IV, and V in the key of F) over an F blues. Staying with the same progression for the remainder of the ninety-minute session on day one, David teaches the class how to manipulate the scale by going up various degrees before descending, starting on chord tones other than the root, beginning phrases on various beats in the measure, and rhythmically ending their bebop lines on the *and of one* and the *and of three*. He also shows his students how, when starting their phrases on non-chord tones, they can restore balance to their lines by adding a half step, syncopating, enclosing chord tones, and more – as detailed in *How to Play Bebop, volume 1*. And he explains and pianistically demonstrates ways to extend their lines, providing examples of such bebop devices as deflection, arpeggiating up and scaling down, and using turns and enclosures.

Going from topic to topic quickly with barely enough time for his students to catch their breath, David has them playing almost continuously, accompanying them on piano all the while. He literally covers weeks of material in just the first day. Although intense, everything is very clear and very practical. And he periodically relieves any tension the class might be feeling via his perfectly timed humorous quips and corny puns. This is his way.

Another staple of this class is David teaching jazz vocabulary utilizing material from bebop heads, particularly phrases built on common harmonic formulae found within, for example, lines that fit over a major chord, a II–V, or a turnaround. Using Miles Davis's "Half Nelson" and Dizzy Gillespie's "Groovin' High" as exemplars, David has his students analyze and memorize pertinent phrases, and transpose them to the keys needed in order to utilize them on both these tunes. He then has them play on "Half Nelson" using "Groovin' High" material and vice versa, along with mixing in each tune's melody and generic bebop patterns learned the day before. Following suit, David teaches his students how to play over "I Got Rhythm" changes by having them mix and match phrases from Charlie Parker's "Anthropology," "Dexterity," and "Moose the Mooch," three quintessential bebop rhythm contrafacts. In no time flat, the students' solos begin to sound less aimless – more like jazz.

The remainder of the week is up for grabs. David may teach tune-learning techniques, post-bop improvisation concepts and vocabulary, or how to practice – depending on the class level, questions raised during the week, and what he feels is most lacking. He'll also take into consideration the number of familiar faces he sees, to make sure that returning students are getting something new. The last day is reserved for review, questions, inspirational advice, and suggestions as to what the students need to do next. Most important, he guides them as to where to find the jazz educational resources necessary for them to continue on their jazz journey. Every year, the class ends with an ardent standing ovation for the master teacher.

David's top combo is equally intense. Having the luxury of having the camp's best six to eight students (determined by audition), David enjoys putting them through the paces two and a half hours per day – sixty minutes in the morning and another ninety in the afternoon. He begins diagnostically, having them play tune after tune on the first day in an effort to ascertain each player's strengths and weaknesses, for this will determine the rest of the week's focus and repertoire. "I'll start with a tune like 'Eternal Triangle' to see if they can read, for one thing, and secondly, what they know," David explains. "Then I'll probably do 'Moose the Mooch.' . . . Then we'll play a couple of blues like 'Relaxin' at Camarillo,' which I'll teach them by ear. . . . Then I'll take a standard like 'Have You Met Miss Jones' or 'Stella [by Starlight].'"[113]

Once he sizes up their abilities, David challenges the musicians throughout the week by removing them from their comfort zones. "For that first session I try to find out what they don't know," David iterates. "And then second session I try to find out what they *do* know and I intend to take that away from them. [For instance], if they can double-time really well, love to double-time, then I won't let them double-time; we don't need to work on that." He'll also have each student play a chorus or two without the rhythm section, making sure that everything is clear – changes, form, time – with no "crutch." Whether you're a horn or rhythm section player (including drummers), David wants to always be able to easily identify what tune you're playing and where you are in the form, whether there's accompaniment or not.[114]

The repertoire for the week will inevitably include such jazz staples as blues, rhythm changes, "All the Things You Are," and "Cherokee," in addition to whatever else David thinks might be most pedagogically appropriate for the particular group at hand. And if they're very advanced, he'll have the students play them in keys other than the original (and in some cases, all keys!). He also has his students learn certain tunes' exact arrangements as recorded on the definitive versions. "I make people learn at least five arrangements where they learn every part [introductions, hits, contrapuntal and harmony parts, backgrounds, vamps, interludes, endings]," David explains. "We take a tune such as [Horace Silver's recording of] 'Nica's Dream.' . . . I want them to know [for instance] what Benny Golson plays; do they hear the difference between the first two times when he plays the major 7th resolving down to the minor 7th or does he stay on the major 7th? . . . I'll play the recording for them."[115]

Although David teaches most everything by ear, he also provides his students with lead sheets as well as fully realized written arrangements, introducing numerous tune types along the way: bop, modal, Latin, modern, fast, slow, $\frac{3}{4}$, $\frac{6}{8}$, and more. He likes to cover a wide variety of repertoire, "including tunes that have some uneasiness in them like 'Stablemates' or tunes that go funny places like 'Along Came Betty.'"[116] In every tune, David insists his students work on their particular deficiencies, such as not using color tones on dominant chords, being unclear on turnarounds, or overusing bebop mannerisms (such as double-time or "favorite" licks).

David also spends a considerable amount of time addressing the rhythm section. First off, he has each member set up close to one another – especially bass and drums – so that all can "see" as well as hear if they're together. While the group is playing, he'll often demonstrate various chord voicings and comping patterns to the pianist. Additionally, he'll urge the pianist and guitarist to practice comping at the same time, finding ways to enhance what the other is doing without getting in each other's way (besides comping separately if musically called for). And, of course, time, groove, interaction, and feel are of the utmost importance in any David Baker rhythm section.

The primary goal for the week is for the members of the ensemble to become more knowledgeable and experienced, substantially improving their playing while becoming a real *group*. "I want them to have the ability to quickly put music together, agree on the changes before they start, agree on the ending," David concludes. "I want them to take away [from their week's work] the camaraderie of watching how they grow from day one which is a bunch of [separate] cats playing, to where by the end of the week we've got one mind."[117]

Although David can count on the level of his theory class and combo being much the same from year to year, his string master class students often run the full gamut from novice to pro. It's not uncommon for his class to include beginners, concertmasters in symphony orchestras who play the instrument beautifully but can't play a lick of jazz, country fiddlers, and seasoned jazz professionals. In years past, if there were any miscellaneous instrumentalists attending the camp, they would be assigned to David's master class as well. "In California [years ago]," David recalls, "I had an accordion – a doctor who played the accordion, another cat who played ukulele, I had a singer, I had a cat who played spoons. And every day all he wanted to play was 'Giant Steps'! . . . I told Jamey that was too much, too much of a grind on the mind."[118] Since then, although they may be at disparate levels, David's string master class students have been violinists, violists, and cellists only.

If the ability range is truly extreme – that is, from raw beginner to experienced pro – David will divide the ninety-minute class period into three thirty-minute sections – beginning, intermediate, and advanced. However, he only does this as a last resort; he prefers to have everyone for the full hour and a half. In most cases there are enough common needs among all the string attendees to warrant putting them in one class.

David always begins with (and emphasizes throughout the week) what he has coined the "fretted" approach to string playing.[119] He teaches movable fingerings in a manner similar to those who play a fretted instrument like guitar or electric bass. For them, finger patterns for the same quality scales and arpeggios (as well as heads, jazz licks, or anything else) in different keys don't change. To transpose, they simply move the left hand to the left or right on the fingerboard. "I'll say, 'Play me an A♭ major scale, three octaves,'" David illustrates. "'Now play me an A scale.' If they start with a different fingering, I'll stop them. I say, 'For our needs, use the same fingering; it's just a half step higher than what it was.'"[120] Once his string students understand the basic principles of "fretted" playing, their world opens up. David immediately has them apply this technique to learning tunes, turnarounds, II–V licks, and, ultimately, improvisation.

Throughout the week, David also provides tutelage on sound, swing, articulation, bowing, and vibrato. Rather than get too technical, he has his students sing jazz heads such as "Doxy," "Sugar," and "Blues Walk" along with the definitive recordings of each, and emulate on their instruments what they just sang. He'll also have them play *while* they sing, suggesting they try to match voice and instrument exactly. Inevitably, owing to the nature of their classical studies, some of the string students will inadvertently overuse vibrato. "Why are you using so much vibrato?" David chides. "Play it just like you sing it!"[121]

As an exercise, he'll often have his students play four bars with vibrato, followed by four bars without, so they can truly hear the difference: "They [need to] understand that vibrato is an expressive device in jazz [whereas] it's a continuum in classical music."[122] By the end of the week, the string players, as well as all of David's Advanced Theory students, are playing in their respective combos with a much better jazz conception than the one they walked in with.

It goes without saying that teaching at Aebersold's camp every summer is self-obligatory for David. Indeed, he has turned down far more lucrative projects over the years that would have overlapped with the Summer Jazz Workshop's dates. "The camp is sacrosanct for me," David attests. "I still love it and would never let Jamey down. I already have it on my calendar for next year."[123]

STEANS INSTITUTE FOR YOUNG ARTISTS AT RAVINIA

In 2000, David was asked to design and direct the inaugural Program for Jazz for the Steans Institute for Young Artists, a now integral component of the world renowned Ravinia Festival in Chicago.[124] He has been chairing this highly visible, prestigious, and educative weeklong summer program ever since. It features fifteen student musicians, mostly in their early twenties, who are amongst the best in the country. "The main stipulation [to be invited to participate in the program]," David clarifies, "is that there is a realistic chance of them having a major career in jazz."[125]

The hand-selected young artists receive a full scholarship to study in Chicago's fully equipped John D. Harza Building with David and an illustrious faculty composed of bassist Rufus Reid and saxophonists James Moody and Nathan Davis.[126] During their seven-day tenure, the invitees partake in combo rehearsals, question-and-answer sessions, and more. The week culminates with a concert open to the public at the Festival, featuring the students performing their original compositions in Bennett-Gordon Hall, a 450-seat, state-of-the-art venue.

Because of his international stature as an artist and educator, David has been given carte blanche to run the program any way he sees fit. This begins with his selecting students who play appropriate instruments to comprise three standard jazz quintets – that is, three pianists, bassists, and drummers, plus six horn players.[127] The artistic focus for the week is twofold: performance and composition – that is, concentration on artistically developing and performing the students' original music. At the same time, sharpening the skills required to be successful bandleaders and sidemen – musically, personally, and commercially – is also of paramount importance. All participants are expected to write as well as play, and lead as well as follow.

On the first day, after a brief introduction, combos are formed in which the students rotate – so that by the end of the second day, everyone has played with everyone else. While getting to know each other musically and otherwise, they receive educative comments from, and are further evaluated by, the faculty. David then assigns each student to one of three quintets – the primary criteria being performance level and who plays best with whom – that will remain intact for the remainder of the week. He also assigns himself and the other teaching artists a particular ensemble to direct, although there is some interchange during the week to allow each combo to work with each faculty member.

The daily schedule consists of combo rehearsal from 9:30 AM to 12:00 PM, a lunch break, a question-and-answer session with the faculty from 1:30 to 3:00 PM, and another combo rehearsal until 5:00 PM. During the Q&A sessions, the students can ask the four faculty members about anything they like. "Since we consider these kids at the brink of a successful career," David explains, "they can talk about anything they want to. They raise questions about copyright, questions about how do you put a group together, playing, getting along with other people, how do you get your tune published, should you join ASCAP or BMI and what do they do? There's a wealth of experience on the stage."[128]

Evenings are open for private lessons, individual practice, writing, informal jam sessions, attending performances by guest artists,[129] and the like. The last night is reserved for the final concert, which features each combo performing a one-hour set of five original tunes, one by each member of the respective quintets. Finally, the concluding Saturday morning is set aside for the students and faculty to watch and together constructively critique the professional quality DVD made of the previous night's concert. Each student is then given a copy of the recording to take home for further examination and insight.

"So far, it's been such a big success," David reminisces. "[The Steans Institute] has supported us completely; we've been treated with the same respect that they treat [the distinguished classical music faculty and students for which the Institute and Ravinia Festival are best known[130]. . . . If I were to wish for anything, [it would be that the program] be lengthier. But, it's more along the line of the real world in that [the students] have only so much time to put together what they do."[131]

PRIVATE LESSONS

David Baker began teaching private lessons in the early 1950s. Barely in his twenties, he set out on the journey that would eventually lead to his becoming one of the most respected jazz pedagogues in the world. It was in those early years when, mostly by trial and error, he began to codify how to teach this music. "I wrote a lot of stuff down," David recalls. "But it never occurred to me that it was ever going to go anywhere beyond that. . . . I was learning as I was going then because I had lots of records, but I didn't [yet] have it in a method book where I could be absolutely consistent when I taught. . . . It was touch and go in the beginning."[132]

Most of David's students at that time came from North Central High School in Indianapolis. "One cat from the school would start studying with me, then I would have all the others who had the ambition to play jazz as my students," David explains. "Basically what I taught was chord to scale relationships and how to play bebop tunes. . . . I charged a dollar and a half an hour."[133]

By the mid-1950s, David had a full teaching load, giving private lessons along with playing. He not only provided weekly instruction to students at his home but went to many of their houses as well. "Sometimes I'd have a whole family [studying with me] because I could teach classical music, too," David remembers. "I had a lot of piano players, sometimes a mother and two kids, whatever. There I would teach the classical side – how to play scales, right fingerings – but more and more [of my students] gravitated towards jazz because that's the place where there were the most gaps . . . I'd teach them II–Vs, turnarounds, tunes."[134]

Besides moms and kids, David's private teaching roster eventually included the likes of Freddie Hubbard, Jamey Aebersold, Ralph Bowen, Gary Campbell, Virgil Jones, and others who went on to have incredible careers in jazz. He even taught tenor saxophone virtuoso James Moody over the phone for a time. David credits these gifted players as being catalysts for his having to come up with and subsequently codify his methods of teaching advanced jazz concepts. "Because they could play so well, I had to find things that challenged them," David explains. "I would stay up for nights before Ralph's lessons, trying to figure out what I was going to do with him."[135]

Among other assignments, David instructed Bowen and others of that ilk to transcribe the masters, learning every nuance there was to learn. "I'd say, 'I want you to learn solos by Hank Mobley,'" David recounts. "'You pick the solos but I want them to be [played in such a way that] if you were standing behind a screen, I'd believe somehow or another that was Hank Mobley playing.' I'd say, 'You make mistakes where he'd make mistakes, change the sound where he would have changed the sound, screw up the time where he would have screwed up the time.'" After a month or so, they'd do this again with another artist, then another. David also contrived novel exercises for his students to practice, like having them improvise on entire tunes using only the notes within the interval of a fifth, forcing them to leave their comfort zones and find new things to play.[136]

Whether teaching at home in Indianapolis in the 1950s, the famed Charles Colin Studio when he lived in New York in the 1960s,[137] or his home studio in Bloomington, Indiana, ever since, David has made private lessons an integral component of his professional activities throughout his career. And although only occasionally and mostly by appointment, David still takes on private students today. These mainly are professional players who need a "tune-up" before making a recording, advanced students who have been recommended by someone of note, or simply someone he feels he'd like to teach, like the talented son or daughter of a colleague. In any case, they must show David that they are serious and are willing to put in the work.

As he has from the beginning, David continues to tailor the lessons to his students' particular needs, covering all necessary fundamentals while striving to lead them in the direction of their own unique voices. Every topic imaginable – bebop language, contemporary language, ear training, tune learning, piano, bass line construction, time feel, solo development, technique, composition, arranging, how to practice, and, especially, the creative process – is on the table. Whatever the subject area during the lesson, the student is always active, playing, emulating, experimenting, continuously on task; and David is always at the piano accompanying and demonstrating – no passive listening to a lecture or someone pontificating found here. And with regard to how much he charges for lessons today, it's $0.00. "I [no longer] need the money; I teach because I want to," David discloses. "It really never would occur to me to charge people for something that I have as a gift."[138]

NOTES

1. Baker, *A New Approach to Ear Training for Jazz Musicians*, 1.

2. An example of jazz ear training software is Big Ears. See www.flat5 software.com.

3. Michael and Randy Brecker are two Indiana University alumni who today are among the most respected names in jazz.

4. David Baker, personal communication, July 27, 2008.

5. Ibid.

6. Before digital technology, David would have his students record LPs onto reel-to-reel tape at 7½ ips (inches per second) – that is, normal speed. He would then have his students play back the recording at 3¾ ips (meaning the tempo would be half speed), making fast or difficult phrases easier to transcribe (most reel-to-reel tape decks include 7½, 3¾, and 1⅞ ips speed controls). Of course, the pitch would be lowered an octave as well, which would be fine for a soprano or alto sax solo; not so fine for a bari sax or bass solo; see Baker, *A New Approach to Ear Training for Jazz Musicians*, 72.

7. Baker, *Jazz Improvisation*.

8. See Gunther Schuller's foreword to Baker, *Jazz Improvisation*, iv.

9. David Baker, interview by JB Dyas, July 25, 2008.

10. Ibid.

11. For example, see Baker, *How to Play Bebop, vol. 2*.

12. David Baker, interview by JB Dyas, July 26, 2008.

13. Ibid.

14. A contrafact is a tune based on the chord progression of an extant composition. For example, there are dozens of jazz tunes that utilize the same chord progression (or variations thereof) as George Gershwin's "I Got Rhythm," a staple in the standard jazz repertoire, such as "Anthropology," "Dexterity," and "Moose the Mooch" (all of which David includes when teaching improvisation). Other common contrafacts include "Donna Lee" (based on "Back Home Again in Indiana"), "Groovin' High" (based on "Whispering"), "Ornithology" (based on "How High the Moon"), "Hot House" (based on "What Is This Thing Called Love?"), and "Dig" (based on "Sweet Georgia Brown").

15. Baker, *How to Learn Tunes*.

16. *Bitonal:* one chord superimposed over another, e.g., a B major triad over a C major triad. *Chromaticism:* improvising using primarily half steps. *Pentatonics:*

five-note scales. *Quartal playing:* improvising using primarily the interval of a fourth.

17. By difficult, I mean tunes that have unusual chord sequences, rapid tempo or harmonic rhythm, complex chords, unusual forms, bitonals, pedal points, or any combination thereof.

18. I had the pleasure of recording "Birdsong" with the David Baker Sextet, of which I was a member in the 1990s (*Steppin' Out,* Liscio Recordings CD LAS-31591). We alternated between using the original "Half Nelson" changes and using David's "Birdsong" bitonal changes – two choruses each, going from bop to modern and back again. Very cool.

19. Baker, *Modern Concepts in Jazz Improvisation,* 121–29.

20. Bebop mannerisms include using bebop scales, bebop licks, quotes from other tunes, blues vocabulary, and inflections such as slides, fall-offs, and grace notes.

21. See Baker, *Practicing Jazz.*

22. Baker, interview, July 26, 2008.

23. Ibid.

24. Dyas, "Master Class," 114.

25. Dyas, "Tune Learning," 70–73.

26. David Baker, interview by JB Dyas, July 19, 2010.

27. Baker, *How to Learn Tunes.*

28. *Riff blues* are based on a repeated phrase in which the phrase is played three times, each lasting four measures (e.g., Sonny Rollins's "Sonnymoon for Two" and Milt Jackson's "Bag's Groove"). *Through-composed blues* have a bebop-like melody and more sophisticated chord progression than traditional I–IV–V blues (e.g., Charlie Parker's "Billie's Bounce" and "Au Privave"). *Altered blues* are unusual in some way, such as in chorus length (e.g., Herbie Hancock's "Watermelon Man"), minor key (e.g., Oliver Nelson's "Stolen Moments"), or chord

progression (e.g., Charlie Parker's "Blues for Alice").

29. Conventional rhythm changes tunes are ones whose chord progression closely reflects the original as penned by George Gershwin on his tune "I Got Rhythm," with perhaps a few chord substitutions; examples include "Anthropology," "Dexterity," and "Moose the Mooch." Altered rhythm changes tunes, on the other hand, are tunes that, while still based on "I Got Rhythm," contain many more chord substitutions and alterations; examples include "Room 608," "Eternal Triangle," and "Crazeology."

30. Dyas, "Tune Learning," 70–73.

31. Dyas, "Master Class, part 2," 82.

32. Dyas, "Master Class," 114.

33. Dyas, "Tune Learning," 70–73.

34. *Indiana University Course Bulletin, 2007–2009,* www.indiana.edu/~bulletin/Indiana Universityb/music/2007-2009/ac6.shtml.

35. Baker, interview, July 26, 2008.

36. Ibid.

37. For more on compromises in academia, see Jorgensen, *The Art of Teaching Music,* 275.

38. Baker, interview, July 26, 2008.

39. Baker, "M582 – The Bebop Era," course packet, available at Mr. Copy, Bloomington, Indiana, www.copysales.com.

40. Ibid.

41. Baker, interview, July 26, 2008.

42. Ibid.

43. Ibid.

44. John Hasse is a music historian, pianist, author, and record producer. He currently serves as curator of American Music at the Smithsonian Institution's National Museum of American History, where he was founding executive director of the Smithsonian Jazz Masterworks Orchestra – an acclaimed repertory band, under the direction of David Baker, spe-

cializing in the music of Duke Ellington and other jazz masters.

45. Baker, interview, July 26, 2008.

46. Ibid.

47. David Baker, interview by JB Dyas, July 30, 2008.

48. Cannonball Adderley, John Coltrane, and Charlie Parker are seminal *jazz* figures; Louis Jordan and Earl Bostic are seminal *rhythm 'n' blues* players.

49. Baker, interview, July 30, 2008.

50. Ibid.

51. Ibid.

52. Baker, "M393 – History of Jazz" and "M395 – Contemporary Jazz and Soul," course packets, available at Mr. Copy, Bloomington, Indiana, www.copysales .com.

53. *Ethnic jazz* is jazz music that utilizes melodic, harmonic, and rhythmic elements – as well as compositions, musical instruments, and musical philosophy – that are associated with various musics from societies other than American. *Liturgical jazz* is jazz music used in the church or with church-related activities, often merging the melodic, harmonic, and rhythmic elements of jazz with liturgical forms such as the mass, cantata, and oratorio. *Third Stream* is a term coined by composer and jazz historian Gunther Schuller to describe a style that is a synthesis of classical music and jazz. See Baker, "M393 – History of Jazz," course packet.

54. Baker, interview, July 30, 2008.

55. Baker, "M393 – History of Jazz" and "M395 Contemporary Jazz and Soul," course packets.

56. Ibid.

57. Baker, interview, July 30, 2008.

58. Ibid. In fact, "Jazz Styles and Analysis" is now two semesters.

59. Baker, *The Jazz Style of Cannonball Adderley; The Jazz Style of Clifford Brown; The Jazz Style of John Coltrane; The Jazz Style of Miles Davis; J. J. Johnson; The Jazz Style of Fats Navarro; Charlie Parker; The Jazz Style of Sonny Rollins.*

60. *Tune types* include blues, ballad, standard, modal, free, jazz original, bebop, Latin, and Afro-Cuban.

61. *Dramatic devices* include such techniques as vibrato, slurs, rips, growls, glissandi, various articulations, alternate fingerings, and harmonics.

62. *Developmental techniques* include simple to complex and complex to simple; single climax or many climaxes; and theme and variations.

63. *Performances practices* include vertical (arpeggio) and horizontal (scalar) approaches; chord and thematic references; use of sequence, call and response, harmonic substitutions, and quotes; use of double time, half time, symmetrical and asymmetrical groupings of notes, and reiterative and non reiterative phrases; the player's relationship to the basic time (e.g., behind, down the middle, or on top of the beat); and melodic style (e.g., folk-like, riff-like, wide and narrow expressiveness, bluesy, bebop, quartal).

64. Berendt, *The Jazz Book.*

65. David Baker, "F318 – Jazz Styles and Analysis," course packet, available at Mr. Copy, Bloomington, Indiana, www .copysales.com. David's list of *important firsts* includes the first jazz recording, classic blues recording, recording by a black band, mixed-race recording session, scat recording, gold record, modal album, use of the word jazz, jazz ensemble on film, and important interracial jazz group.

66. The books to which David is referring are Miller, *Glenn Miller's Method for Orchestral Arranging;* and Alexander, *First Arrangement.*

67. Baker, *Arranging and Composing for the Small Ensemble;* originally published in 1970 by Maher Publications, a division of *DownBeat Magazine.*

68. Chuck Suber was the editor of *DownBeat Magazine* and its related book publications in the 1960s and 1970s.

69. Baker, interview, July 26, 2008.

70. The Nat King Cole Trio substituted guitar for drums, providing another melodic and harmonic voice.

71. In selecting a trio to transcribe, David guides his students not to choose trios such as those led by Bill Evans or Keith Jarrett as theirs involve more free, interactive playing – that is, not trio *arrangements*.

72. Baker, interview, July 26, 2008.

73. Ibid.

74. Ibid.

75. Ibid.

76. Ibid.

77. Ibid.

78. Ibid.

79. Rimsky-Korsakov, *Principles of Orchestration*.

80. Baker, interview, July 26, 2008.

81. Ibid.

82. Estelle Jorgensen, personal communication, August 15, 2008.

83. For more on David's approach to melody construction, see Baker, *Arranging and Composing for the Small Ensemble*, 16–44.

84. David has his students label and categorize each melodic fragment they write. For instance, particular fragments might be more scalar or chromatic in nature, or have a wide interval followed by scale steps or vice versa; a particular phase might be more suited for a classical piece or a Latin tune or bebop head, and so on. The point is that the students label, categorize, and keep in a notebook all melodic fragments they write – and eventually have a notebook full of beginnings of future compositions.

85. See Baker, *Arranging and Composing for the Small Ensemble*, 45–51.

86. *Traditional blues* uses I, IV, and V chords exclusively for the harmony and the blues scale exclusively for the melody. *Riff blues* are based on a repeated phrase in which the phrase is played three times, each lasting four measures (such as Sonny Rollins's "Sonnymoon for Two" and Milt Jackson's "Bag's Groove"). *Altered blues* have a through-composed bebop-like melody and sophisticated chord progression (such as Charlie Parker's "Blues for Alice").

87. See Jorgensen, *The Art of Teaching Music*, 169.

88. Baker, interview, July 26, 2008.

89. The onus is on the students to recruit players (from inside or outside the class) with whom to rehearse and perform their final compositions.

90. Baker, interview, July 26, 2008.

91. Ibid.

92. David has served as musical and artistic director of the Smithsonian Jazz Masterworks Orchestra since 1990. For more information, visit www.smithsonianjazz.org/sjmo/sjmo_start.asp.

93. Saxophonists are expected to be able to double on all the saxophones (including soprano), flute, piccolo, clarinet, and bass clarinet. On occasion, they also might be required to play oboe, English horn, bassoon, alto flute, or recorder. Trumpeters are expected to double on flugelhorn. Bassists are expected to be able to play both upright and electric. If a student does not yet own one or more of the doubles required for a concert, Indiana University makes provisions to lend them what they need for the semester.

94. Necessary appurtenances include all mutes, instrument stands, pencils with erasers, valve oil, extra reeds, guitar cords, picks, amps, extension cords, and the like.

95. Stage left is on the right side of the stage as viewed from the audience.

96. Until 2011, the students are required to wear a tuxedo or concert dress for the two performances presented each semester at the Musical Arts Center

(MAC), Indiana University's 1,460-seat concert hall.

97. David Baker, curriculum vitae, 2010.

98. David Baker, "E470 – Pedagogy of Jazz," course packet, available at Mr. Copy, Bloomington, Indiana, www .copysales.com.

99. Baker, interview, July 30, 2008.

100. David Baker, "E470 – Pedagogy of Jazz," course packet.

101. Baker, interview, July 30, 2008.

102. Ibid.

103. Ibid.

104. Ibid.

105. Baker, Jazz Pedagogy; "E470 – Pedagogy of Jazz," course packet.

106. Jamey Aebersold Jazz Catalog, available at www.jazzbooks.com.

107. JW Pepper Jazz Ensemble Catalog, available at www.jwpepper.com.

108. The Jamey Aebersold Play-Along Series includes over 125 books and corresponding CD recordings. Each set, categorized by artist, tune type, or common chord progressions, features a book containing melodies and chord symbols coupled with an accompanying play-along CD recorded by a professional rhythm section with which to practice the content within. For further information, visit www.jazzbooks.com. For further information on the Aebersold Summer Jazz Workshops, visit www.summerjazzwork shops.com.

109. Baker, Eight Classic Jazz Originals You Can Play; How to Learn Tunes.

110. Jamey Aebersold, e-mail message to JB Dyas, July 23, 2010.

111. Over the past four decades, the Jamey Aebersold Summer Jazz Workshops have been held at colleges and universities in such US cities as Bloomington, Illinois; Champaign, Illinois; Dallas, Texas; Decatur, Illinois; DeKalb, Illinois; Denton, Texas; Dunseith, North Dakota; Elmhurst, Illinois; Greeley, Colorado; Hays, Kansas; Kingston, Rhode Island; Louisville, Kentucky; Miami, Florida; Newton, Kansas; Normal, Illinois; Norman, Oklahoma; San Jose, California; San Ramon, California; and Wayne, New Jersey. They have also been presented internationally in Australia, Canada, Denmark, Germany, England, New Zealand, and Scotland.

112. David Baker strongly believes in "active learning," that is, he has his students play their respective instruments virtually the entire time during his improvisation and theory classes, actively doing rather than passively listening or note taking.

113. Baker, interview, July 19, 2010.

114. Ibid.

115. Ibid.

116. Ibid.

117. Ibid.

118. Ibid.

119. David Baker's "fretted" approach for string players is detailed in his two string books: Jazz Treble Clef Expressions and Explorations; and Jazz Bass Clef Expressions and Explorations.

120. Baker, interview, July 19, 2010.

121. Ibid.

122. Ibid.

123. Ibid.

124. For more information on the Steans Institute for Young Artists and the Ravinia Festival, visit www.ravinia.org.

125. Baker, interview, July 19, 2010.

126. Candidates for the Program for Jazz are identified by faculty members David Baker, Nathan Davis, James Moody, and Rufus Reid via their travels and professional activities throughout the year, as well as by recommendations from other eminent artists and educators. Participation in the program is by invitation only; David Baker makes the final determination as to which candidates are selected.

127. The horn players are generally saxophonists, trumpeters, and trombon-

ists placed in the combos in various combinations. Guitarists, violinists, and other
instrumentalists, if truly exceptional, are
occasionally invited to participate as well.

128. Baker, interview, July 19, 2010.

129. Recent guest performers have
included such artists as Dave Brubeck,
Ramsey Lewis, and Nancy Wilson.

130. For a list of the distinguished classical music faculty at the Steans Institute
for Young Artists, visit www.ravinia.org/
steans_piano_strings.aspx.

131. Baker, interview, July 19, 2010.

132. Ibid.

133. Ibid.

134. Ibid.

135. Ibid.

136. Ibid.

137. Charles Colin Music Publications
website, www.charlescolin.com/studio
.htm.

138. Baker, interview, July 19, 2010.

REFERENCES

Aebersold, Jamey. *Combo Rehearsal Guidelines.* New Albany, Ind.: Jamey Aebersold Jazz, 1980.

Alexander, Van. *First Arrangement.* New York: Capitol Songs, 1946.

Baker, David. *Arranging and Composing for the Small Ensemble: Jazz, R&B, Jazz-Rock,* Revised ed. Van Nuys, Calif.: Alfred, 1988.

———. *David Baker: Eight Classic Jazz Originals You Can Play.* Jamey Aebersold Play-Along Series 10. New Albany, Ind.: Jamey Aebersold Jazz, 1976.

———. *Charlie Parker, Alto Saxophone.* David Baker Jazz Monographs. New York: Shattinger International, 1978.

———. *How to Learn Tunes: The Quick and Easy Method for Remembering Melodies and Chord Changes.* Jamey Aebersold Play-Along Series 76. New Albany, Ind.: Jamey Aebersold Jazz, 1997.

———. *How to Play Bebop, vol. 2.* Van Nuys, Calif.: Alfred, 1987.

———. *J. J. Johnson, Trombone.* David Baker Jazz Monographs. New York: Shattinger International, 1979.

———. *Jazz Bass Clef Expressions and Explorations: A New and Innovative System for Learning to Improvise for Bass Clef Instruments and Jazz Cello.* New Albany, Ind.: Jamey Aebersold Jazz, 1995.

———. *Jazz Improvisation: A Comprehensive Method for All Players,* Revised ed. Van Nuys, Calif.: Alfred, 1988.

———. *Jazz Pedagogy: A Comprehensive Method of Jazz Education for Teacher and Student.* Revised ed. Van Nuys, Calif.: Alfred, 1989.

———. *The Jazz Style of Cannonball Adderley.* Miami, Fla.: CPP/Belwin, 1980.

———. *The Jazz Style of Clifford Brown.* Miami, Fla.: CPP/Belwin, 1982.

———. *The Jazz Style of Fats Navarro.* Miami, Fla.: CPP/Belwin, 1982.

———. *The Jazz Style of John Coltrane.* Miami, Fla.: CPP/Belwin, 1980.

———. *The Jazz Style of Miles Davis.* Miami, Fla.: CPP/Belwin, 1980.

———. *The Jazz Style of Sonny Rollins.* Miami, Fla.: CPP/Belwin, 1980.

———. *Jazz Treble Clef Expressions and Explorations: A New and Innovative System for Learning to Improvise for Treble Clef Instruments and Jazz Violin.* New Albany, Ind.: Jamey Aebersold Jazz, 1995.

———. *Modern Concepts in Jazz Improvisation.* Van Nuys, Calif.: Alfred, 1990.

———. *A New Approach to Ear Training for Jazz Musicians,* Revised ed. Miami, Fla.: Warner Bros., 1995.

———. *Practicing Jazz: A Creative Approach.* New Albany, Ind.: Jamey Aebersold Jazz, 1994.

Berendt, Joachim. *The Jazz Book.* Brooklyn, N.Y.: Lawrence Hill Books, 1997.

Coker, Jerry. *How to Listen to Jazz.* New Albany, Ind.: Jamey Aebersold Jazz, 1990.

Dyas, JB. "Master Class: Methods for Fighting the Epidemic of Tune Illiteracy." *DownBeat* 77, no. 5 (May 2010): 114.

———. "Master Class: Methods for Fighting the Epidemic of Tune Illiteracy, part 2." *DownBeat,* 77, no. 8 (August 2010): 82.

———. "Tune Learning: A Systematic Approach." *Jazz Player* 2, no. 3 (April/May 1995): 70–72.

Hasse, John Edward. *Beyond Category: The Life and Genius of Duke Ellington.* New York: Simon and Schuster, 1993.

Jorgensen, Estelle. *The Art of Teaching Music.* Bloomington: Indiana University Press, 2008.

Miller, Glenn. *Glenn Miller's Method for Orchestral Arranging.* New York: Mutual Music Society, 1943.

Owens, Thomas. *Bebop: The Music and the Players.* New York: Oxford University Press, 1995.

Rimsky-Korsakov, Nikolay. *Principles of Orchestration, with Musical Examples Drawn from His Own Works.* New York, Dover, 1964.

David Baker conducting his winning big band at the French Lick Jazz Festival, 1959.
Courtesy of Jamey Aebersold.

Winning the Notre Dame Jazz Festival, 1964. From right: Dick Washburn (trumpet), David Baker (cello), Jamey Aebersold (alto saxophone), Tom Hensley (piano), Don Baldwin (bass), Everett Hoffman (tenor saxophone), and three representatives from the Notre Dame Festival. *Courtesy of Jamey Aebersold.*

David Baker plays bass with his small group in the studios of WTIU, Indiana University's public TV station, with program host John Joyner, left, 1968. *Courtesy of David Baker.*

Publicity shot from the early 1970s. *Courtesy of David Baker.*

David Baker and trumpeter Dominic Spera sharing a playful moment in the
rehearsal rooms of the IU School of Music in the 1980s. *Courtesy of David Baker.*

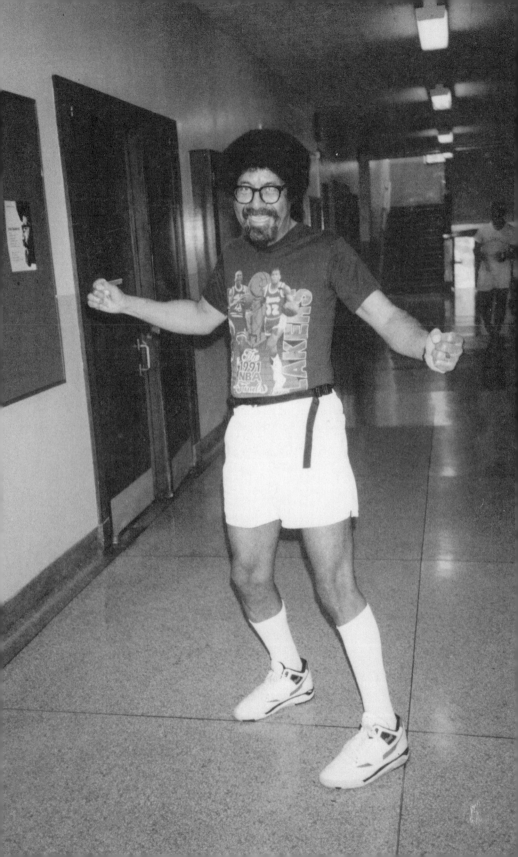

The faculty of the Jamey Aebersold Summer Jazz Workshop at Illinois Wesleyan University, Bloomington, Illinois, after getting into the Marching Band uniform closet, 1980s. *Courtesy of Jamey Aebersold.*

David Baker displays his longtime support for the Lakers. *Courtesy of David Baker.*

David and Lida Baker underneath the billboard for the Johnnie &
Jazz festival in Monaco, June 1992. *Courtesy of David Baker.*

David Baker and Dave Brubeck sharing a cup of tea in Monaco, June 1992.
Courtesy of David Baker.

Honored at the Links Tribute to Indiana African-American Jazz Artists at the
Indiana Roof Ballroom, from left, back, David Baker, J. J. Johnson, Larry Ridley,
David Hardiman; middle, Alonzo "Pookie" Johnson, Killer Ray Appleton, Melvin
Rhyne, Virgil Jones; front, David Young. June 14, 1996. *Courtesy of David Baker.*

David Baker and Dominic Spera discuss the organizational needs of
their students in Monaco, June 1992. *Courtesy of David Baker.*

David Baker with, from left, Lawrence Einhorn, Rev. Theodore
Hesburgh, Otis Bowen, Jane Owen, and Jim Davis, as they receive the
Indiana Living Legends Award, 2001. *Courtesy of David Baker.*

The Baker family at the Indiana Living Legend Award Reception 2001: David
Baker; sister, Shirley Crawford; daughter, April Ayers, and her husband, Brad Ayers;
granddaughter Kirsten Ayers; and wife, Lida Baker. *Courtesy of David Baker.*

David Baker dances with his first wife Jeannie Baker at his Crispus
Attucks High School reunion, 1994. *Courtesy of David Baker.*

David Baker with Joe Wilder and Duncan Schiedt after the
Smithsonian Jazz Masterworks Orchestra performance at the Walker
Theatre, Indianapolis, June 2000. *Courtesy of David Baker.*

Standing ovation by the Indianapolis Symphony Orchestra, under
the direction of Mario Venzago, after the premiere of *Dancing
Shadows,* January 2007. *Courtesy of David Baker.*

David Liebman and David Baker.
Courtesy of Jamey Aebersold.

David Baker delivering a speech at the White House entitled "Jazz – A Reflection of Democracy" as President and Mrs. Bill Clinton and Marian McPartland listen closely, September 18, 1998. *Courtesy of White House Photo Office.*

Publicity shot by Jerry Mitchell.
Courtesy of David Baker.

Living Jazz Legends photograph, taken during the March 3, 2007, Jazz in Our Time Celebration at the Kennedy Center. Front row, seated, left to right: Clark Terry, Frank Foster, Curtis Fuller, Dr. Billy Taylor, Jimmy Scott, Louie Bellson, Marian McPartland, Donald Byrd. Second row, standing, left to right: James Moody, Jimmy Heath, Barry Harris, Nancy Wilson, Benny Golson, Ornette Coleman, Toshiko Akiyoshi, Chick Corea. Third row, sitting onstage, left to right: Phil Woods, Chico Hamilton, Buddy DeFranco, George Russell, Freddie Hubbard, Gerald Wilson, Frank Wess, Dame Cleo Laine. Fourth row, standing, left to right: Al Jarreau, Jon Hendricks, Ahmad Jamal, Dave Brubeck, Wynton Marsalis, David Baker, Paquito D'Rivera, Sir John Dankworth, Michel Legrand. *Photo by John Abbott.*

5

21st Century Bebop

MONIKA HERZIG
AND
BRENT WALLARAB

AS NATHAN DAVIS discussed in chapter 3, the most effective jazz educators are also practitioners with vast experience in the field. Historically, music education methods incorporate modeling as an effective teaching strategy. Some examples are the methods of Shin'ichi Suzuki and Edwin Gordon.[1] In teaching the language of jazz and its improvisatory basis and expressive use of the instrument, modeling has traditionally been a strong element exercised through mentorship and during jam sessions.[2] Baker was well aware of the need to be an active performer and a model for his students when he took the job at Indiana University. Pat Harbison, who had the privilege of being a member of Baker's small groups during his student years, points out, "One demonstration and having to go out and doing it together is worth a thousand hours of rehearsal and someone describing the music and talking about it."[3]

In addition, Baker needed an outlet for his own music. Consequently, he kept his Indianapolis working group that included Mingo Jones, Earl Van Riper, Sheryl Shay, Chuck Carter, Al Reeve, Willis Kirk, and others.[4] But gradually, Baker gathered a group of students at Indiana University to rehearse his music. By the mid-1970s, he had developed the concept of the 21st Century Bebop Band, a performance group that recorded several albums as well as performed on a regular basis for about twenty years.

This chapter explores the unique concept of the group as well as learning experiences and memories of the students and various members over the years. In addition, Brent Wallarab presents a treatise on Baker's jazz composition and arranging techniques. Baker justifies the name and repertoire of the group with the following description: "I considered it a bebop group, but a bebop group with extended roots."[5]

David Baker and Dizzy Gillespie. *Courtesy of David Baker.*

DAVID BAKER'S 21ST CENTURY BEBOP BAND
Monika Herzig

The term "bebop" describes a specific style of jazz that evolved during the early 1940s with a new harmonic, rhythmic, and melodic vocabulary that is still considered the essence of the language of jazz. In fact, Baker expressed in an interview with Kenneth Prouty on the history of jazz education that he considers bebop the *lingua franca* of jazz.[6] A group of musicians – including Dizzy Gillespie, Charlie Parker, Kenny Clarke, Thelonious Monk, and many more who frequented after-hours jam sessions at Minton's Playhouse in New York – was credited with developing the essence of the language. Codifying the chord and scale relationships of the bebop style became the basic building block of the jazz education movement during the 1960s, and can easily be traced in early and recent method books, beginning with George Russell's 1953 treatise *The Lydian Chromatic Concept of Tonal Organization and Improvisation*. In fact, Baker's oeuvre includes three volumes entitled *How to Play Bebop*, and his improvisation method features an eight-note scale that he named the bebop scale.

The trademark of Baker's teaching method is a basic vocabulary of patterns based on the bebop scale that facilitate rhythmically and melodically sound phrasing of improvisatory lines. Baker's many generations of students have jokingly added the lyrics "David Baker Bebop" to the pattern that is usually introduced at the very beginning of the Jazz Improvisation I class.

The bebop era also featured a renewed focus on smaller combos rather than the conventional big bands of the swing era. The smaller units allowed maximal flexibility in developing individual style and innovative musical language, in contrast to the restrictive and uniform

Bebop scale (*How to Play Bebop*, vol. 2).

Bebop pattern, a.k.a. "David Baker Bebop" (*How to Play Bebop*, vol. 3).

structure of the large ensembles. The name 21st Century Bebop Band for Baker's small group is descriptive of his choice of musical language and forward-looking philosophy. Strongly rooted in the bebop tradition, the group featured mostly Baker's innovative compositions and a unique blend of instruments: cello; often flute; trumpet or saxophone; frequently tuba; and a rhythm section including piano, bass, and drums.

The first incarnation of the 21st Century Bebop Band as a combination of faculty and students of Indiana University featured fellow faculty member and tuba virtuoso Harvey Phillips; and students Hunt Butler on saxophone; Kurt Bahn on bass; Steve Ash on piano for one year, followed by Jim Beard; and Keith Cronin on drums. Fellow faculty member Harvey Phillips and Baker met as members of the brass section during the 1959 recording sessions for pianist John Lewis's recording of *The Golden Striker*. Their enduring friendship became the nucleus of the 21st Century Bebop Band. The group proved to be not only a performance vehicle and compositional outlet for Baker, but also a most beneficial learning experience for the students who had the privilege of being part of it. Pianist Jim Beard recalls getting lots of practical training outside of the classroom:

> Outside of the academic environment we had this group and we used to gig in the real world and we would get real money with real cash. And those are things you just don't learn in the classroom. You pack your gear, you schlep it somewhere, you play some tunes, you might sound good, you might sound horrible, but at the end of the night you're paid some money and it's like, "Oh, OK. That's how that works."
>
>   ... We were the band for a prom for one of the high schools. And I kept thinking, "All right, this is really different." We weren't doing "Confirmation" and "Donna Lee," we're more doing "Satin Doll" and Ellington tunes, more the big band ballroom kind of thing, but I remember though thinking, [David Baker's] trying to do this, too.[7]

Fellow jazz faculty member Pat Harbison remembers joining the second incarnation of the group in the early 1980s as a graduate student at Indiana University after spending several years as a professional musician in New York. Although skills such as playing gigs, getting paid, and honing his chops on the bandstand had been part of his daily routine already, he fondly remembers a higher level of combo performance and repertoire development as one of his best learning experiences as a student:

21st Century Bebop Band rehearsal, 1981: Harvey Phillips (tuba), David Baker (cello), Pat Harbison (trumpet), and David Kay (tenor saxophone). *Courtesy of David Baker.*

I think he ran that group the way George Russell had run his sextet. And we'd get together two or three afternoons a week in Harvey's studio and rehearse. I'd get together with David Kay [saxophone] and we'd run the heads and we had frontline sectionals. That was the first time I ever really thought in a combo about where you breathe, how you shape phrases, how you play together. We thought about that in big band, but in the small group the head up to that point was only something we sort of got through to get to the solos. And David being a player/composer, it was the first time I'd been in a small group with a multi-horn frontline where the bandleader as a composer really rehearsed the parts that were rehearsable and then let the parts that were improvised be organic. And seeing how he handled a professional group and got that balance between the composer's/bandleader's vision and letting us be organic as we played. That was the best part of my time here.[8]

Herschel Burke Gilbert, who owned Laurel Records and had worked with Baker previously on some classical projects, suggested recording the jazz group for Gilbert's record company. The first LP recording was simply called *David Baker's 21st Century Bebop Band* (Laurel, LR-503LP) with David Baker (cello), Harvey Phillips (tuba), Hunt Butler (tenor saxophone), Jim Beard (piano), Kurt Bahn (bass), and Keith Cronin (drums) and was released in 1983. Baker lists the selections for this recording:

> We took some standards. I did "Hot House" [Tadd Dameron], but did it in a
> really different kind of way. I did a contrafact on "Back Home Again in Indiana,"
> which I called "Bebop Revisited," a piece called "This One's for 'Trane," and "An
> Evening Thought." But that was a really solid group.[9]

The follow-up recording in 1984 entitled *R.S.V.P.* (LR-504LP) still featured David Baker, Harvey Phillips, and Jim Beard, but added a new crop of students: David Kay (saxophone), Pat Harbison (trumpet), Bob Hurst (bass), and Shawn Pelton (drums). This time the repertoire focused on Baker's original compositions, including "Cahaphi," "Lima Beba Samba," "Jeanne Marie at the Picture Show," "R.S.V.P. Mr. Moody," and "Lerma Samba." The same group was featured on the 1985 release *Struttin'* (LR-505LP) with "Almaco," "The Aebersold Strut," "Padospe," and "Lorob."[10]

A natural side effect of leading a group that includes college students was a constant change in personnel as members graduated and/or pursued new avenues. As a result, the 21st Century Bebop Band had a frequent rotation of players throughout its existence while also retaining a core group of locals. Of course faculty tubist Harvey Phillips became a regular; as did Baker's wife, Lida, on flute; and pianist Luke Gillespie, who arrived in Bloomington in 1975 as a student and is now a fellow jazz faculty member at Indiana University. Before capturing the sound of the new cello and flute-based frontline on *The Harlem Pipes* (Liscio Recording LCD-02032) in 1987, the group went through several more or less permanent incarnations. Some of the members included saxophonists Jack Wilkins and Ralph Bowen, and a young trumpet player named Chris Botti.[11] Jim Beard shares his fond memories of a most fertile period in the Bloomington jazz scene:

> It was a very healthy time there. Chris Botti, Bob Hurst, Shawn Pelton were all
> there at the same time – and Ralph Bowen. I just sort of remember that I was
> learning and gaining experience outside of class as well as just playing gigs and
> having jam sessions and hanging out with the other icons of the Bloomington
> area at that time, even David Miller and Michael Weiss.[12]

What Beard alludes to was an unusually high concentration of talented young jazz students who went on to become leaders in the field. Baker's thorough and effective teaching methods and efforts in providing

James Moody and David Baker with a copy of the 21st Century
Bebop Band recording *R.S.V.P.* *Courtesy of David Baker.*

opportunities for young players paid off as the jazz studies program at
Indiana University developed a reputation for its high quality. The following are just a few examples of the illustrious careers of alumni of the
21st Century Bebop Band and of course the list of accomplishments of
all other alumni of the group as well as all of Baker's many generations
of students is endless and continuously growing. Jim Beard himself is
in high demand as a keyboardist, arranger, composer, and producer;
he often tours with Steely Dan; and has recorded with a long list of jazz
luminaries, including Wayne Shorter, John McLaughlin, John Scofield,
Mike Stern, Dennis Chambers, and Bob Berg. Drummer Shawn Pelton

is a member of the *Saturday Night Live* band on N B C and has collaborated with popular artists such as the Backstreet Boys, Sheryl Crow, Shawn Colvin, Bruce Springsteen, Celine Dion, and Billy Joel. Ralph Bowen is an associate professor of saxophone at Rutgers University, and his recording credits include Orrin Evans, Michel Camilo, and Horace Silver. Trumpeter Chris Botti has become the largest selling American jazz instrumental artist, with four number-one jazz albums as well as several gold and platinum recordings, and Grammy awards. The communal spirit of Indiana Avenue and the formative experiences at the Lenox School of Jazz were thoroughly entrenched in Baker's teaching philosophy, and such accomplishments are living proof for his effective pedagogy. Jim Beard recalls,

> We would do a trio gig – a bass player, myself, and David [Baker] on cello – just once a week playing tunes at like a night club. One night we did a big party at Bobby Knight's house. David put a band together – I think it was Shawn Pelton, Bob Hurst, myself, and David – that was a lot of fun. And David used to hang out a lot, too. A lot of times students would just host their own parties at their house for those who stayed in town and would have a jam session. And David would be invited and he would show up. He always enjoyed very much being in the thick of things.[13]

The 21st Century Bebop Band also performed for larger audiences at auditorium concerts and opening for some of Baker's mentors, such as Dizzy Gillespie and Maynard Ferguson. Early in their careers, he and fellow trombonist Slide Hampton met Dizzy after a concert to express their admiration and tell him that they planned to play a lot of his music. Baker recalls,

> He said, "If you're going to do my music, put something new on it." And of course one of the things that happened was that version I did of "Bebop." Then I did "Hot House," and we did "Groovin' High," a really convoluted version.[14]

An original tribute to his mentor, "Groovin' for Diz," was one of the selections recorded on *The Harlem Pipes,* released in 2003 on Liscio Recordings after the original tapes from the 1987 sessions at Homegrown Studios reappeared many years after the recording date. Additional selections include "The Harlem Pipes," "Birdsong," and "5M Calypso." This incarnation of the 21st Century Bebop Band included David Baker on cello, Harvey Phillips on tuba, Lida Baker on flute, Tom Gullion on

David Baker with 21st Century Bebop Band alumnus Chris
Botti, after Botti's concert with the Indianapolis Symphony
Orchestra, November 23, 2009. *Courtesy of David Baker.*

saxophones, Luke Gillespie on piano, Charles Ledvina on bass, and Scott Latzky on drums. Tom Gullion recalls some of the challenges of playing with such an unusual frontline:

> The music was extremely challenging. The instrumentation is extreme [flute, cello, saxophone and tuba], [and] the harmonies often dense and unexpected. And then once you got past that, you get to test your mettle soloing on some really challenging chord progressions. That said, I thoroughly enjoyed all aspects of this band. It always requires a lot of effort to play David's music – but it is so worth it!
>
> Anyway, it was a fun challenge for me. I have a fairly big saxophone sound and had to bring my volume way down to blend with this instrumentation. I had to be very conscious of the change between soloing with intensity and then coming back down to blend for written parts.[15]

The final full-length recording by the group, *Steppin' Out,* was also released on Liscio in 1992 and initiated by Aebersold Summer Jazz Workshop colleague JB Dyas. JB was teaching at Miami's New World School of the Arts in 1991 and received a grant to engage Baker in a week-long residence at the school and commission a piece for the Miami String Quartet, as well as a suite for the school's jazz sextet. The commissioned piece, entitled *Miami Suite,* was recorded by the New World School of the Arts Jazz Sextet later that year, on an album entitled *First Step.* The suite consists of three tunes that have become frequent features of Baker's concert repertoire: "Tippin'," "Miami Nights," and "Sunfest." The weekend following Baker's residency, *Steppin' Out* was recorded with a combination of regular group members – Lida Baker, David Baker, and JB Dyas on bass – and a local rhythm section featuring David Hammer on piano, Michael DiLiddo on guitar, and Jean Bolduc on drums. JB recalls,

> We recorded it in my home in Pembroke Pines as I owned a beautiful Steinway grand at the time, a piano better than that of any studio we knew of. Producer Peter Yianilos brought over all the gear and engineered it from his truck, which he used for recording live shows. We recorded everything in one day and mixed the next day. We rehearsed and just played tunes in my living room one evening with everything acoustic except for Mike and me playing very softly through our Polytones. Jean's "kit" only included snare drum, high hat, and ride and he only played brushes. David and Lida played unamplified. I remember David having an excellent sound that night and the flute and cello blending perfectly and beautifully because everything was soft. David didn't have to push to be heard nor fight his amplifier. There was such a cool vibe and it truly sounded like a Cool Jazz set, reminiscent of that era. That's the best we ever sounded and we

The David Baker Sextet at the 1992 I AJ E Conference. From left, David Hammer
(piano), Lida Baker (flute), JB Dyas (bass), David Baker (cello), Jean Bolduc
(drums), and Michael DiLiddo (guitar). *Courtesy of David Baker.*

all commented how we wish we could always sound like that. But, unfortunately,
real life, which often means playing in larger venues than my living room and
having to be amplified to be heard would, of course, never permit it.[16]

This specific incarnation of the group, often referred to as the David
Baker Sextet, only did one live performance together, for the 1992 Con-
ference of the International Association for Jazz Education in Miami.
Some combinations of the personnel also later performed at the Jamey
Aebersold Summer Camps as well as local clubs.

Additional recordings that feature David Baker's jazz compositions
and arrangements are a big band recording backing up Indianapolis
vocalist Sheryl Shay, also on Laurel Records, and a release featuring
Baker's string ensemble with the Paul McNamara Trio.[17] Most recently
the Buselli-Wallarab Jazz Orchestra recorded Baker's big band arrangements on *Basically Baker,* a recording cited as one of the best recordings
of the first decade of the twenty-first century by *DownBeat Magazine.*
An analysis of Baker's approach by the co-leader of that group follows.

JAZZ COMPOSITION AND ARRANGING TECHNIQUES
Brent Wallarab

David often points out that writing jazz pieces and arranging for jazz ensemble come easy to him, due to his familiarity with the music and his extensive output in the genre.[18] A comprehensive listing of his jazz compositions and arrangements can be found in the appendices. His method book *Arranging and Composing for the Small Ensemble* has become a commonly used textbook in college classes, and it features a variety of examples of Baker's own pieces and techniques. Baker points out in the introduction to the book that composing and arranging are complementary skills and should be learned simultaneously. Arrangements usually include some newly composed segments in the form of introductions, interludes, codas, and horn lines – and, of course, being able to compose all original materials makes an arranger more versatile and marketable. The following is an examination of Baker's relationship to the blues, commonly used forms, harmonic language, and orchestration characteristics.

Baker and the Blues

Special mention must be made of Baker's thorough and prolific examination of the blues form over his career. With the exception of Duke Ellington, it is difficult to imagine another composer in jazz who has considered the possibilities of the blues as thoughtfully and creatively as David Baker. An examination of his relationship to the blues will illuminate techniques, approaches, and, especially, his general philosophy about music and communication. What we learn from his blues compositions we will discover in all of his compositions and arrangements.

Although many musicians have written large numbers of twelve-bar-blues tunes, few have explored this essential American musical form on such a deep and intimate level as David Baker. In his hands, the blues may be expanded or deconstructed, presented as pure blues or simply gestured at, featured as a single formal structure or exist as a smaller component of a larger form. To Baker, the blues is more than a standard form over which to blow solos. It is the essence of American music, a beautifully balanced and timeless form, similar to the sonnet in poetry. To Baker the blues is where Louis Armstrong, Duke Ellington, Charlie Parker, and J. J. Johnson had some of their finest moments – and is the source for every meaningful development of American popular music. The blues is Baker's music and an obvious choice for him to revisit whether it be for intense abstract experimentation or an expression of his swinging, soulful roots. Baker points out, "We all return to the roots at some point, but I keep going there because it lies at the essence of what we do as jazz musicians."[19]

Baker has always relied heavily on traditional forms, but is not confined or limited by them. In dozens of jazz compositions – such as "Kentucky Oysters," "Honesty," "Terrible T," "Dance of the Jitterbugs," "Roly Poly," "Brother," "Le miroir noir," "Blues for Bird," "The Felix Walk," and "Fuup Blues," to name a few – Baker showcases the blues, which is universally recognized as fundamental in the genetics of jazz. But much like Ellington, who also returned to the blues time and time again in his compositions, Baker trusts in the strength of the form and explores the potential within it as opposed to just presenting it in its original twelve-bar structure. He stretches it, finesses it, expands it, contracts it, knowing that while it may be run through its paces and at times be cleverly disguised, the blues is strong enough to take it. The blues as *lingua franca* offers familiar territory for all participants, both performers and listeners, as Baker experiments with new processes harmonically, rhythmically, formally, and melodically.

As a young trombonist in the George Russell Sextet, Baker contributed an original blues to each recording session.[20] Even at this early stage as an emerging artist it is evident that Baker is determined to discover fresh potential inherent in the standard blues form. "Kentucky Oysters," from the 1960 Riverside album *Stratusphunk,* and "Honesty," from the 1961 Riverside album *Ezz-thetics,* are original blues that provide canvases for experimental improvisation as well as opportunities for Baker to explore form.

"Kentucky Oysters," a bright blues in $\frac{3}{4}$, is expanded to twenty-four bars to accommodate the phrasing. The roots of $\frac{3}{4}$ blues are in gospel music, and jazz musicians had been experimenting with this rhythmic approach for decades – as evidenced by Benny Carter's 1936 "Waltzing the Blues" and Fats Waller's 1942 "Jitterbug Waltz." Although certainly more substantial than novelty pieces, these were rare instances of rhythmic exploration. It was not until the 1950s that new grooves (beyond swing) and time implications (other than $\frac{4}{4}$) were superimposed over the blues and a number of important works emerged using compound meter, including Charles Mingus's "Better Git It in Your Soul," from the 1959 Columbia album *Mingus Ah Um;* Max Roach's "Blues Waltz," from the 1957 Emarcy album *Jazz In $\frac{3}{4}$ Time;* and Dave Brubeck's "Blue Rondo à la Turk," from the 1959 Columbia album *Time Out.* "Kentucky Oysters" is similar to "Better Git It in Your Soul" in that it suggests a down-home southern gospel blues, but it is in Baker's own trombone solo that we find the composer taking the blues where it had never been taken before. His unique approach to soloing on the blues in this recording was spurred as much by necessity as it was by imagination. In Baker's own words, bandleader Russell had been "yelling at us about how we were playing the blues. He said he was sick of hearing us do the same old thing and told us we had better come up with something new. I didn't want to get yelled at anymore so I began working on some ideas I had been playing at for awhile."[21] This idea was to use the dotted-quarter rhythms within a $\frac{3}{4}$ measure, finding the inner half-time $\frac{4}{4}$ swing to superimpose over the faster $\frac{3}{4}$ quarter note. It creates a bi-meter tension with the slower $\frac{4}{4}$ lying on top of the faster $\frac{3}{4}$. Mathematically, the phrases all end at the same places, and it is an incredible effect. One of the initial challenges was to decide if the rhythm section, in part or as a whole, should follow Baker with his metric modulation. The decision for the rhythm section to remain solidly in 3 with Baker alone playing in the new meter and tempo was clearly the right one; it creates incredible tension, yet both meters swing with ease.

Baker's determination to further avoid the wrath of his boss certainly led to remarkable trombone playing, but it is really the composer that emerged. Baker's use of implied half-time duple meter over a triple-meter tune is the rhythmic equivalent of discovering bitonal chords realized out of a standard set of chord changes. We will find time and time again that Baker is a complete musician, and – whether in the role of soloist, composer, or arranger – he consistently seeks new substantive characteristics residing within conventional jazz language.

In 1961's "Honesty," Baker pairs contrasting but eminently compatible improvisational vehicles for the soloists in Russell's sextet.[22] A twelve-bar-blues form is broken up by sections for free improvisation; each soloist plays over both sections. The melody is as soulful as a blues can get with no abstraction and no contrivance, and the unstructured sections are melodyless vehicles for improvisation, providing an environment for soloists to explore and express their voices with complete freedom. Eric Dolphy, David Baker, Don Ellis, and Steve Swallow, in these moments of freedom, present portraits of who they are as musicians, each sounding completely different from one another, and approaching the opportunity for freedom in vastly different ways. Here lies the genius of balancing free jazz with a simple, swinging, unpretentious blues: the blues, in its purest form and with respect to its historical origins, is in itself a vehicle for personalized, free expression of one's story through music. Taking away this structure only frees the musicians further. Baker the composer, through seemingly different techniques (structure and freedom), is simply telling the same story from different perspectives.

In his unrecorded big band version of "Honesty" from the early 1970s, the addition of a third contrasting section, seemingly far removed from the jazz tradition, makes quite a lot of sense in terms of both form and philosophy. This version opens with a brass ensemble, from within the big band, playing material that is written in the style of J. S. Bach. Like the free improvisation sections, the Baroque counterpoint returns throughout the piece to break up the swinging blues choruses. Baker's proclivity for cross germination between jazz and the European orchestral tradition is well known. A common technique he has used is *concerto grosso*, a small group featured significantly between the larger ensemble sections. This is not unknown in jazz, Ellington's *Battle of Swing* (Brunswick/Columbia, 1939) being one of the first examples of this; Baker has used this technique successfully many times. The *ritornello* (the smaller, baroque brass ensemble) provides contrast to both the blues and the free jazz sections. Baker often uses contrasting material to break up the pattern of form repetition, simply to make the experience for both performer and listener more interesting and unpredictable. Before the more structured forms and practices of the Classical period of European music developed, composers from the earlier Baroque period (most notably J. S. Bach) were free to expand, develop, and spin out ideas in an almost improvisatory way. While the material may be from a different musical tradition, the Baroque-style section of "Honesty" philosophically complements the other sections of the piece.

We find the concept of freedom in the blues developed even further in his big band composition "Dance of the Jitterbugs." An altered, extended blues, "Dance of the Jitterbugs" (written almost thirty-five years after "Honesty") features a juxtaposition of structure and anarchy. It stretches this most common vehicle for jazz tunes almost to the breaking point with alterations in length, harmonies, meter, and time feel. Co-leader of the Buselli-Wallarab Jazz Orchestra, Mark Buselli, has the following comments on the composition:[23]

> Brent and I were thrilled that David Baker picked our jazz orchestra to record his music! "Dance of the Jitterbugs" is a great composition that is basically an altered blues up front with added material towards the back. The blues section is 16 bars ... 12 of $\frac{4}{4}$ with the last 4 bars consisting of $\frac{3}{4}, \frac{3}{4}, \frac{2}{4}$, and $\frac{3}{4}$. It feels like a $\frac{12}{8}$ shuffle up front with great use of left hand piano, bass, tuba, and bass trombone.[24]

The extended blues form features an added four-bar turnaround with meter changes and altered harmonies. *DownBeat Magazine* editor Ed Enright points out the effectiveness of Baker's unique approach in his liner notes to *Basically Baker:* "Traditional song forms are altered, as are the chord changes, effectively throwing 'curve balls,' so to speak, to the orchestra – as well as the listener."

The first three soloists (guitar, tenor saxophone, and trombone) use Baker's altered blues structure as the template for their improvisation, allowing the groove and concept to be firmly established well into the piece. About three-fourths of the way into the piece, fragments of the original piano motive are broken up with purely free, unstructured improvisation by the fourth soloist (alto saxophone). The altered harmonies, extended form, and rhythmically asymmetrical turnarounds of the piece up to this point suggest a standard blues form being resisted, as if the structure itself is too restrictive and becomes misshapen by the inner voices struggling to break free. The first set of soloists are steered

"Dance of the Jitterbugs", boogie-woogie bass pattern
played by piano, bass, tuba, and bass trombone;

altered four-bar turnaround;

bass motif and cluster chord;

towards free improvisation by the unstable characteristic of the material they have to work with, but there is still form to be reckoned with,
and it is not until our fourth soloist arrives that the form is demolished
and purely free improvisation reigns. Baker breaks up the form with a
repeated two-bar bass motif followed by a two-bar cluster chord held
by the brass section – inviting Tom Walsh, the saxophone soloist on the
Basically Baker recording, to fill in with open cadences. Mark Buselli
remembers,

> This morphs into the same motif from the top with some great "free" sax work
> by Tom Walsh. This section cascades into a 32 bar double time feel in the drums
> and half time feel in the rhythm [section] . . . very effective! I had fun here having
> a conversation with Tom. A magical moment for me on a super composition![25]

Eventually the free soloing leads us into a new form, a seemingly
altogether new structure based on modal harmonies which are offered
in a less resistant, more contemplative setting. Modal jazz itself was an
attempt toward more melodic freedom, as jazz musicians in the late 1950s

sought ways to be creative without being restricted by rapidly changing harmonies and standard song forms.

> "It's a given," says Baker, "that modal jazz was a step towards freedom. That was even confusing to some at first because what do you do with just one chord when you've been playing tunes with lots of chords your whole life? Miles got it, Bill Evans got it, but some others had a hard time knowing what to do with all this freedom. Ornette finally did away with those confines and went back to melody and the blues. But yes, modal jazz was a major step toward free jazz."[26]

Exploring one scale or mode for long stretches of time presented new opportunities for freer interpretation. Therefore, this portion of Baker's composition is a perfectly logical development, as the overall main concept of "Dance of the Jitterbugs" is the restless nature of the artist – always striving to shed convention and discover originality through freedom. However, the story does not stop there. As the new modal form plays out, it becomes apparent that much of the new material has been developed from the original blues material and upon this realization, the piece returns to the original theme.

Furthermore, in "Dance of the Jitterbugs," we see that Baker's use of harmonic techniques often supports the overall structure and formal development of a piece. A blues form may be extended to sixteen, eighteen or more measures, with harmonic innovations contributing to the logic of the extension. With Baker, it is often in the ninth measure of a blues that we find the development of the form, which makes perfect sense. Whatever sophisticated harmonic treatments are applied to a blues, it is essentially the relationship of the I chord to the IV chord that provides the basic harmonic grounding. By waiting until the ninth bar to expand the blues form, Baker is establishing the harmonic foundation of the blues by modulating to the IV chord in the fifth bar and back to I in the seventh bar. By that time, that fact that he is indeed presenting a blues is firmly established and he is free to expand. In "Honesty" (both the sextet and big band versions) the free improvisation sections flow into the standard swinging blues form at the subdominant, further establishing this important harmonic relationship. Such techniques, which Baker employs frequently, bring the listeners onto familiar ground and help them relate to the experience. Like great artists in any medium, Baker does not try to invent a new, indecipherable language, but reinterprets common vocabulary, maintaining relevance while revealing new perspectives:

> I learned the hard way that you can't try too hard to be different. It doesn't come across. I tried everything to create my own voice from tone rows to set systems. Now I wish those pieces would just disappear! The point is we *all* are different so why try? Build on what came before, borrow from everyone, and you'll still come out in the music. I followed Ornette's lead and decided the best way was to give new life to old forms, focus on the blues, on melody.[27]

David Baker is a gentle, humble man who exudes warmth and geniality toward everyone he meets. This sometimes belies the fact that he is a man of passionate conviction and opinion regarding history, politics, race, and society. Like Armstrong and Ellington, Baker does not wear his politics on his sleeve; nevertheless, he expresses volumes through his music. Even when he is not directly attempting to imply extra-musical notions through his compositions, an artist of his wisdom and brilliance cannot help but tell more about who he is as a man beyond the notes on a score. It seems more often than not that in his exploration of the blues we find Baker in the most telling light of who he is philosophically.

In "Dance of the Jitterbugs" we can interpret varying concepts about music and more. For instance, there seems to be a time in every young jazz musician's life where he or she has to reject the past in order to feel they are developing his or her own voice. In "Dance of the Jitterbugs" we are introduced to a scene in which the blues is in an epic struggle. The conventions of form, phrasing, and melody are there, but as we enter the scene, the blues is being questioned and fought against. Yet after the blues is challenged, rejected, and a new form developed, it becomes evident that the influence of the blues is unavoidable, that jazz as an art form is deeply rooted in this original source. The blues is where every jazz musician comes from. It is in their genes – and fighting it, resisting it, is futile. As in an epic Ellington blues, one can perceive social commentary. In this case, the struggle against conventional form, the acquisition of freedom, the development of new structures and conventions out of the chaos, and a return to the status quo – all are possible considerations. Further metaphors, political or social, can be drawn from this, and it is irrelevant whether Baker was conscious of anything but the music itself.

But as in all great art, the product speaks beyond mere technique to life itself. Everyone interprets art differently, based on individual experience, and art that is especially rich with content allows for more latitude in its interpretation.

In observing how Baker deals with the blues, we find an artist discontent with telling only one side of the story. He wants us to know more than the superficial characteristics – he wants us to know that music, and therefore life, is complex, multilayered, full of potential both realized and unrealized, and laden with what from casual observation seems like contradiction, but in reality is perfect balance and harmony. Knowing Baker's approach to the blues is knowing how he views the human experience, and knowing his music is knowing him.

Form

Along with the blues, the thirty-two-bar song form is another structure that dominates the Baker repertoire. Together with the blues, this structure is what Baker was raised on and represents the laboratory from which jazz musicians have conducted most of their musical experiments – certainly well into the early 1960s. True to his roots, Baker also resides in this lab for much of his work, but constantly reconstructs his space. In "5M Calypso," Baker presents an AABA form, but with an extended bridge and extended A-sections. It is familiar, but totally fresh and engaging, and the techniques used to develop the form feel natural and organic. The first A-section is eleven measures, but it does not feel like an asymmetrical phrase; it is in reality an eight-bar phrase and four-bar phrase with the last measure of the eight-bar phrase overlapping the first measure of the four-bar phrase. This technique is used to allow the phrase to breathe and not feel overly rushed to recapitulate. The second A is a standard eight-bar phrase, which comes as a surprise to the listener. After setting up an expectation for another extended phrase, the natural eight-bar phrase takes the listener by surprise. The bridge for the melody is an eight-bar phrase that is repeated, but upon the repeat, the phrase is extended an additional two bars, creating an overall eighteen-bar bridge.

The first solo section is not a mere repeat of the melody form, although it closely resembles it. The A-sections are identical, but it is at the bridge that Baker gives us something new. Harmonically, the solo bridge

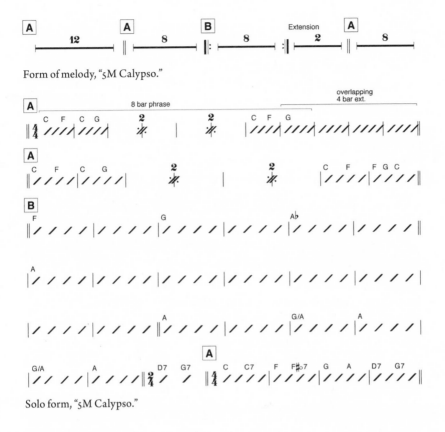

Form of melody, "5M Calypso."

Solo form, "5M Calypso."

begins with the same chords presented along with the original melody of the piece, but it quickly develops, moving to a distant harmony that gives the performer and listener some welcome contrast. The bridge is extended to 20.5 bars (a 20-bar phrase punctuated with a humorous $\frac{2}{4}$ hiccup thrown in) and as it resolves back to the I chord (C major in this case) it is not a final A-section as expected. The soloist wraps up the chorus with the I–I7–IV–#ivo–V–VI–II7–V7 formula that has up to this point acted exclusively as introductory material.

Especially in his later period (c. 1990–present) Baker departs from a repeated formal structure and develops a new, complementary section, usually represented as a new solo section. A blues form or AABA structure (extended or not) may be repeated numerous times in the statement of the main theme and in subsequent solos, but usually around the final third of the piece, a single harmonic idea from the main theme will be extracted and developed as a new contrasting section. Only a

Cm

Cm   Gm△7   G♭m△7 Fm△7   Em△7   E♭m△7   Dm△7   D♭m△7

Cm△7 Bm△7 B♭m△7   G7♭9   G7♭9

Solo form for the second solo section.

seasoned, mature artist can anticipate when an idea has run its course over the length of a composition and must either conclude or evolve. In "5M Calypso" we find this concept executed perfectly. Baker explores the original material – formally and harmonically – with satisfying results, and just when another chorus would become too much of a good thing, he shifts to a contrasting idea, lifting the composition to a new, thrilling level. Organically developed from the main theme, the new material is relevant and always feels natural.

After the pianist and tenor soloist play a couple of choruses, the third soloist (trumpet) finds a shift to a modal C minor solo section, providing a new, contrasting part of the form for further improvisation. The shift from C major to minor is simple, but absolutely enough change to give the piece an exciting, interesting lift just when it is needed. The C minor modal section contrasts with descending chromatic chords, the last of these chords getting us back to the fundamental C harmonic home base.

As in all great art, the development should not draw attention to itself, but rather provide balance and contrast where needed. The shifts, extensions, and modulations in "5M Calypso" are so subtle and so expertly wrought that one doesn't notice them as they happen. The listener is engaged in experiencing the story as opposed to being distracted by technique.

Harmony

Baker's harmonic palate is a rich blend of traditional harmony, daring bitonal substitutions, nonfunctional abstract harmonic colors, and – his musical signature – the diminished scale in every permutation. His ba-

sic harmonic starting point is the bebop and blues vocabulary. In such
pieces as "Jeanne Marie at the Picture Show," "Padospe," "Some Links
for Brother Ted," and "April B," the traditional harmony remains consistent throughout, with perhaps some interludes incorporating the diminished scale. The strength of the melodic and harmonic choices in these
pieces demand little development for them to be effective and satisfying.
It is in their beauty and simplicity that they find their strength. There are
many instances, however, in which Baker presents the opening choruses
of a piece utilizing standard, functional chords directly out of the bebop
lexicon, only to develop the harmony later on. As in his manipulation of
form, Baker establishes his harmonic roots firmly in tradition, only to
reinvent them later on. Baker often develops a complementary bitonal
set of changes to balance out the standard changes, illuminating two different sides of the same piece of music. His pieces often are Janus faced,
being one organism with distinctly different moods residing within.

In his re-working of Tadd Dameron's "Hot House," Baker supplies
the soloists with two sets of chord changes. The first represent the original harmonies from the tune, which itself is a highly altered version of
Cole Porter's "What Is This Thing Called Love?" Baker himself verifies
that Dameron's altered changes are very restrictive, in that they demand
from the soloists a very precise interpretation of every altered harmony.
As Baker puts it, "The melody itself is so specific to the harmony [that]
there is really very little wiggle room for the soloist. You really have to
play exactly what Tadd wrote. It is kind of like being in a straitjacket after
a chorus or two."[28]

To balance out the requirement to play "in a straitjacket," Baker created a set of alternate chords that on the outset seem at least as restrictive
as the original, but are in fact designed to allow the soloist almost abso-
lute freedom. These harmonies are represented by very complex bitonal
chords that discard all function in the traditional sense and sound very
"outside" and abstract. By presenting a very abstruse set of harmonies,
the player is actually released from the confines of the original and is encouraged to improvise freely without having to be precise with the harmony. Baker says, "The [bitonal] harmonies were developed by sounds
I liked. The soloist really can just play freely over them without having
to be locked in."[29]

Reharmonization of "Hot House" by David Baker.

This concept is also represented in the opening statement of his arrangement or more accurately, recomposition. The angular melody of Dameron's tune outlines the altered and extended harmonies, offering little room for reinterpretation. By discarding function altogether as far as harmony is concerned, Baker reorchestrates the theme with abstract, highly dissonant original harmonies. In this case, the composition of new, esoteric harmonies for both solos and in the body of the work is to promote freedom from the restrictive nature of the original.

Original version of "Hot House" by Todd Dameron.

In his composition "Bourne," based on the chord structure of another Dameron original, "Lady Bird," Baker utilizes the procedure of original changes contrasted with extreme reharmonization, but for different reasons. Whereas in "Hot House" the new harmonies are to encourage abstract freedom for the soloist, in "Bourne" the new harmonies (also characterized by bitonal chords) are to be adhered to strictly. Why would Baker, in two pieces based on Dameron originals, apply similar compositional techniques with very opposite outcomes?

The original chord changes in "Bourne" ("Lady Bird") are based on functional ii–V–I progressions with no alterations of any sort. The corresponding melody (for the original Dameron composition as well) is completely diatonic, thereby requiring the harmonies to be unaltered. In the bebop tradition, chord structures are often left unaltered so the soloist is free to alter the harmonies at will. The bassist and pianist (or guitarist) generally walk and comp in the fundamental, lower structures of the chord so as not to influence the soloist too much; by keeping their general harmonic approach simple, they can hear the alterations suggested by the soloist and react efficiently. "Bourne" offers the soloist an unadorned structure for soloing that allows for a different kind of freedom, one in which the soloist can alter or substitute the original harmony at will. Baker's use of complex bitonal reharmonization for this particular piece was developed for three reasons:

1. To balance out the diatonic nature of the original chord changes;
2. To provide a more specific harmony for the soloists to work with, providing contrast; and
3. To develop the tune further, making "Bourne" more of a conceptual composition as opposed to a simple arrangement on "Lady Bird."

Baker confirms that "in this case, the soloists need to stick closely to the bi-tonal harmonies and be as accurate as possible."[30]

To develop bitonal substitutions, Baker uses two basic techniques. The first is based on finding inherent triads from altered pitches or extensions and placing them over roots that are the original roots of the chord changes, a simplified version of the original root movement, or pedal points. There is still a close relationship to the original chords even if the result is dissonant and "outside." For example, a G7 ($\flat$9 $\flat$5) chord can be reduced to a D$\flat$ (triad) over G (bass note or G triad) or a G13 ($\flat$9) chord can be interpreted as an E (triad) over G (bass note). Baker's second technique is derived from an intuitive, aesthetic approach as opposed to a theoretical construct. This strategy evolves from searching

```
 C△                    Fm7       Bb7       C△                     Bm7   E7   Bbm7  Eb7
‖ / / / /  |   ∕.   | / / / / | / / / / | / / / / |   ∕.   | / / / / | / / / / ‖
```

```
 Ab                   Am7       D7        Dm7  G7   Fm7  Bb7   C    Eb    Ab    Db
‖ / / / /  |   ∕.   | / / / / | / / / / | / / / / | / / / / | / / / / | / / / / ‖
```

Original harmonies for "Lady Bird," by Tadd Dameron.

```
 B/C             Ab△+5/Bb   Gb△+5/Bb   D/C        E/C        F    G/E   G    A/Eb
‖ / / / / | / / / / | / / / / | / / / / | / / / / | / / / / | / / / / | / / / / ‖
```

```
 A    Bb/Ab  C/Ab   Db/D       Eb/D       E/G        Gb/G       B/C  D/Eb  G/Ab  C/Db
‖ / / / / | / / / / | / / / / | / / / / | / / / / | / / / / | / / / / | / / / / ‖
```

"Bourne," reharmonized version of "Lady Bird," by David Baker.

for combined tonalities that simply please the composer and provide the momentum or tension that seems most appropriate. The chords may or may not have anything to do with the original harmonies and could be interpreted as functional harmony, but this phenomenon is secondary and often occurs purely by chance. The composer is strictly going by what sounds good without regard to rules or methods. Baker confirms this: "(I) just find sounds or combinations of chords that sound good to me and don't worry about if it follows some rule."[31]

Combining the two techniques, in which some bitonal creations are consciously functional and some are not, is not an uncommon occurrence. For Baker, the final arbiter is the aesthetic outcome: "If it sounds good to me, then it's right."

Baker's use of symmetrical scales, especially the diminished scale, has become a recognizable trait in many of his works for big band. In most cases, he uses this scale in interlude or connecting material. Again, we find tremendous logic in this technique. As in European compositions of the nineteenth century, the diminished sound creates tension; and as it is played out, the desire for release is intensified. Baker's use of various patterns developed from the entire scale offers the same kind of contrast – the tension and yearning for resolution that many composers of the classical European tradition relied upon when developing their pieces. We find that a unique harmonic treatment (regular use of the

Excerpt from "I.U.
Swing Machine," with
diminished scale pattern.

diminished scale in its many permutations) serves the music as much in a formal and structural way as simply a harmonic color. Again, form and harmony are inextricably bound.

Orchestration

As an orchestrator, Baker consistently bridges tradition with innovation. He is both a classicist – utilizing traditional techniques developed by Benny Carter, Fletcher Henderson, Duke Ellington, and others – and an innovator. Baker often employs devices associated with the great writers of the genre, including five-part closed-position saxophone section writing (Benny Carter and Duke Ellington), brass section/sax section call and response (Fletcher Henderson), tuba-grounded small ensemble (Gil Evans and Gerry Mulligan), trombone section comping (Gil Evans), prominent independent bass trombone/tuba (Gil Evans and Stan Kenton arrangers), and a rich, open low brass section providing melody and background (Pete Rugulo and Bill Russo). His love for the genre and its great writers is illustrated by the way he masterfully and seamlessly integrates their techniques. As an innovator, he has established a palate of colors that are purely "Bakerian" devices that bring knowing smiles to the faces of those familiar with his music. From subtle to dazzling, the orchestration techniques employed make a Baker chart as recognizable as one by Thad Jones or Billy May.

As modern big bands developed in the 1960s, the use of mutes became less fashionable – unless, of course, one is discussing Duke Ellington, Count Basie, or the nostalgia bands from the 1930s and 1940s. Basie's band has always used mutes in a very characteristic way – with the brass section in buckets, tight cups, and the occasional harmon mutes for trumpets. The Ellington band was the model for all plunger mute techniques developed thus far, and most bands from the 1960s on who did use mutes merely mimicked Ellington's plunger use or the Basie mute sounds if mutes were used at all. Even Quincy Jones, who used mutes extensively in his big band pieces, employed a very traditional Basie/ Ellington approach. Baker, however, remains one of the few composers of the genre who not only bucked convention and has used mutes consistently, but avoided the Basie/Ellington approach in favor of developing new mute colors.

After the swing era (c. 1935–45) the straight mute almost disappeared from the big band, but it has remained one of Baker's preferred sounds over the decades. This is likely due to Baker's strong orchestral background; the straight mute is almost always the preferred mute for composers of that genre. The unique sound of this mute, along with its virtual extinction from the big band genre, makes it a very recognizable timbre when used by Baker.

A creative mute technique often employed by Baker is combining mutes (cups with straights, straights with plunger, and so on). This is not unprecedented in big band writing; Neal Hefti experimented with this from time to time, most notably in the opening choruses of Basie's "Splanky" (where each member of the seven-piece brass section plays a unison line with a different mutes for each instrument). But there are few other composers in jazz that have explored this as much as Baker. Although often relegated to solo backgrounds, it is one of his more subtle landmark sounds.

A notable observation is that his small group, the 21st Century Bebop Band, has often influenced his *concerto grosso* orchestration for large ensemble, the ritornello often being tuba, trumpet, saxophone, and

Example of Baker's use of straight mutes.

Excerpt from "Cahaphi," ritornello instrumentation.

trombone – a similar instrumentation to his combo sound. His 1982 composition "Cahaphi" features this instrumentation prominently.[32] Baker's orchestration of 1961's "Honesty," originally written for the George Russell Sextet, offers a direct homage to the *concerto grosso* not just in concept, but in harmonic and melodic vocabulary. Although he retains the free sections to complement the blues, he adds sections of composition for a smaller brass ensemble in the style of the great Baroque composers. As discussed in the analysis of Baker's relationship to the blues, we find that a structured blues pairs beautifully both aesthetically (ezzthetically?) and logically with a contrasting free improvisation section.

One of Baker's dazzling orchestration techniques has become something of a musical signature for him. Baker constructs an ascending or descending melodic passage (sometimes both) often covering multiple octaves, which is realized by the entire ensemble, but each individual member of the ensemble executes a solo fragment of the melody. When performed fluently the effect is thrilling, audibly and even visually, in live performance. He uses variations of this concept as well – sometimes with shorter phrases, or sometimes limiting the technique to one section of the band. In most cases, this technique is reserved for interludes, intros, codas, and solo backgrounds, as opposed to orchestrating the main statement of a theme. Diminished and chromatic scales are frequent harmonic choices for this flourish and formally serve to create tension before a return to a stable key center. Although the use of pyramids or

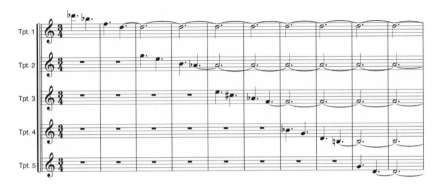

Staggered trumpet section intro, "5M Calypso."

Saxophone section excerpt, "Roly Poly," harmonization of the diminished scale.

staggered entrances is very common in all genres of instrumental composition, Baker's version is instantly recognizable as his and his alone. In most cases, the diminished scale shows up in a Baker piece as a single melodic line, often passed from one voice to another.

In other cases, the melody based on a diminished scale is harmonized in parallel harmony with the diminished scale itself.

Looking at a handful of Baker compositions for jazz big band, we find an innovator who builds new ideas based on the tradition of the music. We find a man of harmonic and rhythmic daring, an orchestrator of great depth and nuance, and an explorer charting expanded forms. But there are times when Baker wishes to do nothing more than swing, plain and simple. A comment made by Baker during a month-long tour in Europe as director of the Smithsonian Jazz Masterworks Orchestra seems appropriate here. The orchestra was treated like celebrities almost everywhere they played, and one meal of fine indigenous cuisine after another was prepared for Baker and the band. At some point well into

the tour, as another culinary extravaganza was being presented to the orchestra, Baker said: "Man, I appreciate the hell out of all this good food,
but I sure could go for some Pa and Ma's [barbecue] right about now!" I
am sure the rest of the band couldn't have agreed more, but it was Baker
who summed it up beautifully.

Great art often aspires to innovation, advanced technique, and virtuosic flourishes, traits usually appreciated by sophisticated audiences.
But at some point, even the most cultivated among us crave simplicity.
Baker's yearning for the soul food of his favorite family-run Indianapolis
barbecue joint in the face of edible works of art from some of the culinary
capitals of the world speaks volumes to how humans crave that which
reminds us of our earthly origins, in spite of our loftier aspirations. The
most refined palate sometimes craves simple comfort food and even the
most cultured musical ears sometimes require the musical equivalent.
Baker's "Some Links for Brother Ted" is a prime example of David's taking the concept of soul food and realizing it in his music. Referencing
Baker's close friend guitarist Ted Dunbar's fondness for sausages, "Some
Links for Brother Ted" does not try to reinvent or reinterpret, but rather
represents the essence of uncluttered, untampered swinging jazz. Remi-
niscent of Art Blakey and the compositions of Bobby Timmons, "Some
Links for Brother Ted" is soul music, satisfying for all the reasons jazz
became popular in the first place: strong danceable rhythms, expressive
yet simple blues vocabulary, and plenty of solo space that encourages
straight-ahead storytelling. An AABA form in F minor, the work cuts to
the chase and starts off with the first chorus of the melody with no introduction. When you have succulent stick-to-the ribs sustenance at hand,
who needs an appetizer? The form never veers, and is never extended or
interrupted by interludes. The harmony, saturated in the blues, holds up
just fine with multiple repetition. The piece is infused with down-home
soulfulness and humor, showing us yet another side of the composer.
Simplicity is often the best choice when telling a story for the ages.

Baker's library includes more than five hundred compositions and
arrangements for jazz ensemble. Probably the best glimpse at the breadth
of his work is the *Basically Baker* recording released in 2007.[33] It is the
first recording that specifically features Baker's jazz writing, with a
variety of compositions written over the course of five decades. Most

performers on the recording are former students and colleagues and intimately familiar with Baker's music and style, which greatly enhances the quality and authenticity of this outstanding collection. The compositions included are "Screamin' Meemies," "Dance of the Jitterbugs," "April B," "5M Calypso," "An Evening Thought," "To Dizzy with Love," "Some Links for Brother Ted," and "The I.U. Swing Machine." It was voted one of the top twenty releases of the first decade of the twenty-first century by *DownBeat Magazine* – a well-deserved honor for the leader of the 21st Century Bebop Band.

NOTES

1. For a rationale on effective modeling in music education, see Haston, "Teacher Modeling as an Effective Teaching Strategy," 26.

2. On the role of jam sessions, see Herzig, "The Jazz Jam Session as a Teaching Tool."

3. Pat Harbison, interview by Monika Herzig, May 6, 2010.

4. David Baker, interview by Lida Baker, June 19–21, 2000, transcript, Smithsonian Jazz Oral History Project, www.smithsonianjazz.org/oral_histories/pdf/joh_DavidNBaker_transcript.pdf.

5. Ibid.

6. Prouty, "The History of Jazz Education," 94.

7. Jim Beard, interview by Monika Herzig, February 11, 2010.

8. Harbison, interview.

9. Baker, interview, June 19–21, 2000.

10. All three of the Laurel releases were released only on LP. Compilation available on CD.

11. Baker, interview, June 19–21, 2000.

12. Beard, interview.

13. Ibid.

14. Baker, interview, June 19–21, 2000.

15. Tom Gullion, e-mail message to Monika Herzig, July 2, 2010.

16. JB Dyas, e-mail message to Monika Herzig, August 25, 2010.

17. *Sheryl Shay: Sophisticated Lady,* Laurel Record LR-506, includes David Baker's composition "An Evening Thought." *Basically Baker,* Larrikin Records LRJ-066, includes David Baker's compositions "Walt's Barbershop," "Mon," "Le Miroir Noir," and "Naptown Strut."

18. Baker, interview, June 19–21, 2000.

19. David Baker, interview by Monika Herzig, November, 21, 2010.

20. Martin Williams, liner notes, *Ezz-thetics.*

21. David Baker, interview by Brent Wallarab, October 19, 2010.

22. From the 1961 Riverside album *Ezz-thetics.*

23. Mark Buselli, e-mail message to Monika Herzig, September 2010.

24. Ibid.

25. Ibid.

26. David Baker, interview by Brent Wallarab, November 12, 2010.

27. Ibid.

28. David Baker, interview by Brent Wallarab, October 19, 2010.

29. Ibid.

30. Ibid.

31. Ibid.

32. Certainly it would appear the combination of instruments for his 21st Century Bebop Band was influenced by the landmark Miles Davis and Gil Evans collaboration from 1949, but the reality is that this instrumentation would have occurred to Baker with or without the existence of *Birth of the Cool.* Baker selected the instrumentation of his combo based on who he wanted to play with and write

for – foremost among them tuba virtuoso Harvey Phillips, who, along with Baker's cello, was the constant voice in the many incarnations of the 21st Century Bebop Band.

33. *Basically Baker.* Buselli/Wallarab Jazz Orchestra. G M 3049, available from G M Recordings website, www.gmrecord ings.com. Licensed to Owl Studios 2011; reissue forthcoming.

REFERENCES

Baker, David. *Arranging and Composing for the Small Ensemble: Jazz, R&B, Jazz-Rock.* Revised ed. Van Nuys, Calif.: Alfred, 1988.

Baker, David. *How to Play Bebop.* Van Nuys, Calif.: Alfred, 1988.

Haston, Warren. "Teacher Modeling as an Effective Teaching Strategy." 93, no. 4 (March 2007): 26–30.

Herzig, Monika. "The Jazz Jam Session as a Teaching Tool." Unpublished survey study, 2009.

Prouty, Kenneth. "The History of Jazz Education." *Journal of Historical Research in Music Education* 26, no. 2 (April 2005): 79–100.

Russell, George. *The Lydian Chromatic Concept of Tonal Organization for Improvisation, volume 1.* 4th ed. N.p.: Beekman, 2001.

6

The Composer

DAVID WARD-STEINMAN

DAVID N. BAKER'S estimated catalog of over two thousand instrumental, vocal, and choral works includes everything from lead-sheet combo jazz arrangements and compositions to big band charts and extended works, from solo and chamber pieces to full-fledged jazz and classical concertos. There are also film and ballet scores as well as works for full symphony orchestra in both jazz and contemporary classical styles. The only genre he hasn't yet assayed seems to be opera. Styles range from straight-ahead modern jazz (mostly bebop) to Third Stream and contemporary classical composition that is only distantly related to jazz.

Baker's reputation was initially established in jazz (as a *DownBeat* poll-winning recipient of their New Star Award in 1962, culminating in that magazine's "Lifetime Achievement Award" in 1987; and confirmed as a National Endowment for the Arts American Jazz Master in 2000, and by the John F. Kennedy Center for the Performing Arts in Washington, D.C., as a Living Jazz Legend in 2007). His work as an educator was honored by his induction into the national *DownBeat* Hall of Fame in Jazz Education, 1994, and by the fact that he is currently Distinguished Professor of Music and chair of the jazz studies department at Indiana University. Baker's significance as a composer of serious concert music will be the subject of this chapter.

At present, recordings of his concert compositions outweigh his jazz recordings, which is surprising given that most people in the music world associate him primarily with jazz. As Brent Wallarab, co-leader of the Buselli-Wallarab Jazz Orchestra that released a CD of Baker originals, puts it, "Much of his music has been recorded, and it is constantly being performed globally, but that music is almost exclusively orchestral or chamber music. We wanted to get the message out that David's big band music is very special and deserves attention."[1] The album in question, *Basically Baker,* was listed in the January 2010 issue of *DownBeat Magazine,* the leading jazz periodical, as being among the "Top 20 Jazz CDs of the 2000s."[2]

The focus here will be on Baker's concert jazz, Third Stream, and contemporary classical compositions. My original idea was to deal with each of these categories separately, but analysis showed that there is rarely a clear-cut division among them; a continuum of techniques and stylistic approaches often blurs any nominal division into categories. Baker uses what he needs as the situation demands, and he does so with internal stylistic consistency and conviction – drawing upon his vast experience as a performer, improviser, big band leader, arranger, composer, and pedagogue. In fact, he points out, "If I am doing a concerto, obviously I learn whatever instrument it is that I'm going to write for. ... I make a point of living with that instrument before I start to write."[3]

Baker's compositions will be discussed selectively by genre or medium, and chronologically within each category. Works chosen are, with few exceptions, published and recorded. I have examined all of Baker's works that were made available to me in these categories, and have chosen the ones I considered most representative or significant for analysis and description, given the space available. (A complete assessment would require several books.) The categories are

1. Piano solos
2. Smaller chamber works (two or three performers)
3. Larger chamber works (four or more performers)
4. Chamber music with jazz rhythm section
5. Song cycles
6. Choral music
7. Orchestral works
8. Concertos

The term "Third Stream," as used in this chapter, requires some explanation. Composer Gunther Schuller coined the term in 1957 to describe, in his own words,

> a musical style which, through improvisation or written composition or both, synthesizes the essential characteristics and techniques of contemporary Western art music and various types of ethnic music. It was originally used for a style that had existed for some years and that attempted to fuse basic elements of jazz and Western art music, these two mainstreams joining to make a "third stream." Since then . . . the term has been broadened . . . to incorporate fusions with other Afro-American music.[4]

Baker's "techniques of contemporary Western art music" include the use of quartal chords and harmony, quartal-secondal harmony, mixed-interval chords, quintal chords, polychords, bitonality, mixed modality, split chords, clusters, cluster harmony, atonal harmony, and even some twelve-tone passages. At the heart of his music is the full vocabulary of jazz that he draws on at will, especially bebop and later styles, but also including rock, gospel, Latin rhythms, and especially the blues. He readily employs blues scales, bebop scales, added-note harmony, parallel block chords, extended tertian harmony (up to the fifteenth, or double octave), major-minor fusion chords, polyrhythms, boogie-woogie basses, call-and-response antiphonal exchanges, and of course improvisation. Baker summarizes his harmonic style as

> pretty much jazz-inflected. It is dodecaphonic very often. It changes according to the needs of the piece that I'm writing. It might be twelve-tone in which harmonies are incidental. It might be vertical. It might be bi-tonal or polytonal. As far as harmony goes, I'm an eclectic.[5]

With this rich palette Baker has concocted a voluminous catalog of pieces and a rich body of work, all of which bears his personal stamp, and

Classical Composer publicity shot, early 1970s. Photo by David Repp.
Courtesy of David Baker.

one that is increasingly recognizable with repeated exposure. Asked to describe his compositional style, Baker again replies,

> Eclectic, but essentially romantic.... I use all the available forms that come out of the tradition – sonata allegro and this kind of thing. I have a strong affinity to ground bass type forms. I like theme and variations very much, and I write theme and variations very frequently. I also use the ostinato forms like the passacaglia. I use all the jazz and pop forms ... and everything else I can get my hands on. Most often, however, ... the form is post facto. I write a piece and then go back to see what the form was.[6]

ANALYSIS OF COMPOSITIONS

Piano Solos

FIVE SHORT PIECES (1970)

These pieces are the most immediately accessible of David Baker's solo piano works. They are indeed short and not too difficult, but there are some rhythmic complexities and polymetric notations that need careful attention, especially in the last movement (see excerpt, next page).

"Rêve" – A one-page "dream" that lasts twenty-five bars with ten changes of time signature. It is through-composed, rhapsodic, and improvisatory in nature. It ends bitonally and unresolved, leading into the next movement.

"To Bird" – Charlie Parker's free-wheeling sax lines are evoked in some right-hand sixteenth-note passages over punctuating augmented fourth chords, major/minor-seventh trichords without roots, augmented elevenths, and so on. This is the most overtly jazz-based movement in the set, both rhythmically and harmonically. But it is not for the casual jazz pianist, who would have to be comfortable with 3 against 2, 6 against 4, 8 against 6, and changing meters ($\frac{5}{8}, \frac{7}{8}, \frac{3}{4}, \frac{3}{8}$, etc.). The movement concludes with a solid C major/minor seventh chord.

"Passacaglia" – This is not a conventional passacaglia. The theme is never obviously stated, nor is there any kind of melodic ostinato. A quarter-note/half-note rhythmic pattern in $\frac{3}{4}$ suggests the historic derivation after the introduction, but it is not a prominent feature in the movement, which is again through-composed and improvisatory in nature.

Five Short Pieces, "Blues Waltz," at letter C.

"Evening Song" – Simple and direct, expressive and "wistful" – as the score is accurately marked. There are three varied strophes framed by a short introduction and coda, with a few polychords in the middle.

"Blues Waltz (née Terrible T)" – This is a jazz waltz over a rhythmic ostinato in the bass. The "Terrible T" of the title was Tillman Buggs, the student captain of the Crispus Attucks High School Band that David Baker played in from 1946–49. There is no clear-cut melodic line, just expanding right-hand figuration that grows increasingly complex rhythmically, such as $\frac{4}{4}$ in the treble clef over $\frac{6}{4}$ in the bass.

SONATA FOR PIANO (1968)
(Commissioned by Natalie Hinderas)

This is the most musically advanced and technically difficult of Baker's piano pieces. It owes little, if anything, to jazz, and resists even Third Stream categorization. It is often complex rhythmically (8 against 3, 8 against 6, with nested and overlapping tuplets producing polyrhythmic counterpoint), but always musical, stylistically consistent, and convincing in its development and unfolding of ideas. This sonata is one of the pinnacles of the David Baker catalog for its boldness and imaginative qualities. Even more remarkable is that it was written away from the piano, while Baker commuted back and forth by train from Bloomington to Atlanta. Baker has said that using the piano limits him because he's not a pianist.

"Black Art" – Rhapsodic and through-composed, the varying textures are mostly dissonant and non-tonal, but stylistically consistent and convincing.

"A Song – After Paul Lawrence Dunbar" – This evocation of the African American poet does suggest something of the emotional range of his poetry in its changing moods, rubato articulations, and expressivity. This is the only movement to carry markings like "tenderly," "somber and with weight," "singing with tenderness," "holding back," and "faster and agitated." It is indeed a "song" and serves perfectly as an interlude and oasis between the turbulent outer movements.

"Coltrane" – This movement is a dazzling toccata that begins with rapid repeated notes that expand to alternating polychordal triads. When it slows down in the middle we hear for the first time some suggestions of the blues in its harmony and melodic figurations, but these are the only overt references to jazz in the entire sonata, and they are subtle. The movement concludes "as fast as possible" in a condensed reverse-recapitulation of the opening material, winding up on middle C as it began.

JAZZ DANCE SUITE (1989)
(Commissioned by Gary Smart)

The movement titles given below are not from the published score, which has none, but from a CD recording by Willis Delony, presumably with Baker's approval.

"Some Sort of Waltz" – A wistful minor-flavored tune is introduced, repeated with varied accompaniment and thickening texture, then moves into a more active contrasting section based harmonically on major-minor seventh chords, voiced as augmented fourths without roots (e.g., F♯–C–F♮– from the bottom up, missing the implied D root). The opening material returns at the end with an arpeggiated accompaniment and ends with a mixed-modal Gm/M7, leaving the B♮ and B♭ sounding alone at the end.

"Solo Dance" – This is a bluesy ballad, simple and poignant, built on eight-bar phrases. The midsection is in a faster $\frac{3}{4}$ time, returning to $\frac{4}{4}$ in the closing section. Because of this, the movement will probably be heard as an ABA ternary form, but the surprising thing is that each of the eight-bar sections in the outer parts has a different theme, growing organically out of the preceding one. There is no literal recapitulation except for a partial da capo at the end. The form, then, is more accurately, A(a b c d)B(e f g)A'(h i a b)–Coda.

"The Jitterbug Boogie" – This is a good example of a Third Stream treatment of a traditional jazz style. This is anything but a traditional

Jazz Dance Suite, "The Jitterbug Boogie,"
first seven measures.

boogie, although the rhythm and walking bass style are clearly evoked, along with mixed-third (major/minor) arpeggios. The rhythms are often complex (4 against 3, 8 against 3), but they develop logically (see above).

"Double Dance" – Although the overall harmonic unifying device of the suite is a chord of mixed modality, fusing major and minor in an augmented-ninth voicing, this movement is harmonically adventurous and only evokes the major/minor chord in passages of augmented octaves or minor ninths. Instead we have extended tertian chords (thirteenths), polychords, quartal and quintal voicings, and dissonant arpeggiations over pedal points or rhythmic accompanying ostinatos. The overall form is ternary, but Baker's recapitulations are never literal – always varied and further developed. A catchy calypso-flavored tune is prominent in this movement and drives it to the end.

Smaller Chamber Works (Two or Three Performers)

SONATA FOR CELLO AND PIANO (1973)

This is a full-fledged, nineteen-minute, three-movement sonata that owes little, if anything to jazz, or even Third Stream extensions. It takes its place among Baker's catalog of contemporary concert pieces that

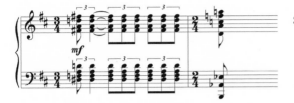

Sonata for Cello and Piano,
first movement,
second measure.

would not be out of place on any program of new or recent music. It is uncompromising and at times austere, but ameliorated by often lyrical and expressive elements.

David Baker is himself a cellist, although this was not his first instrument, and this sonata was written for the great cellist and Indiana University professor Janos Starker, who helped edit the cello part. The latter is of course very idiomatic for the instrument, the piano part rather less so. There are occasionally bursts of notes to be played rapidly – and at least one chord that is literally unplayable as written, but it is worth the effort and must be arpeggiated (see above).

The first movement opens with a fast cello ascending scale in D major which is punctuated in the second bar with piano chords containing "split" thirds (both major and minor) as well as "split octaves" (D and D♯) – see example above. The resulting minor seconds become increasingly important as the movement unfolds. The first page of the score is introductory to an expansive cello theme at letter A that will be brought back later, at letter H. A contrasting theme follows ("Energetic") that is also recapitulated later in the same key. New developmental material occurs in between the exposition and recapitulation sections. When the principal material returns, the piano part is completely different and takes over the theme from the cello. The harmonic language is often triadic based, but it is by no means "functional" or traditionally tonal, although the pitch D is centric to the movement.

The second movement is slow and begins with a long cello solo that implies E minor tonality. The piano enters with a lyrical line in D major, superimposed over the E minor accompanying figures in the cello. Both parts become increasingly chromatic as the lines are developed. There is a long cello cadenza followed by a return of the original piano theme, this time played in thirds with the cello. As the movement draws to a close, there is a surprising four-octave, whole-tone rapid scale in the piano,

Sonata for Cello and Piano, second movement, final six measures.

followed by a Lydian hybrid scale leading to cluster chords in the piano that resolve to a cadential quartal chord with E on top.

The third and last movement varies widely in tempo, texture, and style. The form is roughly an ABCBA arch, each section characterized differently as suggested above. The tempo begins fast, then slows to "Restful" before resuming. What is most surprising about this movement is the unexpected jazz element (the B section) that even evokes "Night Train" subtly in its shuffle rhythm:

Sonata for Cello and Piano, third movement, final two measures.

Sonata for Cello and Piano, third movement, letter J.

Rehearsal for *Singers of Songs, Weavers of Dreams*. From left: David Baker, Janos Starker, George Gaber. *Courtesy of David Baker.*

The C section ("Restful") is lyrical and waltz-like. When the B section returns (letter J) it is abbreviated, but the "Night Train" shuffle rhythm is even more explicit. The ending is dynamic and brilliant.

There is also a composition for cello and percussion (*Singers of Songs, Weavers of Dreams*) written for Indiana University faculty percussionist George Gaber and cellist Janos Starker, which they performed in Carnegie Hall. Baker describes this work as "not jazz, but jazz-influenced."

SONATA FOR CLARINET AND PIANO (1989)

This piece might be described as "concert jazz," fully written out and based on jazz forms and progressions. The harmonic language is mostly conventional and tonal, not yet venturing into "Third Stream" waters, but appropriate for the material. It was originally written for a student of Indiana University Professor James Campbell's, then taken up by Campbell himself; he has also recorded it.

"Blues" – The first movement is the simplest of the three. There are eight sections lasting either sixteen or twelve bars, each with a change of tempo and mood in a short movement lasting less than five minutes, and only the opening material (after the introduction) returns at the end. The introductory clarinet solo and main theme with accompanying triadic harmony in the piano contrasts starkly with the swing section, in boogie-woogie piano octaves in the bass that follows. This is a brusque change of pace that lasts only sixteen bars before slowing down to a different rhythmic pattern in triplets. This pattern lasts only twelve bars before it, too, changes character and tempo for another twelve bars. At letter F the piano begins a block-chord section of parallel dominant seventh chords with added sixths that invite antiphonal responses from the clarinet. Sixteen bars later the meter changes to $\frac{3}{4}$ and the tempo changes again. The piano plays a two-bar ostinato in the bass that outlines a G7 chord under sustained major- or minor-seventh parallel chords in the right hand that move against it. Over this the clarinet plays a sustained lyric line. The next sixteen-bar section is slow (half-time) and built over a simple B♭ minor arpeggiated bass that finally breaks away from the swung eighth notes or triplets. This sets the stage for a reprise of the opening material that takes us to the end of the movement with a slight extension. The blues progression and structure obviously dictated the variation approach in this movement, though the variations might have been more elaborated to establish themselves convincingly.

"Loneliness" – This movement is the gem of the sonata, the heart and core of the piece that justifies the other movements, and the one that Baker himself is most fond of. He says his slow movements "are almost always my most successful."[7] This one stands apart and above the outer movements in a manner not unlike the slow movement in Ravel's Piano Concerto in G Major. Here Baker allows his melodic gift to soar unfettered. The line unfolds naturally and convincingly, exploiting the full range of the clarinet, which is accompanied by simple arpeggiated F minor expanding lines in the piano, quartal chords, and added-note tertian chords. The F minor tonality departs at the end for E♭ minor, but only to set up the key of the next movement, which is F major.

"Dance" – This movement is bright and tuneful, and suggestive of calypso, a favorite rhythm of Baker's. The piano reverts to the boogie bass, the tempo slows and the pattern changes, this time suggesting a montuna before the return of the opening material, rounding off the extended ternary form.

The piano part in this sonata has been arranged for organ by Faythe Freese, and this version is retitled *Sonata for Clarinet and Organ*.

ROOTS II (1992) FOR VIOLIN, CELLO, AND PIANO
(*Commissioned by and dedicated to Menahem
Pressler and the Beaux Arts Trio*)

Roots, which preceded this trio, was composed in 1976, and two of its movements ("Incantation" and "Sorrow Song") have been taken over into the new trio, *Roots 11,* which now replaces the first *Roots.* The impetus for the revision came from a notice from the Beaux Arts Trio to Baker that they planned to record it in two weeks, whereupon Baker shifted into high gear to revise the piece and replace the movements he was unhappy with. He has provided ample notes about this piece for the definitive CD recording by the Beaux Arts Trio who commissioned it, and I won't repeat them here except to confirm that the polystylistic sources he acknowledges are very well integrated into a consistent whole, and that the contrasting movements make powerful individual statements that coalesce synergistically into a greater culmination. This is an important piece in Baker's catalog, and he was no doubt inspired by the commission from a great ensemble as well as the opportunity to pay homage to his own African American roots.

"Incantation" – This movement is driven by a low E rhythmic pedal point in the piano bass that supports quartal chords in the right hand, then later parallel thirds in the violin and cello. The music builds relentlessly and picks up speed; the bass drops out briefly, changes pitch, and returns to support a cadential stacked-thirds chord (a minor fifteenth framed by E on the top and bottom). The bass drone is meant to "evoke the mood of voodoo rites from ancient African traditions," according to Baker.

"Dance in Congo Square" – Surprisingly, this begins as a slow dance that "seeks to capture the spirit and vitality that . . . continued to reveal itself even in the condition of slavery." It is more poignant than exuberant, and when lively melodies are introduced, a dissonant element very quickly undercuts the joyful one, leading directly into the

"Sorrow Song" – This movement was often excerpted by the Beaux Arts Trio and performed as an encore. According to Baker, it "sums up the musical elements of the black church as exemplified in spirituals, laments and church house moans. It is the plaintive cry of a downtrodden people." The title says it all.

"Boogie Woogie" – This addition to the piece is really a Third Stream stylized boogie, and it works wonderfully in this context. Baker's other uses of the boogie-woogie bass have been much more literal and faithful to the model, but this one is driving, fragmented, elusive and allusive, and set in minor mode. With its fast-driven tempo, there is nothing rollicking or playful about it. Baker means business here, and this boogie is a revelation. It gains power from the restrained dynamics and muted strings (the dynamics never rise above *piano* except for the very opening bass line), but the undercurrent of restless movement transfigures the form and transcends it. This movement was often used as a crowd-pleasing encore by the Beaux Arts Trio.

"Jubilee" – meant to "cap the suite in a mood of unbuttoned celebration with a complex and vigorous expression of energetic elation." But it does more than that. The piano solo in major seconds harks back to a similar passage in the second movement; the piano scale passages in octaves echo a similar passage in the strings from the fourth movement. The perfect fifths in the bass that end the "Sorrow Song" are picked up in the bell-tone fifths that begin the last movement, and all sorts of subtle links unify and sum up the suite. The final chord contains a flatted-fifth dissonance (spelled as a $CM7^{\sharp 9\sharp 11}$ or B-over-C polychord), a bebop calling card and perhaps a little rain on the Jubilant parade, which would be symbolically and programmatically appropriate, considering the extra-musical subject matter.

Most audiences associate American-style concert music with composers such as Gershwin and Copland, and if we discount Gershwin and jazz for the moment, the concert classical composers most associated with Americana are (besides Copland) Charles Ives, Roy Harris, Virgil Thomson, William Schuman, Leonard Bernstein, and a few others. No African American classical composers have made the list – with the possible exception of William Grant Still – and this is an oversight that has impoverished us. This piece of David Baker's is an authentic piece of Americana, and a major work with a distinctly different voice to boot. It deserves to take its place in the pantheon of works exemplary of the American spirit and experience.

JAZZ SUITE FOR VIOLIN AND PIANO (1993)

This is an extended sixty-eight-page composition of Third Stream concert jazz, fully written out but requiring stylistically knowledgeable classical performers who can swing. It is both light and serious, at times hard-driving and intense, and at times reflective and intimate. It is a major contribution to the literature that should be more widely known and played.

"Minton's" takes its name from a well-known New York jazz club usually associated with the early development of bebop. This is a fast movement, similar to all the others, except for the central third movement, and there isn't a single standard triad or jazz chord in the entire piece. Instead we have mostly linear "dissonant" counterpoint in two or three parts with occasional thickening in the piano. The major seventh interval

Jazz Suite for Violin and Piano, first movement, "Minton's": (top) measures 19–20; (middle) measures 45–48; (bottom) measures 2–4.

figures prominently, sometimes spelled enharmonically as a diminished octave. This interval will invert to a minor second and expand to a minor ninth by octave displacement, all permutations of a [0–1] minor second cell.

The form is fluid, approximately ABA'–(Development)–B'A'', but there are no literal recapitulations, only continued development each time a motive returns.

"Harlem, Saturday Night" [Passacaglia] begins with a four-bar ostinato in the bass that one could well imagine being played by a string bass. After two iterations, the right hand enters with punctuating mixed-interval dissonant tetrachords, followed by a simple violin melody – all very soft and "mysterious" as the score instructs. There is a crescendo and climax that introduces a new section in $\frac{3}{4}$ where the passacaglia theme

Jazz Suite for Violin and Piano, third movement, "Perfume/
Perspiration," letter A, measures 35–41.

vanishes for nineteen bars, then returns, fragments, disappears again,
turns into a boogie bass in octaves, and re-establishes itself in time for
the ending, but remains unresolved, vanishing "mysteriously" on the
upper leading tone (Neapolitan) to the tonic. (The first note of the next
movement resolves the hanging A♭ by beginning on G, the tonic of the
passacaglia.)

"Perfume/Perspiration" (above) is the slow movement of the suite. It
begins with a long unaccompanied solo by the violin in G minor. There
is a sly nod to the twelve-tone theme of the Berg Violin Concerto in
an arpeggio that includes the first eight notes of Berg's tone row, followed by the remaining four as dyads. The piano enters with tetrachords
(all containing a minor second), which expand to pentachords echoed
by augmented minor seventh chords in the left hand, becoming quite
thick.

A passage in three-part chromatic counterpoint follows, leading to
a simplified harmonic modulation to F, prepared by its split-third domi-

Jazz Suite for Violin and Piano, fifth movement, "52nd Street," first two systems, measures 1–4.

Jazz Suite for Violin and Piano, final two measures (167–68).

nant (C minor/major), a cadence that will return at letter H in the modu-lation back to the tonic G minor. This is significant structurally because the movement ends on another split mode chord, this time G♭ minor/major, or enharmonically F♯ minor/major, the leading tone to G. This parallels by inversion the cadence at the end of the previous passacaglia movement and frames the tonic G of this movement with its chromatic leading tones on both sides of the tonic (F♯/A♭, resolving into G). This helps tie all the movements of the suite together by relating them tonally at a Schenkerian structural level.

"Jamaican Jam" begins on C in the bass, linked by the dominant-functioning G minor tonality of the previous movement. This is a pun-gent calypso with a lighthearted tonal theme that is always harmonized dissonantly, never according to the implied harmonies of the melody. The rhythm is sustained through a series of variations whose harmonies always contain minor seconds or split thirds. The pianist needs a large stretch to reach the walking bass major tenths. There is a solo violin cadenza before a contrapuntal accelerando to the tonally ambiguous end – a trichord cluster of E♭–E–F spread over four octaves.

"52nd Street" was the birthplace of bebop, the "Broadway of Jazz" south of Harlem and home to many renowned jazz clubs. Baker's "52nd Street" is a large ternary ABA form that grounds the entire suite most firmly of any of the movements in post-bebop jazz, or rather a Third

Stream extrapolation of it. The harmonies are rooted in extended tertian chords and parallel quartal chord formulations of up to six parts (see measures 1–4 above).

The extended middle section departs from extended tertian chords (often in dominant $7^{\sharp9}$ formulations) and harks back to the preceding movements in its chromaticism, triadic arpeggiations, and contrapuntal textures. The varied reprise of the opening material leads to a trademark Baker coda that gets "gradually faster and faster" to the end. The final chord echoes the ending of the first and third movements, a Cmaj7 chord that includes an augmented eleventh and sharp ninth above it, notes that enharmonically make it another split third major/minor chord, this time with the bebop signature sound of the flatted fifth on top ($\sharp11$).

The entire suite is tightly integrated with interlocking movements and materials. Just as the first, third, and fifth movements end similarly, so do the intervening second and fourth movements, each of which leads on to the next. The harmonic language is stylistically consistent and though not often tonally explicit, can be shown to derive from rootless tetrachord formulations usually containing flat seventh and sharp ninth components, and sometimes a thirteenth. The final movement makes these more explicit. There is nothing mechanical or routine about the musical forms, either. There are no exact recapitulations of any of the material, which returns only to be varied and developed further in very imaginative ways. Because of this, the forms sound more rhapsodic and improvisatory than sectional, even though they are satisfactorily rounded off by the return of familiar material in truncated or further developed iterations. There is neither padding nor wasted notes, just continuous invention at a very high level that deserves attention.

AND THEN . . . (2001)
FOR BASS CLARINET AND PIANO

This piece is a welcome addition to the scanty literature actually composed for bass clarinet and piano. It is a three-movement composition that is idiomatically written for the instruments and looks as if it would be great fun to play. The score is transposed for the bass clarinet, although this is not indicated (a frequent omission in Baker's scores with transposing instruments), and must be determined by analysis.

"The Song Also Rises" – and begins with a bass clarinet solo (eighteen bars); when the piano enters, the clarinet theme is transposed up an octave and becomes the highest voice while the piano adds a simple bass line accompaniment. This is exactly the same procedure as the opening of his 1997 "Variations and Passacaglia," although of course the material is different. The textures increase in density from monophony to two-part polyphony, three-part octave-doubled monophony, two-part homophony, four-part homophony as accompaniment, and so on with great variety that is never static. Tertian and quartal chords plus their combinations provide the harmonic basis, which evokes jazz as well as neoclassic harmony and linearity. The movement climaxes with bell tones in open fifths played in the piano accompaniment that echoes the ending of "Jubilee" in *Roots II*.

"On Wings of Song" takes flight with ascending tertian piano arpeggios that etch minor seventh and thirteenth chords on C and then Eb. After the intro, the piano provides a simple arpeggiated bass figure as accompaniment to a gradually unfolding clarinet line (which returns in varied form to end the movement). The rhythmic density increases as well, arriving at clarinet triplets against piano quadruple sixteenth notes. At letter L the pianist is invited to "fake cluster (black keys)" within the boundary notes given! Baker favors extended tertian harmony in this piece, up through minor thirteenth chords topped with the double octave, although added-note triads and quartal chords are also employed.

"The Apprentice's Sources" ends with a polychord Ab over A♮ under a stratospheric altissimo concert Ab in the clarinet, which is approached by a chromatic glissando – probably the only way to get there safely! Triplets dominate in this movement, appearing on all but five pages of the twenty-four.

Larger Chamber Works (Four or more performers)

HOMAGE À L'HISTOIRE (1994)
(Commissioned by James Campbell)

The instrumentation is exactly the same as Stravinsky's *Histoire du soldat* – clarinet, bassoon, cornet (although Baker replaces this with a trumpet), trombone, percussion, violin, contrabass – because it was written as a companion piece as well as an homage. Baker's movement titles are given below, and the Stravinskyan counterparts are in brackets, though Baker's order of the internal movements is different. The style might be described as Franco-American – "French Six" neoclassicism without Stravinsky's sharp dissonances but with a subtle underlay of American pop/jazz phrasing and rhythms. Stravinsky's "Ragtime" and "Tango" movements, although based on American and Argentine models, are stylized to the point where the original sources are barely recognizable and only hinted at. Baker's "Lindy Hop" and "Samba" are logical substitutions, and much closer to the mark.

"Little Parade March" ["The Soldier's March"] – suggests the character of the model, but the bass lines can't help swinging gently with a lilt that is all American.

"Waltz" ["Waltz"] – pop style with mostly straightforward tertian harmonies; becomes more chromatic and active in the middle with some rhythmic hemiola.

"Lindy Hop" ["Ragtime"] – this is set primarily to blues changes that contain some minor seconds evoking Stravkinsky's usage without literally quoting anything.

"Samba" ["Tango"] – more authentic stylistically than Stravinsky's adaptations, and swings discreetly.

"Little Song" ["The Devil's Song"] – wistful waltz, short and tuneful.

"Grande March" ["Triumphal March of the Devil"] – This movement contains the only literal quotation from Stravinsky's *Histoire du soldat,* and that only lasts two bars. The snare drum is used in a more Sousa march–style than in the Stravinsky, but the latter's spirit still lingers. Baker uses his ensemble in a more soloistic fashion than if he were scoring a big band homophonic chart, and that works well in this piece. Baker's neoclassicism in this suite is more pop/jazz based than, say, Copland's, and owes less to Stravinsky than the other American neoclassicists (such as Piston, Persichetti, Schuman, Kubik) do.

FANTASY (1994)
FOR FLUTE, CLARINET, BASSOON, ALTO SAX,
TENOR SAX, VIOLIN, VIOLA, GUITAR, BASS

This is a one-movement 45-page concert jazz piece commissioned by Janis Stockhouse for her Bloomington (Indiana) High School North ensemble. The alto sax, guitar, violin, and bass players are invited to improvise over blues changes in the middle and on scales later. No timing is given and a recording was not available. Of note is a bassoon ostinato in bars 141–44 that evolves into a seven-beat ostinato spread over a $\frac{4}{4}$ plus $\frac{3}{4}$ bar (between bars 191–92):

Fantasy (1994): (a) bassoon, measures 141–44;

(b) bassoon, measures 191–92.

THEME AND VARIATIONS FOR
WOODWIND QUINTET (1970)
WOODWIND QUINTET NO. 1,
WOODWIND QUINTET FROM *THE BLACK FRONTIER* (1971)

These are short one-movement works for woodwind quintet (flute, oboe, clarinet, horn, and bassoon) in undated manuscripts in the collection of Indiana University's Cook Music Library. They are simple and straightforward, and easily playable by intermediate or advanced students. These quintets were originally part of the score for *The Black Frontier* – a four-episode television documentary about the role of African Americans in the settling of the American West. Quintet no. 1 ends with a decrescendo and an instruction to "blow air thru horn and jiggle keys," a nice contemporary touch.

Chamber Music with Jazz Rhythm Section

SUITE FOR CELLO AND JAZZ TRIO (1994)
(Commissioned by Ed Laut)

"Swagger," "Meditation," "Slow Blues," "Calypso" – This suite, written a year after the *Jazz Suite for Violin and Piano* to fill out the other side of an LP recording, is as different from it as Mars is from Venus. It is neither Third Stream nor purely contemporary classical music, just written-out jazz for cello and rhythm section, much in the spirit of the Claude Bolling suites for various instruments and rhythm section. The harmonies are straightforward extended tertian, and could be notated easily with traditional chord symbols – unlike those in the suite that preceded it. The outer movements are exuberant, high-spirited, and fun. "Meditation" is apparently a slow ballad (no tempo or character is indicated in the score) in minor mode and $\frac{3}{4}$ time – simple and poignant, but not sentimental. "Slow Blues" seems somewhat out of place here. It is notated in $\frac{12}{8}$ and features constant rock-like triplets in the right hand. The concluding "Calypso" is very different from the one in the *Suite for Violin and Piano*: this one is much less complex, less difficult and demanding, and flaunts its charms winningly. Great fun!

HERITAGE: A TRIBUTE TO GREAT CLARINETISTS
(1996), FOR CLARINET, VIOLIN, PIANO, AND BASS

Transcriptions of solos by the clarinetists evoked here are quoted and incorporated into the framework provided by David Baker. Only the violinist is not required to improvise.

"Buddy and Beyond" – is a tribute to bebop great Buddy DeFranco. Chord changes and bass line from Miles Davis's "Half Nelson" are used for a set of variations, similar to the chaconne/passacaglia Baroque form.

"Artie" – is Artie Shaw, of course, and some of his solos from "Special Delivery Stomp" have been transcribed and included in this movement.

"BBBB" – refers to the blues players Buster Bailey and Barney Bigard. A Louis Jordan solo from "Ain't Nobody Here but Us Chickens" is the "glue which holds the movement together."

"BG" – celebrates Benny Goodman, whose solos from "China Doll" are quoted.

ASPECTS OF ANDY (1998), FOR CLARINET, PIANO, BASS AND STRING QUARTET
(In memory of Andrew Mayne Upper)

This three-movement work "combines elements of classical music with influences from Baker's African-American roots. Each of its three movements incorporates improvisational elements for clarinet, piano and bass."[8] The first movement swings easily, the second movement is a slow pensive ballad, and the last movement, only slightly faster, unwinds over a typical Baker bass ostinato followed by block chords in the piano. Then a melodic line in the clarinet overlays the foundation, picks up the tempo, and begins to swing with improvising piano, pizzicato bass, and clarinet soaring on top. The opening material returns to round off the movement.

Song Cycles

THROUGH THIS VALE OF TEARS (1986) FOR HIGH VOICE, STRING QUARTET, AND PIANO
(Composed for and dedicated to William Brown)

This song cycle is a tribute to Martin Luther King, Jr., and a commentary on his assassination. The movements "Thou Dost Lay Me in The Dust of Death" and "Now That He Is Safely Dead" are recast from Baker's 1968 cantata *Black America*. The unnumbered movements are bound separately and the order has not been specified.

"Deliver My Soul" – features a fast tempo, AA^1B^2 form, where the B section invites the soloist to double the violins' octave passage work with ad lib scat syllables.

"Thou Dost Lay Me in the Dust of Death" – is a slow piece, initially a cappella, then strings enter. There is no piano in this short three-page movement.

Through This Vale of Tears, "Sometimes I Feel Like a Motherless Child," measures 10–13.

"If There Be Sorrow" – begins with a slow piano solo introduction featuring minor seconds, the voice enters in broken phrases over a continuous piano ostinato. The text is by poet Mari Evans.

"Sometimes I Feel Like a Motherless Child" – features a wordless vocal solo requiring the singer to reach a high A. The strings enter with mixed-mode major/minor chords. Expanded chromatic cluster chord (minor ninths) over a surprising eight-note cluster chord in the strings mark the piano entrance, voiced as double-stopped perfect fifths that result in nine simultaneous pitch classes – the most dissonant sonority in the cycle so far, and used here for expressive purposes that introduce the title text. The piano continues with [0,1,5] trichords over the minor ninth dyad sustained in the bass (see example above).

Baker uses word painting very expressively in this setting. When the singer first reaches "a long way from home" in the text (bar 21), the strings soar away from the key center in four-part mixed-interval chords. At the last utterance of the text, the strings and voice double the tonic A in octaves on the word "home," but the piano adds a dissonant chromatic cluster that suggests being still "a long way from home."

"My God, Why Hast Thou Forsaken Me?" The text is taken from Psalm 22, which also provides the texts of "Thou Dost Lay Me in the Dust" and "Deliver My Soul." Baker continues to use chromatic cluster chords in the accompaniment, linking the texts of this song with the preceding "Sometimes I Feel Like a Motherless Child." These chords expand to less dissonant quartal-secondal chords and then minor seventh chords. The text "Why art Thou so far from helping me" is set in unison octaves; the absence of harmonic support here suggests the barrenness and loneliness in the text. The final line of text – "and find no rest" – is set to agonizing string and vocal glissandi that take the voice for the first time up to a high C (C6 [referencing middle C as C4], the highest note in the cycle and the only time it is used) before resolving down to the F minor tonic.

"Now That He Is Safely Dead" features the text by Indianapolis jazz pianist and poet Carl Hines. The first six pages are set to a one-bar basso ostinato figure in the piano and cello, the first part of a binary form. The song ends with the singer speaking the text "A dead man's dream!" over octave harmonics in the strings. "Parades to Hell" follows.

ALABAMA LANDSCAPE (1990–91) FOR
BARITONE AND SYMPHONY ORCHESTRA
(Commissioned by William Brown)

The manuscript score is not dated, but the premiere is recorded as being February 9, 1991, so we might assume that Baker began the fourteen-minute, one-movement work in the preceding year. The piece is a setting of the poem of the same title by Mari Evans, an African American poet and writer friend of the composer – one whose works he has frequently set to music. It was commissioned by the Columbus (Indiana) Pro Musica and premiered by Michael Gordon, baritone soloist, under the direction of

David Bowden. Baker considers it "one of my strongest works," and has also made a version of the same piece for tenor soloist William Brown, who recorded it with the Czech National Symphony Orchestra under the direction of Paul Freeman, a frequent conductor and champion of David Baker's music.

The source poem is described by Dan McKinley, the critic who reviewed the premiere performance, as having been written

> as an angry response to the legal system's failure to punish acts of alleged police brutality. Evans begins with a slave's daring escape through a hostile countryside, and she relates that flight to contemporary struggle: "History repeated, history relearned, history relived." The past is "still swollen" and the present is "savagely contrived" with "sanctioned lynchings." In his music, Baker allows such rage to have a chilling effect, but instead of emphasizing the poem's violence, he chooses to focus on the continuing quest for freedom. He uses the phrase "black man running" as a recurring textual motive, varying its musical moods to suggest that striving for justice may take many forms.[9]

The music is intense, foreboding and dramatic, seamlessly melding four sections into a dramatic and powerful statement that is one of Baker's strongest works. The vocal part includes spoken lines, *Sprechstimme*, and of course sung lines that are all rendered convincingly and compellingly by William Brown in the recording. The final lines of text–

> Who is it bides the time and why? And for how long? There will be no one left
> For . . . ovens

– are punctuated by a dissonant chromatic cluster stinger in the brass, followed by a single quotation of the opening phrase in the bass.

LIFE CYCLES (1998)
(Commissioned by William Brown)

Life Cycles is a setting of six poems by Terrence Diggory for tenor, horn, and strings (the same instrumentation as Benjamin Britten's *Serenade*), also available for tenor, horn, and piano. The vocal settings are invariably syllabic, with only occasional melismas of two notes and no more. Metronomic tempo marks are given at the beginning of each song, but no indication of the character or mood, though the titles of course provide a clue.

"Night Song" – There is no indication in the score as to whether the horn part is transposed, and the part could be read either way initially, but later entries and range suggest that it is indeed transposed for horn in F. "Night Song" begins with a two-bar, three-note ostinato in arpeggiated fifths in the cello and bass. Upper strings then superimpose a three-chord polyharmonic ostinato, setting a dark mood for the opening text, "The sun deserved to die." The horn provides mostly dissonant counterpoint. The textures vary frequently and sustain interest. Belltone double-stopped fifths in the strings provide contrast in the middle, followed by a new ostinato in the bass and parallel seventh chords in the upper strings. The movement ends a tritone away from where it began, but the French horn bitonally evokes the opening tonality ("in the distance").

"Surface" – an expressive tone poem about the sea that begins with arpeggiated sixteenth-note figures in A♭ major, played by the cello and bass as an undercurrent to a text about the sea surface. The upper strings join the current bitonally in B over A in the cello and bass. The midsection slows down and the strings sustain a spread-out chromatic cluster (D–E–F–F♯–G–B) under the vocal text "from where we stand we see the violence." The opening arpeggios return in A minor but finally cadence in D minor.

"Autumn Moral" – a colorful setting of a nature poem with effective word painting; for example, "a sheet of silver" is followed by a quick ascending chromatic flourish by the 1st violin; "bare branches trace the clouds" is accompanied by scattered sixteenth-note triplets, and when "frost-brittle leaves filter down," the violins start a very soft complex chromatic descent in parallel tritone sextuplets. The tenor reaches his highest note, a C♭, on the word "fist." The same pitch recurs only once (in the last bar), set to the word "compassion."

"What It Means When Spring Comes" – It means that Baker trots out his freshest and most interesting harmonies! The first twenty-four bars feature sustained diatonic string clusters, arranged in divisi thirds that fill in a complete octave. The bass chimes in with perfect fifths a twelfth below the octave cluster. Then the voice lilts in accompanied by a lively counterpoint in the horn. A two-bar quintal pattern in the bass sets up the next ostinato, high strings enter with added note triads (B♭

over C), the horn offers a disjunct counterpoint, and the voice enters to stabilize it all. The cluster chords return, slightly more dissonant with bell tones from the horn, then followed by close harmony in the strings, a disjunct line in the tenor, and finally a sustained quintal chord at the end "that gave a meaning to the seasons."

"Saints and Hermits" – The tenor tells us "where saints are" by leaping in fifths up to a high B♭, followed by the C♭ from "Autumn Moral" descending on "beasts crave to be" – the beasts getting the higher note. The song picks up a steadier tempo at letter B over another of Baker's two-bar bass ostinatos in $\frac{3}{4}$ (C♯ minor). "But hermits hunger at the close of day" is then introduced by rapid thirty-second-note Lydian scales in the strings over fifth a step below, implying E♭ minor ninth harmony. A slow contemplative passage ends the song, at which point the tenor reaches his highest note, a countertenor C over a dissonant chord on the word "prey."

THE PLACE WHERE THE RAINBOW ENDS
(2000) FOR SOPRANO, TRUMPET, TENOR SAX,
TROMBONE, TUBA, AND PERCUSSION

These are settings of poems by Paul Laurence Dunbar, the great African American poet, and the accompaniment for mixed ensemble is the most unusual of Baker's song cycles. Trumpet, tenor sax (doubling alto), and trombone are mainstays even in small jazz ensembles, but the tuba is not – although Miles Davis famously incorporated it in his classic jazz album *Birth of the Cool*. But this is not exactly a jazz score – there is no improvisation anywhere in it – and the percussionist, absent in the first song, only plays drum set in the last song, where he is asked to provide a "quasi-rock feel." These songs do, however, use the harmonic vocabulary of jazz and Broadway to a certain extent, even though the two-octave vocal part and chromatic writing is beyond the ability of the average jazz or cabaret singer. This is certainly concert music, and music to be taken seriously through the alembic of jazz, rather than contemporary classical music or even Third Stream.

Two of the songs were later adapted for *Songs of Living and Dying* (2003), a cycle for a very different kind of ensemble. None of the songs are numbered, so the preferred order, if there is one, is unknown.

"A Song" – begins rather slowly and somberly in F minor, although the harmony is never purely triadic or functional. The opening music for "Thou art the soul of a summer's day, / Thou art the breath of the rose" is more contemplative than the text might suggest, but Baker is anticipating the next lines: "But the summer is fled / And the rose is dead."

"To a Dead Friend" – This song was later rescored and transposed down a third for alto voice, cello, and piano in the set called *Songs of Living and Dying*. This setting is more colorful, however, especially in its use of percussion. Divided arpeggios in thirds spell out an Am11 chord ending in the double octave, or fifteenth (=Am15) to open this song, and its elegant tracery underlies the first part of the song.

"Sympathy" – This is a setting of Dunbar's famous 1899 poem that includes the well-known line "I know why the caged bird sings," popularized by Maya Angelou's autobiography of the same name.

"The Place Where the Rainbow Ends" – is bright and cheery. Since the harmonies are more fully fleshed out in the later version for alto voice, cello, and piano they will be discussed below.

"We Wear the Mask" – The latent jazz potential of the ensemble is finally called into play, and the percussionist is given a rock/jazz role to fill. But this is not carefree "smooth jazz": it is used to give an ironic twist to the text "We wear the mask that grins and lies, / It hides our cheeks and shakes our eyes." Even so, it swings with a nice groove over a two-bar tuba ostinato, supporting block chords in the rest of the ensemble that underlay the vocal line which is often lower than the trumpet part (here and elsewhere) and will require careful balancing unless the singer is amplified.

SONGS OF LIVING AND DYING (2003) FOR
ALTO VOICE, CELLO, AND PIANO

The sources for the texts of these songs are not identified in the score, although we know that Paul Laurence Dunbar wrote the poems for the two songs adapted from the earlier cycle – "The Place Where Rainbow Ends" and "To a Dead Friend" and Langston Hughes is the probable author of the others. Originally for soprano, tenor, and piano, the songs are among Baker's favorites, and have been rescored for alto, cello, and piano in the recorded version, wherein the cello is totally independent of the piano, and is most often allied with the voice. The cello is now Baker's own performing vehicle, and he knows it well and how to write effective idiomatic parts for it, even while mostly supporting the voice at the unison or a harmonic interval, and occasionally in homorhythmic counterpoint.

This cycle is more optimistic than the preceding one, whose texts were all dark and foreboding. Songs 2 and 4 are bright and cheerful, 1 is equivocal, 3 and 5 are darker and perhaps sadder, 6 (the last) is ambiguous and something of a fusion of the two contrapuntal moods: the text is dark and monitory, but the accompaniment attempts a kind of jazzy cheering up before giving way to the darker mood of the protagonist. The song ends on a dark bitonal dissonance: F7 over F♯. But this cycle has a broader emotional range than the previous one.

"Forever" – An arpeggiated bass provides the initial underpinning in this song, giving way to major triads over dissonant basses as the cello doubles and supports the vocal line. When the alto sings, "The slow stroke of the clock of rime I had not heard," instead of bell tones or chimes, the piano imaginatively springs loose for a dazzling solo run in sixteenths, sextuplets, and quintuplets before scurrying back to the accompanying underbrush.

"The Place Where the Rainbow Ends" is in a trichordal piano solo using the same cells again [0,1,5] over parallel perfect fifths in the bass that give way to more euphonious parallel thirds. This is an echo of where the rainbow had begun harmonically with extended tertian chords of thirteenths and fifteenths, all in a very fast tempo. This song was rescored and adapted from an earlier version of *The Place Where the Rainbow Ends* for soprano and a quasi-jazz ensemble – but not transposed, although it is high for an alto.

"To a Dead Friend" – This song has been transposed down a third from its previous incarnation in *The Place Where the Rainbow Ends* for soprano and combo, which better fits the alto voice range. Here the cello parallels the voice in harmonious sixths or occasional octaves, but is always supportive like a dear friend, never disagreeing with independent counterpoint. The piano, absent from the first version, is given an expansive decorative role with running patterns of sixteenth notes.

"To Satch" – How about a stylized boogie bass in $\frac{3}{4}$? Satchel Paige, the honoree, probably would have liked that, and that's what Baker gives him for an accompanying ostinato. There are subtle quotations from "Take Me Out to the Ball Game" sprinkled through the song (set to "I'll reach up and grab me a handful of stars"), confirming that Satchel Paige, and not Louis "Satchmo" Armstrong, is the intended honoree. The song ends with a spoken query, "How about that?" and Baker punctuates his answer with one of his favorite chords, three pairs of simultaneous minor-ninth dyads in the cello and piano that are a permutation of a filled-in P5 chromatic cluster.

"Trifle" – No tempo is given for this $\frac{3}{4}$ waltz-like setting, but a waltz tempo would work. The cello is again paired with the voice in unisons alternating with sixths or thirds, but pausing unresolved on major seconds as the song continues, finally cadencing on a perfect fifth over a quintal chord in the piano.

"Without Benefit of Declaration" – "Mama don't cry" is the spoken exhortation at the beginning of this song, which seems to be a eulogy for a dying one. But the text is ambiguous: "Mama don't cry, yonder you will lie, in exchange for a guy . . . " The piano holds a polychord while the voice and unison cello land on the minor seventh of the upper triad (F over F♯).

WITNESS – SIX ORIGINAL COMPOSITIONS IN SPIRITUAL
STYLE (2005 ADAPTION FOR SOPRANO AND ORCHESTRA)
(Original [1990] version commissioned by the Plymouth Music Society)

These settings are simpler than the previous cycle harmonically, as befits their material and intent, but they are not without interest and vitality. There is a wide range of emotional expression and content in these deeply felt settings, which Baker modestly dismisses as "another recycled work." The first version of Witness was scored for bass voice and contrabass viol (!), and in that form it was premiered by Jubilant Sykes and Gary Karr.

"We Has a Hard Time" – The opening is characterized by three-way antiphonal exchanges among cello (arco, doubled at the unison by pizzicato bass), upper strings, and the voice. Not until nine pages into the song do all the strings play together, and even then the pizzicato bass remains independent, finally joining the rest homophonically at letter G. The harmony here is made with major and minor seventh chords. Only the final phrase unites voice and all the strings in a unison rhythmic assertion.

"Didn't My Lord Deliver Daniel" – A two-bar, seven-beat basso ostinato opens this spiritual and drives it for the first half of the song, while the voice delivers short phrases ending in fermatas and chordal accompaniments. The final cadence is ironic, pitting "Daniel" against a minor second before it releases him.

"Death Is Riding" – A unison-octave string passage opens this spiritual in a quick tempo. The accompaniment is mostly homophonic and sets the final "don't grieve after me" to an ascending overlapping arpeggio that ends in a perfect fifth with the voice.

"Sorrow Song" – The voice is totally absent in this setting, where the string section is allowed to carry the burden. Baker has used this title before (in *Roots II*), but this is a different piece. Again, a one-bar ostinato in $\frac{3}{4}$ serves as underpinning for the arching high melodic line with inner harmonies filled in by the middle strings. Simple, direct, and affecting.

"And He Never Said a Mumbalin' Word" – The title phrase, "And he never said a mumbalin' word," is set ten times strophically with minor variations on each repetition, ending on a diminished chord.

"My Lord, What a Morning" – An earlier, very different setting of this spiritual is for tenor solo and mixed chorus a cappella (2000). This version, a third lower (and faster) than the earlier setting, is a jubilant and happy one – a triumphant setting to end the cycle. Some of the vocal lines are doubled at the unison and octave by the strings, which provide a sense of unity and propulsion. A rhythmic figure in the strings is repeated four times, which also helps energize the song. The tempo slows in the middle, but regains momentum until the culminating allargando that accompanies the triumphant phrase "when God calls his children home!"

Choral Music

BLACK AMERICA: TO THE MEMORY OF MARTIN
LUTHER KING (1968, SEVERAL REVISIONS) FOR
JAZZ ENSEMBLE, NARRATORS, CHORUS (SATB),
SOLOISTS, AND STRING ORCHESTRA

The piece was originally written after the assassination of Martin Luther King, Jr., and in memory of him. Immediately after the tragic event, Baker was searching for music by black composers to play at a tribute concert. To his dismay he realized that there was nothing available and proceeded to write this piece as well as start the Black Music Center at Indiana University. The initiative sparked a host of seminars addressing cultural, political, and sociological concerns; a series of recordings; as well as further research centers focusing on black music and culture.[10]

The four movements are entitled "The Wretched of the Earth (Machinations, Missionaries, Money, Marines)"; "Kaleidoscope"; "125th Street"; and "Martyrs: "Malcolm, Medgar, Martin" and utilize texts from traditional and biblical sources as well as poems by Stanley Warren, Langston Hughes, Pauli Murray, Carl Hines, and Claude McKay. In a 1969 *DownBeat* interview with Mike Bourne, Baker comments on the premiere of the piece:

> As a whole piece of art, I wanted everybody who listened to know that I was, first of all, angry at the senseless murder of Dr. King. And secondly, I wanted to register musically and with words – in every way I know – that I was hurt. Still, I wanted everybody to know that a lot of love was there and that I didn't think this was the end of the world, or that it was the end of relationships between black and white. All through there was that element of hope that there must be a way somewhere. . . . I refuse to give up his dream, though, and refuse to think there isn't a way, because I know from my own experiences that there is a way.[11]

THREE CHORAL PIECES IN SPIRITUAL STYLE (2000) FOR
TENOR SOLO AND MIXED CHORUS (SATB) A CAPPELLA

These are informal settings, bound separately and not numbered. David Baker has suggested the following order if all three are done together, as indeed they should be:

Three Choral Pieces in Spiritual Style, "See How They Done My Lord," measures 49–51.

"My Lord, What a Morning" – This spiritual begins with the tenor solo singing the first phrase unaccompanied. The chorus enters "a little faster," repeating the opening text. The third stanza is antiphonal, solo (punctuated by perfect fifths in the basses) then choir with sopranos divided. After a fermata pause, the tempo slows, the chorus drops dynamically and vocalizes on "Oo" under a wide-ranging tenor solo. The chorus takes the next stanza (1st sopranos take a high C for "world on fire"), then the tenor joins in, doubling the soprano melody down an octave. The tenor returns for a solo stanza followed by two-part chorus, then full chorus for the final lines. When the tenor returns, he doesn't merely repeat his opening material; rather he is given the remaining part of his text to complete the thought – "My Lord, what a morning when the sun refused to shine" becomes "My Lord, what a morning when the sun refused to shine and God called His children home." Every stanza is scored differently in a variety of textures, with no literal repetition. Baker is endlessly inventive and easily sustains interest throughout this setting.

"See How They Done My Lord" – The opening phrase is given to low four-part divided male chorus, which continues under the tenor solo.

The fortissimo climax is reached on the word "pierced," a high B♭ for the tenor and the sopranos. The only real departure from tertian functional harmony in the three choruses occurs here at the change of text to "Hammers ringing," echoed by "Ham'ring, ham'ring . . ." (see example above). Here the basses sing deep accented tritones while the divided tenor section claps and doubles the tritones in major seconds on the off beats. The female half of the chorus enters on split-root diminished octave triads (B♮ up to B♭, enclosing D and F).

The final cadence, on "not a word," resolves deceptively on an E-A-B-E chord (bottom up), with the fourth replacing the usual mode-defining third.

"When I'm Dead" – begins with another unaccompanied tenor solo, soon counterpointed by the choral basses in a chromatic rhythmic line. The chorus enters and divides for greater density, subsiding in hummed chords when the tenor solo returns. The final chord includes a suspended fourth, echoing the end of the preceding spiritual, but this time it resolves up to the fifth while another voice supplies the minor third.

EPISCOPAL MASS FOR THE FEAST DAYS OF BISHOP ABSALOM JONES (2003)

This is a jazz Mass, a setting of the *Missa brevis* texts in English without the Credo, and it joins the very small circle of memorable settings in jazz style by Joe Masters and Lalo Schifrin. (There is the famous Congolese Mass, *Missa Luba,* and it swings with African rhythm and percussion, but it is not, strictly speaking, a jazz Mass.) Baker's scoring is for boys' choir, mixed chorus SATB, combo (rumpet, alto sax, trombone, baritone sax), and rhythm section (piano, bass, drums). Only the rhythm section improvises; all other parts are completely written out. The choral writing is not too difficult and could be done by good church choirs (and has!). There are no vocal solos and few divided parts. The congregation is even invited to join the singing at several points. The instrumental parts require jazz experience and ability, but they are not virtuosic or exceptionally difficult either. In performance the *Mass* is exciting and uplifting, and has been known to attract a far broader congregation than is usually in attendance. The *Mass* has not yet been performed in a non-church concert setting, but there is no reason why it could not serve both sacred and secular functions.

"Kyrie" – The rhythm section opens with a four-bar basso ostinato, harmonized triadically in B♭ minor. The boys' choir enters a cappella with the opening lines in one part, then divided in two parts followed by the full chorus in four-part harmony over the bass ostinato which has just returned; next the boys' choir adds their voices to the full ensemble, which now pauses on a DM/m7♯^{5} chord under a fermata. This detail is important in two ways: it shows that Baker never repeats a texture or setting when the text is repeated and might allow it, but always finds something different and fresh to do with the material; secondly, he resists the obvious temptation to add a crescendo to the increasingly dense textures, but instead holds everything down to a pianissimo, which is even more effective and pregnant with possibilities. The meter now changes from a fast $\frac{4}{4}$ to an even faster $\frac{3}{4}$, the rhythm section drops out and the combo presents a chorale-like homophonic section expanding outward to trumpet and baritone extremes, and upward from *pp* to *ff*. The choirs respond a cappella, the rhythm section answers in slower tempo with Gm9 arpeggios in the piano, and so on with continually varied settings of the limited text ("Lord have mercy, Christ have mercy"), culminating in an octave ascent in the sopranos to a resounding E-minor chord.

"Gloria" – begins with the rhythm section, then the whole combo enters. The main tonality is F minor with a chromatically rising and subsiding fifth of the chord (C–C♯–D–E♭–D–D♭–C). The boys' choir begins in unison, and the mixed choir joins in with octaves (plus congregation ad lib) and then exchanges antiphonal responses with the boys' choir, adding harmony in the process. A "gentle" passage in triplet rhythm provides a brief interlude before the return of the opening material as the congregation is again invited to join the singing. The form is a rondo, ABACA–Coda.

"Sanctus/Benedictus" – This fast movement opens with the rhythm section and piano in open bell-tone fifths that cover the full range of the keyboard as they set the stage for the unison choral entry that follows. The texture is very transparent, omitting any intervals of thirds or sixths, and the "Hosanna"s are even spoken at one point, as the piano bell-tones continue to anchor the chorus for the next six pages. At the first break in this pattern the congregation is invited to join the choir on the melody line. But it is not until bar 76 that the piano plays any full chords, and there are only five before reverting to open fifths, at which point the choir reverts to unison song and the congregation rejoins them. "Hosanna" is set to leaping major sevenths in imitative choral antiphony, giving way to a triple spoken utterance of the text over bell tones in the combo with blues-scale improvisation in the piano. The cadential phrase sets "in the highest" on the highest soprano note, a B♭, and the ensemble chimes in with a final Gm6 chord.

"Agnus Dei " – A very fast ensemble introduction requires the pianist to "improvise wildly (clusters, scales, chords)" over the combo's syncopated punctuations. After a sudden break, the tempo drops by half and the piano plays parallel quartal chords over open fifth bass dyads. The sopranos enter over this, then are joined harmonically by the rest of the choir. The combo responds antiphonally in varying textures. There is an a cappella passage in two-part counterpoint, then three parts, then four (three-part homophony against an independent bass line). The opening quartal passage in the piano returns to accompany pyramidal entries in the chorus which then reprises and develops its opening material. The final statement begins with chorus and combo in unison octaves, expands harmonically, then cadences on a choral four-octave D while the combo moves against this and finally resolves to D major, the same tonality as the Gloria and the only movement to end with a pure major triad. The overall form is ternary.

THE GROWTH SINGLE SEED (2004) FOR MIXED
CHORUS SATB, STRING QUARTET, AND RHYTHM
SECTION (GUITAR, PIANO, BASS, DRUMS)

This is a single-movement, concert jazz setting of a poem by John Ha. The title is adumbrated in the opening two-bar snare drum roll, which simply crescendos from pianissimo to fortissimo and back. The poem is a rather transparent metaphor for the growth of a seed "showing the light of hope to everyone" once it is fully grown. The form is set respectfully by Baker who observes the ritornello line "Nothing more and nothing less" with fermatas or changes of tempo and texture after every recurrence.

The opening choral phrase starts and ends with a tritone, all parts moving up or down to fill in a tritone that shifts upward by a tritone. There doesn't seem to be any structural or symbolic significance in this, however, since it never recurs, unless the tritone is the Diabolus of doubt that splits the octave into the "single seed" of growth, harmonic development, and . . . "hope?"!

After the first ritornello and fermata, Baker starts a two-bar rhythmic ostinato in the bass, one of his favorite devices. The piano and guitar add punctuating trichords [0,1,5], the strings sustain a four-octave pedal point on F for twenty-four bars, and the chorus projects the next stanza in two-part antiphonal exchanges between the men and women. The ostinato modulates up a half-step to F♯ for the next twelve bars until the chorus reaches the next ritornello, "Nothing more and nothing less." At this point the tempo slows, the meter changes to $\frac{12}{8}$, and the texture changes to gently undulating quintal triplets as the text "transforms to a new level" is sung. This section concludes with the fourth iteration of the textual ritornello, another fermata and change of tempo (letter G, "faster") and the return of the rhythm section, which ad libs in G minor as the chorus sings the next phrase:

> The spring ends and the seasons bring the sunny, sunny summer
> Slowly the seed starts to grow and grow ever so much
> That little light of hope starts to shine
> And suddenly the dramatic change begins
> Everything is going perfectly for the little sapling

until it runs into a fermata and stops. The tempo slows again, the strings sustain an A♭m6th chord, and the rhythm section starts to "Rock à la Miles' Fusion band" as requested. The chorus sings the next lines of text, and

> The seed starts changing and transforming to a new creation
> The little seed is now adorned by human beings
> The little seed is fully grown showing the light of hope to every one.

Another pause while the piano plays quintal arpeggios that introduce the final statement of the ritornello:

> Hopeful it seems
> nothing more and nothing less.

Orchestra

KOSBRO – A PIECE FOR ORCHESTRA (1973)
(Commissioned by Paul Freeman)

The title is an acronym for "Keep on Steppin', Brothers," and one might expect a jazz, blues, or some kind of ethnic piece from the title, but to the contrary, this piece is a dynamic steamroller, high energy with relentless drive and only traces of jazz influence in a few passing major/minor augmented chords. Parts are even dodecaphonic. There is a dazzling recording by Paul Freeman and the Czech National Symphony that grabs you by the ear and does not let go for over eleven minutes. This piece could hold its own on any concert of contemporary music, and should be a staple in the symphonic repertory. Baker is not to be pigeonholed!

Kosbro is loosely cast in a single-movement sonata form, with a slightly slower section in the middle where a twelve-tone theme emerges, but the energy level doesn't drop and the breakneck tempo (quarter note = 168 beats per second) soon resumes and drives relentlessly to a quadruple forte climax on the last note, a resounding brace of D octaves at maximum range (the first trumpet in B♭ has a written high E above the staff). Baker contents himself with calling it "another piece which is full of melody,"[12] but there is a lot more to it than that, and it is one of his very best pieces.

LE CHAT QUI PÊCHE (1974)
(Commissioned by the Louisville Orchestra, for wordless soprano, jazz quartet, and orchestra)

This piece was released on the Louisville Orchestra's First Edition Records series in 1975 and features five movements:

"Soleil d'Altamira" (The sunshine of Altamira) – This salsa-flavored piece features the soprano voice on a lively melody evoking the image of sunny afternoon on the beach. Most notable is a strong saxophone solo by Jamey Aebersold on the difficult and uneven chord progression.

"L'odeur du blues" (The scent of the blues) – the piano sets up the flavor of a smoky blues bar, followed by the saxophone leading the orchestra through this slow $\frac{12}{8}$ blues section.

"Sons voilés" (Veiled sounds) – The voice certainly produces some haunting, extremely high sounds throughout in call and response technique with the orchestra with rather atonal melodies.

"Guadeloupe calypso" – The percussion section sets up the happy calypso feel with the voice singing unison melodies with the trumpets.

"Le miroir noir" (The black mirror) – a wild jazz fusion piece featuring the Fender Rhodes keyboard and electric bass in the style of then-popular fusion group Weather Report.

The cast of soloists for the recording of the Louisville Orchestra for the First Edition Series in 1975 features Linda Anderson, soprano; Jamey Aebersold, alto saxophone; Dan Haerle, piano; John Clayton, bass; and Charlie Craig, drums.

IMAGES OF CHILDHOOD (1998)

Baker writes that this piece

> is one of only a handful of compositions I have written in the last 20 years which
> was not written on commission. I thought it would be fun to write a piece about
> my memories of growing up in the Indianapolis of the late 1930s and early 1940s,
> and Images of Childhood was the result. As with most of my music, while the
> titles of the work and its movements are programmatic, there was no attempt to
> connect them to specific events, people, or things; rather, the piece was inspired
> and driven by fleeting memories, shifting impressions and the nostalgia of
> carefree times, childhood friends, and a nurturing environment.[13]

Stylistically it is tonal, tuneful, straightforward and accessible rather than challenging, which is fitting considering the subject matter. Baker doesn't indicate timings on his scores, nor complete transposition information (for example, the trumpets are evidently in B♭ but this is not indicated, whereas clarinets in B♭ are indeed specified).

"Maypole" – The harmonies tend toward simplicity despite occasional extensions like the opening pyramidal thirteenth/fifteenth

Images of Childhood, "Follow the Leader," third movement, orchestral tutti.

chords. Baker will often set up ostinato chordal accompaniments that underlie the melodic lines that are shared among the remaining instruments. The final cadence is on a Gmaj7 chord.

"Lazy Summer Days" – This is the most successful and satisfying movement. A quintal arpeggiated ostinato provides the initial underpinning for triadic strings doubled at the octave by celeste, which in turn supports a clarinet and woodwind symmetrical period of four four-bar phrases, which are further developed and passed around the orchestra. The orchestration is colorful and soloistic, without a single tutti.

"Follow the Leader" begins with a unison-octave, full-orchestra statement of the most interesting theme in the suite so far, one that leaps and turns in on itself, quickly using up all the notes of the chromatic scale, but not in twelve-tone or serial fashion (see example above).

What follows is imitative fugal counterpoint at descending minor seconds ("Follow the Leader"). The theme then gets broken up antiphonally and passed around the orchestra. At Baker's specified tempo (quarter note = 208 beats per second) the pace is dizzying indeed – especially in the sixteenth-note passages – and ends abruptly and dramatically.

REFRACTIONS (1998) FOR STRING ORCHESTRA
(Commissioned by Paul Freeman)

This piece exists in three versions, first for cello quartet (commissioned by Janos Starker, 1993), later expanded to eight-part cello choir (1996) – really a double quartet (probably spaced antiphonally, as the score layout implies) – and then finally for full string orchestra. There are three movements in each version.

The composer states,

> Like virtually all of my large classical works, [Refractions] is romantic in nature, yet influenced by my background as an African-American and a jazz musician. Both the title and the titles of its three movements . . . are intended to be descriptive as well as euphonious.[14]

The scoring is mostly thick and homophonic in texture, and the three movements share such closely related material that there is little to differentiate them except a fast-slow-fast tempo scheme. Baker considers *Refractions* to be a "companion piece to *Alabama Landscape.*"

"Crescent" – opens with a familiar Baker figure, the quintal bass arpeggio one-bar ostinato, followed by violas adding a minor third to the mix. The form is roughly a rondo, ABA'CA. The C section at letter G is interesting harmonically, consisting of discrete dyads in thirds that use seven different stacked pitches initially, then later eight different pitches just before the end.

"Crepuscule" – opens with the same figure as the first movement transposed to C from F and is very similar in its material to the first movement, but in a slower tempo. The first theme is structured and phrased like a popular song (ABA), then a variant of it appears slightly faster in E♭ with a fifth in the arpeggiated bass oscillating between perfect and augmented. The next variant states the theme in canon for four bars before transitioning to a faster midsection that introduces a contrasting subject in the lower strings while the upper strings provide a homophonic punctuation in trichords of major thirds over a minor second [0,1,5], a favorite formulation of Baker's. The opening theme returns in tempo with unaccompanied violins in octaves – a welcome respite from the mostly tutti scoring. The overall form is compound ternary, ABA'.

"Convergence" – opens with eighth-note triplets scattered throughout the string section, interspersed with chordal passages (six-note divisis over open fifths). A long singing line emerges in the 1st violins, characterized by a rhythmic figure used in the preceding movements – a dotted quarter followed by an eighth tied to a half note or longer. The form is approximately ABACA–Dev.–A, and each reprise is marked by continued variation and development.

MASQUE OF THE RED DEATH BALLET (1998)
FANTASY ON THEMES FROM MASQUE
OF THE RED DEATH BALLET
SUITE FROM THE MASQUE OF
THE RED DEATH BALLET (2002)
"BASED ON A STORY BY EDGAR ALLEN POE"

"The Masque of the Red Death" was first a classic short story by Poe; in 1998 it became the subject of a ballet produced by the Indiana University Ballet Theatre with music by David Baker, which in turn resulted in two musical spinoffs – a short one-movement Fantasy (the only version to be commercially recorded so far) and a more substantial Suite from the ballet from which it was extracted. The Fantasy was actually a "conductor's cut" from the Suite, made by Paul Freeman to fit the time available for a CD released in 2006.

The music is neither jazz nor Third Stream based, but is tonal and programmatically functional. The Dies Irae chant from the Requiem Mass is quoted as a death motif to accompany the plague called the Red Death, symbolized by a masked intruder who has been ravaging the countryside. The score is colorful and suitably ominous: a notable touch is the wind machine at the close to "depict the complete and utter desolation that remains."[15]

Concertos

CONCERTO FOR FLUTE, STRING QUARTET, AND JAZZ BAND (1970)

This is a full-fledged, three-movement concerto in Third Stream concert jazz style. Curiously, the solo flute part (doubling alto flute) requires no improvisation at all, just a virtuoso classical technique with an ability to swing and play jazz phrases convincingly. The full range of the flute (both flutes) is utilized, all the way up to the double high C. The instrumentation is also unusual in that a string quartet is called upon only in the second movement. The jazz band required is a large one with sections of five (five saxes, five trumpets, and four trombones plus tuba) and the usual rhythm section, which carries most of the improvisational load by improvising the accompaniment based on chord symbols.

After a slow introduction and opening theme in the first movement, the tempo picks up and a nine beat $(\frac{4}{4} + \frac{5}{4})$ ostinato in tuba and bass sets up the next section, an octave-doubled long line in flute, soprano sax, tenor sax, and trumpet. The next section is a flute solo with drum set accompaniment in double time, marked *cooking*. A long free development section (so labeled) follows, leading to a literal recapitulation of the opening material and a coda consisting of a solo flute cadenza that leads into the next movement.

The second movement is a passacaglia, or rather four passacaglias in sequence. The first theme (sixteen bars) is stated by trombones in chorale harmonization (cf. Brahms's Fourth Symphony, last movement chaconne), slow tempo, then picked up by the muted string quartet. Subsequently the tempo increases, the meter changes from $\frac{3}{4}$ to $\frac{4}{4}$ and a new four-bar jazz ostinato is introduced by the string bass. The tempo slows and the string quartet returns with a third bass passacaglia theme, back in $\frac{3}{4}$. After an interlude the tempo picks up once more, the meter changes back to $\frac{4}{4}$, and the string quartet introduces a fourth ostinato theme in octaves, four bars long. This takes us up to the ending where the original theme is recapitulated in a coda.

The third movement, marked "As fast as possible (half-note = 168)," will probably push everyone to their limits. After introductory riffs there is a long overlapping chromatic scale in the band that ascends from low C in the tuba all the way to a 1st trumpet high G above the staff. After that, a metric modulation reduces the tempo by a third and things ease a bit into a section marked "funky," meters changing freely with the phrasing. This is a complex movement with a lot of variety and high energy. The concerto is a unique work and a major contribution to the literature.

CONCERTO FOR VIOLIN AND JAZZ BAND (1970)
(Commissioned by Josef Gingold)

In a 1970 interview with David Shank for WFIU Public Radio, violinist Josef Gingold described his attraction to the music:

David Baker and Joseph Gingold, 1970. *Courtesy of David Baker.*

When he first showed me these sketches, I was intrigued by what I saw. I realized immediately that there was not only an artist, but an artisan. He knew his craft and I liked what I saw. He showed me the score, it all looked great on paper. And about three or four weeks prior to our first concert we had a rehearsal. I was just swinging along with those youngsters. I'm only sorry that I couldn't turn the clock back forty years.[16]

The solo violin, like the solo flute in its concerto, is not required to improvise, but it may be even harder to find a classical violinist, which this requires, who can also play written-out jazz convincingly when it is called for. The improvisational elements are embedded in the parts for the jazz band. There are several elaborate cadenzas and much for the violin to do, and Baker is to be commended for providing these two concertos as a challenge and opportunity for classically trained musicians who want to stretch out into jazz.

CONCERTO FOR CELLO AND CHAMBER ORCHESTRA (1975)

This is one of several pieces written for the great cellist Janos Starker, and it was premiered by him shortly after it was finished. The instrumentation is for one each of the woodwinds, two horns, two percussion and strings, but omits orchestral cellos from the string section to avoid acoustic confusion. The score estimates the duration at fifteen minutes, but the recording by the Czech National Symphony Orchestra takes all the movements slower than indicated in the score, and it lasts almost twenty-two minutes. Baker describes the three-movement concerto as

> coloristic and dramatic. The first movement is lyrical in nature, featuring the cello in a somewhat transparent environment, ending with harmonics. The second movement opens with an extended solo cello recitative in which all of the principal thematic material of this movement is presented. The first theme is reminiscent of the material from the first movement; and special effects, including glissandi in the upper strings and the use of exotic percussion, create an impressionistic atmosphere. The third movement is jazz-influenced. The first theme uses the harmonic progression from "Back Home Again in Indiana" and is introduced over a series of rhythmic interjections. The second theme is a clever and charming 12-tone row conceived by Starker and incorporated into this movement over a rhythmic bass line.[17]

The second movement is very colorful and imaginative in its scoring. The third movement really requires a cellist who understands jazz rhythms and can "swing" convincingly. I have not heard Starker's performance, but the Czech cellist who recorded it is a little stiff and "square" in the jazz sections.

CONCERTO FOR TWO PIANOS, JAZZ BAND,
STRINGS, AND PERCUSSION (1976)
*(Commissioned by Charles Webb and Wallace
Hornibrook for the Webb-Hornibrook Duo)*

Baker's program notes for the original LP recording are unusually detailed, and worth quoting in full:

> This is the eighth in a rather unique series of concerti involving the classical
> music (western art music) area and jazz band. It is in many respects the most
> individualistic of the lot. Among its unique features are: an unusual instrumen-
> tation; the fusion of jazz, rock, folk and art music elements; the combination
> of improvisational and written elements; the unusual use of conventional and
> exotic instruments in movement two; the unusual use of the harmonic structure
> of George Gershwin's "warhorse" "I Got Rhythm"; the cyclical use of material;
> and finally the totally authentic and convincing use of the jazz materials by both
> solo pianists.
>
> Among the basic problems that had to be addressed were the integration of
> the soloists with the accompanying instrumental forces, achieving balance, and
> composing a work that is convincing as both jazz and art music.
>
> Once the seed for a large-scale work for two pianos was planted by Charles
> Webb, the young and dynamic dean of Indiana University's School of Music, I
> followed my established routine of studying as many diverse works in the genre
> as possible. My own biases and musical tastes led me to return again and again to
> the Bartok concerto for two pianos, percussion, and orchestra transcribed by the
> composer from his *Sonata for Two Pianos and Percussion*.
>
> Each of the three movements is designed to place the two pianos in a com-
> pletely different setting:
>
> > Movement One – the two pianos, jazz band and percussion ensemble;
> > Movement Two – pianos, string orchestra and percussion;
> > Movement Three – the total forces.

Baker continues:

> The outside movements are the most heavily jazz influenced and both share a
> high percentage of the same raw material. The slow movement shows the great-
> est degree of indebtedness to Bartok's concerto [for two pianos, percussion and
> orchestra], more in instrumental choices and spirit than in content and form.[18]

CONCERTPIECE FOR VIOLA AND ORCHESTRA (1989)
(Commissioned by Karen Elaine)

"Of the 20 concerti I have written, this one is arguably the most ambitious," says Baker of this three-movement, thirty-two-minute work. He goes on to describe it as

> one of the most virtuosic, involves the largest orchestra, is the grandest in terms of emotional sweep, and is very much in the tradition of the major string concerti of the Romantic Era. Unlike most of my works this concerto shows virtually no hint of a conscious jazz influence; my references are more obviously Bartok, Tchaikovsky, and Shostakovich. It is very much reminiscent of the tune-filled works of an earlier time.[19]

Baker's description is very accurate and unapologetic. The themes are indeed pretty, evoking not only Tchaikovsky but even Samuel Barber's violin concerto, and Baker's concerto is full of graceful touches and colorful orchestration.

The concerto was commissioned by Karen Elaine, who gave the premiere in 1991 at Indiana University. Baker made a viola-piano reduction of the piece, probably for rehearsal purposes, but I have performed that version with Karen Elaine, and can report that it is idiomatic for the piano despite being an orchestral reduction, and was fun to play.

JAZZ SUITE FOR CLARINET AND SYMPHONY
ORCHESTRA: THREE ETHNIC DANCES (1992)
*(Commissioned by and dedicated to The Akron
Symphony Orchestra, Alan Balter, conductor)*

This piece "might be loosely called a Thirdstream work," according to David Baker. It was written "to showcase Balter's skill as a classical and jazz clarinetist and the orchestra's versatility in both idioms. . . . The work's title and the names of the individual movements reflect their allegiance to black music traditions. Each of the three movements is heavily indebted to and influenced by a dance form issuing from a black aesthetic."[20]

"Jitterbug" begins with fast xylophone and snare drum sixteenth notes (all on F for the xylophone) that continue for eight pages of score (forty-eight bars), punctuated by syncopated stabs in the bassoons and pizzicato basses, all confirming the tonic F. This is in fact the same introduction and tempo that Baker used in the orchestral work *Kosbro* in 1973, but it develops differently here and not as relentlessly. The piano and jazz bass circle chromatically around F, the piano in broken "boogie" octaves that weren't used in *Kosbro*. Sections of the orchestra enter gradually until the full orchestra is in – winds and violins sustaining a lyrical line, brass punctuating. At the climax the orchestra drops out for the solo clarinet entry on a notated altissimo B♭ that descends to the bottom of the clarinet range and then back up to the mid-range. The piano then accompanies the clarinet solo discreetly before resuming the boogie broken-octave bass. The clarinet is instructed to swing the eighth notes, and is given chord symbols over the written-out lines, inviting improvisation. Short phrases and punctuations are exchanged among clarinet, piano, and percussion (triangle and xylophone). The tempo slows for a contrasting section in $\frac{3}{4}$ featuring long lyric clarinet lines accompanied by soft strings. After a pause the opening material returns, closing the ternary ABA form.

"Slow Drag" starts with clarinet triplets accompanied by pizzicato jazz bass. Strings enter with block chords – triads initially, expanding to four-part chords. The clarinet part becomes more active with long sixteenth note runs accompanied by triplets in the piano and bass (doubled at the unison by French horns). The tempo soon picks up as well and the clarinet drops out as the piano improvises over chord changes. Then the pace slows and the mood changes (the score is marked "Slower, melancholy"). A bluesy melodic line in violins and winds is counterpointed by rapid sixteenth-note scale figures and interjections by the clarinet, leading to a very fast "double time" section over a two-bar ostinato in the piano and bass (a favorite device of Baker's). The meter shifts to $\frac{3}{4}$ for eighty-four bars, then back to $\frac{4}{4}$ for the final twenty-seven. Baker intends this latter change as a metric modulation, dotted-half note equaling the new quarter note, which would slow the apparent tempo down by two-thirds, since the quarter note provides the unit of propulsion. This section serves as a transition to a recapitulation of the opening material, rounding the movement off very nicely.

"Calypso" – Maracas in eighth notes provide the pulse and Caribbean color from the beginning, while divided cellos play multiple-stop arpeggios "quasi guitar." A long ascending chromatic scale in the orchestra covers six octaves before reversing. The meter changes to $\frac{3}{4}$ and the clarinet begins a long chromatic scale in triplets doubled by the marimba at the unison. This leads to a new groove that settles in with three percussion, clarinet solo, harmonic accompanying strings, and piano improvising to chord changes "in Calypso style." The ending is dynamic, dramatic, and loud. This is a very rich Calypso, intricate and inventive, that turns it into something substantial for concert purposes.

CONCERTO FOR TUBA AND ORCHESTRA – THE B'S (1997)
(Commissioned by Daniel Perantoni)

The movement titles in this concerto reflect Baker's fondness for alliteration, and "each is intended to be descriptive as well as euphonious."[21] And no doubt "euphonious" is a pun on the tenor tuba, or euphonium.

"B's" – The three Bs in question are not the standard classic ones but Brahms, Bartók, and Berg. Baker "pays homage to these three," he says, "through the use of quotes, gestures, and harmonies, all the while creating a showcase for Mr. Perantoni, one of the most versatile and highly respected tuba virtuosi of our time."

"Berceuse" – a "contemporary cradle song or lullaby," with "sweeping romantic lines" and "lush cushions of sound." This is a tender, waltz-like song in B♭ minor, later changing to $\frac{4}{4}$ with hints of major mode in chromatically moving inner lines. The $\frac{3}{4}$ time and mood return, but with different material.

"Blues" – "utilizes the blues form, gestures, and scales, but altered in various ways to display the multi-faceted artistry of the soloist. . . . The jazz-like allusions in this movement to the signature gestures of such artists as Charles Mingus, Dizzy Gillespie, Charlie Parker, and Cannonball Adderley are most convincingly rendered."[22]

This blues is in F minor and is characterized by a two-bar rhythmic ostinato in the bass, high violin pedal points, and a snare drum pattern of sixteenth notes – all as underpinning for long lyric tuba lines. The tuba part is very high, as it is elsewhere, necessitating dropping some of the passages an octave. The final chord is a D major diatonic cluster in the orchestra (using all seven notes of the diatonic scale) over an A pedal; the orchestra drops out, leaving the tuba with the last note, a tonic A and major third to the opening F minor key.

Saxophone Concertos

The *Concerto for Alto Saxophone and Symphony Orchestra* (1989, rev. 2004) was commissioned by Tom Walsh and is solidly in the jazz idiom. Its extended three-movement, fast-slow-fast form with obligatory improvisation make it Third Stream rather than its harmonic language, which is tonal, functional, and rather conservative for Baker, who writes that this concerto is

> one of only a handful of my compositions which calls for a soloist who is
> equally skilled in handling both the classical and jazz languages. In most of my
> "Thirdstream" works the "improvised" sections are written out so that I can
> be assured of a realization which fits my artistic vision for the piece. This work,
> however, is designed to provide a point of departure for the exceptional improvi-
> sational skills and imagination of Thomas Walsh, whose formidable talents as an
> interpreter of contemporary classical music and as one of today's brightest and
> most imaginative jazz soloists make him the ideal artist to create the concerto's
> definitive first performance.[23]

The extended opening solo cadenza is totally improvised from the instruction "At the beginning the solo alto plays in and out of tempo using A-blues combinations of major thirds and half steps gradually establishing tempo, key and mood into letter A," where a written-out solo for the sax continues for fourteen bars before the orchestra enters. On the recording, Tom Walsh does this beautifully and seamlessly, and his playing throughout is lucid and burnished. The concerto itself seems rhapsodic and improvised compositionally, but serves admirably as a vehicle for a stellar soloist.

Between 1985 and 1991, Baker was commissioned to write four additional saxophone concerti for specific jazz artists. The first one, written for Lee Konitz in 1985, was never premiered, but the subsequent three for Dexter Gordon and the New York Philharmonic (1987), Ernie Krivda and the Ohio Chamber Orchestra (1988), and Howie Smith and the Cleveland Chamber Symphony (1992) received successful premieres and subsequent performances and recordings. In an article for the *In-*

ternational Jazz Archives Journal (1993), Baker discusses similarities and differences between the works and his inspirations and strategies.[24] The opportunity for writing several commissions for similar instrumentations in such a short amount of time is rare and a unique opportunity to build a cumulative repertoire and knowledge in one idiom. Owing to his background as a jazz artist as well as close familiarity with the style of the featured saxophone artist, Baker was able to write each piece focusing on the strengths, preferences, temperament, and personality of the soloists. In fact, Michael Drexler confirms the successful fusion of music and personality in his review of Ernie Krivda's premiere of the *Concerto for Saxophone and Chamber Orchestra*:

> The magic of this piece is the success in which Baker has allowed Krivda to be himself and still keep the structure and feeling of a concert piece that is heavily influenced by European music.[25]

Most notable of this group of pieces is *Ellingtones: A Fantasy for Saxophone and Orchestra* (1987). Baker pays tribute to Duke Ellington, who, in his own words, "has long been my hero and whom I consider one of the greatest composers of the twentieth century."[26] His skillful mosaic of literal statements of Ellington compositions to medleys of fragments as well as original melodies based on characteristic elements of Ellington themes provides a familiar, yet open framework for soloist Dexter Gordon to showcase his trademark robust tone as well as melodic improvisations. In one of his last public appearances, Gordon recorded an expanded version of this piece with the Tokyo Philharmonic (1989) that unfortunately was never released.

CONCERTINO FOR CELLULAR PHONES AND SYMPHONY ORCHESTRA (2006)

This odd work was commissioned by the conductor of the Chicago Sinfonietta and the Czech National Symphony Orchestra, Paul Freeman, who decided to launch the Sinfonietta's third decade "with something completely different." In the Prague airport he "saw so many people using cell phones for last-minute conversations before boarding their flights that he thought there must be some way of combining this technological accomplishment with music."[27]

Baker readily undertook the task of composing the piece with audience participation, and one of his Indiana University graduate assistants, Aaron Vandermeer, appeared as no doubt the first cell phone soloist to perform with an orchestra. A review of the premiere described it as sounding

> like an aviary gone mad. Scores of cellular phones trilled and twittered, beeped and burbled all at once inside a concert auditorium.... The orchestra onstage was unfazed. The composer was delighted.... A device similar to a traffic light signaled the audience members to activate their rings – red for the balcony, green for the orchestra seats – at various points in the piece.... Four amplified mobile phones were onstage.... The score was filled with classical tunes suggested by a ring-tone Web site.... At one point, Mr. Baker turned the tables. Oboes and flutes imitated a cell ring. The tuba groaned with irritation.[28]

The concertino is framed by an orchestral tutti chromatic cluster that cuts off the audience's ringing phones and resolves to a triple forte unison-octave D at the end of the piece while the cell phones compete. In between are many collaged quotations from the classic repertoire that get interrupted periodically on cue by the audience. I have not heard the piece performed, but the score had me in stitches. Baker said,

> This is the first time in my career that I have a piece that's finished, and I have no way of knowing what the results will be. There's just no way to replicate 1,000 cell phones going off at once.... There's a wonderful balance between [chaos and organization] because that's how our lives are. Moving from the known to the unknown is very exciting.[29]

It's a tribute to Baker's youthful open-mindedness and sense of play that at age seventy-four he would undertake an adventure like this, totally without precedent in his previous voluminous catalog as far as I know. There is far too little humor and fun in the concert hall these days, and Baker has made a marvelous, audience-pleasing contribution to the genre:

> "Sometimes we take everything so seriously that we forget there's a real world out there that's not life and death," he says, adding, "there's nothing more deadly than a passive audience."[30]

Amen.

Coda

The thirty or so works discussed here form barely the tip of David Baker's titanic musical iceberg, which has been floating innocuously alongside the ship of his other endeavors for many years without garnering the comprehensive critical attention it deserves. His prodigious output is unprecedented in the jazz world and also in contemporary composition, especially considering his active life as a performer, author, conductor, and pedagogue – in all of which he has excelled with great distinction.

Baker's writing skills are expressed most frequently and eloquently in his many concertos, by far the most numerous of his chosen genres and hence the closing section of my chapter. In addition, it should be noted that there is usually not one concerto per instrument but often two, one in Third Stream or concert jazz style paired with another in contemporary classical style, as exemplified by these pairings:

1. Concerto for Cello and Chamber Orchestra / Concerto for Cello and Jazz Band
2. Jazz Suite for Clarinet and Symphony Orchestra / Concerto for Clarinet and Orchestra
3. Concerto for Violin and Orchestra / Concerto for Violin and Big Band, etc.

His African American roots are often reflected in the texts he chooses for songs and choruses (almost always by African American writers), in the titles of many works, and in the themes that have inspired him. He is also deeply respectful of his peers in the jazz world, and has honored many of them with dedicated works and quotations. He has been fortunate in having his music played by world-class virtuoso performers in both the classical and jazz worlds, many of whom have commissioned him repeatedly. None of this would have happened without Baker's talent and genius, of course – but his humanity, humility, and altruism have undoubtedly contributed greatly to his success in the world, and have endeared him to everyone fortunate enough to know him.

NOTES

1. "IU Jacobs School of Music Faculty and Alumni Featured on *Basically Baker* CD," Apr. 23, 2010, newsinfo.iu.edu/web/page/normal/14234.htm.

2. *DownBeat* 77, no. 1 (January 2010), 42. The tabulation cites 4–1/2- and 5- star reviews of outstanding CDs from the past decade, referencing the Baker review from its September 2007 issue.

3. Baker and Baker, *The Black Composer Speaks*, 24–25.

4. Schuller, "Third Stream," 773.

5. Baker and Baker, *The Black Composer Speaks*, 26.

6. Ibid.

7. Baker, interview by Monika Herzig, May 18, 2010.

8. Thomas Wolf, liner notes, *David Baker at Bay Chamber Concerts,* Cala Records, 2002.

9. Liner notes, *Paul Freeman Introduces . . . David N. Baker, vol. 5,* Albany Records Troy 377, 2000.

10. David Baker, interview by Lida Baker, June 19–21, 2000, transcript, Smithsonian Jazz Oral History Project, www.smithsonianjazz.org/oral_histories/pdf/joh_DavidNBaker_transcript.pdf.

11. Bourne, "Defining Black Music," 105.

12. Baker and Baker, *The Black Composer Speaks*, 25–26.

13. Liner notes, *Paul Freeman Introduces . . . David N. Baker, vol. 8,* Albany Records Troy 499, 2002.

14. Liner notes, *Paul Freeman Introduces . . . David N. Baker, vol. 5,* Albany Records Troy 377, 2000.

15. Liner notes, *Paul Freeman Introduces . . . David N. Baker, vol. 12,* Albany Records Troy 843, 2006.

16. Josef Gingold, interview by David Shank, *Jazz: Past, Present, Future; Com-*mentary by David Baker and Josef Gingold, WFIU, May 31, 1970.

17. Liner notes, *Paul Freeman Introduces String Concertos, vol. 10,* Albany Records Troy 559, 2003.

18. Liner notes, *Concerto for Two Pianos, Jazz Band, Strings & Percussion,* Laurel Record LR-115, 1982.

19. Liner notes, *Paul Freeman Introduces String Concertos, vol. 10,* Albany Records Troy 559, 2003.

20. Liner notes, *American Voices: The African-American Composers' Project,* Telarc CD-80409, 1995.

21. Liner notes, *Paul Freeman Introduces . . . David N. Baker, vol. 5.*

22. Ibid.

23. Liner notes, *Paul Freeman Introduces . . . David N. Baker, vol. 12,* Albany Records Troy 843, 2006.

24. Baker, *From the Composer's Perspective.*

25. Drexler, "David Baker's 'Concerto for Saxophone,'" 38.

26. Baker, "From the Composer's Perspective," 105.

27. Quoted in John Von Rhein, "Concertino for Cell Phones and Orchestra," *Chicago Tribune,* October 8, 2006, www.publicbroadcasting.net/michigan/artsmain/article/2/1083/977161/Classical/Concertino.for.Cell.Phones.and.Orchestra/.

28. Quoted in Daniel J. Wakin, "Horns Up, Bows Ready, Cellphones On." *New York Times,* October 3, 2006, www.nytimes.com/2006/10/03/arts/music/03cell.html.

29. Quoted in Cynthia Martens, "Ladies and Gentlemen, Please Turn Your Cell Phones ON," Trustees of Indiana University website, September 28, 2006, newsinfo.iu.edu/news/page/normal/4063.html.

30. Ibid.

REFERENCES

Baker, David. "From the Composer's Perspective: Three Saxophone Concertos." *International Jazz Archives Journal*, 1, no. 1 (1993): 104–13.

Baker, Lida Belt, and Baker, David. *The Black Composer Speaks*. Metuchen, N.J.: Scarecrow Press, 1978.

Bourne, Mike. "Defining Black Music: An Interview with David Baker." *DownBeat* 36, no. 19 (September 18, 1969): 104–13.

Drexler, Michael. "David Baker's 'Concerto for Saxophone' Premiered by Ernie Krivda." *Saxophone Journal* 13, no. 1 (Spring 1988): 38–39.

Schuller, Gunther. "Third Stream." *The New Grove Dictionary of Music and Musicians*, edited by Stanley Sadie, 18:773. New York: Macmillan, 1980.

7

David Baker and the Smithsonian: A Personal Perspective

JOHN EDWARD
HASSE

I FIRST MET DAVID BAKER in fall 1973, when I arrived at Indiana University to pursue a doctorate in ethnomusicology.[1] Even though I would earn my degree in the Graduate School rather than in the Music School, where he taught, David was a huge factor in my decision to attend IU. Unknown to me at that time was how significant he would turn out to be in my life and career, and how important he would become to the Smithsonian Institution.

Over the course of my studies leading to MA and PHD degrees, I took just about all the courses I could from David, including F321: Jazz Improvisation; M393: History of Jazz; M395: Contemporary Jazz and Soul Music; M593: Advanced History of Jazz; M582: The Bebop Era; M584: Research in the History and Analysis of Jazz: Miles Davis and John Coltrane. Although I had taken a course or two in jazz at my undergraduate alma mater, Carleton College, studying with David was eye-, ear-, and mind-opening. He was highly organized and systematic in his approach: a thorough syllabus announced the week-by-week progression and he adhered to it religiously. His exams combined drop-the-needle identification of recordings with traditional true/false and multiple-choice questions, and were themselves models of organization. (I still have my copious handwritten notes on his lectures, all his syllabi, and all the tests I took from him.)

David galvanized my interest in jazz. He was such a passionate, articulate, and effective educator – the phrase "master teacher" doesn't even do him justice – that I soon began to see him as a role model: an academic who performed, wrote, published, lectured, advocated, and inspired. Who could do all that better than David Baker?

In fact, some years later, when Bernice Johnson Reagan, as Director of the Program in African American Culture of the Smithsonian's National Museum of American History, brought David to do a lecture on improvisation, she remarked that he was "the best teacher of *anything*" she had ever encountered.[2] Coming from someone who maintained very high standards and was known as candid and tough minded, this was praise of the highest order.

A few years earlier, in New York, I had had the good fortune to take private lessons in jazz piano with two great practitioners – Jaki Byard and Roland Hanna (who later became Sir Roland Hanna, when the government of Liberia knighted him). From each I learned a lot. But when I enrolled in David Baker's jazz improvisation course, I was thunderstruck; on the very first day, he explained the relationships of scales to chords. I confess that during that initial class, I learned more from David than I had in months of lessons with Byard and Hanna. That's how organized and incisive David Baker is.

In 1984, the Smithsonian's National Museum of American History created a new curatorship to specialize in twentieth-century American vernacular and popular music, and I was hired to fill that position.[3] Immediately I sought to put to work the learning, perspective, and judgment that David had taught me. One of my very first acquisitions was the custom-built, angled-bell trumpet of Dizzy Gillespie. When I spoke at the packed press conference at which Gillespie formally presented

TABLE 1. DAVID BAKER AND THE SMITHSONIAN: A CHRONOLOGY

1984	David Baker's ex-student/mentee John Hasse arrives at the Smithsonian to assume the new position of curator of American Music, and begins to apply knowledge gained from studying with David.
1985	The Smithsonian's National Museum of American History acquires the trumpet of David Baker's mentor, Dizzy Gillespie.
1986	A national conference on jazz is held at the Wingspread Conference Center in Racine, Wisconsin, under the leadership of David Baker; among the speakers are Baker and the Smithsonian's Martin Williams.
1987	The National Museum of American History receives its first federal appropriation for jazz, to acquire and catalog the massive Duke Ellington Collection.
April 1988	The Duke Ellington Collection is moved from a warehouse in New York to the Smithsonian.
1990	Smithsonian Institution Press publishes *New Perspectives on Jazz*, edited by David Baker, comprising papers from the 1986 Wingspread Conference.
October 1990	Congress authorizes the establishment of the Smithsonian Jazz Masterworks Orchestra (SJMO) – the Smithsonian's second federal appropriation for jazz.
October 1990	Baker takes the Indiana University Jazz Ensemble to the Smithsonian to perform an Ellington concert for the annual conference of the College Music Society (CMS).
January 1991	The International Association for Jazz Education (IAJE) conference in Washington, D.C., features a mini-conference on Ellington, and Baker speaks on a panel discussing jazz repertory.
May 19, 1991	SJMO debuts at the National Museum of American History (NMAH), begins a summer season of seven free weekend concerts.
August 1991	Nationally syndicated newspaper columnist David Broder urges Congress to provide more funding for the SJMO so it can perform in other cities.
1991	SJMO plays "Concert for Congress" on Capitol Hill.
1992	The Smithsonian secures a $7 million grant from Lila Wallace–Readers Digest Fund, and establishes ten-year partnership called America's Jazz Heritage.

May 22–23, 1992	David Baker conducts the SJMO in "Stompin' at the Smithsonian," two nights with the sixteen-member Big Apple Lindy Hoppers and veteran swing dancers Norma Miller and Frankie Manning, master classes, dance demonstrations, and a dance floor for the audience.
June 19, 1993	SJMO performs at the White House Jazz Festival.
July 26, 1993	Writing about the White House Jazz Festival in *The New Yorker*, Whitney Balliett calls the SJMO "the best jazz repertory band in the country."
1993	First Jazz Masterworks Editions (JME) are published: Ellington's *Daybreak Express* and *Sepia Panorama*.
October 15, 1993	Under David Baker, the SJMO performs at Harlem's Apollo Theater, in conjunction with the Smithsonian's *Beyond Category* traveling exhibition.
1993	Ken Kimery joins staff, works on the Smithsonian Jazz Oral History Program and the Smithsonian Jazz Masterworks Orchestra.
February 1994	David and Lida Baker interview J. J. Johnson for the Smithsonian Jazz Oral History Program.
1994–95	SJMO tours the United States, under John Gingrich Management.
1994	*Jazz Smithsonian* radio series begins, hosted by Lena Horne.
1995	Third JME is published: *Take the "A" Train*.
1995	SJMO *Demo Disc* issued, with ten tracks from the radio series *Jazz Smithsonian*.
Spring 1996	Gunther Schuller resigns as musical co-director of the SJMO; David Baker takes sole reins as musical and artistic director.
August 2, 1996	SJMO performs for the Cultural Olympiad at the Olympic Games in Atlanta.
September 1996	*Smithsonian* magazine publishes a lengthy article about the SJMO.
1996	NMAH issues the SJMO's first CD, *Big Band Treasures, Live*, with support from America's Jazz Heritage (AJH) and Nissan: its twenty tracks were conducted by David Baker and Gunther Schuller and taped in concert from 1993 to 1996.
1999	SJMO begins touring under the management of SRO Artists.
April 29, 1999	SJMO performs Duke Ellington's Sacred Concerts at the Washington National Cathedral on the night of Ellington's hundredth birthday.
July 1999	SJMO does "world tour" of Canada, Europe, and Turkey, performing a show called the "Cotton Club Revue."

TABLE 1. *continued*

September 1999	SJMO performs a tribute to Ellington, including *Suite Thursday,* at the Monterey Jazz Festival.
November 1999	James Zimmerman becomes executive producer of the SJMO; Ken Kimery becomes producer.
2000	David Baker becomes music co-editor for the series Essential Jazz Editions, a collaboration among Jazz at Lincoln Center, the Smithsonian Institution, the Library of Congress, and Warner Brothers Publications. Five editions of Louis Armstrong's music are issued.
June 2000	David Baker sits for full interview by Lida Baker for the Smithsonian Jazz Oral History Program.
July 2001	The NMAH announces a new initiative – an annual, national jazz month called Jazz Appreciation Month (JAM), to be observed each April.
2001	With David Baker as music co-editor, Essential Jazz Editions issues its set of five scores and parts titled *Music of the 1930s, Part 1.*
January 2002	David Baker, then president-elect of IAJE, participates in a panel discussion on Jazz Appreciation Month at the IAJE conference in Long Beach – along with Willie Hill, President-Elect of Music Educators National Conference (MENC); Tim Owens, executive producer, NPR Jazz; and JAM founder John Edward Hasse.
2002	Under music co-editor David Baker, Essential Jazz Editions issues its set of five scores and parts titled *Music of the 1930s, Part 2.*
2003	Smithsonian Folkways Recordings begins planning a book and CD set, *Jazz: The Smithsonian Anthology;* David Baker becomes part of the executive committee.
2003	Essential Jazz Editions issues five scores and parts, *Music of the 1940s, Part 1,* with David Baker as music co-editor.
2003	Ken Kimery takes over as head of the Smithsonian Jazz Oral History Program.
2004	Smithsonian Folkways Recordings issues *Tribute to a Generation: Salute to the Big Bands,* its seventeen tracks were recorded live by the SJMO from 1992–98 (Smithsonian Folkways SFW40817).
2005	Ken Kimery takes over as SJMO Executive Producer.
2005	*Louis Armstrong Education Kit,* co-authored by David Baker and Luvenia George, is issued by the Museum.
2005	*Music of the 1940s, Part 2,* a set of scores and parts for five classic works, is issued by Essential Jazz Editions; David Baker is music editor.

February 2008	Under the sponsorship of the US State Department, the SJMO tours Egypt; the theme is "Jazz on the Nile."
July 2008	MCG Jazz issues *Live at MCG,* a CD/DVD recorded live at Manchester Craftmen's Guild in Pittsburgh, in April 2005, under the baton of David Baker.
September 2008	David Baker interviews Quincy Jones for the Smithsonian Jazz Oral History Program.
September 2008	The SJMO tour of Egypt is discussed in "Jazz on the Nile: The Smithsonian Takes the Nation's Jazz Band to Egypt," a *DownBeat* article by Hasse.
June 2010	David Baker does research at NMAH for Quincy Jones's American Music Curriculum.
September 2010	David Baker conducts the SJMO in a twentieth anniversary performance for the Congressional Black Caucus Foundation's annual Jazz Forum and Concert, organized by Rep. John Conyers and Cedric Hendricks.
March 2011	Smithsonian Folkways issues *Jazz: The Smithsonian Anthology,* a 6-CD, 111-track set packaged with a two-hundred-page book. David is the author of four track essays and a member of the five-person executive committee that chose the selections.

his instrument to the nation, it was David's judgments on Gillespie that informed my remarks. When, beginning in 1985, I had the opportunity to lead the Smithsonian's efforts to acquire Duke Ellington's archives, again, it was what I had learned from David that provided a framework for my further learning about Ellington.[4] David's influence would inspire one aspect of my Smithsonian work after another.

JAZZ MASTERWORKS EDITIONS AND ESSENTIAL JAZZ EDITIONS

Jazz Masterworks Editions was a pioneering series of authoritative printed versions of jazz classics. The initiative came out of Oberlin College and the National Museum of American History. David recalls,

That had its genesis with Fred Starr, President of Oberlin.... I went out to do an evaluation of their school. Gunther [Schuller] had already been there. Fred started talking then about, why not publish some – what he was calling "urtext" editions of works by Ellington, works by Fletcher Henderson, and that kind of thing. It seemed like a pipe dream to me at the time, but he pursued it with Roger Kennedy, who at the time was head of the [Smithsonian Institution's National]

TABLE 2. ESSENTIAL JAZZ EDITIONS CO-EDITED BY DAVID N. BAKER

EJE SET	TITLE	RECORDING ARTIST	RECORDING YEAR	TRANSCRIBER
Music of the Louis Armstrong	"Cornet Chop Suey"	Louis Armstrong	1926	Randy Sandke
	"Hotter Than That"	Louis Armstrong	1927	Randy Sandke
	"Mahogany Hall Stomp"	Louis Armstrong	1929	Randy Sandke
	"Tight Like This"	Louis Armstrong	1928	Randy Sandke
	"West End Blues"	Louis Armstrong	1928	Randy Sandke
Music of the 1930s, Part 1	"Big Jim Blues"	Andy Kirk	1939	Brent Wallarab
	"For Dancers Only"	Jimmie Lunceford	1937	Brent Wallarab
	"From A-flat to C"	John Kirby	1938	Joey Sellers
	"Lonesome Road"	Tommy Dorsey	1939	Joey Sellers
	"Symphony in Riffs"	Benny Carter	1933	Brent Wallarab
Music of the 1930s, Part 2	"Avalon"	Jimmie Lunceford	1935	David Berger
	"King Porter Stomp"	Benny Goodman	1935	David Berger
	"South Rampart Street Parade"	Bob Crosby	1937	David Berger
	"Sweet Sue, Just You"	Don Redman	1937	David Berger
	"Swingtime in the Rockies"	Benny Goodman	1936	David Berger

Music of the 1940s, Part 1			
"Cupid's Nightmare"	Cab Calloway	1940	David Berger
"The Hour of Parting"	Benny Goodman	1940	David Berger
"Yard Dog Mazurka"	Jimmie Lunceford	1941	David Berger
"Loose Lid Special"	Tommy Dorsey	1941	David Berger
"Flying Home"	Lionel Hampton	1942	David Berger
"Cool Breeze"	Billy Eckstine	1947	David Berger
"Dance No. 5, Liberian Suite"	Duke Ellington	1947	David Berger
"Mango Mangüé"	Charlie Parker with Machito	1948	Michael Philip Mossman and Omar Castaños
Music of the 1940s, Part 2			
"Robbins' Nest"	Claude Thornhill	1947	David Berger
"Sidewalks of Cuba"	Woody Herman	1946	David Berger

> Museum of American History.... Of course it was logical to call in Gunther
> Schuller, who had done a lot of work along these lines, because he had had reper-
> tory orchestras – ragtime orchestras and [jazz] repertory orchestras. And the
> same thing [applied] with Martin Williams, who had tried to have transcribed
> all the stuff that was on the [*Smithsonian Collection of Classic Jazz*], which again
> would have been "repertory."[5]

Roger G. Kennedy, who was director of the Museum from 1979 to
1992, was an admirer of the Library of America, which was founded in
1979 to publish America's most significant writing in definitive editions.
Kennedy asked me to help him pull together the aforementioned experts
to explore whether a similar enterprise could be mounted to publish
America's jazz classics. And so I contacted David and invited him to join
a conversation that included Kennedy, S. Frederick Starr, the eminent
composer-conductor-author Gunther Schuller, and the Smithsonian jazz
critic and record producer Martin Williams. Kennedy secured a modest
startup grant from the Rockefeller Foundation, and the Museum undertook additional fundraising. The group of five became an executive board
and decided to begin the series with Ellington, especially as the museum
had just acquired about a hundred thousand pages of unpublished music
composed by Ellington and his colleague Billy Strayhorn. The king of
Thailand, a devoted jazz fan, sent a contribution; and initial funding
came also from a federal appropriation.[6]

A ripple of excitement went out in the cultural world, as the *Wall
Street Journal, Washington Post, Chicago Tribune,* and other news media
took note of this new initiative.[7] As someone who had conducted and
taught Ellington's music for years, David's expertise and suggestions
were invaluable. Three editions of works recorded by Ellington were
issued: "Daybreak Express," the powerful 1933 evocation of an express
train; "Sepia Panorama" (1940), which for a short period was Ellington's
signature tune; and "Take the 'A' Train," the 1941 Strayhorn composition that quickly became Ellington's theme song.[8] As innovative and
worthwhile as these critical editions were, they were not considered
"sexy" by funders, and raising outside funding proved to be difficult to
the point that after the initial three editions, no more were published.
But about twenty years after the project was established, the three Jazz
Masterworks Editions (JME) publications are still in use in the United
States and abroad.

In the late 1990s, the idea of creating a national series of authoritative jazz editions, which had begun with Jazz Masterworks Editions, was revived by joint agreement between the Smithsonian's National Museum of American History and Jazz at Lincoln Center (JALC). A partnership was formed among JALC, the National Museum of American History, the Library of Congress, and Warner Brothers music publications. My colleague Ken Kimery became project director for the Smithsonian's part of the collaboration. I served as text editor, and the partnership produced thirty publications – covering jazz from the 1910s through the 1940s – before it, too, ran out of funds. Like the Jazz Masterworks Editions, each publication included a conductor's score with a historical essay and performance suggestions, and separate parts for all the instruments. Wynton Marsalis, and – beginning in 2000 – David were music co-editors, checking and double-checking the work of the transcribers who painstakingly notated the music from the original recordings. Under David's musical oversight, and drawing on his peerless ears and sharp eyes, twenty-five editions were issued (see table 1), ranging from Louis Armstrong's landmark 1928 recording "West End Blues" to "Mango Mangüé" as recorded by Charlie Parker with Machito and His Orchestra in 1948. David said, "All jazz players, regardless of their stylistic preferences, can learn a great deal by studying the masters of this music."

SMITHSONIAN JAZZ MASTERWORKS ORCHESTRA

Once the museum acquired the Duke Ellington Collection in 1988, it was memories of David's brilliant conducting of the Indiana University jazz band that helped fire my imagination.[9] I dreamt that the Smithsonian could have its own jazz orchestra, whose first mission would be to bring alive the old, fading manuscripts of Ellington and breathe new life into them, to make the manuscripts "sing."[10] A big band was the dream, because it is the ultimate expressive medium for jazz composers such as Ellington, and within jazz, a big band provides by far the widest range of dynamics, sonorities, and tonal colors.

I gave considerable thought to the idea, wrote several documents to develop a rationale, came up with a name for the band, and began talking up the idea. Roger G. Kennedy, then the Director of the National Museum of American History, warmly embraced the concept. Word of this idea began to spread, and when it reached the ears of Diane Blagman, then chief of staff for United States Congressman Bob Carr, it found a supporter.[11] When word reached Congressman John Conyers, an ardent advocate for jazz, and his jazz advisor, Cedric Hendricks, it found two champions. In 1987, Representative Conyers had won passage of a concurrent resolution, HR 57, declaring jazz "a rare and valuable national American treasure to which we should devote our attention, support and resources to make certain it is preserved, understood and promulgated."[12] He and Cedric Hendricks were looking for the next thing that Congress could do to begin to build a stronger institutional foundation for the music, and seized upon the Smithsonian – which at that point had a twenty-year record of accomplishment in jazz, including the publication of the *Smithsonian Collection of Classic Jazz*[13] and other significant recordings, and the acquisition of the Duke Ellington Collection.

I had been harboring high hopes that not only would this dream become a reality but that one of my musical heroes, David Baker, would serve as conductor. The Smithsonian got a kind of sneak preview of David's approach to conducting Ellington in September 1990. I had lobbied and persuaded the College Music Society (CMS), which was holding its annual conference in Washington, D.C., to devote several sessions to Duke Ellington, the city's native son. On October 27, 1990, the Museum hosted a symposium that I organized, "Duke Ellington: A Retrospective," and David participated in two presentations, "Recreating Ellington's Masterworks" and "Integrating Ellington into the College Music Curriculum." At the CMS's invitation, and knowing that the concert would be held at the Smithsonian, the Indiana University School of Music sent David Baker and the Indiana University jazz band to perform "A Concert of Duke Ellington Masterworks, 1927–1967."

In the audience that evening were Gunther Schuller and Martin Williams, eminent jazz authorities who had argued that a repertory band couldn't play ballads authentically, because doing so would require a player to exactly recreate the original solo on the recording. But when student alto saxophonist Shannon Hudgins recreated Johnny Hodges's stunning solo on Ellington's "Warm Valley," recalls David, "both were convinced that it could be done."[14] David managed to change the minds of two leading jazz experts who had given much thought to how to perform Ellington. As a result, they joined me in supporting the idea of David's role as conductor of a Smithsonian jazz orchestra. "There was something magical that evening," David recalls, "and the very fact that the concert was in an almost sanctified environment" imbued it with influence.[15]

With the support of Congressmen Carr, Conyers, Ralph Regula, and Sidney Yates, in October 1990, the US Congress passed legislation authorizing the establishment of a national jazz band – the Smithsonian Jazz Masterworks Orchestra – and provided $242,000 for a season of free public concerts.[16] And thus the ensemble became the big-band-in-residence at the Smithsonian's National Museum of American History.

I asked director Kennedy if he would appoint David conductor and musical director and Kennedy agreed, inviting David to lead the band. In a typically magnanimous gesture, David said that he would accept the position if Schuller were named co-director. David recalls, "I had had a chance to study [Schuller's compositions], and across the years we became fast friends. That culminated in my asking him to be a part of the Smithsonian Jazz Masterworks Orchestra when that was formulated. He was already kind of the senior member of the Jazz Masterworks Editions. . . . Gunther [is] a continuing friend. We are close enough friends that we can fight when we need to fight."[17] David was also named a senior consultant in jazz. In that capacity, he has kindly lent his advice on many musical matters over the years.

In a preview of the band's first season, which began in May 1991, the *Washington Post* quoted Schuller as saying, "If a music is not played by living, breathing, emotionally expressive people, that music will eventually die. No music can exist solely in archival museum form."[18] This is a view that David has wholeheartedly endorsed.

It was with great anticipation that the SJMO played its first concert – on May 17, 1991, at the Museum's Carmichael Auditorium.[19] Baker and Schuller shared conducting duties, each leading the band through three short sets. The *New York Times* sent its jazz critic, Peter Watrous, to attend the first concert. "The result was more than culturally important, it was fairly spectacular musically as well," he wrote. "The music, after being embalmed on recordings, suddenly came alive."[20]

David returned to visit the music of Sy Oliver on July 20–21, and, on August 3–4, Chick Webb, Count Basie, and Duke Ellington. (The SJMO's Washington concerts are summarized in table 3.) The band wowed another noted journalist – the syndicated columnist David S. Broder:

> The impact of these live performances is everything the showmen, scholars, and politicians who brought this small miracle to pass imagined it might be. It is electrifying.
>
> Important as authenticity of performance is to him as a scholar and teacher, Baker told me, "It's even more important to me as a musician." Classical quartets that play Haydn, Mozart and Beethoven "strive to be faithful to the composer's intent," he said. "How many times does Sy Oliver or Basie or Ellington have that respect afforded to them?"
>
> Serious as the purpose may be, the concerts themselves are sheer joy. Earlier this month, Baker told one casually dressed audience, "We're in a museum, but John [Hasse] has got clearance for head-nodding, foot-stomping and butt-shaking, so go ahead." And they did. "This music is precious," Baker remarked later, "because we want to preserve it. But this ain't precious music. This is robust, living, vivacious music. It crosses all demographic lines. I watch little kids and their parents, old people, black people, white people – they all get it. . . . It's music that transcends time and place."[21]

Make no mistake about it: this music requires musicians with superb skills and exceptional versatility. Playing repertoire is extremely difficult. In the course of one evening, one player might have to switch from the musical equivalent of the comic Falstaff to the doomed Hamlet to the impish Puck to the star-crossed Romeo, or from the tragic Willy Loman of *Death of a Salesman* to the wacky Kramer of *Seinfeld*. "This is great," said saxophonist Steve Wilson in 1996, at the time an SJMO regular. "It's essential to the grandeur of this music to hear it live. Playing this is humbling. It's as difficult as anything I've ever had to do."[22] "There's a lot more to it than just reading the notes," said former SJMO trombonist Brent Wallarab. "You have to understand what the musicians were trying to get across emotionally and spiritually. You put yourself in their heads, but then play your interpretation."[23]

Throughout the history of jazz, great emphasis has been placed on achieving one's own sound. This artistic quest is so strongly ingrained in jazz musicians that many are unwilling to set aside their sonic approach and play the music of a different figure or an earlier style. It is an exceptional individual who doesn't mind subjugating his or her ego to approach to the goal of playing someone else's music in the manner of the original. It takes a singular musician to relish the challenge of mastering Johnny Hodges's sound, or Miles Davis's attack, or James P. Johnson's figurations. Only a special kind of player can read the music flawlessly and also improvise, when called upon, in the original style. In its several hundred concerts to date, the SJMO has been grooming players, giving them more practice and experience in this highly demanding pursuit.

Discerning listeners of the SJMO came to realize that although recording technology allows the modern listener to hear nearly a century of music by the masters of big band jazz, there is nothing like experiencing the thrill of an exciting live performance up close and personal. There is no substitute for being able to see with one's own eyes which instruments and which soloists are creating this sonority, or that tonal color, or a certain blend of sounds. There is nothing like the immediacy and directness of a live performance, nothing like the magic of performers interacting with a living, responding audience.

As every performer knows, the interchange between performer and audience can be unpredictable and sometimes magical. In a live performance the audience can affect the course of events. That influence empowers an audience and creates a yin-yang relationship with the performers. That's why live performance is so vital and why in our high-tech age, it remains irreplaceable. The Smithsonian Jazz Masterworks Orchestra dedicated itself to the proposition that the great classics of big band jazz deserve to live on through informed performances before live audiences.

Besides the joy of playing and hearing old music spring to life again, the SJMO offers other pleasures. In some cases, an original recording was poorly performed. The band perhaps didn't have enough rehearsal time, or was forced to make the recording in just one take, or there was some other musical shortcoming. In contrast, the SJMO often has had the luxury to rehearse and get it "right."

Sometimes the original performance was poorly recorded. Using modern twenty-four-track recording technology for its radio and recording projects, the band brought out (and the audience could hear) aspects of the music that were simply hidden before – intricacies of part writing, subtle shifts in tonal colors, and the like.

Sometimes the SJMO, or soloists within the band, can bring a new interpretation to an old work. Sometimes the SJMO will restore material that was in the original composition, but was omitted in the recording because of time constraints. And sometimes the SJMO will find a vintage piece that was never recorded and will give it its premiere public performance, broadcast, and recording.

What sets the SJMO apart from other big bands? The band is a repertory band in two senses. First, it is a repertory company of musicians. As in a theatrical repertory company, where not every performer is needed in every production, performers are drawn from a core group for each performance, depending on the needs of the program. Second, the band canvases the classic, enduring repertory of big band jazz to select works of special significance, appeal, or timelessness. Unlike the "ghost" bands which replicate the music of a single band – such as the Duke Ellington Orchestra or the Count Basie Orchestra – the SJMO has the same freedom and flexibility as a symphony orchestra in selecting and performing historic music written for its medium.

Several other aspects of the SJMO distinguish it from all other bands. The fact that it was congressionally chartered gives it the imprimatur of the United States government – no small thing. In addition, it's the only jazz band headquartered in a museum, specifically the National Museum of American History. As a result, its goals align with the Museum's – specifically to link to the Museum's permanent collections, to make American musical history come alive, to provide historical context for its selections, and to engage in educational outreach to frame the music and reach young audiences.

One of the most enjoyable tasks of the band is turning on young people to music that preceded them by decades. Reviewing the band's concert on May 18, 1991, the *Washington Post*'s Mike Joyce wrote, "The evening ended with a long and well-deserved standing ovation, but perhaps the most telling praise paid the ensemble – and jazz repertory groups in general – came afterwards. That's when two members of the audience who appeared to be in their early twenties were overheard extolling the great virtues of [Bennie] Moten's music as they walked down Constitution Avenue. Sixty years after its prime, they spoke of the music in the present tense."[24]

The museum management very much admired David Baker's musical and leadership skills. In the summer of 1991 three of us – NMAH director Spencer Crew, James Weaver, chairman of the Division of Musical History, and I – flew to Chicago to meet with David, then teaching at Jamey Aebersold's jazz camp in the suburb of Elmhurst, to woo him into joining the museum staff on a fulltime basis. David replied that he was extremely flattered, but he loved teaching so much that he would remain at Indiana University, but stay involved in the orchestra as a conductor.

At the time, a few other jazz "repertory" big bands were in existence, such as the Jazz Arts Group in Columbus, Ohio;[25] the American Jazz Orchestra in New York;[26] and the Classical Jazz at Lincoln Center Orchestra.[27] But what had gotten lost in most big band performances was the historically vital, tight connection between the music and dancing. So on May 22–23, 1992, we presented an innovative concept, which – with a nod to Harlem's Savoy Ballroom and the Chick Webb anthem, "Stompin' at the Savoy" – I dubbed "Stompin' at the Smithsonian." We brought the Big Apple Lindy Hoppers from New York City, along with noted swing dancer Norma Manning and swing dancer and teacher Frankie Manning. Before the SJMO performance, the dancers showed their steps and conducted a master class for Washington hoofers. As a result, people flocked to the SJMO performance, swinging and jumping. David, I could tell, was having a ball.

Over the years, he proceeded to explore the music of one major figure after another, starting with mainstays of the swing era, such as Fletcher Henderson, Chick Webb, Count Basie, Jimmie Lunceford, Artie Shaw, Glenn Miller, Tommy Dorsey – not to mention Duke Ellington and Billy Strayhorn – and gradually moved forward in time. He has devoted special concerts to Louis Armstrong, the "territory bands," Mary Lou Williams (with pianist Geri Allen as guest soloist), Woody Herman, Dizzy Gillespie, Thelonious Monk, Stan Kenton, the "Latin tinge" (jazz compositions influenced by Latin American rhythms), Miles Davis and Gil Evans, Bill Russo, Oliver Nelson, Bill Holman, Benny Carter, and such composer-arrangers as Maynard Ferguson, Thad Jones, and John

Dankworth who wrote in a modern idiom and were celebrated in the Smithsonian's five-CD set, *Big Band Renaissance.*[28]

Among the most memorable concerts in Washington was the band's performance, conducted by both Schuller and Baker, for the second White House Jazz Festival. Bill Clinton hosted a jazz concert on June 28, 1993 – fifteen years to the day after Jimmy Carter hosted a jazz concert on the South Lawn. Three pickup groups, two led by Wynton Marsalis and Illinois Jacquet, performed in the main tent, but *New Yorker* jazz critic Whitney Balliett complained that "one of the world's premier ensembles, the Smithsonian Jazz Masterworks Orchestra, situated on the balcony of the White House, played before most guests arrived."[29]

For the first few years, Baker and Schuller divided conducting duties, occasionally splitting a concert between them, but more often alternating concert weekends. They employed two contrasting approaches to rehearsing and performing. Schuller liked to rehearse each piece in sections, going over each segment until it sounded right, building a polished performance from small units into a whole. Baker preferred an opposite approach. He focused first on the whole and then the parts – that is, to run through the entire piece, occasionally working on difficult passages. Schuller, with a long career as conductor of classical music, preferred that the audience not applaud after solos. Baker, steeped in the jazz tradition, encouraged the audience to move their body parts during the performance and applaud after solos. Baker pointed out in 1996: "When people just sit there and don't respond, I say, 'No, no! Don't listen to us as though we are an artifact. Listen to us and *react.*'"[30] The two musical directors got along well, but eventually differences emerged over band personnel and other issues. By spring of 1996, Schuller had made a decision to depart the SJMO and turn his energies elsewhere. Baker recalls,

> When we were at odds with the direction that it was going to go, it really needed to have a single – probably a single vision for what the orchestra was going to be. ... I was – despite the fact that Gunther had been my teacher in composition – I was the senior person in this particular instance. He left voluntarily. He was not asked to leave. He chose to leave, to pursue other things.[31]

Program cover, Smithsonian Jazz Masterworks Orchestra.
Courtesy of the Smithsonian Jazz Masterworks Orchestra.

Where does a band such as this one acquire its music? The SJMO encountered a problem that would not face the establishment of a symphony or chamber orchestra: the almost complete lack of published orchestrations in authentic versions. So the band turned to transcriptions, meaning notations painstakingly extracted from the original recordings. Making accurate transcriptions is an acquired skill that few musicians can master. Most difficult of all is transcribing the music of Duke Ellington, because he composed with highly personal, unusual instrumental voicings. Very few musicians possess the "ears" to hear precisely what Ellington wrote, although once the Smithsonian acquired and made available to researchers the vast trove of Ellington scores and instrumental parts, making the transcriptions became less onerous and more accurate.[32] At the very beginning, the band leaned on transcriptions that Baker and Schuller had in their libraries, some of which they themselves had done. David Berger, Andrew Homzy, Mark Tucker, Jeff Lindberg, and Brent Wallarab also contributed transcriptions.

By 2011, the SJMO had assiduously developed a library of over 1,200 pieces and a repertory ranging widely over the history of jazz, from the 1920s through the 1990s, focusing on works that are the best of their type and that have stood the test of time.

In the band's early years, funding from the Lila Wallace–Reader's Digest Fund supported recordings of the band's concerts to be broadcast on *Jazz Smithsonian*.[33] The series, produced by Tim Owens, was an artfully compiled stream of programs that featured SJMO performances, excerpts from Smithsonian oral histories, and commentary by the incomparable Lena Horne, who was a close friend of Billy Strayhorn and many other musicians whose music was featured by the SJMO.[34] The series premiered in January 1994 on 170 radio stations. It was broadcast in forty-five states as well as Panama, New Zealand, Australia, and India. Each show was one hour in length. In 1995, it was the most successful jazz series ever distributed by its network, Public Radio International. The series ran through 2001 with up to thirteen shows per season.

The SJMO has released two CD recordings and one DVD. The first CD, *Big Band Treasures, Live* (1996) was recorded live in concert in Washington between 1993 and 1996, and featured twenty tracks of music by

Cab Calloway, Duke Ellington, Billy Strayhorn, Lionel Hampton, and others.[35] The second CD, *Tribute to a Generation: A Salute to the Big Bands of the WWII Era* (2004), included seventeen selections by Artie Shaw, Duke Ellington, Lionel Hampton, and other 1940s favorites, recorded live in concert in Washington between 1992 and 1999.[36] The ninety-minute DVD *Live at MCG* was videotaped in concert at Manchester Craftsmen's Guild Jazz in Pittsburgh, from April 14–17, 2005, and the sixteen selections include music of Oliver Nelson, Quincy Jones, Woody Herman, Benny Carter, J. J. Johnson, Dizzy Gillespie, Mary Lou Williams, and others.[37] The two CDs included performances conducted by either Baker or Schuller; the DVD features only Baker conducting the SJMO. In the latter, Baker introduces each track with a bit of history and context, just as he typically does in live performance.

An ensemble as robust as the SJMO takes enormous behind-the-scenes work. After Congress provided the startup funding, the Museum tapped me to oversee it as executive director. During the early years, my principal assistants were Dottie Green and Jonathan Yardley. In 1994 and 1995, respectively, Ken Kimery and James Zimmerman were hired and paid their dues as the band stepped up its touring. Kimery soon learned that David's "fanbase was really large. People would out of the blue come up to him and acknowledge his reach – they were fans of his or were musicians themselves."[38] Kimery continues, "Touring with David is always great. . . . He's one of the guys. He comes from being a performing musician and he's never lost that. So when you're on the bandstand with him or traveling with him, he's one of the guys. Puns and all, he's one of the guys."[39]

In 1992, the SJMO started touring with concerts in Charleston, South Carolina, the Ravinia Festival, and the Festival at Sandpoint. A notable performance took place on October 15, 1993, at Harlem's famed Apollo Theater, once a pivotal venue for big bands. That day, the Smithsonian's traveling exhibition "Beyond Category: The Musical Genius of Duke Ellington" opened at the Museum of the City of New York.[40] Under Baker's leadership, the SJMO performed an all-Ellington program in celebration of the composer and bandleader. As "Beyond Category" toured to ten cities altogether, the SJMO performed in a number of them: Dallas, Chicago, Los Angeles, Kansas City, and Atlanta. The Atlanta appearance on August 2, 1996, at the 1996 Olympic Games was the result of the only official invitation of the Cultural Olympiad to a jazz ensemble (besides Wynton Marsalis's small ensemble). The audience response at Atlanta's Symphony Hall was ecstatic.

As the centennial of Duke Ellington's birth approached in 1999, programs to celebrate his legacy were prepared throughout the country and around the world. As an orchestra that was conceived as a means of bringing Ellington's music alive, and whose home base housed the world's largest collection of Ellington music, the SJMO took a leadership role in recognizing the centennial. On February 5, 1999, the orchestra performed at the Kennedy Center a "Duke Ellington One-hundredth Birthday Celebration," with an all-star lineup of guest artists: trumpeter Clark Terry and drummer Louie Bellson, both alumni of the Duke Ellington Orchestra, saxophonist/flutist Frank Wess, and singers Dianne Reeves and Kevin Mahogany. In addition, the Billy Taylor Trio was on the bill.

On Ellington's actual one hundredth birthday, April 29, 1999, David conducted the band in a performance of selections from the Ellington's Sacred Concerts at the Washington National Cathedral, the nation's second-largest such building, perched on the highest ground in the city. The SJMO was joined by two singers who had actually sung the Sacred Concerts with Ellington – Queen Esther Marrow and DeVonne Gardner – as well as Kevin Mahogany. The fresh-faced Morgan State University Choir sang the choral parts, and eighteen-year-old tap-dance sensation Noble Potts contributed his visually arresting, percussive footfalls. Here were all the makings of a memorable night: the nation's jazz orchestra, performing in the National Cathedral a couple of miles from Ellington's birthplace, in the nation's capital, on the centennial of one of the nation's greatest creative artists, performing his sacred music before a huge stained-glass rose window and arches and flying buttresses reaching up towards heaven. For me it was a thrilling and highly moving performance, and although I sat in the second row, through much of the concert I could not see because tears of profound emotion were filling my eyes. I was reminded of what a young girl told Ellington after hearing one of his Sacred Concerts: "You know, Duke, you made me put my cross back on!"[41]

Smithsonian Jazz Masterworks Orchestra performance of Duke
Ellington's Sacred Concerts at the Washington National Cathedral
with the Morgan State University Choir, April 29, 1999. *Photo by Hugh
Talman, courtesy of the Smithsonian Jazz Masterworks Orchestra.*

During summer 1999, the band undertook an ambitious international tour, performing an all-Ellington program across Canada and
Europe, and as far as Istanbul. "The Cotton Club Revue" included vintage film clips and photographs, dancing, and instrumental pieces by the
SJMO, creating a multidimensional experience for the audiences. The
revue played major festivals such as the North Sea Jazz Festival (Hol-
land), San Sebastián (Spain), Pori (Finland), Antibes (France), and at
concert halls such as the Barbicon Theater, London.[42] The dances were
choreographed by Chester Whitmore. The band members joined local
musicians in jam sessions in Istanbul and Amsterdam.

Who were and are the musicians of the SJMO? When it comes to
staffing the orchestra itself, the Museum makes the selections, relying
on the recommendation of the musical director(s). In the band's early
years, maestros Baker and Schuller made recommendations of musicians they knew and trusted. Several colleagues and former students

Smithsonian Jazz Masterworks Orchestra, with dancer Chester Whitmore.
Courtesy of the Smithsonian Jazz Masterworks Orchestra.

of Baker's were chosen – among them Larry Wiseman, Brent Wallarab, Shannon LeClaire (formerly Hudgins), and Randy Salman, all from Indiana. Other musicians (table 5) had played with famous big bands; for example, trumpeter Joe Wilder brought a wealth of experience from his years with the big bands of Jimmie Lunceford, Count Basie, and Benny Goodman. These players provided a direct link to the traditions of some of the greatest big bands and passed along their knowledge to other members of the SJMO.

In the band's early years, there were still active musicians who had played with the great big bands – Jimmie Lunceford, Count Basie, Duke Ellington, Woody Herman, and others – and the SJMO had the privilege of employing a number of them (see table 5). These players brought road-vetted "chops," stylistic insights, and deep-in-the-tradition knowledge that enriched the band's performances and created a direct connection with the original bands whose music the SJMO performed. Over the years, as some of the older players retired or rotated out, they passed along some of that knowledge to younger players who rotated into the band.

In addition to the SJMO regulars, the band has worked with a distinguished group of guest soloists: trumpeter/flugelhornist Clark Terry, drummer Louie Bellson, pianist Geri Allen, saxophonist/flutist James Moody, saxophonist Frank Foster, and trumpeter Randy Sandke. The SJMO had the privilege of employing veterans of the Ellington, Basie, and other bands. Noted musicians such as trumpeter Byron Stripling and pianists Dick Hyman and James Williams have performed with the band.

Over the years, the orchestra turned increasingly to musicians living in and around Washington, D.C., which is the home to a bevy of extremely talented players, many of whom play or formerly played with one of the US military bands, such as the US Army Blues, the Navy Commodores, and the Airmen of Note (see table 6). These bands are known for selecting only top-notch players with superb sight-reading and musical skills. The SJMO now comprises a pool of gifted musicians, mostly from around Washington, D.C., whom David and Executive Producer Ken Kimery can draw upon, depending on the specific requirements of the repertory. Kimery, whose first training was as a percussionist, took over the drum chair in 2005, ably powering the rhythm section and keeping the band swinging.

In July 2002, David conducted two concerts of the music of his one-time employer and longtime friend Quincy Jones. Jones was seated in the audience both nights, beaming. At one point, David invited Jones to take the stage and guest conduct three numbers. Jones became so animated conducting this superb ensemble that he, even at age sixty-nine, jumped six inches in the air, mid-tune, twice. The musicians and the audience responded with great enthusiasm to his passion.

In 1999, after a decade of working on this ensemble, I decided to turn my energies to other curatorial responsibilities, and Ken Kimery took

TABLE 3. SJMO CONCERT HISTORY: WASHINGTON, D.C., 1991–2010

DATE	CONDUCTOR	PROGRAM THEME	VENUE[1]
May 17–18, 1991	David Baker	Music of Duke Ellington, Jimmie Lunceford, Count Basie, Benny Goodman, Duke Ellington, and Bennie Moten	Carmichael Auditorium
June 29–30, 1991	Gunther Schuller	Music of Duke Ellington, Dizzy Gillespie, and Woody Herman	Carmichael Auditorium
July 20–21, 1991	David Baker	A Tribute to Sy Oliver, the Arranger for the Jimmie Lunceford and Tommy Dorsey Orchestras	Carmichael Auditorium
August 3–4, 1991	David Baker	The Music of Chick Webb, Duke Ellington, and Count Basie	Carmichael Auditorium
August 30–31, 1991	David Baker	A Retrospective of the Inaugural Season, Chick Webb, Jimmie Lunceford, Tommy Dorsey, Count Basie, Benny Goodman, Duke Ellington, Woody Herman, and Dizzy Gillespie	Carmichael Auditorium
October 8, 1991	Gunther Schuller	A Concert for Congress: The music of Benny Goodman, Duke Ellington, Woody Herman, and Dizzy Gillespie	Carmichael Auditorium
October 8, 1991	David Baker	A Concert for Congress: The music of Chick Webb, Jimmie Lunceford, Tommy Dorsey, and Count Basie	Carmichael Auditorium
May 22–23, 1992	David Baker	Stompin' at the Smithsonian: The music of Duke Ellington, Count Basie, Glenn Miller, Jimmie Lunceford, Tommy Dorsey, Chick Webb, Artie Shaw, Charlie Barnet, Dizzy Gillespie, Woody Herman, and Benny Goodman	Andrew W. Mellon Auditorium
June 20–21, 1992	Gunther Schuller	Music of Duke Ellington, Artie Shaw, and Benny Goodman	Marian and Gustave Ring Auditorium
July 18–19, 1992	David Baker	The Gillespie Connection: Music of Dizzy Gillespie, Earl "Fatha" Hines, Cab Calloway, and Billy Eckstine	Marian and Gustave Ring Auditorium

July 25–26, 1992	David Baker	Music of Fletcher Henderson, Benny Carter, Erskine Hawkins, and Glenn Miller	Baird Auditorium
August 8–9, 1992	Gunther Schuller	Music of Benny Goodman, Artie Shaw, Lionel Hampton, the John Kirby Sextet, and Duke Ellington	Carmichael Auditorium
August 29–30, 1992	Gunther Schuller	Music of Duke Ellington, Count Basie, Charlie Barnet, McKinney's Cotton Pickers, and Horace Henderson	Carmichael Auditorium
May 7–8, 1993	David Baker	A Tribute to Duke Ellington and Billy Strayhorn	Carmichael Auditorium
May 8–9, 1993	David Baker	The Music of Billy Strayhorn, Duke Ellington, Tommy Dorsey, Artie Shaw, Benny Goodman, Woody Herman, Chick Webb, Count Basie, Charlie Barnet, Jimmie Lunceford, and Glenn Miller	Carmichael Auditorium
June 12–13, 1993	David Baker	Music of Duke Ellington, Artie Shaw, and Count Basie	Carmichael Auditorium
July 3–4, 1993	Gunther Schuller	Music of Duke Ellington, Don Redman, Lionel Hampton, and Earl Hines	Carmichael Auditorium
July 31 and August 1, 1993	David Baker	Music of Duke Ellington and Dizzy Gillespie	Carmichael Auditorium
August 28–29, 1993	Gunther Schuller	Music of Duke Ellington, Tommy Dorsey, Harry James, and Hal McIntyre	Carmichael Auditorium
May 7–8, 1994	David Baker and Gunther Schuller	Music of the Erskine Hawkins, Artie Shaw, Earl Hines, Chick Webb, Benny Carter, Tommy Dorsey, Duke Ellington, and Benny Goodman Orchestra	Carmichael Auditorium
June 18–19, 1994	David Baker	Territory Bands "Plus": Bennie Moten, Andy Kirk, Teddy Hill, Harlan Leonard, Claude Hopkins, Casa Loma, Lloyd Hunter, Jimmie Lunceford, James P. Johnson, and Mary Lou Williams	Carmichael Auditorium
June 24–25, 1994	Gunther Schuller	Music of Artie Shaw, Claude Thornhill, and Stan Kenton	Baird Auditorium

TABLE 3. *continued*

DATE	CONDUCTOR	PROGRAM THEME	VENUE[1]
July 30–31, 1994	David Baker	Music of Stan Kenton and Duke Ellington	Baird Auditorium
September 17–18, 1994	David Baker	Music of Chick Webb, Cab Calloway, Duke Ellington, and Jimmie Lunceford	National Theatre
April 29–30, 1995	David Baker	Go Harlem: A Tribute to Mary Lou Williams, Chick Webb, and Duke Ellington	National Theatre
May 20–21, 1995	David Baker	The Big Band in Transition: From Swing to Bebop – The music of Chubby Jackson, Dizzy Gillespie, Woody Herman, Billy Eckstine, Eliot Lawrence, Boyd Raeburn, Claude Thornhill, and Lionel Hampton	National Theatre
June 24–25, 1995	Gunther Schuller	Miles Davis, Birth of the Cool, and More	Lincoln Theatre
August 12–13, 1995	David Baker	A Salute to Sy Oliver and the Orchestras of Jimmie Lunceford and Tommy Dorsey	Lincoln Theatre
June 22–23, 1996	David Baker	The Spanish Tinge: The music of Woody Herman, Duke Ellington, Stan Kenton, Miles Davis, Billy Verplanck, and Dizzy Gillespie	Lisner Auditorium
July 27–28, 1996	David Baker	Strayhorn Discoveries, Ellington Evergreens, and Armstrong Rarities	Lincoln Theatre
September 21–22, 1996	David Baker	The Big Band Renaissance: Big Band Jazz from the '40s to the '90s – the music of Count Basie, Woody Herman, Harry James, Maynard Ferguson, Herb Pomeroy, Dizzy Gillespie, Thad Jones, Duke Pearson, John Dankworth, and Miles Davis	The Duke Ellington School of the Arts
October 5–6 1996	David Baker	Miles Davis, Gil Evans, J. J. Johnson, and Michel Legrand	Lincoln Theatre
July 19–20, 1997	David Baker	Celebrating Benny Carter on His Ninetieth	Lincoln Theatre

Date		Event	Venue
August 16–17, 1997	David Baker	Blues and the Abstract Truth: The Music of Oliver Nelson, featuring guest artist Oliver Nelson, Jr.	Lincoln Theatre
September 13–14, 1997	David Baker	Monk's Mood and Early Autumn: The Music of Thelonious Monk and Woody Herman	Lisner Auditorium
November 15, 1997	David Baker	The Sounds of Color: Concert for the Jerome and Dorothy Lemelson Center for the Study of Invention and Innovation	Lisner Auditorium
July 18–19, 1998	David Baker	Windows and Mirrors: African American and Jewish American Connections in Jazz – the music of Count Basie, Duke Ellington, Benny Goodman and Artie Shaw	Lincoln Theatre
August 15–16, 1998	David Baker	Duke Ellington: Suite Sixteen Plus Six	Lisner Auditorium
September 26–27, 1998	David Baker	Count Basie and the Music of Neal Hefti featuring guest artist Frank Foster	Lincoln Theatre
February 5, 1999	David Baker	Duke Ellington One-Hundredth-Birthday Celebration featuring guest artists: Clark Terry, Frank Wess, Louie Bellson, Billy Taylor Trio, Dianne Reeves, and Kevin Mahogany	Kennedy Center
April 29, 1999	David Baker	Duke Ellington: Hallelujah! A Sacred Concert	Washington National Cathedral
January 28–29, 2000	David Baker	Bebop in the New Millennium featuring guest artist James Moody	Kennedy Center
May 7–8, 2000	David Baker	The Musical World of Mary Lou Williams featuring guest artist Geri Allen	Kennedy Center
March 9–10, 2001	David Baker	The Legacy of Louis Armstrong featuring guest artists Miles Griffith, Delores King Williams, and Randy Sandke	Lincoln Theatre
July 20–21, 2001	David Baker	The Big Band Magic of Quincy Jones: Composer, Arranger and Bandleader featuring Quincy Jones as guest conductor	Lincoln Theatre

TABLE 3. *continued*

DATE	CONDUCTOR	PROGRAM THEME	VENUE[1]
April 25–27, 2002	David Baker	A Tribute to Ella Fitzgerald	Coolidge Auditorium, Lincoln Theater, Carmichael Auditorium
July 26–27, 2002	David Baker	The Music of Bill Holman and Bill Russo	Carmichael Auditorium, Lincoln Theater
February 7–8, 2003	Charlie Young	Portrait of Julian "Cannonball" Adderley	Carmichael Auditorium
March 7, 2003	Scott Silbert	Jeni LeGon: Tappin' at the Smithsonian	Carmichael Auditorium
April 5, 2003	David Baker	The Treasures of Benny Carter	Carmichael Auditorium
April 18–19, 2003	Randy Sandke	Celebrating Bix Beiderbecke on His Centennial	Carmichael Auditorium
July 18, 2003	Charlie Young	Keter Betts 75th Birthday Celebration	Carmichael Auditorium
April 2–3, 2004	David Baker	A Tribute to Benny Carter: Music from the Archives	Carmichael Auditorium
May 29, 2004	David Baker	A Salute to the Big Bands of the WWII Era	Flag Hall, National Museum of American History
April 23, 2005	Loren Schoenberg	Big Band JAM	Carmichael Auditorium
June 19, 2005	David Baker	The Big Band Renaissance: From Harlem to Hollywood	Baird Auditorium
October 29, 2005	Loren Schoenberg	From Harlem to Hollywood: Duke Ellington	Carmichael Auditorium
November 3, 2005	Chuck Redd	The Music of the Modern Jazz Quartet and Milt Jackson	Baird Auditorium
November 15, 2005	David Baker	Concert for Smithsonian Contributing Members	Baird Auditorium
February 26, 2006	Charlie Young	From Harlem to Hollywood: Benny Carter	Carmichael Auditorium
April 2, 2006	Loren Schoenberg	From Harlem to Hollywood: Ella Fitzgerald	Carmichael Auditorium

Date	Name	Title	Venue
August 16, 2006	David Baker	Big Band Works of Quincy of Jones	Baird Auditorium
February 24, 2007	David Baker	Benny Carter Centennial Celebration	Baird Auditorium
April 1, 2007	Anthony Brown	A Salute to Art Blakey and the Jazz Messengers	Baird Auditorium
April 28, 2007	David Baker	Big Band Jam: Mixed Bag of Repertoire	Voice of America Auditorium
May 20, 2007	David Baker	Such Sweet Thunder	Concert Hall, John F. Kennedy Center
September 15, 2007	David Baker	Duke Ellington Jazz Festival	Lincoln Theater
February 8, 2008	David Baker	The Big Band Renaissance: Big Band from the '40s to the '90s	Baird Auditorium
April 7, 2008	Scott Silbert	The Music of Johnny Hodges and his Small Ensemble	Voice of America Auditorium
April 7, 2008	Scott Silbert	The Music of Johnny Hodges and His Small Ensemble	Childers Recital Hall, Howard University
April 26, 2008	David Baker	Big Band JAM: Willis Conover Memorial Concert with a Tribute to Quincy Jones	Voice of America Auditorium
December 13, 2008	David Baker	Swingin' in the Holidays	Voice of America Auditorium
January 18, 2009	Charlie Young	The Smithsonian Jazz Masterworks Quartet	Rasmuson Theater
February 21, 2009	David Baker	The New Jazz Standards	Baird Auditorium
April 4, 2009	Charlie Young	Revisiting Miles Davis's *Kind of Blue* and His Modal Period	Baird Auditorium
April 6, 2009	Charlie Young	50th Anniversary of Miles Davis's *Kind of Blue*	Childers Recital Hall, Howard University
July 9, 2009	David Baker	World Copyright Conference	Mellon Auditorium, Washington, DC

TABLE 3. continued

DATE	CONDUCTOR	PROGRAM THEME	VENUE[1]
September 18, 2009	Charlie Young	Harlem Renaissance Festival	Lincoln Theater
October 24, 2009	Charlie Young	Portrait of Julian "Cannonball" Adderley and the Riverside Years	Baird Auditorium
December 4, 2009	David Baker	Swingin' in the Holidays	Baird Auditorium
April 8, 2010	Tom Williams	*Hub-Tones*: The Life of Freddie Hubbard	Childers Recital Hall, Howard University
April 10, 2010	Tom Williams	*Hub-Tones*: The Life of Freddie Hubbard	Baird Auditorium
April 27, 2010	Scott Silbert	Big Band JAM: 3rd Annual Ella Fitzgerald Birthday Tribute, featuring Delores King-Williams and Afro Blue	Sylvan Theater
May 16, 2010	David Baker	You Heard It First at the Apollo: A Mid-century Sampler	Baird Auditorium
July 23, 2010	David Baker	The Lady Who Swings the Band: Mary Lou Williams Centennial Celebration	Baird Auditorium
September 16, 2010	David Baker	Congressional Black Caucus Foundation Jazz Concert	Washington Convention Center
October 23, 2010	Scott Silbert	Artie Shaw and His Gramercy Five	Rasmuson Theater
December 4, 2010	David Baker	Holiday Concert	Epiphany Church
February 12, 2011	David Baker	Big Band Revival	Baird Auditorium

Note:

1. Carmichael Auditorium is in the Smithsonian's National Museum of American History. The Ring Auditorium is in the Smithsonian's Hirshhorn Museum. Baird Auditorium is in the Smithsonian's National Museum of Natural History. The Rasmuson Theater is in the Smithsonian's National Museum of the American Indian. Other auditoria listed here are not part of the Smithsonian.

over the position of producer; James Zimmerman became executive producer. By 2005, the SJMO came under the sole management of the ever-
capable, kinetic Ken Kimery. Under Kimery's management, the band
has consolidated its roster of top-flight musicians from the Washington,
D.C., area; solidified its relationships with other parts of the Smithsonian; built new collaborations with presenters such as Pittsburgh's MCG
Jazz and broadcasters such as the Voice of America; collaborated on a
DVD of the band; reinvigorated its domestic touring; and begun working
with the US State Department on foreign tours.

Of the band's many tours, one unquestionable highlight was its
week-long tour to Egypt in February 2008.[43] The tour came together
with funding from the US State Department and with corporate spon-
sorship raised by Egyptian impresario Ibrahim Hegazy and the Cairo
Opera House.

This was neither the first American jazz band to perform in Egypt nor
the first State Department–sponsored jazz tour there. In January 1961,
Louis Armstrong performed at an orphanage in Cairo. A now-famous
photo shows him blowing his trumpet up the face of the Sphinx. Other
visiting American jazz artists have included Sun Ra, Dizzy Gillespie,
and Herbie Hancock. But this was evidently the first State Department
tour to Egypt by an American big band and the first time American jazz
dancers had toured with a jazz band.

The band consisted of artistic and musical director David Baker;
trumpeters Tom Williams, Joey Tartell, Brian McDonald, and Lenny
Foy; trombonists Sam Burtis, Brent Wallarab, John Jensen, and Rich
Dole; saxophonists Scott Silbert, Antonio Parker, Charlie Young, Randy
Salman, and Leigh Pilzer; bassist James King; pianist Harry Appelman;
and drummer and SJMO executive producer Ken Kimery. Singer Delores
King Williams and dancers Chester Whitmore and Shaunte Johnson
rounded out the ensemble. Collectively, the members possessed hundreds of years' experience performing with everyone from Stan Kenton
to Tito Puente. I went along as the SJMO's founder and as a lecturer on
Louis Armstrong.

The tour was under the honorary patronage of Suzanne Mubarak,
wife of the then–prime minister, and received red-carpet treatment. We
were escorted everywhere by two to four armed security men – two on

the band bus, and two in a car traveling behind the bus. The Egyptian government wanted to ensure that nothing bad happened to our rather visible delegation, and nothing did.

The day after our arrival, the band made its Egyptian debut, auspiciously, in front of the Sphinx and the Great Pyramids of Giza. For many in the entourage, this was unquestionably the high point of the tour. David says, "If I had dreamed to lead a band at the Pyramids and in front of the Sphinx, I would not have expected the dream to come true."

At the beginning of the performance, before the sound mix was adjusted, the trumpets could barely be heard. Trumpeter Joey Tartell complained to fellow trumpet man Brian McDonald, who replied, "Joey, the Sphinx. The *Sphinx*!" Performing almost in the shadow of this great figure put everything into perspective. The sound mix was not the only challenge: wind gusts kept whipping across the desert, repeatedly sending music from maestro Baker's stand skittering across the stage. With typical humor, David told the audience, "Wind 12, band 0."

The band launched into Ellington's "Rockin' in Rhythm," first heard in 1931, and made it sound fresh and compelling all over again. On "Satin Doll" and "Take the 'A' Train," dancers Whitmore and Johnson came onstage in colorful period costume and wowed the audience. During Basie's "Jumpin' at the Woodside," the irrepressible Whitmore jumped off the stage and grabbed several female members of the audience and whirled them around. The performance was met with sustained applause and two standing ovations. Afterwards, Egyptian teenagers thronged the stage, seeking autographs and photos with the performers.[44]

The news media turned out in full force to cover this historic concert, including about thirty radio, TV, newspaper and magazine reporters. The concert was covered by *Al-Ahram*, Egypt's leading daily newspaper, wire services Reuters and the Middle East News Agency, Nile TV, Channel 1 and Channel 2. The *Daily News* ran a lengthy story and color photos. "The backdrop was incredible," it wrote. "The band was superb."[45] Even the Arabic satellite station *Al Jazeera*, which has often angered Western governments for its coverage of al-Qaeda, gave the concert favorable coverage, footage which it repeated for several days. Via television, the band reached millions of people in the Middle East. The tour was already

Smithsonian Jazz Masterworks Orchestra in front of the pyramids.
Courtesy of the Smithsonian Jazz Masterworks Orchestra.

turning into a public relations bonanza for the band, the Smithsonian, and the United States, exceeding all expectations.

If there was a theme for this tour, it demonstrated, said tour guest Joe Lamond, President and CEO of National Association of Music Merchants (NAMM), "once again the incredible power of music to break down every conceivable barrier." American jazz showed that it can communicate, move, and inspire people beyond all divides of race, nationality, religion, language, and age. As tour impresario Hegazy put it, "We all spoke the same language – the language of music and joy."[46]

At the American University in Cairo, maestro Baker led a workshop for young Egyptian musicians. Aided by trumpeters Tartell and Foy, and the SJMO rhythm section, David gave pointers to a series of twenty-something pianists, singers, and saxophonists brave enough to perform for this illustrious musician, a watchful audience, and TV cameras. (The band was followed everywhere it went by one or two documentary crews.) Kimery demonstrated cymbal technique and snare technique to a novice drummer. Each apprentice seemed grateful for the rare opportunity to receive instruction from these American masters.

This six-person team then went to the Cairo Opera House to conduct a master class with a big band – one of the very few in Egypt – led by trumpeter Magdy Boghdady. The Boghdady jazz band read through some American charts – "April in Paris," "In the Mood," and others. Under David's nimble and assured guidance, these players' renditions improved markedly, sounding much more rhythmic and idiomatic.

At the largest hall of the Cairo Opera House, the SJMO performed two concerts in honor of the hall's twentieth anniversary, the first a matinee for eight hundred disadvantaged and orphaned children. They reacted with fervor to the performances, with calls and shrieks of delight. The evening concert drew a well-dressed audience, which responded very positively to the music and to the Lindy Hop and other sensual dancing. The repertory included the Ellington-Strayhorn "Isfahan," Gillespie's "Manteca," the Basie band's "'Deed I Do" and "Tickle Toe," and Quincy Jones's crowd-pleasing "Soul Bossa Nova." When Louis Armstrong's name was announced from the stage, a cheer went up from the audience. Under the headline "Reaching Sublime Heights," *Al-Ahram,* Egypt's leading daily, wrote,

> The Smithsonian Jazz Masterworks Orchestra's recent Egyptian concerts made a delicious musical cocktail, imaginatively conceived, brilliantly performed, and very exciting. . . . The concert presented by the Smithsonian Jazz Masterworks Orchestra must have been one of the most ravishing jazz concerts ever presented at the Opera . . . a pure jazz experience, a meeting of spontaneity and virtuosity.[47]

The final public performance was a concert at the stunning Opera House in the ancient Mediterranean port of Alexandria. Again, an enthusiastic audience extended a standing ovation.

What did we accomplish with this tour? We brought the power of American music, rooted deeply in American history, to new audiences; projected a very positive image of our country and its creativity, diversity, history, and culture, at a time when the United States urgently needs a better image abroad and especially in the Middle East; helped student and professional musicians better understand the American art form of jazz; touched the hearts and minds of thousands of people; generated extensive and very positive press coverage in the Arab world; and won many new friends across the divide of culture, religion, and language. "The concerts and outreach events," said Helen Lovejoy, US cultural attaché in Egypt, "powerfully promoted shared values and cultural exchange between Egypt and the US, leading to calls for a return tour and bringing a message of hope and joy through the unique American musical form of jazz to millions throughout the Middle East via extensive media coverage." The tour struck many as a triumph – for the music, the band, the Smithsonian, and for the United States.[48] We all felt good about engaging in cultural diplomacy, as did Louis Armstrong back in 1961, when he played in Cairo.

Looking back at their experiences working with David over the years as conductor and musical director, Kimery and Silbert offer praise and insight. In recalling touring with David, Kimery offers observations on David's gift for communication, commitment, and inclusion:

> We were all one family and there was a bond. And even though, in all families you have a little undercurrent or challenges of the moment, there's always a way to pull together. So the communication is really good. And that speaks to who David is. That's why David's family is so extended. Because he is so much committed to who you are and committed to paying attention and getting to know about you and learn about you and bring you into his life.... David is very much a team player, giving everyone ownership. His sense of generosity prompts the musicians to respond wonderfully. He rehearses you, but he expects you to have a voice and to be part of the conversation. It's not just "This is the way it is, and that's it." He wants feedback, he wants investment. I've been in many bands; especially in a large ensemble, the more people you put in a setting, the more it can become like a dictatorship. David was always able to balance it, to guide you down the path but also allow you to be part of the discussion.[49]

Saxophonist Scott Silbert comments on the mentoring and contagious passion that characterizes Baker:

> David Baker is by far the greatest jazz musician/educator that I have ever had the pleasure to have worked with. He has all of the attributes of a great teacher. He has lived the history by working with and knowing many of the giants of jazz. He is extremely passionate about teaching and sharing his boundless knowledge. David loves what he does and it shows. One of my fondest memories is watching David run a jazz improvisation clinic for a band in Omaha. The band, which easily numbered close to 100 high school kids, was on the school auditorium stage, and within minutes David had not only showed them some of the basic tenets of jazz, but he had them playing through the blues! And this went on for close to an hour. It was an amazing display of David's passion for sharing his love and

TABLE 4. SJMO CONCERT TOURING

DATE	CONDUCTOR	LOCATION	OCCASION/THEME
April 4, 1992	Gunther Schuller	Charleston, S.C.	For the Smithsonian Associates National Board
June 12, 1992	Gunther Schuller	Ravinia Festival	
July 31, 1992	Gunther Schuller	The Festival at Sandpoint, Idaho	
February 10, 1993	David Baker	The Supper Club, New York	For *Smithsonian* magazine
October 15, 1993	David Baker	Apollo Theater, New York	In conjunction with the opening of the Smithsonian's *Beyond Category* touring exhibition on Ellington
September 20, 1994	Gunther Schuller	Topeka Performing Arts Center, Topeka, Kans.	Community Concerts Association
September 22, 1994	Gunther Schuller	Coronado Theater, Rockford, Ill.	As above
October 7, 1994	Gunther Schuller	Miller Theater, New York	As above
October 17, 1994	Gunther Schuller	Portland Civic Auditorium, Portland, Ore.	As above
October 19, 1994	Gunther Schuller	Capitol Theater, Yakima, Wash.	As above
November 7, 1994	David Baker	Thomas Wolfe Auditorium, Asheville, N.C.	As above
November 8, 1994	David Baker	Blumenthal Performing Arts Center, Charlotte, N.C.	As above
November 9, 1994	David Baker	High Point Theatre, High Point, N.C.	As above
January 24, 1995	David Baker	Gammage Auditorium, Arizona State University, Tempe, Ariz.	As above
January 25, 1995	David Baker	Sundome, Sun City, Ariz.	As above

Date	Performer	Venue	Event
January 28, 1995	David Baker	South Bay Center for the Performing Arts, El Camino, Calif.	As above
January 30, 1995	David Baker	Bayfront Plaza Auditorium, Corpus Christi, Tex.	As above
February 3, 1995	David Baker	McCain Auditorium, Manhattan, Kans.	As above
February 4, 1995	David Baker	Hancher Auditorium, Iowa City, Iowa	As above
February 8, 1996	David Baker	California Plaza, Los Angeles	America's Smithsonian, 150th anniversary exhibition
February 8, 1996	David Baker	Los Angeles Convention Center, Los Angeles	America's Smithsonian, 150th anniversary exhibition
February 11, 1996	David Baker	DuSable Museum, Chicago	Duke Ellington *Beyond Category* exhibition
April 9, 1996	David Baker	H. Roe Bartle Convention Center, Kansas City, Mo.	America's Smithsonian 150th Anniversary Gala
April 10, 1996	David Baker	Bakersfield Convention Center, Bakersfield, Calif.	Community Concerts Association
April 11, 1996	David Baker	Richland High School, Richland, Wash.	As above
April 12, 1996	David Baker	Paramount Theater, Denver Colo.	As above
April 13, 1996	David Baker	Folly Theater, Kansas City, Mo.	Duke Ellington *Beyond Category* exhibition
April 14, 1996	Bobby Watson	Centennial United Methodist Church, Kansas City, Mo.	Jazz in the Sanctuary
June 10, 1996	David Baker	New York Coliseum, New York	America's Smithsonian 150th Anniversary Gala
August 2, 1996	David Baker	Atlanta Symphony Hall, Atlanta, Ga.	Cultural Olympiad

TABLE 4. *continued*

DATE	CONDUCTOR	LOCATION	OCCASION/THEME
August 20, 1996	David Baker	Rhode Island Convention Center, Providence, R.I.	America's Smithsonian 150th Anniversary Gala, featuring the SJMO Quintet
August 21, 1996	Loren Schoenberg	Waterfront Jazz Festival, Providence, R.I.	Jazz Festival; SJMO Quintet
October 15, 1996	David Baker	St. Paul Convention Center, St. Paul, Minn.	America's Smithsonian 150th Anniversary Gala; SJMO Quintet
December 5, 1996	David Baker	George R. Brown Convention Center, Houston, Tex.	America's Smithsonian 150th Anniversary Gala
December 7, 1996	David Baker	Caruth Auditorium, Dallas, Tex.	Duke Ellington *Beyond Category* exhibition
March 25–26, 1997	David Baker	Sarasota Jazz Festival, Sarasota, Fla.	
April 2, 1997	Ken Kimery	Portland Exposition Center, Portland, Ore.	America's Smithsonian, 150th anniversary exhibition
September 27, 1997	David Baker	Center for the Arts, Midland, Mich.	Community Concerts Association
September 28, 1997	David Baker	Frauenthal Center, Muskegon, Mich.	As above
September 30, 1997	David Baker	Paramount Theater, Cedar Rapids, Iowa	As above
October 25, 1997	David Baker	Municipal Auditorium, Charleston, W.Va.	As above
November 21, 1997	David Baker	Civic Center, Great Falls, Mont.	As above
September 28, 1998	David Baker	Carpenter Center, Richmond, Va.	Count Basie and the Music of Neal Hefti

Date	Performer	Venue	Description
September 30–October 2, 1998	David Baker	Terrace Theater, Long Beach Convention Center, Long Beach, Calif.	Public Corporation for the Arts: Three-day residency educational program, Big Band Explosion!
January 26–27, 1999	David Baker	Center for the Arts, Scottsdale, Ariz.	Duke Ellington: 100th Birthday Celebration
January 30, 1999	David Baker	California Center for the Arts, Escondido, Calif.	Best of repertoire
February 28, 1999	David Baker	Philharmonic Center, Naples, Fla.	A Centennial Tribute to Duke Ellington
March 1, 1999	David Baker	Homestead, Fla.	Community Concert Association
March 13, 1999	David Baker	Lansdale, Pa.	Community Concerts Association
April 3, 1999	Loren Schoenberg	Hering Auditorium, Fairbanks, Alaska	Fairbanks Concert Association, A Centennial Tribute to Duke Ellington
April 4, 1999	Loren Schoenberg	Evangeline Atwood Concert Hall, Anchorage, Alaska	Anchorage Concert Association, A Centennial Tribute to Duke Ellington
April 7, 1999	David Baker	University of Tennessee, Knoxville	
April 8, 1999	David Baker	Oscar Mayer Theatre, Madison Civic Center, Madison, Wisc.	Duke Ellington: A Centennial Tribute
April 9, 1999	David Baker	Sangamon Auditorium, University of Illinois, Springfield	As above
April 10, 1999	David Baker	Millikin University, Decatur, Ill.	As above
April 11, 1999	David Baker	College of DuPage, Chicago	As above

TABLE 4. *continued*

DATE	CONDUCTOR	LOCATION	OCCASION/THEME
April 16, 1999	David Baker	Wharton Center for the Performing Arts, Michigan State University, East Lansing, Mich.	As above
April 17, 1999	David Baker	Madame Walker Theatre Center, Indianapolis, Ind.	As above
April 18, 1999	David Baker	Macomb Center, Detroit, Mich.	As above
April 20, 1999	David Baker	Luther College, Decorah, Iowa	As above
April 21, 1999	Loren Schoenberg	Viterbo College, Lacrosse, Wisc.	As above
April 23–24, 1999	Loren Schoenberg	Lied Center for Performing Arts, University of Nebraska, Lincoln	As above
July 1, 1999	David Baker	The Jazz Festival Jack Singer Theater, Calgary, Alta.	Cotton Club Revue, an all-Ellington concert
July 2, 1999	David Baker	Orpheum Theater, du Maurier International Jazz Festival, Vancouver B.C.	As above
July 3, 1999	David Baker	Centennial Theatre, Saskatoon, Sask.	As above
July 9, 1999	David Baker	Cultural Theater, Istanbul, Turkey	As above
July 10, 1999	David Baker	North Sea Jazz Festival, The Hague, Netherlands	As above
July 11, 1999	David Baker	Cotton Club Revue, Théâtre Antique, Vienne, France	As above
July 12, 1999	David Baker	Teatro Jovellanos, Gijon, Spain	As above
July 15, 1999	David Baker	Giardini del Frontone, Perugia, Italy	As above
July 17, 1999	David Baker	Jazz Festival, Pori, Finland	As above

July 18, 1999	David Baker	Kirjurinluoto Park, Helsinki	As above
July 19, 1999	David Baker	Jazz aux Remparts, Bayonne, France	As above
July 20, 1999	David Baker	39e Festival International de Jazz, Pinède Gould, Antibes, France	As above
July 24, 1999	David Baker	Barbican Theatre, London, UK	As above
March 25, 2000	David Baker	University of Massachusetts, Amherst	
June 3, 2000	David Baker	Dodd Auditorium, Mary Washington College, Fredericksburg, Va.	
June 17, 2000	David Baker	Indy Jazz Festival, Indianapolis, Ind.	Legends of Indianapolis
September 5–6, 2000	David Baker	Brooks Center Clemson University, Clemson, N.C.	100 Years of Jazz
October 14, 2000	Loren Schoenberg	Stevens Center, Winston-Salem, N.C.	100 Years of Jazz, with guest vocalist Chirs Murrell
January 12–13, 2001	David Baker	IAJE Conference, New York	NEA Jazz Masters
April 20, 2001	David Baker	Eisenhower Auditorium, Pennsylvania State University, University Park	100 Years of Jazz
April 22, 2001	David Baker	Tri-C Jazz Festival, Severance Hall, Cleveland, Ohio	SJMO, featuring Rosemary Clooney
July 7, 2001	David Baker	Farthing Auditorium Appalachian State, Boone, N.C.	100 Years of Jazz
September 15, 2001	Loren Schoenberg	King Hall, State University of New York College at Fredonia	As above
October 17, 2002	David Baker	Free Library of Philadelphia	SJMO and the Philadelphia Connection, featuring Joe Wilder

TABLE 4. *continued*

DATE	CONDUCTOR	LOCATION	OCCASION/THEME
August 5, 2003	David Baker	Musical Arts Center, Indiana University–Bloomington	Big Band Renaissance: Evolution of Jazz Since the Swing Era
October 6, 2003	David Baker	Blumenthal Performing Arts Center, Charlotte, N.C.	As above
October 7, 2003	David Baker	Johnson C. Smith University, Charlotte, N.C.	As above
October 8, 2003	David Baker	Rowe Recital Hall, University of North Carolina, Charlotte	Big Band Renaissance: Evolution of Jazz Since the Swing Era
October 18, 2003	David Baker	Providence, R.I.	
August 14, 2004	David Baker	Musical Arts Center, Indiana University–Bloomington	A Centennial Celebration of Count Basie and His Orchestra
November 13–14, 2004	David Baker	Krannert Center, University of Illinois, Urbana-Champaign	
April 14–17, 2005	David Baker	Manchester Craftsman's Guild, Pittsburgh, Pa.	From Harlem to Hollywood: Big Band Jazz from the 1940s to the Present
June 6, 2005	David Baker	Ravinia Festival, Highland Park, Ill.	As above
August 13, 2005	David Baker	Musical Arts Center, Indiana University–Bloomington	As above
June 10, 2006	David Baker	Clifford Brown Jazz Festival, Wilmington, Del.	
August 12, 2006	David Baker	Musical Arts Center, Indiana University–Bloomington	
November 15–17, 2006	David Baker	Tennessee Performing Arts Center, Nashville	

Date	Performer	Venue	Notes
January 11, 2008	David Baker	IAJE Conference, Toronto	With guest artists NEA Jazz Masters Joe Wilder, Paquito d'Rivera, and Cándido Camero
February 7, 2008	David Baker	Paramount Theater, Charlottesville, Va.	
February 9, 2008	David Baker	Kresge Auditorium, DePauw University, Greencastle, Ind.	Big Band Works of Quincy Jones
February 13–20, 2008	David Baker	Cairo and Alexandria, Egypt	"Jazz on the Nile," with support from the US State Department
July 19, 2008	Scott Silbert	Shenandoah Valley Music Festival, Orkney Springs, Va.	Shenandoah Music Festival Summer Concert Series
April 22, 2009	David Baker	Victory Theatre, University of Evansville, Evansville, Ind.	
April 24, 2009	Charlie Young	George Washington High School Auditorium, Danville, Va.	Danville, Va., Concert Association
July 23, 2009	Scott Silbert	Shenandoah University, Winchester, Va.	For National Jazz Workshop
February 28–29, 2010	David Baker	Manchester's Craftsmen's Guild, Pittsburgh, Pa.	Tribute to Ella Fitzgerald
April 12–14, 2010	Scott Silbert	Durham Museum, Omaha, Nebr.	For Jazz Appreciation Month

TABLE 5. SJMO MUSICIANS WHO PLAYED WITH THE FAMOUS BIG BANDS

MUSICIAN	INSTRUMENT	BIG BAND EXPERIENCE
Art Baron	trombone	Duke Ellington, Illinois Jacquet, Frank Wess
Keter Betts	bass	Woody Herman
Sam Burtis	trombone	Tito Puente
James Chirillo	guitar	Benny Goodman
Jerry Dodgion	saxophone	Benny Goodman, Thad Jones–Mel Lewis, Dizzy Gillespie
Sir Roland Hanna	piano	Thad Jones–Mel Lewis
Dick Johnson	clarinet	Charlie Spivak, Woody Herman, Artie Shaw[1]
Benny Powell	trombone	Lionel Hampton, Count Basie, Thad Jones–Mel Lewis
Rufus Reid	bass	Thad Jones–Mel Lewis
Jerome Richardson	reeds	Gil Evans, Quincy Jones, Thad Jones–Mel Lewis
Chris Royal[2]	trumpet	Duke Ellington
Loren Schoenberg	tenor sax	Benny Goodman, Benny Carter
Joe Temperley	baritone sax	Woody Herman, Duke Ellington,[3] Thad Jones–Mel Lewis
Joe Wilder	trumpet	Les Hite, Lionel Hampton, Jimmie Lunceford, Count Basie
Britt Woodman	trombone	Duke Ellington, Oliver Nelson, Dizzy Gillespie, Toshiko Akiyoshi–Lew Tabackin
Charlie Young	alto sax	Duke Ellington[4]

Notes:
1. Dick Johnson played with and led the Artie Shaw "ghost band."
2. Chris Royal played in the Duke Ellington Orchestra after Ellington's death, under the direction of Ellington's son, Mercer Ellington.
3. Joe Temperley played in the Duke Ellington Orchestra, under the direction of Mercer Ellington.
4. Charlie Young played in the Duke Ellington Orchestra after Ellington's death, under the direction of Mercer Ellington.

TABLE 6. SJMO MUSICIANS WHO HAVE PLAYED WITH US MILITARY BIG BANDS

MUSICIAN	INSTRUMENT	BIG BAND	SERVICE BRANCH
Pete BarenBregge	reeds	Airmen of Note	Air Force
Jim Carroll	saxophone	us Army Band, "Pershing's Own"	Army
Doug Elliott	trombone	Airmen of Note	Air Force
Luis Hernandez	saxophones	Commodores	Navy
Dudley Hinote	trombone	Airmen of Note	Air Force
Bill Holmes	trombone	us Army Blues	Army
Jen Krupa	trombone	Commodores	Navy
Brian MacDonald	trumpet	Airmen of Note	Air Force
Bill Mulligan	saxophones	Commodores	Navy
Tony Nalker	piano	us Army Blues	Army
Matt Niess	trombone	us Army Blues	Army
Daniel Orban, Jr.	trumpet	United States Marine Band	Marines
Kenny Rittenhouse	trumpet	us Army Blues	Army
Scott Silbert	saxophones	United States Navy Band	Navy
Dave Steinmeyer	trombone	Airmen of Note	Air Force
Harold Sumney	drums	United States Army Band	Army
Liesl Whitaker	trumpet	us Army Blues	Army
Dolores King Williams	vocals	United States Army Band	Army
Steve Williams	saxophone	Commodores	Navy
Tom Williams	trumpet	us Army Blues; Jazz Ambassadors	Army
Charlie Young	saxophone	United States Navy Band	Navy

knowledge with all of these kids. And he brings that same passion and love to the stage every time he leads the Smithsonian Jazz Masterworks Orchestra. It is an honor and a privilege to work with *and* learn from David.[50]

In fall 2010, the Smithsonian Jazz Masterworks Orchestra celebrated the twentieth anniversary of its founding. With David playing a key role throughout its two decades, the Orchestra can claim the following accomplishments:

- It has performed more than three hundred concerts in thirty states and in ten countries, and its radio series reached listeners in forty-five states and five countries.
- The sjmo has made the jazz archives "sing," bringing alive dusty old arrangements and breathing new life into them.
- It has methodically built a vast library of more than twelve hundred transcriptions and orchestrations with considerable musical and temporal range.
- The Orchestra has helped train a generation of musicians in the craft and art of playing the classic repertory of jazz with care, authenticity, and appeal.
- The sjmo has projected the Smithsonian and the National Museum of American History to audiences across the nation and, through tours and broadcasts, around the world.
- The band has diversified the Museum's audiences, and brought jazz classics of the past to new young audiences.
- By deploying a jazz orchestra, the Smithsonian has, in effect, again given its coveted cultural seal of approval to classic jazz, and has helped pave the way for the establishment of other jazz "repertory" orchestras.
- Through its comprehensive program booklets, with extensive notes, and through David's customary historically informed spoken introductions of all the pieces he conducts, the sjmo has set a very high standard for educating its audiences.
- Through educational workshops, master classes, and teacher training, the sjmo has broadened participation in playing jazz and the sharpened skills of young performers.

SMITHSONIAN JAZZ ORAL
HISTORY PROGRAM

In 1993, the Smithsonian secured a grant from the Lila Wallace–Reader's Digest Fund to establish a ten-year partnership called America's Jazz Heritage. The grant of $7 million set three new records, becoming the largest grant that the Lila Wallace–Reader's Digest Fund had ever given, the largest grant the Smithsonian had ever received, and the largest grant

J. J. Johnson and David Baker, May 1988, after Johnson received an honorary doctorate from Indiana University. *Courtesy of David Baker.*

ever given for jazz. My roles were to work as one of the three grant writers (along with Betty Teller and Nancy Fischer), and – once the grant was awarded – to serve as co-director along with Betty Teller. A series of traveling exhibitions were the main product, and the funds also helped create educational materials, develop a new website for Smithsonian jazz, and establish the Smithsonian Jazz Oral History Program (SJOHP).[51] I took on the responsibility of establishing the procedures and standards for conducting oral histories: match musicians with interviewers who are steeped in their legacies and who have or can quickly establish rapport with the informants; offer the informants an honorarium for the time they might otherwise be devoting to paying musical engagements or gigs; offer an honorarium to the interviewer for the preparation and interviewing; record the interviews on the highest-quality medium available; and transcribe the interviews if budget allowed. And I created an editorial style sheet for all transcribers to use.

Thus began a program that has, as of 2010, captured the life stories of more than 160 jazz figures. Many of the interviews were conducted by composer-percussionist Anthony Brown, trained in ethnomusicology and a gifted oral historian. Since 2003, the program has been directed by Ken Kimery, who has forged a strong relationship with the National Endowment for the Arts while overseeing a lengthy series of interviews with NEA Jazz Masters as well as with other musical figures.[52] Many of these interviews he also documented on video as well and ensured that the interviews were included on the Smithsonian Jazz website and deposited in the Museum's Archives Center to be available to any researcher. David Baker provided counsel at many points.

David has thrice played a role in the SJOHP. Early on in the life of the program, in February 1994, David and his wife, Lida Baker, conducted a lengthy interview with trombonist J. J. Johnson, a boyhood friend of David's and an inspiration to David and many a trombonist.[53] In June 2000, Baker sat for a lengthy oral history with someone who knows him better than anyone does – his wife, Lida.[54] And in September 2008, Baker carried out an interview with his longtime friend Quincy Jones.[55] Baker values these interviews highly:

That's one of the really important things about the oral history project the Smithsonian's doing: having an opportunity to capture something that you cannot recapture when the person is gone. I don't care how many people you talk to as secondary and tertiary sources, there will be information that you cannot glean. It was very interesting for me to listen when the interview was proceeding with J. J. [Johnson] and to think that I felt I really knew J. J. as well as anybody could, because I have idolized him all my life, and then to find time and time again misconceptions, and things that I didn't know about J. J., that even though there's the book out, there are things that we didn't know about that aren't in that book [*The Musical World of J. J. Johnson*], and nuances in a live interview that cannot possibly be in a book. So this has been a major, major thing for me to see this the Smithsonian Jazz Oral History Project grow, and it's another reason why I'm hoping that this will thrive.[56]

These life interviews are unique and valuable additions to the historical record because they tend to be methodical reconstructions of the informant's life, told in their own words, unedited, and related in their own voices. The spoken word conveys so many subtleties that printed words cannot convey. And long after all of us have passed into distant memory, the voices of jazz masters such as David Baker, J. J. Johnson, and Quincy Jones will remind us of their struggles, their triumphs, their greatness.

SMITHSONIAN BOOKS

David has taken a leading role in two books issued by the Smithsonian. The first was as editor of a collection of position papers and responses presented at a 1986 conference organized by the National Jazz Service Organization.[57] Such luminaries as Gunther Schuller, Dan Morgenstern, Amiri Baraka, Stanley Crouch, Gary Giddins, and Martin Williams were contributors and the different perspectives of such experts provided passion and sparks. "What happened is, inadvertently," recalls David, "[that] the book's appeal was people being adversarial. Because they picked people who had 180-degree differences." But the "ad hominem" arguments, he felt, were "a weakness in the book."[58]

In 2001, the Smithsonian's National Museum of American History entered into a partnership with the US Department of Education and, with a grant from its Fund for the Improvement of Education, the Museum produced the *Louis Armstrong Education Kit*.[59] This book provides teachers with background, lesson plans, and tools to educate middle and high school students (grades 5–12) about the figure who is, in my judgment, the single greatest, most influential musician in American history. The kit, co-authored by Luvenia A. George and David Baker, was published as an eighty-eight-page spiral-bound book and included a CD of Armstrong's music. Three thousand copies were distributed free of charge to educators.[60] "It's very handsomely done and I think the kit is very important," avers David. "Without any doubt, even just on his mass of accomplishments, Louis dominated fifty years in a way nobody else could have, and sometimes he was not given credit." The kit has proven popular with educators around the country.

JAZZ: THE SMITHSONIAN ANTHOLOGY

When it was first published in 1973, *The Smithsonian Collection of Classic Jazz* revolutionized the appreciation and teaching of jazz. Until then, there was no reliable anthology of jazz. The existing record anthologies either were restricted to the archives of but one record label (imagine an anthology of English literature limited to the back catalog of but one publishing house!) or were bootlegs. It took the Smithsonian Institution to persuade all the major record labels to open their vaults and to select recordings not on the basis of their commercial success (that is, sales figures) but on the basis of historical and music merit. The main argument was that by attaching the Smithsonian's name to the product, jazz would become more respectable as an art form, both in higher education and in the nation at large.

The SCCJ struck a powerful chord among the public, teachers, students, and librarians. Indeed the set sold so many copies it went "double platinum."

The influence of this boxed set of recordings has been enormous and unprecedented:

- It paved the way for the establishment of major jazz programs at the Smithsonian, Lincoln Center, Kennedy Center, and many other institutions;

created countless opportunities for community members to enjoy a better quality of life, secure hope for the future and reach their full potential. OHA will continue his work of building a brighter future for generations to come.

On behalf of the residents of California's 9th Congressional District, Mr. Jon Gresley, I salute you. I congratulate you on your many achievements, and I wish you and your loved ones all the best in this next chapter of life.

HONORING   THE   SMITHSONIAN JAZZ MASTERWORKS ORCHESTRA: 20 YEARS OF ENGAGEMENT, EDUCATION, AND EXCELLENCE

HON. JOHN CONYERS, JR.

OF MICHIGAN

IN THE HOUSE OF REPRESENTATIVES

Tuesday, September 14, 2010

Mr. CONYERS. Madam Speaker, in 1990, the Congress recognized the importance of jazz in American culture when it authorized the establishment of the Smithsonian Jazz Masterworks Orchestra (SJMO).

As the Nation's jazz orchestra, the SJMO regularly performs the great works of jazz. Throughout its 20 years, the orchestra has distinguished itself as one of the crown jewels of the Smithsonian—which is itself, a pre-eminent national treasure.

The band has performed for audiences at the Smithsonian Institution, Kennedy Center, White House, U.S. Capitol, Harlem's famed Apollo Theater, the 1996 Olympic Games in Atlanta, and prestigious music festivals like Ravinia and the Monterey Jazz Festival. The ensemble has traveled prolifically and performed at many American schools and colleges, as well as in Canada, Europe, and the Middle East. On a 2008 State Department-sponsored tour of Egypt, the Orchestra won many new friends for the United States. After an outdoor performance at the Pyramids and Sphinx, the Cairo Daily News raved, "The backdrop was incredible, the band was superb."

Other critical reaction has been enthusiastic. Wrote The New York Times: "Culturally important. . . . spectacular musically. After being embalmed on recordings, the music suddenly came alive." Syndicated columnist David S. Broder wrote, "The impact of these live performances is everything the showmen, scholars, and politicians who brought this small miracle to pass imagined it might be. It is electrifying. . . ."

While the SJMO is not the only jazz orchestra in America, it is unique. As the only federally-chartered jazz orchestra, it enjoys a position of prestige and influence. As the only such ensemble with resident status at a museum, it's in a unique position to bring the jazz legacy to life.

The Smithsonian Jazz Masterworks Orchestra educates the public about the history and development of jazz as an art form and means of entertainment. It promotes a greater appreciation for jazz as a valuable American treasure by performing jazz masterworks, and presenting educational activities that engage the public with this great music.

Further contributing to its status, the orchestra is led by the internationally famous Maestro David Baker—the world's leading jazz educator, author of over 70 books and 400 arti-

cles, and recent recipient of the prestigious American Jazz Masters Award given by the National Endowment for the Arts.

Madam Speaker, the orchestra has special expertise in engaging and educating its audiences—young and old—about this vital part of American culture. I am pleased to recognize its service and accomplishments over the past 20 years.

IN HONOR OF LANCE CORPORAL JAMES M. FERRARA

HON. JOHN H. ADLER

OF NEW JERSEY

IN THE HOUSE OF REPRESENTATIVES

Tuesday, September 14, 2010

Mr. ADLER of New Jersey. Madam Speaker, I rise today to congratulate Lance Corporal James M. Ferrara who received the Navy and Marine Corps Achievement Medal for meritorious duty on March 13, 2010. While on duty as patrolman at the Marine Corps Base in Quantico, Virginia, Lance Corporal Ferrara was dispatched to the base motor pool after he received reports of an injured person. Without hesitation, Lance Corporal Ferrara rushed off to the scene and quickly identified the victim who was suffering from a severe laceration with substantial loss of blood. Drawing upon his extensive emergency medical training, Lance Corporal Ferrara immediately delivered first aid, and probably saved the victim's life.

The men and women of our Armed Forces serve with an incomparable sense of duty. They are willing to sacrifice their lives to keep our country safe and free. In his service, Lance Corporal Ferrara exemplified the bravery and courage routinely displayed by those who serve in our military. The residents of New Jersey's Third District are grateful for the service of Lance Corporal Ferrara.

Madam Speaker, I ask my colleagues to join me in congratulating Lance Corporal Ferrara for his bravery and responsiveness under challenging circumstances.

IN HONOR OF LATINO COALITION AGAINST DOMESTIC AND SEXUAL VIOLENCE, INC.

HON. ANDRÉ CARSON

OF INDIANA

IN THE HOUSE OF REPRESENTATIVES

Tuesday, September 14, 2010

Mr. CARSON of Indiana. Madam Speaker, today I rise to recognize the Latino Coalition Against Domestic and Sexual Violence, Inc. for their dedicated service to Latino communities in 92 counties across Indiana.

The Latino Coalition, founded as a nonprofit corporation in 2004, has worked to eliminate domestic and sexual violence by focusing on the contributing conditions affecting Latino communities and immigrant populations in Indiana. Today, the Latino Coalition is the only statewide coalition of its kind in the United States that addresses the causes of domestic violence and sexual assault in the Latino community. Due to the tireless efforts of the Latino Coalition, men and women throughout Indiana have been able to extricate themselves from violent relationships, protect their children and improve their self confidence. This organiza-

tion serves as a model for other groups seeking to reduce the incidence of domestic and sexual violence in the United States.

Today, I ask my colleagues to join me in honoring the Latino Coalition for its distinguished efforts in improving the quality of life for victims of domestic violence and their families in the Latino community. This organization serves as an example to community organizations everywhere.

FINDINGS OF THE CHAIRMAN OF THE COMMITTEE ON EDUCATION AND LABOR RELATING TO EFFICIENCY AND REFORM PURSUANT TO H. RES. 1493

HON. GEORGE MILLER

OF CALIFORNIA

IN THE HOUSE OF REPRESENTATIVES

Tuesday, September 14, 2010

Mr. MILLER of California. Madam Speaker, in fulfillment of House Committee chair responsibilities per H. Res. 1493 (111th Congress), below are "findings that identify changes in law that help achieve deficit reduction by reducing waste, fraud, abuse, and mismanagement, promoting efficiency and reform of government, and controlling spending within Government programs" the Committee on Education and Labor authorizes. The measures discussed below are pending before Congress. If enacted, the legislation would promote efficient government and allow the agencies and departments within the jurisdiction of the Committee to more effectively serve the public.

In addition to the pending measures discussed below, this Congress has already enacted changes in the law in the Committee's jurisdiction that will significantly reduce the deficit. Specifically, the Student Aid and Fiscal Responsibility Act, included with health insurance reform in last year's Health Care and Education Reconciliation Act of 2010 (H.R. 4872), will save billions of taxpayer dollars in needless subsidies to banks lending to students. The Committee shares jurisdiction over the health care reform law enacted earlier this year through H.R. 4872 and H.R. 3590, the Patient Protection and Affordable Care Act. Among other things, these reforms reduce the rate of increase in government health care expenditures, encourage prevention and wellness, and shift to new effective health care payment mechanisms. The Congressional Budget Office reports that they will reduce the deficit by $143 billion over the next 10 years and by $1.2 trillion in the following 10 years.

A. MINE SAFETY—ROBERT C. BYRD MINER SAFETY AND HEALTH ACT OF 2010 (H.R. 5663)

Recent mine disasters and subsequent investigations and reviews have highlighted that the Mine Safety and Health Administration (MSHA) does not have the authority it needs to efficiently enforce the Nation's mine safety laws.

Under current law, MSHA may only subpoena documents and witnesses as part of an investigation of a mine disaster if the material is to be used in a public hearing. This has hamstrung MSHA's efforts to efficiently receive relevant documents in a timely manner. The Byrd Act would grant MSHA authority to subpoena documents and testimony without regard to whether the material is for a public

---

- The anthology became the cornerstone of every good jazz record (and later) CD collection – whether at schools, libraries, or in private homes;
- It established the leading canon of jazz recordings;
- Virtually every jazz textbook was organized around the SCCJ's recordings; and
- It helped educate more than a generation of college students.

The SCCJ was revised in 1989 and remastered in 1992. It remained in print for twenty-five years, but in 1999 all the licenses expired and the album went out of print. In 2000, I began to push for a new anthology to be created, and in 2002, I teamed with Smithsonian Folkways to develop one. At my urging, Folkways invited David Baker to become a member of a core five-person committee that, after considering recommendations from an international advisory survey, made the final selections of the 111 tracks. The committee met several times in person and by phone. Baker's input was integral to the selection process. He also contributed essays on four tracks: Cannonball Adderley's "Work Song," John Coltrane's "Giant Steps," Stan Kenton's "23 Degrees North, 82 Degrees West," and "King of the Road," recorded by Jimmy Smith and Wes Montgomery. The resulting book and six-disc set, *Jazz: The Smithsonian Anthology*, was published in March 2011, to generally glowing reviews.[61]

LIFE AND LEADERSHIP LESSONS

Finally, I'd like to acknowledge David's generosity of spirit and encouragement. In the late 1990s, troubled by the under-appreciation of jazz in the country of its birth, and inspired by the success of Black History Month, I conceived of the idea of a national "month" for jazz – Jazz Appreciation Month. Of course, jazz should be recognized and celebrated every month of the year, but designating a month for it, I reasoned, could provide a focus for awareness, a hook for the news media, and a platform for a nationwide celebration. Among the first people I ran the idea by was my longtime mentor, David Baker. He immediately saw the value and potential of the idea, and lent his warm support.

There is no manual for starting a "month," and I found the learning curve to be essentially vertical. There were challenges and obstacles on the road, and one organization even threatened to steal the idea and make it highly commercial, which I felt would have cheapened and diminished it. David kept urging me on, and the Museum took up the cause, announcing it at a press conference on July 2001.[62] For David's steadfast support, I will always be grateful. As of 2011, JAM is celebrated in all fifty states and in forty countries. I feel that, whatever JAM achieves in the future, David will be a part of that success.

The Smithsonian itself recognized his leadership. For his extraordinary service to the Nation through the Smithsonian, David Baker was awarded the Institution's highest honor, the James Smithson Founder's Medal in 2002.

Since 2000, I have been giving a presentation on "Leadership Lessons from the Jazz Masters," based on the inspiration from the likes of Louis Armstrong, Duke Ellington, and Miles Davis. David himself is a master and an inspiration to me and to many, many others. To summarize the leadership and life lessons I have learned from David:

· Keep music central to your life;
· Never stop practicing;
· Listen closely not only to the music, but to the people around you;
· Focus on the big picture;
· Be inclusive and generous of spirit;
· Proclaim your passion;
· Devotedly pass your knowledge on to the next generations;
· Readily offer encouragement;
· Maintain a sense of humor under all circumstances;
· Never stop being creative, never retire; and
· Give thanks for each and every day.

For these admirable examples and the many other ways that David has inspired me, I will be eternally grateful to him.

NOTES

1. I wish to thank David Baker, Lida Baker, and Ken Kimery for their generous help providing information and sharing memories for this chapter; and Ann Moore and Salomone Baquis for their assistance in proofreading it.

2. Bernice Johnson Reagan, personal communication.

3. Stokes, "Tracing the Music," C7.

4. After several years of negotiation between the Museum and with the Ellington estate, and considerable preparation by Museum staff, the Duke Ellington Collection arrived at the National Museum of American History in April 1988. Paul, "Collection Holds Clues to the Genius of Duke Ellington," A4.

5. David Baker, interview by Lida Baker, June 19–21, 2000, transcript, Smithsonian Jazz Oral History Project, www.smithsonianjazz.org/oral_ histories/pdf/joh_DavidNBaker_ transcript.pdf.

6. *Department of the Interior and Related Agencies Appropriations Bill,* US House of Representatives, 101st Cong., 2nd session, Committee Print, 1991, Report, September 11, 1990, 137.

7. Reich, "Keeping the Jazz Flame Alive"; Point, "Future of Jazz Blaring Bright"; Fuller, "Big Band Transcription Project Begins"; Orgill, "In Search of the Real Ellington Sound"; Harrington, "All That Jazz, at Smithsonian," and "On the Beat."

8. The three works were published as Smithsonian Jazz Masterworks Editions. See Smithsonian Jazz website, www .smithsonianjazz.org/pdfs/Masterworks Editions Order Form.pdf.

9. Portions of the discussion of the Smithsonian Jazz Masterworks Orchestra are excerpted from my liner notes to *Big Band Treasures, Live.*

10. There had been an earlier Smithsonian Jazz Repertory Ensemble, which both Bob Wilber and Gunther Schuller had conducted. Under Schuller, the ensemble made a recording for the Smithsonian Collection of Recordings of Ellington's *Symphony in Black,* which was recorded live in concert in May 1980, and reviewed in *Stereo Review.* Under Bob Wilber, the ensemble made a recording of a live concert of May 1979, issued by the Smithsonian Collection of Recordings as *Music of Fats Waller and James P. Johnson,* which was also reviewed in *Stereo Review.* Preceding the SJRE was the 1973–81 National Jazz Ensemble, pioneered by bassist Chuck Israels, and the 1974–80 New York Jazz Repertory Company, founded by George Wein. See Stewart, *Making the Scene,* 63–69.

11. Bob Carr was then the chair of the Congressional Arts Caucus and a member of the House Appropriations Committee.

12. House Concurrent Resolution 57, 100th Congress, was passed on December 4, 1987. For the complete text, see www .hr57.org/hconres57.html.

13. The *Smithsonian Collection of Classic Jazz,* selected and annotated by Martin Williams, was published by the Smithsonian Collection of Recordings in 1973. The anthology gained influence to the point that it defined something of a canon of jazz recordings and nearly all college-level jazz textbooks organized their listening examples around the SCCJ's selections.

14. Baker, interview, June 19–21, 2000.

15. David Baker, interview by John Edward Hasse, July 24, 2010, Washington, D.C., tape recording in possession of author.

16. See "Smithsonian Announces Jazz Expansion," 13.

17. Baker, interview, June 19–21, 2000.

18. Harrington, "Smithsonian Jazzmen."

19. The auditorium is named not for fellow Hoosier (and Bloomington) musician Hoagy Carmichael, but for Leonard Carmichael, the seventh secretary of the Smithsonian, who served from 1953 to 1964.

20. Watrous, "The Smithsonian's Jazz Orchestra."

21. Broder, "Real Jazz."

22. As quoted in John Edward Hasse, liner notes, *Big Band Treasures, Live,* 7.

23. Ibid, 6.

24. Joyce, "Big Band Sound."

25. The Jazz Arts Group was founded in Columbus, Ohio, by Ray Eubanks in 1975. Its big band is now known as the Columbus Jazz Orchestra.

26. The American Jazz Orchestra was founded in New York in 1996 by jazz critic Gary Giddins. Due to funding problems, it disbanded late in 1992. See Watrous, "Jazz Group."

27. This ensemble set the stage for the Jazz at Lincoln Center Orchestra, which later became the Lincoln Center Jazz Orchestra.

28. *Big Band Renaissance: The Evolution of the Jazz Orchestra; The 1940s and Beyond.* Washington, D.C.: Smithsonian Collection of Recordings, 1995.

29. Balliett, "Jumpin' at the White House."

30. Santiago, "When This Jazz Band Plays," 80.

31. Baker, interview, June 19–21, 2000.

32. The task is still quite difficult, for several reasons. None of the band's music in the Ellington Collection is complete and ready to perform: Ellington never wrote out a piano part or drum part. In addition, he was one to tinker with his band's "charts" throughout a recording session, so that what appears on paper does not fully or accurately represent what a recording captured. In jazz, typi-

cally the urtext is considered to be the recording, not written music.

33. In 1992, the Smithsonian announced a $7 million grant from the Lila Wallace–Readers Digest Fund to create a ten-year initiative called America's Jazz Heritage – a series of traveling exhibitions, radio programs, oral histories, and educational projects. See Harrington, "Smithsonian Jazz Program Gets $7 Million."

34. Mercedes Ellington, granddaughter of Duke Ellington, was the host during the series' last season of broadcasts.

35. It was issued by the National Museum of American History, Smithsonian Institution, as RJ0044.

36. This was issued by Smithsonian Folkways Recordings as SFW40817.

37. DVD MCGJ3004 is available through MCG Jazz in Pittsburgh.

38. Ken Kimery, interview by John Edward Hasse, October 4, 2010, Washington, D.C., tape recording in possession of author.

39. Ibid.

40. Jefferson, "Critic's Notebook."

41. Ellington, *Music Is My Mistress,* 282.

42. Davis, "The Cotton Club Revue."

43. The following discussion of the Egypt tour is excerpted from Hasse, "Jazz on the Nile."

44. "The Smithsonian Jazz Masterworks Orchestra: Swingin' at the Pyramids," YouTube video, 5:28, posted by "JEH1001," April 19, 2008, www.youtube.com/watch?v=whGqUMmbAzo.

45. Michaela Singer, "A Jazzy Afternoon at the Pyramids," *Daily News Egypt,* February 17, 2008, www.dailystaregypt.com/article.aspx?ArticleID=11927. A brief *Smithsonian* magazine article is available at www.smithsonianmag.com/arts-culture/atm-jukebox-200805.html.

46. Hasse, "Jazz on the Nile," 21.

47. Amal Choucri Catta, "Reaching Sublime Heights," *Al-Ahram Weekly*, February 28–March 5, 2008, weekly.ahram .org.eg/2008/886/cu6.htm.

48. A fifteen-minute documentary about the tour was made by the Egyptians. It can be seen in various versions, such as these: "Smithsonian Jazz Masterworks Orchestra in Egypt: Part 1 of 'Jazz on the Nile'" and "Smithsonian Jazz Masterworks Orchestra in Egypt: Part 1 of 'Jazz on the Nile,'" YouTube videos, 9:31 and 5:31, posted by "JEH1001," June 22, 2010, www.youtube.com/watch?v= yZO9kVaAjlA and www.youtube.com/ watch?v=lrmVJ72F6X4; and "sjmo in Egypt," YouTube video, 10:01, posted by "kendrum100," November 12, 2009, www .youtube.com/watch?v=E_wcMxPet6I.

49. Ken Kimery, interview by John Edward Hasse, October 4, 2010.

50. Scott Silbert, e-mail message to John Edward Hasse, November 2, 2010.

51. This amounted to, in a sense, the re-establishment of a program that existed at the Smithsonian in the 1970s and 1980s, funded by grants from the National Endowment for the Arts. See www .smithsonianjazz.org.

52. The jazz oral history program was first coordinated by Jessie Adkins. Subsequently, Anthony Brown was program director, assisted by Lisa Stewart. Later, Matt Watson ran the program, followed by Katea Stitt, and then Kimery took over.

53. J. J. Johnson, interview by Lida Baker and David Baker, February 26–27, 1994, transcript, Smithsonian Jazz Oral History Project, http://www.smithsonian jazz.org/oral_histories/pdf/joh_JJJohn son_transcript.pdf.

54. Baker, interview, June 19–21, 2000

55. Quincy Jones, interview by David Baker and Ken Kimery, September 7, 2008, transcript, Smithsonian Jazz Oral History Project, http://www.smithsonian jazz.org/oral_histories/pdf/Jones.pdf.

56. Baker, interview, October 4, 2010.

57. Baker, *New Perspectives in Jazz*.

58. Baker, interview, October 4, 2010.

59. George and Baker, *Louis Armstrong Education Kit*.

60. The kit continues to be available on the Smithsonian Jazz website, www .smithsonianjazz.org.

61. Schudel, "Smithsonian Set Updates Jazz Anthology"; Wolk, "Swing States."

62. Hasse, "Launching Jazz Appreciation Month." See also Trapps, "Picking a Month to Celebrate Jazz"; "Quincy Celebrates Jazz."

REFERENCES

Baker, David N., ed. *New Perspectives in Jazz*. Washington and London: Smithsonian Institution Press, 1990.

Balliett, Whitney. "Jumpin' at the White House." *New Yorker* 69, no. 23 (July 26, 1993): 77+.

Broder, David S. "Real Jazz." *Washington Post*, August 28, 1991, A23.

Davis, Clive. "The Cotton Club Revue." *Times* (London), July 26, 1999, 45.

Ellington, Duke. *Music Is My Mistress*. Garden City, N.Y.: Doubleday, 1973.

Fuller, Patricia. "Big Band Transcription Project Begins." *DownBeat* 56, no. 4 (April 1989): 11.

George, Luvenia A., and David Baker. *Louis Armstrong Education Kit*. Washington, D.C.: Smithsonian Institution National Museum of American History, 2005.

Harrington, Richard. "All That Jazz, at Smithsonian." *Washington Post,* October 10, 1990, D7.

———. "On the Beat: Convening in the Name of the Duke." *Washington Post,* January 9, 1991, C7.

———. "Smithsonian Jazz Program Gets $7 Million." *Washington Post,* May 22, 1992, D2.

———. "Smithsonian Jazzmen: Federally Funded Orchestra to Debut." *Washington Post,* April 25, 1991, C2.

Hasse, John Edward. "Jazz on the Nile: The Smithsonian Takes the Nation's Jazz Band to Egypt." *DownBeat* 75, no. 9 (September 2008): 20–21.

———. "Launching Jazz Appreciation Month." *Jazz Education Journal* 34, no. 5 (March 2002): 40–42, 44–45.

Jefferson, Margo. "Critic's Notebook; Ellington: Beyond Category." *New York Times,* October, 15, 1993, C25.

Joyce, Mike. "Big Band Sound." *Washington Post,* May 21, 1991, C2.

Orgill, Roxane. "In Search of the Real Ellington Sound." *Wall Street Journal,* August 8, 1989, A8.

Paul, Angus. "Collection Holds Clues to the Genius of Duke Ellington; Manuscripts at the Smithsonian Reveal the Composer's Methods." *Chronicle of Higher Education* 35, no. 7 (1988): A4+.

Point, Michael. "Future of Jazz Blaring Bright as New Talent Gains Exposure." *Austin American Statesman,* January 6, 1989, C3.

"Quincy Celebrates Jazz." *Jet,* August 6, 2001, 10.

Reich, Howard. "Keeping the Jazz Flame Alive." *Chicago Tribune,* December 25, 1988, 18.

Review of *Duke Ellington's* Symphony in Black *and Other Works. Stereo Review* 47, no. 3 (March 1982): 111.

Review of *Music of Fats Waller and James P. Johnson. Stereo Review* 46, no. 4 (April 1981): 93.

Santiago, Chiori. "When This Jazz Band Plays, It's Not Just Music – It's History." *Smithsonian* 27, no. 6 (September 1996): 74–80.

Schudel, Matt. "Smithsonian Set Updates Jazz Anthology 38 Years Later," *Washington Post,* March 27, 2011, E8.

"Smithsonian Announces Jazz Expansion." *Jazz Educators Journal* 23, no. 4 (Summer 1991): 13.

Stewart, Alex. *Making the Scene: Contemporary New York City Big Band Jazz.* Berkeley and Los Angeles: University of California Press, 2007.

Stokes, W. Royal. "Tracing the Music." *Washington Post,* August 27, 1985, C7.

Trapps, Tynisa E. "Picking a Month to Celebrate Jazz." *Los Angeles Times,* July 20, 2001, 11.

Watrous, Peter. "Jazz Group, a Guest of High Art, Seems Lost on a Trail it Blazed." *New York Times,* December 10, 1992, C15, C18.

———. "The Smithsonian's Jazz Orchestra Makes Its Debut in Washington." *New York Times,* May 20, 1991, C11, C13.

Wolk, Douglas. "Swing States: How to Make a New Jazz Canon in Six Easy Steps," *Time* 177, no. 13 (April 4, 2011): 74–75.

8

Social Engagement

WILLARD JENKINS   AS IS NO DOUBT crystal clear by this point, David Baker is a quintessential modern music renaissance man. An award-winning educator, composer, musician, bandleader, and recording artist, David Baker has given tirelessly in service to jazz music in particular and the arts in general. His years as a stellar composer and as a sideman in such auspicious settings as his fellow NEA Jazz Master George Russell's challenging Lydian chromatic tableaux, not to mention what is perhaps his crowning achievement – nurturing young talent on the university level – also constitute *service* par excellence. But let us consider the many off-bandstand ways David Baker has given of his expertise, wit, and considerable grace on behalf of jazz music.

Throughout his career in service to jazz – hallmarked in the

twenty-first century by his distinguished educating and directorship of
the Smithsonian Jazz Masterworks Orchestra and its ongoing record of
preserving the legacy of the music's most distinguished composers – David Baker has been passionate about the need to sustain the art form.
"And that perpetuation is in the hands of our young people," he says, adding that people like himself have the responsibility of providing succeed-
ing generations "the truth from our griots."[1] In West African tradition,
a griot is a historian, a sage whose charge is to maintain an oral history
of the tribe or village, and to readily disseminate that history through
various vehicles of expression. David Baker's career has marked him as
a jazz griot.

As a senior member of the jazz community, one keenly aware of the
mysteries of mortality, Baker has witnessed the passing of many fellow
comrades and griots of this music, and for him the alarm bells sound
when yet another master passes on to ancestry. "We're losing what's remaining of the people who were the progenitors of the music," he insists.
Baker believes we must collectively "do something to make sure those
traditions are preserved, while we're getting them in truth from people
who were there, much like the perpetuation of the legends in an African
tribe when you're talking about the griots." That is how Baker views the
passing of those masters who were around to witness, or instigate nearly
every significant change in the music. And despite what to some might
appear to be a sense of cleaving to those traditions, David Baker clearly
recognizes the need for jazz music to experience constant evolution:
"Any time a music starts to stagnate, it's gonna die."

David repeatedly cautions against the dangers of placing boundaries
around jazz: "I just think that putting boundaries to the music is easy
enough to do, but Ellington said, 'Don't put the music in a box.' I think
Clark Terry said, 'The difference between a groove and a grave is just
a couple of letters.'" One of Baker's burning suggestions is "investing
money in trying to establish situations where old and young musicians
come together," in mentoring relationships.

Obviously David Baker has given a great deal of thought, energy, and
tireless work to the perpetuation of this art form on a variety of service-
oriented fronts. One wonders, as he developed his craft as a musician,
composer, and educator, at what point did he begin to seriously invest in

service to the art form, and why? In typical self-deprecating fashion, he pleads innocence: "I think the decision was made for me because I was drafted into service. As someone who was a goody two-shoes in school, I got things thrust upon me that I would not always anticipate doing. Like I didn't start out to try to put together the jazz program at IU [Indiana University]; Jerry Coker had been teaching jazz courses [before Baker came along], but then Dean Bain asked me to put together a jazz program. Then I understood a little bit how that led up to the appointments to the NEA and the National Council on the Arts. I think the good idea is to be prepared when that circumstance takes place."

NATIONAL ENDOWMENT FOR THE ARTS

The groundwork for David Baker's career in service to jazz was obviously laid long before, but his first opportunity to exercise those chops arrived in the nascent stages of the National Endowment for the Arts (NEA). The independent agency was formed in 1965 as our nation's "public agency dedicated to supporting excellence in the arts, both new and established; bringing the arts to all Americans";[2] its first dynamic chairperson was Nancy Hanks. The NEA's headquarters, in the venerable Old Post Office building in downtown Washington, D.C., was subsequently rechristened the Nancy Hanks Center. Hanks assumed chairmanship of the Endowment in 1969.

At the time jazz music was just beginning its struggle for a piece of the rock, wrestling against the misconception that it was still part of the popular music market, which had not been the case since at least the heyday of the so-called "swing era," and even then that designation was arguable considering the creative arc of the music. Meanwhile the so-called "classical" art forms – orchestral and chamber music, dance, and theater – had early Endowment support. Along came David Baker and a handful of other jazz stalwarts to figuratively shake things up, curiously appointed as members of what was then known as the "Folk-Ethnic" category; a kind of catchall grouping that supposedly would serve as a place of refuge for those music forms not quite considered "classical" or art music.

Says Baker, "Those very first panel meetings – we're talking late '60s – at that time they were giving maybe a million dollars to sympho-

nies and ballets, and the entire money for the Folk-Ethnic panel, which
I chaired with Milt Hinton, Jimmy Owens and those guys, that whole
amount was minuscule by comparison. I don't remember the exact number, but it was enough to show me that jazz was not being afforded the
same kind of position in the music world that classical music was."

Poet and jazz writer A. B. Spellman, who authored *Four Lives in the
Bebop Business,* and who served a distinguished career at the Endowment as director of a variety of programs before retiring in 2005, recalls
those days of struggle for jazz at the NEA as a time when not only was
jazz struggling for recognition in the fine arts realm, but the Endowment
staff was also in need of some schooling. At the time Baker was appointed
chair of the Folk-Ethnic panel,

> Billy Taylor was on the National Council on the Arts and he recommended
> Dave and Jimmy [Owens]. He valued their intelligence, articulation, activism
> and strong principles. Both were strong personalities, but with different styles,
> and they were capable of guiding an NEA staff that had little knowledge of jazz.
> I believe that the jazz support at the Endowment came about in large part as a
> result of their participation.[3]

Typically modest, Baker suggests that his tenure at the NEA had
as much to do with the fact that he was "stationary" in his position at
Indiana University, as opposed to other activist-minded jazz artists who
were constantly out on the performance circuit:

> Consequently, because they could locate me all of the time here at IU, they
> would ask me to be on the panels more quickly than somebody like Cannonball
> [Adderley], who they had to chase down. Antoinette Handy [the late former
> director of the NEA music program] was very instrumental in picking people
> for panel work who she thought would take the time. Since I didn't have a major
> career playing the music, I was stationary at the school, and she knew that I
> didn't have any axes to grind either. At that time I hadn't built any kind of large
> performing career, except with George Russell. So it was the luck of the draw a
> lot of the times that I would get in those kinds of Endowment panel work, and
> one inevitably led to the other.

Modesty aside, it's clear from the tenor of the times in arts funding
that while NEA support for the jazz field was in its infancy, Baker, Owens
and other representatives of the jazz field were also on board to guide the
Endowment staff in matters of support for the art form. Furthermore, the
jazz community at the time was largely uninformed and ill equipped to
access arts funding. In that sense David Baker was a pathfinder. "I think

it was partially that," he says, "but the other thing they were respond-ing to was any criticism aimed at them about them *not* doing what they should for American music in general."

Baker quickly recognized that he was not only a representative of the jazz field, but also a voice for American music in general:

> As Quincy Jones has said so many times, you can go anywhere . . . Japan, China, Romania . . . and the music that you hear that is common to everybody is not often the folk songs, but it's American music . . . whether it's American jazz, American blues, hip-hop or whatever. I heard A. B. Spellman say once that anywhere there was music on a Saturday night, you could trace it back to the jazz diaspora.

As the NEA sought guidance from Baker, Owens, and others from the jazz field on matters of funding support, Baker saw openings for the music as a means of elevating the Endowment itself:

> I also think they were looking for things which were high profile enough to en-able them to say, "This is what we're doing for jazz." For instance, when they ran that study that Harold Horowitz did in 1985 on the jazz audience, I think it was as much publicity as it was devotion to the music.

That particular survey was undertaken by the NEA, which commis-sioned the US Census Bureau to collect information on the participation of adult Americans in a wide range of arts and culture activities, includ-ing jazz, in 1982.[4] That unprecedented survey categorized four means of jazz audience participation: attending live performances, listening to recordings, listening to the radio, and watching television. By those four criteria, the survey measured the jazz audience at that time at ap-proximately 54 million individuals, practically one-third of all Ameri-can adults; the largest sector of that 54 million consumed their jazz via recordings. Needless to say, this was hopeful news for much of the jazz community.[5]

NATIONAL COUNCIL ON THE ARTS

David Baker's next station in his arts services journey was his 1987–94 appointment to the National Council on the Arts, the quasi-board of the National Endowment for the Arts. Not strictly designed as a board of governors per se, the National Council on the Arts is charged with advising the chairman of the NEA – who also chairs the Council – on agency policies and programs. The National Council's primary responsibility is reviewing and making recommendations to the chairman on grant applications, the various funding guidelines for those grants, and leadership initiatives. A. B. Spellman puts the National Council on the Arts in context: "They are primarily advisory. The only thing that they can decide is which grants get rejected; they recommend the ones to be funded to the Chairman, but he/she may decline grants that they have supported. The Chairman may not, however, fund an application that the Council has rejected. They may advise policy and budget priorities, but the Chairman doesn't have to listen to them. This sometimes frustrates them as these are people who are not accustomed to board authority," a fact that becomes clear just scanning the distinguished roster of former members of the National Council on the Arts.

Though the NEA would likely shy away from such a pure designation, fact is, David Baker was essentially *the* representative from the jazz field on the Council during his tenure. And it is Baker's sense that once again he owed his appointment to the ever-vigilant D. Antoinette Handy:

> She never told me this, but I believe Antoinette came up with the notion that there ought to be jazz representation on the National Council on the Arts. As far as jazz is concerned, on the National Council prior to my tenure there was Duke Ellington, Gunther Schuller, Billy Taylor, then me.

In the days of David's tenure on the National Council, and even more so prior to that tenure, there was still very much the matter of convincing the Endowment and fellow members of the National Council on the fact of jazz as a fine art form. "I don't think we ever got full cooperation from the National Council as far as jazz goes," Baker lamented.

Spellman contextualizes the tenor of those times during Baker's National Council tenure thus: "Dave was the second jazz musician to serve on the council after Billy [Taylor]." Baker suggests that Ellington's National Council tenure was purely ceremonial: "I would doubt that Ellington ever went to a meeting." Of the uphill battle waged on behalf of jazz as a fine art form, Baker says, "Jazz's relationship to the nonprofit scene was pretty contentious during Billy's term, with the arts establishment unapologetically holding that [jazz] was commercial music and

A. B. Spellman, David Baker, and Billy Taylor. *Courtesy of David Baker.*

had no place in the world of serious music; with Gian Carlo Menotti, composer and erstwhile artistic director of the Spoleto Festival declaring that jazz would never appear on his stages."[6]

Apparently Menotti was not alone in his objections to jazz sitting at the serious music table during those days of National Council deliberations. Spellman explains,

> This was a common point of view in those days. Billy had a couple of allies on the Council like Gunther Schuller and Charles McWhorter, a hip Republican lawyer and kingmaker. Dave didn't have such allies [during his tenure] but the establishment had become slightly less hostile. There was one Council member, a classical pianist and *New Criterion* contributor named Samuel Lipman, who had held that jazz didn't belong, but he admitted during one meeting that he had

learned a lot from Dave, and after all, you only had to listen to the early Ravel
piano concertos to see jazz's influence, as if that was the issue.

Baker takes a broad brush to his days on the National Council,
suggesting that his tenure was more about representing a broader constituency, and that his term "continued the notion that there needed to
be somebody there to represent American music." Spellman is more
pointed in his assessment when asked if Baker was indeed on the Council
to represent the jazz field: "Certainly. But he could not have been so effective if he had been unable to comment authoritatively on other kinds
of art. His credentials as a composer of classical music and professor at
a major conservatory were crucial to his standing."

In addition to Baker's various jousts on behalf of jazz at National
Council meetings, his stint marked perhaps the most politically charged
period in the history of the National Endowment for the Arts. It was during Baker's term that massive controversy arose over the Endowment's
funding of such heavily debated visual arts projects as the lightning rod
photographer Robert Mapplethorpe's exhibit, "Robert Mapplethorpe:
The Perfect Moment," with what some viewed as its sadomasochist images; and photographer Andrew Serrano's deeply provocative piece "Piss
Christ," a depiction of a cross suspended in the photographer's urine.
Both had been supported in some measure by Endowment funding.
The ultraconservative wing of the legislative branch, which at the time
believed its ideology represented mainstream America, began flexing
its muscles in opposition to the NEA, threatening the agency's very existence. Meanwhile, the boiling point for the Mapplethorpe exhibit was
reached in Cincinnati, Ohio, as vehement public protests erupted in
opposition to and support of its run at that city's Contemporary Arts
Center. Baker characterizes those times on the National Council as turbulent indeed:

> The Mapplethorpe exhibit was the last straw. People came and stood outside
> the Old Post Office [where we were meeting] and picketed us; we had a police
> escort. I felt at that time that Americans weren't really ready to be respectful of
> the diversity in the arts. Then you had [Council] people who maybe didn't have
> the background to deal intelligently with such controversy.

These contentions and the roiling dialogue that ensued had a very
unfortunate upshot: the dissolution of NEA grants to individual art-

ists. Baker and other Council members apparently found that a palat-
able compromise, and when one considers the alternative – the death of
the Endowment – perhaps it was a deeply regrettable compromise. Says
Baker:

> One of the things I was surprised they were able to do, which helped dilute
> some of the anti-Endowment fervor, was to discontinue giving individual artist
> grants; because with the individual artist grants I think the NEA had less control
> . . . unless they were able to establish some way of tracking the individual grants,
> making sure the grants were spent properly, and there was consistency. . . . We
> had made a lot of decisions that were not the most informed decisions, in terms
> of individual grants.

Meanwhile, establishing jazz as one of the fine arts was an ongoing
negotiation. Some of the work done by people like Baker and others who
were part of NEA panels, and the resulting policy discussions that took
place once a panel's slate of proposals has been reviewed and vetted, was
also meant to differentiate jazz's various stylistic approaches: "Because
to compare an Ellington piece with something which is so far afield that
it's got nothing to do with African American music, it's like a lost cause."
Baker remembers,

> During that tenure we had Council members who were arguing about things
> that basically came out of the civil rights movement. Those arguments were
> never couched in racial language, but it was things that had to do with race, and
> people arguing against what they wrongly viewed as "set asides" on the grounds
> that this is a "democracy"; the same things that were happening with Dr. King
> when he was trying to deal with some of the most dramatic civil rights changes
> that we've seen.

Let's say David Baker might argue about the fact that jazz should be
supported at certain levels at the NEA. Would counterarguments suggest
that we can't have quotas? "It was never put that bluntly, but in my mind
that's what it was about. They would find a psychological or a political
reason to not go in that direction. Remember, with the Council we didn't
make the initial decisions to fund or not to fund; we had to adjudicate
those decisions."

Recalling the old Sam Greenlee novel that was so widely read among
black college students in the 1970s, and subsequently made into a motion
picture with a music score by Herbie Hancock, one wonders if during

his National Council tenure as the jazz rep whether he ever felt like the spook who sat by the door.[7] When asked this, Baker laughs.

> What I did feel like sometimes was a voice screaming into the wind. There would be people on the Council like Gregory Peck or Robert Stack who rarely spoke, but when they spoke it would be a sentence or a paragraph that really had an impact. A lot of people told me when I first came on the council, "Look, you don't have to talk all the time; you don't have to talk just because somebody else is talking. Wait until you have something specific that you have in mind, something you really want to fight for, then bring it up . . . and look for allies." I learned a lot about listening and I learned a lot about reaching compromises – compromises that did not destroy an idea but meant you had to make concessions so you could get along, assuming that maybe you'll need that vote when you bring up something. So if I took anything away from that experience at all it would be consensus building. I did a lot of listening, and I think out of that I'm able to better function in the world I live in now.

NATIONAL JAZZ SERVICE ORGANIZATION

Consensus-building skills are certainly tools that came in handy at Baker's next two jazz-service stations. In 1985 Baker took up the hopeful mantle of leading (as first and only board chairman) a gallant, but ultimately failed effort to establish the National Jazz Service Organization (NJSO).[8] Developed through significant NEA support as a means of finally establishing a national service organization for jazz, along the lines of what the American Symphony Orchestra League, Chamber Music America, and Dance/USA meant to their respective art forms, NJSO was primarily hatched and nurtured through two momentous think-tank conferences at the Johnson Foundation facility Wingspread in Racine, Wisconsin. Again, a familiar figure was a driving force. "Antoinette Handy called a meeting," recalls Baker. "She said, 'Why don't we get together some of the best minds in jazz and we'll meet up at Wingspread?' It was intended just to explore ideas."

Among the participants was an impressive cross-section of the jazz field at the time: Muhal Richard Abrams, Billy Taylor, Bruce Lundvall, arts administrator (and Ornette Coleman kin) James Jordan, Donald Byrd, Larry Ridley, and Congressman John Conyers, Jr., were part of its distinguished roster. David Baker explains, "At this time it really was groundbreaking because when they asked us, 'What is a service organization?' I don't think any one of us could have told them the model we were going to use, what it is supposed to do, and how does it work."

A second such Wingspread conference yielded the NJSO volume *New Perspectives on Jazz* including a series of introductory editorials on the conference and the state of jazz in 1986 by Baker and such other participants as Congressman John Conyers, Jr. The bulk of the book is a series of commissioned papers and follow-up reactions or rebuttals from Gunther Schuller, Olly Wilson, Gary Giddins, Dan Morgenstern, Billy Taylor, Jimmy Lyons, George Butler, and Martin Williams on various aspects of the then-current state of the art form. The controversial highlight of the conference (or the "heavyweight championship," as Conyers announced at the time) was a paper read by Amiri Baraka and a subsequent vitriolic rebuttal read by Stanley Crouch. Things reached such a heated state that a fistfight nearly broke out between the two combatants. Also included, and perhaps the most valuable chapter of all, is then-director of the Endowment's Research Division Harold Horowitz's detailed analysis of the aforementioned survey.[9] Proceeds from the sale of *New Perspectives on Jazz* were earmarked to benefit NJSO.

What they resolved at that initial Wingspread confab was a sweeping mission statement: "To nurture the growth and enhancement of jazz as an American art form." They included "all forms of jazz music in its definition of jazz and recognizes it as a gift to the world through the Afro-American experience. NJSO educates, informs, communicates, and networks to enhance the status of jazz." In hindsight David Baker believes the organization was doomed by a critical lack of focus. And that lack of focus was perhaps exacerbated by a momentous grant the organization achieved in 1991. "You can have a vision, but a vision without action is marking time," Baker suggests.

That year, in partnership with the New England Foundation for the Arts, NJSO was granted an unprecedented sum of $3.4 million for a four-year project to establish a national jazz network of jazz presenting organizations, which would ideally become a jazz touring circuit. Baker's sense is that this grant, coupled with the organization's overly broad mission, was NJSO's ultimate undoing in 1995:

Second Wingspread conference of the National Jazz Service
Organization, 1986. Billy Taylor, Harold Horowitz, David Baker, and
Congressman John Conyers, Jr. *Courtesy of David Baker.*

We were bailed out a little bit by the Lila Wallace–Reader's Digest Fund, but I
think it became like an albatross, because if we hadn't had that money we might
have been encouraged to try to find a funding source that was going to be a continuing source. I think there was a good mix of brainpower on the board, people
who could get along with each other about what we were going to do because I
don't think we were wedded to any particular style of jazz. But none of us could
contribute full time to this. I think maybe we were naïve; we just didn't have all
the business sense. Somewhere there should have been someone . . . even if it was
a silent or distant partner . . . who said, "Hey, look. You have such a good idea,
here's what Eli Lilly, here's what Ford . . . can do to help you." I think [corporate
angels] might have done that if NJSO had been something about new music – and
I'm not talking about jazz music, but new American music that the symphony
orchestras were going to play. I don't think there was even a board or organization consensus as to which is the most important music to be concentrating on.
People have different ideas about what jazz is supposed to be, and if those ideas
don't somehow coalesce, then you're left struggling; we didn't have an angel.

INTERNATIONAL ASSOCIATION
FOR JAZZ EDUCATION

David Baker's next service stint came in 2002, when he served as president of an organization with a specific focus on education – which at the time appeared robust, but which may have ultimately met its own sad demise by trying to be all things jazz to all people – the late International Association for Jazz Education (IAJE). Originally christened the National Association of Jazz Educators (NAJE), and later rechristened the International Association of Jazz Educators, then the International Association for Jazz Education, IAJE was founded in 1968 and went bankrupt in 2008; it closed its doors for good in March 2009.[10] Recently it has been succeeded by the new Jazz Education Network, which held its inaugural conference in May 2010, at which David Baker gave the keynote address.

NAJE was founded as something of an offshoot of the old Stan Kenton band camps. As such, not only was it narrowly focused on jazz education, it was also quite stylistically focused on the Kenton oeuvre, and rather lily white in its early administration and membership – incongruous with the historic origins of jazz music in the African-American experience. When David Baker was elected president of IAJE in 2001, he was the fourth in a succession of African American presidents that began with Warrick Carter, then Bunky Green, and Ron McCurdy, each of whom were musicians and university-level jazz educators. Baker recalls,

> At the time we were still in the throes of Stan Kenton and neophonic jazz. We had seen the jazz education situation as teachers teaching teachers to teach teachers to teach teachers, with positions not going to people who had some experience playing the music. When they asked me if I would take the position of president, my first question was "Is it going to be a point of stasis where we're standing still?"

And despite the organization's international outlook intentions, Baker believes that the United States was "still the leader of the world as far as changes, formative changes in the music. That had been denied by a lot of people; I got tired of reading in magazines where 'If jazz is gonna be good, it's going to come from Europe, Japan or somewhere else.'"

Despite that cautionary note, Baker still thinks that expanding the organization's reach from national to international was a prudent move, "because we know there were people in other countries that did acknowledge that America was the birthplace of this music. I'm not sure it was most accurate to use the term 'America's Music,' but I think it certainly was very, very high on the pole representing what this music was supposed to stand for in the world." Evidence suggests that IAJE's troubles began when it broadened its mission in an effort at becoming a sort of umbrella organization for the art form, adopting a dramatically expanded perspective for their very successful annual conference out of the ashes of the old *Jazz Times* conventions in what may have been a misguided effort at being about all things jazz.[11] Regardless of causal factors, "We know IAJE had a troublesome ending," Baker says with resignation.

He modestly insists that in so many of these cases where his expertise was called upon by jazz and arts service efforts, it was merely a matter of his being in the right place at the right time, but clearly they have been valuable learning experiences to which he has devoted great energy. Baker points out,

> Giving service to jazz is something that I enjoy doing, even though I have never learned how to say no to somebody who needs something from me. My life's lesson to kids now is to go to wisdom sources whenever you can, take advantage of these jazz masters that we're going to be losing at some point. We're trying to expose people to as much truth as we can by going back to these sources. For me it's about bringing together the knowledge that I've accrued teaching for fifty years and being able to disseminate that knowledge to kids where they're able to change. There's no point in me worrying about what's been done and [what] I can't do, but to profit from the mistakes I've made.

NOTES

1. All conversation excerpts with David Baker throughout this chapter are part of an interview conducted by Willard Jenkins in May 2010.

2. "NEA at a Glance," National Endowment of the Arts website, April 2009, www.nea.gov/about/Facts/AtAGlance.html.

3. All conversation excerpts with A. B. Spellman throughout this chapter are part of an interview conducted by Willard Jenkins in July 2010.

4. Horowitz. *Public Participation in the Arts: Research Note #16*, National Endowment of the Arts website, May 27, 1986, www.nea.gov/research/Notes/16.pdf.

5. Horowitz, *The American Jazz Music Audience*, Education Resources Information Center website, 1986, eric.ed.gov/PDFS/ED280757.pdf.

6. That barrier was obliterated in the 1980s when producer Michael Grofsorean instituted a jazz component at the Spoleto Festival.

7. Greenlee, *The Spook Who Sat by the Door*.

8. Willard Jenkins served as executive director of the National Jazz Service Organization 1989–94, leaving a year prior to the organization's dissolution.

9. Horowitz, *The American Jazz Music Audience*.

10. Ratliff, "A Jazz Lifeline to Academia Is Severed."

11. A good summary of speculations on the cause can be found in Hopkins, "IAJE."

REFERENCES

Baker, David N., ed. *New Perspectives on Jazz*. Washington, D.C.: Smithsonian Institution, 1990.

Greenlee, Sam. *The Spook Who Sat by the Door*. New York: R. W. Baron, 1969.

Hopkins, Marc. "IAJE: Miseducation." *Jazz Times Magazine* 38, no. 6 (July/August 2008): 6.

Horowitz, Harold. *The American Jazz Music Audience*. Washington, D.C.: National Jazz Service Organization, 1986.

———. *Public Participation in the Arts: Research Note #16*. Washington, D.C.: National Endowment of the Arts, 1986.

Ratliff, Ben. "A Jazz Lifeline to Academia Is Severed." *New York Times*, April 26, 2008.

Spellman, A. B. "Four Lives in the Bebop Business." New York: Pantheon Books, 1966.

9

Coda

MONIKA HERZIG

THE CODA OF A MUSICAL piece is a separate movement that creates a memorable ending to a composition while incorporating previous stylistic elements and themes. In fact, Merriam-Webster defines a coda as a concluding musical section that is formally distinct from the main structure or a concluding part of a literary or dramatic work.[1] Similarly, this concluding chapter features a summary piece on the impact and future of jazz education, observations on David Baker's effective strategies and personality traits, and his keynote address at the inaugural Jazz Education Network conference, May 20–22, 2010. Most importantly, this finale is not an ending, but a look ahead into the future of jazz and jazz education.

TWENTY-FIRST-CENTURY JAZZ EDUCATION

As we review the legacy of David Baker, it is clear that his influence goes well beyond the jazz field as a prolific master composer in classical as well as jazz styles, as arranger and performer, conductor, historian, author, administrator, and – of course – pedagogue. In fact, Nathan Davis, director of jazz studies at the University of Pittsburgh, points out that Baker could easily hold the position of composer-in-residence at any major university.[2] Nevertheless, being widely recognized as the "B" in the ABCs of jazz education (Jamey Aebersold, David Baker, and Jerry Coker), Baker has especially succeeded in making jazz available and accessible to generations of jazz students globally as well as codifying a universal approach to jazz pedagogy. Indiana University Associate Professor of Woodwinds Tom Walsh notes,

> But, I mean, in terms of teaching, certainly every day that I teach I'm paying homage to David Baker. There's no doubt that huge amounts of what I teach comes from David. And there comes a point where you don't even remember where you learned something or how you learned something. And I have this experience of starting to think something is my own . . . then I'll open up one of his books and I am like, "Oh! There it is. It's been there all along. Oh, yeah, I guess I did learn that from David." So, you know, it certainly perpetuates my teaching.[3]

Pat Harbison, professor of jazz studies at Indiana University, confirms Baker's success in codifying the language of jazz and explaining the need for preserving its oral traditions for future generations:

> He [David Baker] has codified a lot of these things that he learned by the oral tradition and now the oral tradition virtually doesn't exist. He has created an academic discipline, and pedagogy, and methodology for us to convey that information and passing that cultural code forward. It's almost like breeding wild animals in the zoo once they're extinct in the wild. It's not quite that desperate yet, but if he hadn't done that we would be looking at a nearly extinct population in the wild, I think. . . . An oral tradition only needs to have one lost generation and it's gone.[4]

Stuart Nicholson confirms Harbison's speculations. He points out that as more and more mostly self-taught master musicians departed, the last traces of a true oral tradition also disappeared, and we now live in the age of the college-educated jazz musician.[5] Nicholson also points towards a discrepancy of academic training versus audience demands in the music market, in which the consumer decides to buy music based on personal attraction to the sound rather than the artist's level of education. Further criticism is directed towards a lack of individuality and originality of performers coming off the "jazz-education production line."[6] Guitarist John Scofield confirms in an interview for *Jazz Times* magazine that he noticed such shortcomings in young players.[7]

Asked about the concern that academia may be stifling the growth of jazz, Baker strongly denies such possibilities. In his view, academia provides not only the possibility for jazz musicians to preserve the history but also the opportunity to develop new directions and new repertoire without the pressures of having to make financial profits for a record company or club owner:

> First of all, I think that that's absolute nonsense. For instance, classical music hasn't stopped growing because it's in academia. Otherwise you wouldn't have all the new music programs that play music by contemporary composers. And I think you have the best of both worlds in an academic situation because for example, I always see my role as twofold: one to preserve, the other to nurture. So at the same time I'm talking about Benny Carter, Oliver Nelson, or George Russell I'll also talk about where it is going. I think the people who are most frightened about that are the people who have the most to lose if jazz is a part of academia.[8]

Similar concerns about jazz as a living art form have been raised recently, based on the results of the fourth Survey of Public Participation in the Arts conducted by the National Endowment of the Arts in 2008.[9] Results indicated the following tendencies, as extracted in Terry Teachout's provocative article for *The Wall Street Journal* questioning the commercial survival of jazz:[10]

- In 2002, the year of the last survey, 10.8 percent of adult Americans attended at least one jazz performance. In 2008, that figure fell to 7.8 percent.
- Not only is the audience for jazz shrinking, but it's growing older – fast. The median age of adults in America who attended a live jazz performance in 2008 was forty-six. In 1982 it was twenty-nine.

- Older people are also much less likely to attend jazz performances today than they were a few years ago. The percentage of Americans between the ages of forty-five and fifty-four who attended a live jazz performance in 2008 was 9.8 percent. In 2002, it was 13.9 percent. That's a 30 percent drop in attendance.
- Even among college-educated adults, the audience for live jazz has shrunk significantly, to 14.9 percent in 2008 from 19.4 percent in 1982.

Although these numbers sound alarming on first sight, indicating a dwindling and aging audience, it is important to consider the population sample and the overall economic tendencies at the time of the survey. In the last quarter of 2008, the American economy had been in recession for six months and declining participation in arts events was noticeable across all art forms, most likely due to strained financial resources.[11] However, arts participation via the Internet was on the rise, indicating a shift in consumer habits. Finally, younger audiences frequent smaller clubs and outdoor events rather than the typically more expensive and elite performing arts venues sampled for this survey. For example, NEA Jazz Master Ornette Coleman performed as part of the 2007 Bonnaroo lineup, which featured a sold-out audience of eighty thousand youngsters; this festival is certainly not categorized as a jazz festival for survey purposes.

During two extensive interviews in 1997 and 2008 on the current state and future of jazz and jazz education, Baker expressed the following key points.[12] In response to the question on the economic viability of jazz as an art form and becoming a jazz musician, Baker indicated that excellence in education certainly produces good results. He also believes that the commercial world now has aligned closely with academia for job opportunities and new directions. The high placement of graduates in jazz studies from the Indiana University Jazz Department is living proof of its outstanding reputation and high quality of education:

> We have a hell of a rate with placing our students. Many of them perform at the highest level like Bob Hurst. I can't tell you how many students are on cruise ships. We've got students in the service, dozens of students who are teaching in

public schools, not all jazz, but jazz is part of what they do. So I would say that just being from Indiana University already gets you a foot in the door. I think we probably have a better placement rate than some other places do. For instance, from the twenty or more people who auditioned for the saxophone position at Berklee, Shannon Hudgins [LeClaire] got the job. And Billy Pierce told me that there was nobody that was anywhere near Shannon's level because Shannon could do all the repertory stuff, she could play modern stuff, she could teach, and she could play classical music. She played the music from her classical recital and that blew the jury away. Nobody else had been made to do that. Consequently, Shannon walked away with the job.

Another career opportunity for college graduates is joining one of the professional touring ensembles, such as the Woody Herman Band, the Count Basie Band, or the service bands (such as the US Army Blues). Most leaders now find prospective members by scouting the major jazz programs rather than picking up performers in local clubs. David points out,

> Woody Herman told me once: "Look, if somebody has to learn, I would prefer they learn from somebody who knows how to teach." And then he put a post-script on it, just like Maynard does. He said, "Virtually every band I've had for the last twenty years included predominantly players who came out of the college bands." Every year in the spring I would get a call from Woody's manager, asking, "Do you have two tenor players? Do you have a drummer?" And it wasn't just me. That call went to [the] Eastman [School of Music] to Bill Dobbins, to [the University of] North Texas to Dan Haerle, because they realized that the feeder systems, just as it is in the NBA with basketball and in the NFL with football, are in the colleges – because that's the only place where you get slave labor, where somebody can learn.

One major emphasis of the Indiana University jazz program is to prepare students to be versatile in performing different styles of music and knowledgeable about other music-related fields. Such versatility pays off in today's highly competitive market. Baker cites examples of students who worked as tune detectors for BMI or made a living transcribing country and western pieces to be registered for copyright. He admits that the job market is changing and performance opportunities in traditional jazz clubs have decreased. But other opportunities have developed such as performing at colleges or other venues, such as coffeehouses and of course teaching at the secondary and college level. Many jazz musicians have succeeded in finding ways of making a living

by creating new performance opportunities at nontraditional venues or
creating income from related areas such as music copying or providing
corporate entertainment. In the 1997 interview, David observes,

> The venues have changed. I'm just saying that if it's a prerequisite for teaching,
> it's a problem. If, however, you're willing to accept that the venues have changed,
> your performance might be in a college atmosphere. It might be in a repertory
> band like the band that I lead [the Smithsonian Jazz Masterworks Orchestra]. It
> might be playing in coffeehouses. If you're willing to accept a change in venues,
> then there is a market. If you're trying to hold on to that old business of Fifty-
> second Street, your stomach is going to be growling really loud because you will
> be hungry all the time. Also, people are starting to realize that they might get a
> job as a librarian with a major orchestra or they might get a job doing whatever.
> People are so busy trying to be performers and that's a very, very limited avenue.

Differing opinions exist on the teaching of jazz in academic settings.
In an investigation on the elements of jazz piano pedagogy, jazz pianist
Clare Fischer expressed strong reservations about the teaching of jazz,
whereas colleagues Jeff Hellmer and Bill Cunliffe believed that the inclusion of jazz in academia is a positive development and helps sustain
jazz as an art form and support more jazz musicians economically.[13] A
similar discussion appeared in the *New York Times* in conjunction with
the 2007 IAJE conference in New York.[14] Even with the change in venue
and such an emphasis on jazz teaching and performing in academic settings, Baker sees no dangers to a continued development of the creative
and subjective aspects of jazz. On the contrary, he believes that having
a college position allows many jazz musicians to pursue their creative
interests without financial concerns, as do contemporary classical composers. Students also have the opportunity to get their arrangements and
compositions performed by capable ensembles and develop their skills
and individual styles without commercial pressures. Baker exemplifies
this with the following statements:

> That's why you [Monika Herzig] wrote so much music for big band while
> you were here [as a doctoral student at Indiana University], because if you're
> going to New York you'll have to pay somebody to rehearse your music or put
> together a rehearsal big band. You have to get people to come from all over town
> to rehearse. If they don't show up, what are your options? You don't have any
> sanctions like, "If you don't show up I'm not going to let you play any more in my
> rehearsal band." Come on. Give me a break. So it seems to me that the keeper of
> the flame now is academia just like for a composer. Do you know any composer

who is making a fulltime living and is not associated with a college or some kind of university situation? I really don't know. I'm sure there are some, but most of them are emeritus. They already have retired. [Coleridge-Taylor] Perkinson, one of the great composers in America today, worked hard to have the security of a college job which would allow him to have health benefits and a steady income so that he could write music. I have no illusions about this. I have more music recorded than any composer on this faculty, but it's because I do so many other things that I can afford to write.

Baker strongly believes in the obligation of academia to keep jazz alive. Now jazz musicians can, instead of competing with each other, work together in spreading the message of jazz, due to the support of the academic system:

> Ten years ago there wouldn't be somebody with a doctorate sitting here who cares enough about where the music came from, that you would take your time to do this [analyze the past, present, and future of jazz education]. Ten years ago you would have been so busy trying to make sure that nobody else got in your way of a job that probably you wouldn't have thought about how to perpetuate, how to make sure that this music stays alive. I fought with myself when they offered me the job at the Smithsonian. I said, "I don't really need this. I don't want to do this." But I got in the door. We started out doing music from 1928 to 1938. Then it was 1928 to 1942 and now this last season I did music that was written in 1976. That's a hell of a span from 1928 to 1976 and every time I add ten years to it I'm getting closer to our time. Pretty soon repertory music will mean music written over a month ago. That's not that farfetched. When I chose to do Oliver Nelson, it was basically because Oliver had been neglected and it's important music. When I chose to do Benny Carter, [it was] not quite for the same reasons because Benny hasn't been neglected, but all his early music had been neglected. So it seems to me that all of us have a hell of an obligation as keepers of the flame. What it is that President Kennedy said? "Ask not what your country can do for you. Ask what you can do for your country."

In discussing the role of the college jazz educator, Baker also points towards some new challenges for the future. The increasing number of high school jazz programs now provide students entering college with a strong basis of skills and knowledge. A higher skill level creates new challenges for the college educator, such as finding ways to help students get past their technical skills and find ways to become creative and refine their playing style. Baker explains,

> It means that I start on a different level. It means that I have to find ways to let them be creative, to let them get beyond their superior technical skills. To be

truthful, if I auditioned now with where I was as a trombone player, I wouldn't get into school. Where my ear was when I got into school, I wouldn't even pass the theory test. Yes, the skills are up but that doesn't mean you shouldn't go out in the streets and learn how to use those skills. The first part of the equation is to get the skills and have them, but the second part of the equation is what you do with them. There is a parable in the Bible about the man who gave his sons ten talents each. Two of the sons used their money to buy grain and plants and one had put his talents under a barrel so that they wouldn't be stolen. And the lesson of the parable was you don't hide your talents under a basket. You use them to bear fruit. And I really believe that my role as a teacher is to help kids maximize their talents. That's why I'm so impatient with students. When students don't give me everything that they got to give me, then I take it as a personal offense.

Of course, Baker is always observing his students' progress and looks for educational needs and problems to be solved. In light of the recent expanded emphasis on the combo program at Indiana University, he detected a need for teaching performance etiquette and conventions on the bandstand. In the 2008 interview, he points out,

I find out that the kids come out of here, but they don't know commonsense things. For instance, they don't know how to start a tune. They don't know how to end a tune. And I get so tired of hearing them ending like a play-along (sings ending of "Take the 'A' Train"). You'd think that's all that we have. When kids go out on the gig and they do decide to extend the ending of "Bye, Bye, Blackbird," but then they don't know how to end and it keeps going and it keeps going. Nobody knows how to count off, and then there's the body language. How do you indicate to another player that you're finishing your solo? How do you indicate to another player that you're going to extend it? Do you do it orally, do you do it by mouth? How do you communicate the changes? So this book [I'm writing] is addressing [all of] this. First I'm looking at all of the pieces that have standardized introductions and endings like "All the Things You Are" or "Star Eyes" and things like that. See, I didn't used to teach the bebop scales because I assumed everybody would learn them the way I did. And then I found out they didn't. They had to really learn them. And so consequently I started writing books. I don't write a book that I don't think anyone needs. But if I see that it's something I need to teach, then I assume that other people will also need to have it to teach.

Finally, Baker talks about his dedication to education. He points out that he became an educator because he wanted to give back the opportunities that had been provided to him from mentors such as Dizzy Gillespie. Creating an educated audience for jazz is an essential strategy to keep the music alive and growing:

I feel like I have to give something back. That's why I went all these years sitting on all these boards of directors where I could not get grants or anything to help me, because I felt I needed to give something back to Dizzy who didn't have to give me a scholarship to Lenox. I was nothing. But somebody said, "Hey, I believe I ought to take a chance on you." That's why this wall [in David Baker's office] is full of Dizzy Gillespie [pictures and photographs], because somebody believed in me and somebody was willing to reach out. People ask me, "Look, of the seventy books or so that you have written, you don't get enough credit for being the person who started all this." And I tell them, "I don't have time to worry about money. I can't spend any more money than I've got. I got enough to eat, I got a nice house, I got people that I care about, I have friends that I love, I have students that I care about, I'm healthy, I have a granddaughter that I absolutely adore. What more do I need? If it were about money, I would have been a nuclear physicist. Then I would really have some money. I probably would also be counting the days from the first day I started the job until the day I was going to retire with my gold watch. This is about love. There is no glory and a halo over your head when you help somebody learn to play. My educational philosophy is about perpetuation of the music."

BAKER REKAB

The following is a variety of interview excerpts collected from David Baker's peers, colleagues, and students during 2009 and 2010. All of these are responses to the question of what they think makes Baker such an effective teacher and leader and pinpoint special traits of his personality. Mihaly Csikszentmihalyi, a leader in research on creativity, points out how documenting the story and creative process of outstanding minds helps us understand and grasp the process of creative thinking and provides guidance for future generations. Similarly this segment provides a profile in creativity.[15]

Reflecting Csikscentmihalyi's findings, Baker certainly has a strong drive to create and produce, thus often living in a state of flow where the creative energy surpasses even the need to eat and sleep. The appendixes in this book document his most prolific output and his wife, Lida Baker, comments on the challenges of living with such a high energy personality:

> Suddenly I was living with somebody who didn't seem to need to sleep that much. And I would try to stay up at night and keep him company and get up when he was getting up. He was trying to teach me how not to sleep. . . . I just

couldn't understand how somebody wouldn't need any rest. And I said, "Don't you need to stop and have some down time, have some recreation time?" And he said, "No, what I do when I need a rest is, I switch to a different activity." And that's what he still does. For example, if he gets tired, he'll stop practicing and sit with his headphones on and work through some scores that he needs to learn.[16]

Fellow jazz educator and past president of the Jazz Education Network, Mary Jo Papich, exemplifies Baker's generosity with this story from his 2002–2005 presidency of the International Association for Jazz Education (IAJE):

> I got to see the budget reports at the beginning [of my tenure as president-elect of the IAJE]. The presidents were only allowed to spend so much a year for travel. ... They got a stipend that they weren't supposed to go over. Some of them went beyond it. David Baker utilized zero money throughout his presidency. And I'm sure he's the only president who's ever done that. He never spent a dime of IAJE money.... And I think that's extremely admirable.[17]

Bassist and Rutgers University Professor Emeritus Larry Ridley has a similar report on Baker's willingness to give:

> I was a guest professor at the University of Natal.... I was only supposed to go over there for a short period, and I ended up staying a couple months ... and the students were wonderful. And I called David transatlantic and I said, "David, there's a need here. And I want to stay on and to do what I can to help Darius [Brubeck] working with these young South African musicians." David packed up a box of books and all kinds of stuff – recordings and everything – and sent that to me. That's my brother.[18]

In 1966, fellow jazz educator Jerry Coker recommended to Indiana University School of Music Dean Wilfred Bain that he should hire David Baker, as he would be able to bring all factions together and make a "big production." This prophecy has been confirmed not just in the academic setting of Indiana University, but as a global ambassador for jazz. Poet and author A. B. Spellman observes a similar gift for diplomacy:

> Fact of the matter is that it took America almost a century to forgive jazz for its origins. And Billy [Taylor] and then David [Baker] were crucial in getting that achieved. So at first David was so unassuming and such an easygoing person that I thought, "Oh, man, this one is not going to be the fighter that the music needs." But I was entirely wrong. He had a way of picking the right spots and saying exactly the right thing with exactly the right force and clarity. And one of the first things he said is that "I have no doubt that when the history of American music in the twentieth century is written that Charlie Parker, Louis Armstrong,

Duke Ellington will be right up there on top as the greatest American musical artists." And he was prepared to defend it. And again, his voice was a very important voice because he could argue with the symphonic people because he knew that music so well. So he could argue with them on their terms. I've got a lot of respect and friendship with David Baker.[19]

Baker's diplomacy and advocacy for jazz as a national treasure and viable art form also have been recognized by former chairman of the National Endowment for the Arts Dana Gioia:

I first met David shortly after I became chairman when he arrived in my office. ... David arrived in my office for two apparent reasons. The first was simply to meet the new chairman of the NEA; and second, to serve as sort of an ambassador, or even a lobbyist ... for the jazz field. And we had a long, friendly conversation about music, about jazz, about music education. And from that first meeting I had a reaction, which I think is a pretty common reaction, which was that this is just a great guy, a great human being, a great musician, a great music teacher, and a great soul.[20]

What Baker's students and colleagues appreciate is that beyond his vast amount of knowledge about music and advocacy for the field, he also has unique stories and historical anecdotes to back up his points. His background as a world-renowned performer with roots in the history of jazz deserves much respect. Director of jazz studies at DePauw University and longtime member of the Smithsonian Jazz Masterworks Orchestra Randy Salman comments on that fact while reflecting on Baker's conducting styles:

But there's a certain amount of respect. Not only would I respect him anyway because of who he is and what he stands for, but yes, he was there. He went through the trenches; he transformed it. He automatically gets my respect, a little above and beyond someone who's really a stellar, bright, incredible musician, but maybe hasn't had that kind of historical perspective.[21]

Such respect and authority could easily create a distance from students and colleagues. But according to multiple testimonies, Baker has a strong sense of family and inspires through his warm and welcoming nature. Associate Professor of jazz studies at Florida International University Gary Campbell recalls the importance of becoming part of the jazz family:

You know, if you're just a child and ... you're playing music and listening to records and fantasizing about playing music and all this and trying to learn off of listening to records and the radio and all this, then to start on a regular basis to start taking a lesson with somebody who is part of this world, that's a big step. It's like finding something, or being found, too.[22]

Executive producer of the Smithsonian Jazz Masterworks Orchestra Ken Kimery confirms such sentiments:

What I find also for me to be very inspiring is David's family is a very extended family. We've traveled throughout the country, we've traveled internationally, and I can't tell you a time that I haven't run into somebody that is part of that extended family, that David has taught in some way and is just thoroughly excited about what David has afforded them and their personal growth. That says something about him to me as somebody who has been very unselfish in his giving, to be able to help the cause, help those who are interested in learning about the music, helping them grow and then continue to be there as a partner in this growth process. There are very few people who have that capacity and really are committed to that, and I've been here sixteen years, and I've never seen anything but that.[23]

Furthermore, Kimery reflects that "David's most lasting impact is that he's not just a teacher. He's committed to that individual as a teacher, as a friend, a mentor, forever."

David's wife, Lida Baker, confirms his genuine and warm nature, admitting that her initial attraction was based on this personality trait:

He was just this incredibly kind, genuinely nice person, very friendly, very outgoing, very nice to everybody. It didn't make any difference if you were the president of the university or if you were a custodian. That impressed me enormously. I already knew that he was a wonderful composer, a teacher, a per- former, a writer, before I ever really knew him. But when I first met him and was just observing how he behaved and acted with people, I was just so impressed with how kind and generous he was.[24]

Some musicians were hesitant to share their knowledge and skills, especially during the beginnings of the jazz education movement. As Nathan Davis points out in chapter 3, his fellow musicians in Paris were resistant about teaching jazz and cautioned him about selling out when he decided to accept a teaching position in the late 1960s.[25] Jazz educa- tor and entrepreneur Jamey Aebersold confirms Baker's unusual level of commitment to teaching and sharing his craft, recalling his student days at Indiana University:

Back there when I was going to college – and I hope I don't get off track – I didn't ask a lot of people who really played well at IU any questions, because I knew that they would not give me answers or they would brush me off or fluff me off. Or say something like, "Well, if you can't hear, you don't need to get it." I knew that's what was going to be the answer. But with David I never got that. David would tell you; whatever he knew he would tell you. And, if he didn't know he'd tell you to go ask somebody else. He'd direct you to the right person. And I think that's extremely important because back then in the late '50s and '60s the idea of sharing information wasn't universal in the jazz community.[26]

Beyond creating a sense of family and a willingness to share, much of Baker's effective teaching can also be attributed to his encouragement to his students to develop their individuality and independence in learning. *Saturday Night Live* drummer Shawn Pelton observes this of his student days at Indiana University:

> I always thought that David did have a sense of vision about planting seeds in his players. You know, about reaching for something that's different.

Indiana University Associate Professor of Jazz Studies Luke Gillespie expressed his gratitude for Baker's guidance to find independence:

> I asked him if I could have a private lesson. One was at the end of my undergraduate time and the other was towards the beginning of my master's. I took four years off, so there were about four years between those lessons. I can tell you – I don't have the copy with me right now; it is at home. In my first lesson with him – in fact, in both lessons – he worked with me for an hour and a half to two hours each time. I wrote notes down on just one sheet of paper those things he told me to work on and practice, and those things took easily two to four years to practice. Each lesson lasted two to four years. Wow!! I thought this was amazing. You're used to people giving you a lesson and then the next week and so forth. So that made me realize he acted like he was like a musical coach, a facilitator. He wanted to allow me or show me as he tried to show his students to learn to teach myself. He will give you some materials and some tools but you have to do it. He's not going to paint the painting for you. And this reminds me of one of the things he said in his jazz improvisation textbooks. I remember vividly the last sentence of the preface or foreword, "Every student is encouraged to bring something of his or her own personality to everything, whether it is a scale or a tune, someone else's composition or your own. . . . Bring something of your own personality when you play." And that struck me. Why did he say that in an improvisation class? I didn't understand it at eighteen, but I realize now that improvisation is not just simply regurgitated material but putting your own stuff on the music. So, two lessons, and each one lasted at least two to four years.[27]

When saxophonist Randy Salman first started his teaching job at DePauw University, he observed Baker's approach to pedagogy during classes and private lessons in order to formulate his own curriculum and philosophy:

> The other thing that always inspired me, that I thought was very interesting, was even though he was concrete in what he wanted you to do, if you did something good he would incorporate your approach or at least he would say, "Hey, that was really great. That isn't what I would usually do, but man, that sounds wonderful," or whatever. So in a way he's dogmatic in trying to present the materials and the language. On the other hand, he's very flexible and has that information, understands that it is a personal music, and it is about individual freedom and all of that.[28]

Lida Baker confirms having observed many times over the years David's unique gift of quickly analyzing the strengths and needs of any student. Furthermore, he immediately tailors his pedagogical strategy to offer the best materials and guidance needed in any particular situation:

> I was always really impressed at how he seemed to be able to guide people. He seemed to be able to really put his finger on what would be the most helpful thing to say to a young soloist, for example, or a person who was just struggling with some problem or somebody who just really had a personality characteristic that might turn out to make them not quite so employable later on or make them not quite so easy to work with. . . . It's just so impressive to watch him work with players of all levels and ability, all different commands of the English language. He seems to be able to genuinely help anybody that comes to him for help.[29]

Beyond being flexible and understanding individual needs, Baker has succeeded in codifying the language of jazz and successfully communicating its ingredients. As Grammy-nominated vocalist and fellow educator Janet Lawson points out,

> There are lots of jazz educators. There are lots of jazz books. But David knew how to cut through and say exactly what it was that would give you what you needed. I think that's his genius.[30]

Multiple Grammy Award–winning trumpeter Randy Brecker attributes much of his early progress to private lessons with David Baker between 1962 and 1964:

> It was a fascinating time for me because he helped codify stuff that I had learned but I didn't know the terminology and I didn't know how to apply certain scales to chords. So, it was a very fertile learning period for me.[31]

And saxophone master James Moody sums it all up:

That's what I'm saying! You know, I know somebody's brilliant when I see them or hear them, you know, so, give me a little bit of that![32]

The importance of modeling as part of effective music pedagogy was discussed early in chapter 5 as one Baker's inspirations to start the 21st Century Bebop Band. The trait that Baker has modeled from early on as a key factor to success is discipline in focusing on a task as well as managing time. Fellow educator and Crispus Attucks High School graduate Tillman Buggs recalls this example:

> He had the discipline to go on and do what had to be done. He had the discipline. I remember one summer school we were down in Bloomington, and he didn't know how to swim. So we'd go swimming after a class, and within a few days David was swimming. He kept going, figuring it out. So I thought about it. This guy is special. He doesn't let anything stop him. And the same thing was true back in theory class in high school. He was a year behind [me], as I mentioned. Mr. Merrifield taught the class. At that time David had played the tuba, the baritone, and hadn't gotten to the trombone, which are all bass-clef instruments. In theory, you have to play more than those. He didn't know the treble clef at the time. And most of the people in the class were piano players; at least they knew both clefs. But it was just a matter of time. He picked it up and ran away with it. Of all the people in the class, he has probably done more than any of us that were there. So I just take my hat off.[33]

A conversation with David Baker, no matter if it's casual storytelling or intellectual discussion, invariably includes some puns and word games. In fact, as Indiana University jazz studies colleague Tom Walsh suspects,

> Anybody who's around David for any amount of time starts using puns more frequently. There's no doubt about that. And, that's part of his intelligence and his curiosity just as a person. It's really astonishing how much he absorbs and processes in terms of books that he reads, and his range of interest in terms of even just TV shows and basketball and movies somewhat – he's not a movie buff per se – but if there's a new book out and somebody has sent him a copy, he's looked it over. And he can tell you what it's about and give you an opinion about whether it's well written or not. And that curiosity and kind of active mind, it extends to just the way he likes to engage in word play, so puns are a big part of that and all the storytelling and jokes and all that.[34]

Indiana University reference librarian David Lasocki recalls the following example of word play:

David Lasocki, teasing: "Still composing, David"?

David Baker: "Better composing than decomposing."[35]

Baker's first wife, Jeannie, remembers all the word games the family engaged in during car rides:

> When we'd go to Indianapolis, all of us, we would read words backwards on the signs or whatever you'd see. So that was always a big thing. And then another thing David used to do when driving . . . he'd tap out a beat on the [steering] wheel and they'd have to figure out what tune it was. So that was always a thing that we would do clear to Indianapolis and back to [Bloomington]. And it's amazing how many tunes you can name just from the pattern.[36]

Baker is well aware of his frequent engagement in word play. In fact, he points out that finding puns and quotes is a great way to keep the mind sharp and active:

> I get into puns and into word play, because what makes something funny sometimes is the context you put it in. Fact is, all jokes are a kind of creative magic. The pun is creative magic. You take what is the pun – the word – and all of a sudden it shifts its meaning. Consequently, I try to devise as many different techniques for making myself stay sharp about how I use material. When I play, nothing pleases me more than when I'm playing and all of a sudden I come up with a double quote.[37]

David Baker's daughter, April, was the first string player to graduate from the Indiana University jazz studies program in 1982. She runs a private violin studio in Bloomington and performs frequently in orchestras as well as chamber ensembles. April confirms Baker's exemplary discipline and recalls strict daily family practice sessions early in the morning before school started, as well as required attendance at everyone's performances up to this day. Furthermore, the family was often called upon for help in completing Baker's scores and manuscripts. Balancing a fledgling music career with family life is a quite common demand for young musicians and rarely dealt with in teaching methods. Jeannie Baker has some anecdotes that shouldn't necessarily serve as models, but remind us of the importance of community and family, something David Baker values most of all:[38]

> Once I had hidden Christmas gifts in the closet. And then he, when April was smaller and he was in between bouts with the hospital and things he was, of course, the one taking care of her. And I came home and he's wearing his sweater and she's already got hers. Once I had picked up a cake for her birthday and she must have been going to be one [year old] and was just on the table. And when I

came home she was sitting on the table, you know, with chocolate cake all over her. And once she was sitting with all the guys [who were] smoking and rehearsing at the house and she was drinking out of the beer cans they had put their cigarette butts in. And then when they had rehearsal in the club when George Russell would come, he [David Baker] would take her pillow with him and she would go to sleep in a booth, or something. And once, I guess she had gotten right in front [of him when he was playing] George Russell's music. She was standing right in front of him, going [holds hands over ears]. He said, "It must be good because April hates it." And if he forgot her pillow, he would really be in trouble then. And then he went shopping only once for our car. I would never let him do it again. He bought a Fiat with, you know, no front end. It's like a little miniature station wagon but with no front end. And he would drive around and April would be standing next to him leaning on him drinking a malt, you know. And people would tell me they saw him. But he was the caregiver. And she survived, so I guess it was okay.

KEYNOTE ADDRESS AT THE INAUGURAL CONFERENCE OF THE JAZZ EDUCATION NETWORK, MAY 21, 2010, ST. LOUIS, MISSOURI

Thank you, Mary Jo, for those very kind words. It is an honor and a privilege to be standing here in front of all of you at the inaugural conference of this wonderful new organization, the Jazz Education Network.

Because of the tireless efforts of many talented and selfless people, the constituencies that make up our jazz education family – teachers, students, performers, and industry – have once again been brought together under one roof for the benefit of us all.

We owe a deep debt of gratitude to our president, Mary Jo Papich, our president-elect, Dr. Lou Fischer, the original steering committee and mentors, the founding and charter members, the executive board, the board of directors, and many others who have contributed their time and talents to the formation of this organization and to making this inaugural conference possible.

Would you please join me in thanking all of them for their hard work on our behalf?

I don't know about the rest of you, but for the past several years, January has been a difficult month for me in the absence of our annual gathering. For many of us, our IAJE time was more than a convention of clinics, performances, lectures, demonstrations, exhibits, and the like. It was a family reunion – a time for renewing personal and professional bonds, catching up with longtime friends and colleagues, making new friends and professional and personal connections, and continuing to learn and learn and learn.

What a joy it is to have the opportunity to gather together again to pursue our shared passion for jazz education and to support the goals and ideals of the Jazz Education Network!

I have been asked to speak today on our conference theme: Shaping the Future of Jazz Education. I think that we can agree that we are living and working in challenging times. All of us – teachers, performers, presenters, publishers, journalists, and others – have been affected in ways we could not have imagined just a few short years ago.

But think of it this way. We who have dedicated our lives to jazz and jazz education have faced challenging times before. We must not lose heart, and we *will not* lose heart! Remember how far we have come!

Jazz is no longer stigmatized as a lesser music, a music without value, a music which was said to corrupt and defile not only those who played it but also those who listened to it. Those of us of my generation remember a time when, if you were attending college and studying music, you could lose your practice privileges for playing jazz in the music building. In some schools, you could even be expelled and sent home! At Lincoln University in Jefferson City, Missouri, where I had my first teaching job, even faculty members were not exempt. I was told in no uncertain terms by the Dean of the school, "No jazz in the big house!"

As I said in an article in the January 2010 issue of *JazzEd* magazine, in my opinion the state of jazz education today has never been healthier, never been better.

Here are some of the reasons:

· More schools than ever have jazz bands or jazz programs. In looking at our conference schedule, all levels are represented by clinics and/or performances – K through 8, middle school, high school, performing arts school, and college.
· Jazz also has a home in institutional settings other than schools. Here are four examples:

1. The jazz orchestras attached to institutions like Lincoln Center in New York City and the Smithsonian Institution in Washington, D.C.

2. The jazz bands which are a part of the musical performing ensembles in the various branches of the military. One of the finest, the Army Blues, performed brilliantly on last night's concert.

3. In jazz clubs. For example, Blues Alley in Washington, D.C., runs an educational outreach program for the benefit of aspiring young jazz musicians in the District of Columbia and the surrounding areas.

4. The jazz programs supported by the National Endowment for the Arts, including grants, the American Jazz Masters Fellowship awards, and the Jazz Masters in the Schools program

· Because more schools are offering jazz programs, there are now more teachers who are well prepared to deal effectively with a variety of elements of jazz instructions, including directing large and small ensembles, and teaching improvisation, theory, ear training, composition, and arranging. Also, more performers are getting involved as artist-teachers, to the benefit of students at all levels.

· Along with the increase in programs and teachers, the number of talented young players has also increased. In my travels throughout the country, I have seen firsthand a higher level of ensemble performance and improvisation at festivals, competitions, and clinics.

· This is also a time when more jazz materials and resources are available to students, teachers, and researchers than ever before. Even a cursory glance through the numerous catalogs of published compositions and arrangements for jazz ensembles reveals a wealth of materials for bands of all sizes, instrumentations, and levels. Instructional materials in a wide range of formats including books, DVDs, CDs and CD-ROMs, and so forth are abundant. Recordings, including reissues and previously unissued tracks, are accessible in a variety of

formats – so accessible, in fact, that when Quincy Jones gave the
commencement speech at Indiana University last week, when
he was awarded an honorary doctorate, part of the pledge he
had the graduating seniors recite included a promise to stop
downloading music illegally! Research collections at major
repositories, like the Library of Congress and the jazz archives at
Rutgers University, continue to grow; and oral history projects
like the one at the Smithsonian Institution's National Museum
of American History provide invaluable insights into the lives
and work of numerous jazz artists through their own words.

· In spite of the current economic environment, the May 2010
issue of *JazzEd* magazine lists seven pages of summer jazz
programs which will run this summer. Also continuing to run
are a number of select programs in which young jazz musicians
identified as having exceptional potential have the opportunity
to study in environments designed to help them develop in all
aspects of the jazz experience. These include programs such as
those of the Thelonious Monk Institute, the Brubeck Institute,
the Steans Institute for Young Artists at the Ravinia Festival,
Betty Carter Jazz Ahead at the Kennedy Center, and many
others.

· Competitions held by schools and festivals at the local, state,
and national levels, and those sponsored by entities such as
DownBeat Magazine, the American Pianists Association, Jazz
at Lincoln Center, the Thelonious Monk Institute, ASCAP,
and BMI continue to provide awards, scholarships, cash prizes,
recording contracts, performance opportunities, and other
rewards to up-and-coming jazz performers and composers.

Now let's look at some things that I think we need to address in looking at the future of jazz education:

1. It is crucial that we encourage our students to get the best
   all-around musical education possible, and to be prepared to
   work in a wide variety of musical environments. This includes
   teaching them to *listen* – this is why we have two ears and only

one mouth! – and to learn about the historical and cultural context in which the music to which they are listening was created.

2. It is paramount that we promote awareness of how jazz has altered the musical and cultural environment of the twentieth and twenty-first centuries, and will be likely to do so in an even greater way in our time and beyond.

3. Borrowing these words from a Clinton White House presentation entitled "Jazz as a Metaphor for Democracy," in which I was a participant, "We must continue to promote jazz as a means of breaking down cultural, ethnic, language, musical, gender, age, and other demographic barriers."

4. In educational institutions we must continue to widen the scope of the musical environment to include all areas of jazz, from the earliest styles – which, because of their temporal distance, have tended to be less accessible and less desirable as performance sources – to the most advanced present-day styles and everything in between.

5. I would like to see the standard and quality of teaching elevated by encouraging all teachers to perform and understand the imperatives of the performance of jazz.

6. I would like to see us avoid the treadmill of students who become teachers who teach other students to become teachers without the benefit of intervening experiential opportunities.

7. I would like to see us get away from the notion that there is only one way to teach the various aspects of this music, whether it be history, improvisation, arranging, composing, styles and analysis, and so forth.

8. I would like to see us continue to view the music as a shifting, living organism. We must keep an open mind and not be impervious to change. Change is as natural as breathing, and today's seemingly endless verities often become tomorrow's fads and follies.

9. We must be constantly aware of the ever-changing musical, cultural, political, and economic landscape. It is important to envision the future in such a way that we will not continue

to provide students with skills and preparation for jobs which will have become obsolete by the time they have finished their matriculation. We must find a way to tailor information in such a way as to be relevant to the subjects which they will teach, and give them information that they can use.

10. A lot more attention should be given in the classroom to the business side of jazz. This is something that affects every constituency in this music. This includes issues like health care, retirement, taxes, recording, publishing, marketing, contracts, web design, and other areas. Very often only the artistic concerns of the music have been addressed, leaving these other matters to those who may or may not have the best interests of the music and the musicians at heart.

In closing, let me leave you with this final thought:
    Vision without action is daydreaming.
    Action without vision is marking time.
    But vision PLUS action can change the world.
So now let us go forward, with vision plus action; and like the phoenix which rose transformed and triumphant from the ashes, we, too, through the Jazz Education Network, can change the world.
Thank you.

NOTES

1. "Coda," *Merriam-Webster,* www.merriam-webster.com/dictionary/coda.

2. Nathan Davis, telephone conversation with Monika Herzig, July 8, 2010.

3. Tom Walsh, interview by Monika Herzig, May 4, 2010.

4. Pat Harbison, interview by Monika Herzig, May 6, 2010.

5. Nicholson, *Is Jazz Dead?* 100.

6. Ibid., 101.

7. Primack, "Joe Henderson and John Scofield," 60.

8. David Baker, interview by Monika Herzig, September 1997.

9. Williams and Keen, *2008 Survey of Public Participation in the Arts.*

10. Teachout, "Can Jazz Be Saved?"

11. Compare overall tendencies in Williams and Keen, *2008 Survey of Public Participation in the Arts.*

12. The following interview excerpts are from Herzig's September 1997 interview with David Baker investigating the past, present, and future of jazz education; and a follow-up on the topic in August 2008.

13. Herzig, "Elements of Jazz Piano Pedagogy," 59–62.

14. Chinen, "Jazz Is Alive and Well."

15. Csikszentmihalyi, *Creativity,* 10.

16. Lida Baker, interview by Monika Herzig, August 30, 2010.

17. Mary Jo Papich, interview by Monika Herzig, August 6, 2009.

18. Larry Ridley, interview by Monika Herzig, January 11, 2010.

19. A. B. Spellman, interview by Monika Herzig, January 10, 2010.

20. Dana Gioia, interview by Monika Herzig, October 5, 2009.

21. Randy Salman, interview by Monika Herzig, July 7, 2009.

22. Gary Campbell, interview by Monika Herzig, July 7, 2009.

23. Ken Kimery, interview by Monika Herzig, August 18, 2009.

24. Lida Baker, interview.

25. See Nathan Davis's essay on the early generation of jazz educators in chapter 3.

26. Jamey Aebersold, interview by Monika Herzig, August 22, 2009.

27. Luke Gillespie, interview by Monika Herzig, May 6, 2010.

28. Salman, interview.

29. Lida Baker, interview.

30. Janet Lawson, interview by Monika Herzig, January 10, 2010.

31. Randy Brecker, interview by Monika Herzig, January 11, 2010.

32. James Moody, interview by Monika Herzig, June 16, 2009.

33. Tillman Buggs, interview by Monika Herzig, August 8, 2009.

34. Thomas Walsh, interview.

35. E-mail exchange between David Lasocki and Monika Herzig, July 5, 2010.

36. Jeannie Baker, interview by Monika Herzig, May 11, 2010.

37. David Baker, interview by Lida Baker, June 19–21, 2000, transcript, Smithsonian Jazz Oral History Project, www.smithsonianjazz.org/oral_histories/pdf/joh_DavidNBaker_transcript.pdf.

38. "But I don't ever forget that the most important things are family, health, and those things that we have no control over, except in a certain measure" (Baker, interview by Lida Baker, June 19–21, 2000).

REFERENCES

Chinen, Nate. "Jazz Is Alive and Well – In the Classroom, Anyway." *New York Times,* January 7, 2007, A1.

Csikszentmihalyi, Mihaly. *Creativity: Flow and the Psychology of Discovery and Invention.* New York: Harper Perennial, 1997.

Dobbins, Bill. "Jazz and Academia: Street Music in the Ivory Tower." *Bulletin of the Council for Research in Music Education* 96 (Spring 1988): 30–41.

Herzig, Monika. "Elements of Jazz Piano Pedagogy." PHD diss., Indiana University, 1997.

Nicholson, Stuart. *Is Jazz Dead? Or Has It Moved to a New Address?* New York: Routledge, 2003.

Porter, Lewis. "Jazz in American Education Today." *College Music Symposium* 29 (1989): 134–39.

Primack, B. "Joe Henderson and John Scofield." *Jazz Times* 26, no. 10 (1996): 60.

Teachout, Terry. "Can Jazz Be Saved?" *Wall Street Journal,* August 8, 2009, W14.

Williams, Kevin, and Keen, David. *2008 Survey of Public Participation in the Arts.* National Endowment for the Arts Research Report 49. Washington, D.C.: National Endowment for the Arts, 2009.

APPENDIX A

List of Compositions

INTRODUCTORY NOTES Although David Baker has written hundreds of arrangements on the compositions of other composers, this list covers only his own compositions.

The designation "jazz ensemble" is used for compositions that are strictly jazz compositions. David Baker wrote nearly all of the compositions with this designation for big band and also arranged many of them for a variety of smaller jazz ensembles.

ABRAHAM LINCOLN IN INDIANA (2008)
Narrator and chamber ensemble (trumpet, alto saxophone/clarinet, tenor saxophone, baritone saxophone, trombone, piano, bass, and drums).

Narrator's script written by David Baker. Nine movements: I. When Indiana Was the Frontier; II. Clearing Fields and Splitting Rails; III. On the Death of Loved Ones; IV. Boys at Play; V. And He Read Himself to Sleep; VI. Sunday Go to Meetin'; VII. Becoming His Own Man; VIII. A Country Boy; IX. Of Times Gone By. Commissioned by the Indiana Abraham Lincoln Bicentennial Commission.

ABYSS (1968)
Song cycle for soprano and piano. Text by Carole Wright. Four movements:

I. Perception; II. Observation; III. Introspection; IV. Penetration.

ADUMBRATIO (1971)
Jazz ensemble. Also published in an arrangement for jazz nonet (trumpet, alto saxophone, tenor saxophone, trombone, baritone saxophone, guitar, piano, electric bass, and drums) by Three Fifteen West Fifty-Third Street Corp. in their Dave Baker Jazz Rock Series (Charles Colin Publications).

THE AEBERSOLD STRUT (1982)
Jazz ensemble.

AFRO-CUBAN SUITE (1954)
Band. One movement.

AN AFTER HOURS LAMENT (1990)
Jazz ensemble.

AL-KI-HOL (1956)
Jazz ensemble.

ALABAMA LANDSCAPE (1990)
Bass-baritone and orchestra. Text by Mari Evans. Commissioned by William Brown. Published by Lauren Keiser Music.

THE ALARM CLOCK (1973)
Tenor and piano. See THE BLACK EXPERIENCE (1973).

ALMACO (1982)
Jazz ensemble.

ALMOST (1973)
Jazz ensemble. For lead sheet, see
Baker, *Advanced Improvisation.*

AN ALMOST DEATH (1975)
Soprano and chamber ensemble.
See GIVE AND TAKE.

ALTO (2002)
A concerto for saxophone and jazz
ensemble. Commissioned by Bruce
Jordan and Sinclair Community College.

AND HE NEVER SAID A
MUMBALIN' WORD (1990)
Baritone and contrabass. See WITNESS:
SIX ORIGINAL COMPOSITIONS
IN SPIRITUAL STYLE (1990).

AND THEN . . . (2001)
Bass clarinet and piano. Three move-
ments: I. The Song Also Rises; II. On
Wings of Song; III. The Apprentice's
Sources. Commissioned by Howard Klug.

ANDY JACOBS'S CAMPAIGN
SONG (1972)
Incidental music for a television show.
Commissioned by Andrew Jacobs, Jr., for
use in his 1972 Congressional campaign.

ANGEL'S GLOW (2005)
Jazz ensemble.

ANJISA (1973)
Jazz ensemble. For lead sheet, see
Baker, *Advanced Improvisation.*

ANOCAL (2005)
Jazz ensemble.

ANY HUMAN TO ANOTHER (1973)
Chorus (SATB) and piano.
Text by Countee Cullen.

APOCALYPSE (1964)
Jazz ensemble.

APRIL B (1959)
Jazz ensemble. Also published in an
arrangement for jazz nonet (trumpet,
alto saxophone, tenor saxophone,
trombone, baritone saxophone, guitar,
piano, electric bass, and drums) by
Three Fifteen West Fifty-Third Street
Corp. in their Dave Baker Jazz Rock
Series (Charles Colin Publications).
For lead sheet, see Baker, *Arranging and
Composing for the Small Ensemble.*

APRIL IN AUGUST (1996)
Jazz ensemble.

APRIL'S SMILE (2008)
Jazz ensemble.

ASPECTS (1998)
Jazz ensemble.

ASPECTS OF ANDY (1998)
Clarinet, bass, jazz piano, and
string quartet. Three movements.
Commissioned by James Campbell.

AT TWILIGHT (1996)
Jazz ensemble.

AU DEMAIN (1973)
Jazz ensemble.

AUCON (1973)
Jazz ensemble.

AUEV (1973)
Jazz ensemble.

AUJOURD'HUI (1973)
Jazz ensemble.

AULIL (1973)
Jazz ensemble. Jazz septet arrangement
published by Studio PR (trumpet, alto

saxophone, tenor saxophone, trombone, piano, bass, and drums). Also arranged for brass quartet (trumpet, trombone, euphonium, and tuba) by Norlan Bewley. For lead sheet, see Baker, *Advanced Improvisation*. In addition, a play-along track and lead sheets (for concert key treble clef, concert key bass clef, B♭, and E♭ instruments) can be found in the book and CD set *David Baker: Eight Classic Jazz Originals You Can Play*, Jamey Aebersold Play-Along volume 10.

AUTUMN'S DREAMS (1990)
Jazz ensemble. Published by Walrus Music.

THE AVENUE (2001)
Jazz ensemble. Scheduled for publication by Sierra Music.

BAKER'S SHUFFLE (1970)
String orchestra. Published by Creative Jazz Composers.

BALLADE (1967)
F horn, alto saxophone, and violoncello. Commissioned by Peter Gordon.

BASH (1972)
Jazz ensemble.

THE BEATITUDES (1968)
Chorus (SATB), soloists, narrator, jazz ensemble, string orchestra, and dancers. Biblical text. Twelve parts: I. Instrumental Prelude; II. Vocal Introduction; III. Blessed Are the Poor in Spirit; IV. Blessed Are They That Mourn; V. Blessed Are the Meek; VI. Blessed Are They That Hunger; VII. Blessed Are the Merciful; VIII. Blessed Are the Clean in Heart; IX. Blessed Are the Peacemakers; X. Blessed Are They Who Suffer Persecution; XI. Blessed Are Ye When Men Shall Revile You; XII. Instrumental Postlude.

Commissioned by Christian Theological Seminary; Indianapolis, Indiana.

BEBOP REVISITED (1974)
Jazz ensemble. For lead sheet, see Baker, *Advanced Improvisation*.

LA BELLE FLEUR (1964)
Jazz ensemble.

BILY (1974)
Jazz ensemble.

BIRD (TO THE MEMORY OF CHARLIE PARKER) (1970)
Jazz ensemble. Four movements: I. The Blues; II. In Beauty; III. Bird's Lady; IV. Past-Present-Future.

BIRDSONG (1984)
Jazz ensemble. Also arranged for orchestra; see JAZZ SUITE FOR CHAMBER ORCHESTRA AND RHYTHM SECTION.

BLACK AMERICA: TO THE MEMORY OF MARTIN LUTHER KING, JR. (1968; HAS UNDERGONE SEVERAL REVISIONS)
Cantata for jazz ensemble, narrators, chorus (SATB), soloists, and string orchestra. Four movements: I. The Wretched of the Earth (Machinations, Missionaries, Money, Marines); II. Kaleidoscope; III. 125th Street; IV. Martyrs: Malcolm, Medgar, Martin. Texts include the following: Black Man, White World (Stanley Warren); The Burying Ground (traditional); I Dream a World (Langston Hughes); Sorrow Is the Only Faithful One (Pauli Murray); Now That He Is Safely Dead (Carl Hines); Thou Dost Lay Me in the Dust of Death (Biblical); If We Must Die (Claude McKay). For many years a recording of this work was broadcast annually by Voice of America on the anniversary of Dr. King's death.

BLACK CHILDREN (1970)
Chorus (SATB), unaccompanied. See
FIVE SONGS TO THE SURVIVAL
OF BLACK CHILDREN.

THE BLACK EXPERIENCE (1968)
Television theme music. See SON MAR.

THE BLACK EXPERIENCE (1973)
Song cycle for tenor and piano. Text
by Mari Evans. Seven movements:
I. The Alarm Clock; II. A Good
Assassination Should Be Quiet; III. The
Insurgent; IV. I Who Would Encompass
Millions; V. The Rebel; VI. Status
Symbol; VII. Early in the Mornin'.
Commissioned by William Brown.

THE BLACK FRONTIER (1971)
Music for the National Educational
Television [NET] series *The Black
Frontier.* Four one-hour shows: The
New Americans; The Cowherders; The
Buffalo Soldiers; The Exodusters.

BLACK MAN, BLACK WOMAN (1969)
Jazz ensemble. Based on music from
I HEARD MY WOMAN CALL.

BLACK THURSDAY (1964)
Jazz ensemble. Also published in an
arrangement for jazz nonet (trumpet,
alto saxophone, tenor saxophone,
trombone, baritone saxophone, guitar,
piano, electric bass, and drums) by
Three Fifteen West Fifty-Third Street
Corp. in their Dave Baker Jazz Rock
Series (Charles Colin Publications).
For lead sheet, see Baker, *Arranging and
Composing for the Small Ensemble: Jazz,
R&B, Jazz-Rock.* In addition, a play-along
track and lead sheets (for concert key
treble clef, concert key bass clef, Bb,
and Eb instruments) can be found in
the book and CD set *David Baker: Eight
Classic Jazz Originals You Can Play,*
Jamey Aebersold Play-Along volume 10.

BLACK-EYED PEAS AND
CORNBREAD (1970)
String orchestra. Published by
Creative Jazz Composers.

BLUE STRINGS (1970)
String orchestra. Published by
Creative Jazz Composers.

BLUES (1966)
String orchestra. Published by
Creative Jazz Composers. This
piece is an arrangement of "Deliver
My Soul" from PSALM 22.

BLUES (1966)
Violin and piano. This piece is an
arrangement of "Deliver My Soul" from
PSALM 22 and is published by Lauren
Keiser Music under the title "Blues"
("Deliver My Soul"). The recordings
of this piece list the title as "Blues."

BLUES FOR BIRD (1972)
Jazz ensemble. For lead sheet, see
Baker, *Advanced Improvisation.*

BLUES FOR D. P. (1999)
Jazz ensemble.

BLUES ODYSSEY (2006)
Tuba ensemble. Commissioned by
Winston Morris for the fortieth an-
niversary of the Tennessee Technological
University Tuba Ensemble.

BOOCHIE (1985)
Incidental music for the play
Boochie by Mari Evans.

THE BOOGIE JOOG
Jazz ensemble.

DE BOOGIE MAN (1973)
Jazz ensemble.

BORDERLINE (1972)
Soprano, string quartet, and piano.
See SONGS OF THE NIGHT.

BORDERLINE (1972)
Soprano, string quartet, and piano.
The Samuel Coleridge-Taylor String
Quartet recorded eight movements of
the twelve-movement song cycle SONGS
OF THE NIGHT on their CD *Calvary*
under the title BORDERLINE. The
movements they recorded are Night:
Four Songs; Fragments; Kid Stuff;
Poppy Flower; Gethsemane; Religion;
Now That He Is Safely Dead; and End.

BOSSA BELLE (1973)
Jazz ensemble. Also, a play-along track
and lead sheets (for concert key treble
clef, concert key bass clef, B♭, and E♭
instruments) can be found in the book
and CD set *David Baker: Eight Classic
Jazz Originals You Can Play,* Jamey
Aebersold Play-Along volume 10.

BOUGALOO (1971)
Jazz ensemble.

BOURNE (1984)
Jazz ensemble. Published
by Walrus Music.

BROTHER (1973)
Jazz ensemble. Published by
Walrus Music. For lead sheet, see
Baker, *Advanced Improvisation.*

BRUSHSTROKES (1966)
Theme music for the television
show *Brushstrokes* (WTTV;
Indianapolis, Indiana).

BUCK (1975)
Jazz ensemble.

THE BUFFALO SOLDIERS (1971)
Television score. See THE
BLACK FRONTIER.

BUS RIDE (1973)
Jazz ensemble. For lead sheet, see
Baker, *Advanced Improvisation.*

CAHAPHI (1982)
Jazz ensemble. Published by Walrus
Music. Also arranged for five saxophones
and rhythm section; this arrangement
is published by Advance Music. Also
arranged for orchestra. Also arranged
for brass quartet (trumpet, trombone,
euphonium, and tuba) by Norlan Bewley.

CALYPSO-NOVA #1 (1970)
Jazz ensemble. Also published in an
arrangement for jazz nonet (trumpet,
alto saxophone, tenor saxophone,
trombone, baritone saxophone, guitar,
piano, electric bass, and drums) by Three
Fifteen West Fifty-Third Street Corp.
in their Dave Baker Jazz Rock Series
(Charles Colin Publications). Also
published in an arrangement for string
orchestra by Creative Jazz Composers.

CALYPSO-NOVA #2 (1971)
Jazz ensemble. Also published in
an arrangement for string orchestra
by Creative Jazz Composers.

CATALYST (1966)
Jazz ensemble.

CATHOLIC MASS FOR PEACE (1969)
Alternate title: VOTIVE
MASS FOR PEACE.
Chorus (SATB) and jazz ensemble.
Five parts: I. Entrance Antiphon; II.
Give Peace to Your People; III. Congre-
gational Refrain; IV. Great Amen; V.
Recessional (Psalm 150). Commissioned
by the National Catholic Music Educators
Association.

CATPIAB (2005)
Jazz ensemble.

CATTIN' (1971)
Jazz ensemble.

CCP
Jazz ensemble. Published by
Creative Jazz Composers.

CELEBRATION IN THREE
MOVEMENTS (1992)
Jazz ensemble. Commissioned by the
Indiana University School of Law in
commemoration of its sesquicentennial.

CELEBRATION SUITE
Jazz ensemble. Three movements: I.
Sunburst; II. A Crystal Tear; III. Jam
Session. Published by Walrus Music.

CFB (1972)
Jazz ensemble. For lead sheet, see
Baker, *Advanced Improvisation.*

CHAIN REACTION (2005)
Jazz ensemble.

CHANGES (1996)
Jazz ensemble.

CHARIOTS (1972)
Jazz ensemble.

LE CHAT QUI PÊCHE (1969)
Jazz ensemble. Also published in an
arrangement for jazz nonet (trumpet,
alto saxophone, tenor saxophone,
trombone, baritone saxophone, guitar,
piano, electric bass, and drums) by
Three Fifteen West Fifty-Third Street
Corp. in their Dave Baker Jazz Rock
Series (Charles Colin Publications).

LE CHAT QUI PÊCHE (1974)
Orchestra, soprano, and jazz quartet
[alto/tenor saxophone, piano, bass,
and drums]. Text by David Baker.
Five movements: I. Soleil d'Altamira;
II. L'odeur du blues; III. Sons

voilés; IV. Guadeloupe-Calypso;
V. Le miroir noir. Commissioned
by the Louisville Orchestra.
Published by Associated Music.

CHE (1969)
Jazz ensemble.

CHECK IT OUT (1970)
Jazz ensemble. Also published in an
arrangement for jazz nonet (trumpet,
alto saxophone, tenor saxophone,
trombone, baritone saxophone, guitar,
piano, electric bass, and drums) by
Three Fifteen West Fifty-Third Street
Corp. in their Dave Baker Jazz Rock
Series (Charles Colin Publications).

CINQUATRE (1964)
Jazz ensemble.

CLEGRE (1973)
Jazz ensemble.

COLLAGE: ODE [OWED!]
TO STARKER (1999)
Cello orchestra. Commissioned
by Wyatt Sutherland for Janos
Starker's seventy-fifth birthday.

COLTRANE IN MEMORIAM (1967)
Jazz ensemble. Four movements:
I. Lachrymose; II. Blues; III.
Apocalypse; IV. Lachrymose.

CONCERTINO FOR CELLULAR
PHONES AND ORCHESTRA (2006)
Commissioned by Paul Freeman.
Published by Lauren Keiser Music.

CONCERTO FOR ALTO SAXOPHONE
AND ORCHESTRA (1989)
Commissioned by Thomas Walsh.
Published by Lauren Keiser Music.

CONCERTO FOR BASS VIOL
AND JAZZ BAND (1972)
Bass viol, jazz ensemble, string quartet,
and solo violin. Four movements.
Commissioned by Gary Karr.

CONCERTO FOR BRASS QUINTET
AND ORCHESTRA (1987)
Commissioned by Top Brass.
Published by Subito Music.

CONCERTO FOR CELLO AND
CHAMBER ORCHESTRA (1975)
Three movements. Commissioned
by Janos Starker. Published
by Associated Music.

CONCERTO FOR CELLO
AND JAZZ BAND (1987)
Commissioned by Ed Laut. Published
by Lauren Keiser Music.

CONCERTO FOR CLARINET
AND ORCHESTRA (1986)
Commissioned by Michael Limoli.

CONCERTO FOR FLUTE
AND JAZZ BAND (1971)
Three movements. Flute/alto flute,
jazz ensemble, and string quartet.
Commissioned by James Pellerite.

CONCERTO FOR FOURS (1980)
Solo quartet (flute, cello, tuba, and
contrabass), tuba quartet, contrabass
quartet, and percussion quartet.
Commissioned by Barry Green.

CONCERTO FOR SAXOPHONE AND
CHAMBER ORCHESTRA (1987)
Tenor saxophone, piano, bass, drums, and
chamber orchestra. Three movements:
I. Jubilee; II. Spiritual; III. Ostinato/
Blues Waltz. Commissioned by Ernie
Krivda. Published by Subito Music.

CONCERTO FOR TROMBONE,
JAZZ BAND, AND CHAMBER
ORCHESTRA (1972)
Commissioned by Thomas Beversdorf.

CONCERTO FOR TRUMPET, STRING
ORCHESTRA, PERCUSSION,
AND JAZZ BAND (1988)
Commissioned by Dominic Spera.
Published by Lauren Keiser Music.

CONCERTO FOR TRUMPET AND
WIND ENSEMBLE (1996)
Commissioned by David Coleman.

CONCERTO FOR TUBA AND
ORCHESTRA (1998)
Three movements: I. B's; II.
Berceuse; III. Blues. Commissioned
by Daniel Perantoni.

CONCERTO FOR TUBA, JAZZ
BAND, PERCUSSION, CHOIR,
DANCERS, SLIDES, AND
TAPE RECORDERS (1975)
Text by David Baker. Commissioned
by Harvey Phillips.

CONCERTO FOR TWO PIANOS,
JAZZ BAND, STRINGS, AND
PERCUSSION (1976)
Three movements. Commissioned by
Charles Webb and Wallace Hornibrook
for the Webb-Hornibrook Duo.
Published by Lauren Keiser Music.

CONCERTO FOR VIOLIN
AND JAZZ BAND (1969)
Three movements. Commissioned
by Josef Gingold. Published
by Lauren Keiser Music.

CONCERTO FOR VIOLIN AND
SYMPHONY ORCHESTRA (2006)
Commissioned by Diane Monroe.

CONCERTPIECE FOR TROMBONE
AND STRINGS (1991)
Trombone and string orchestra.
Commissioned by the Camerata
Orchestra for trombonist Dee Stewart.
Published by Lauren Keiser Music.

CONCERTPIECE FOR VIOLA (1989)
Viola and orchestra. Also scored for
viola and piano. Commissioned by
Karen Elaine [Bakunin]. Published
by Lauren Keiser Music.

CONTRASTS (1976)
Violin, violoncello, and piano. Four
movements: I. Passacaglia; II. A Song; III.
Episodes [CEI/CCP]; IV. Kaleidoscope.
Commissioned by the Western Arts Trio
[Brian Hanly, violin; David Tomatz,
violoncello; Werner Rose, piano].
Published by Lauren Keiser Music.

THE COWHERDERS (1971)
Television score. See THE
BLACK FRONTIER.

CREATE IN ME A CLEAN
HEART (1967)
Chorus (SATB) and jazz septet.
See LUTHERAN MASS.

CUZIN' DUCKY (1973)
Jazz ensemble.

CUZIN' LARRY – THE CHAMP (1973)
Jazz ensemble. For lead sheet, see
Baker, *Advanced Improvisation.*

CUZIN' LEE (1973)
Jazz ensemble. For lead sheet, see
Baker, *Advanced Improvisation.*

DABD (1973)
Jazz ensemble. For lead sheet, see
Baker, *Advanced Improvisation.*

DAKIAP (1973)
Jazz ensemble.

DANCE
(Clarinet; classical piano; and jazz trio
of piano, bass, and drums) This piece is
an adaptation by David Baker for James
Campbell of the last movement of his
SONATA FOR CLARINET AND PIANO.

DANCE OF THE JITTERBUGS (1994)
Jazz ensemble.

DANCING SHADOWS (2007)
Orchestra. Three movements: I. Dancing
Shadows; II. Fading Memories; III.
Fleeting Images. Commissioned by the
Indianapolis Symphony Orchestra.

DAVE'S WALTZ (1957)
Jazz ensemble.

DAYDREAMS AND DETOURS (2002)
Clarinet trio and orchestra. Three move-
ments. Commissioned by Trio Indiana
[James Campbell, Eli Eban, and Howard
Klug] and the Camerata Orchestra.

DE BOOGIE MAN (1973)
Jazz ensemble.

THE DEACON (1994)
Jazz ensemble.

DEATH IS RIDING (1990)
Baritone and contrabass. See WITNESS:
SIX ORIGINAL COMPOSITIONS
IN SPIRITUAL STYLE (1990).

DELIVER MY SOUL (1966)
Chorus (SATB), narrators, jazz
ensemble, string orchestra, and
dancers. See PSALM 22.

DELIVER MY SOUL (1986)
Tenor, string quartet, and piano. See
THROUGH THIS VALE OF TEARS.

DELIVER MY SOUL (1968)
Alternate title: BLUES
Violin and piano. Adaptation of "Deliver My Soul" from PSALM 22. Published by Lauren Keiser Music.

DIDN'T MY LORD DELIVER
DANIEL (1990)
Baritone and contrabass. See WITNESS: SIX ORIGINAL COMPOSITIONS IN SPIRITUAL STYLE (1990).

DIGITS (1972)
Jazz ensemble.

DO DE MI (1965)
Jazz ensemble.

A DOLLAR SHORT AND
A DAY LATE (1964)
Jazz ensemble.

THE DREAM BOOGIE (1970)
Chorus (SATB), unaccompanied. See FIVE SONGS TO THE SURVIVAL OF BLACK CHILDREN.

DREAM STEPS (2005)
Jazz ensemble.

DREAMS AWAY (2005)
Jazz ensemble.

THE DUDE (1962)
Violoncello and piano.

THE DUDE (1962)
Jazz ensemble. Also published in an arrangement for jazz nonet (trumpet, alto saxophone, tenor saxophone, trombone, baritone saxophone, guitar, piano, electric bass, and drums) by Three Fifteen West Fifty-Third Street Corp. in their Dave Baker Jazz Rock Series (Charles Colin Publications).

DUET FOR ALTO
SAXOPHONES (1990)
Three movements. Published by Lauren Keiser Music.

DUO FOR CLARINET
AND CELLO (1988)
Three movements. Commissioned by the Ronen Chamber Ensemble for David Bellman and Ingrid Fischer-Bellman. Published by Lauren Keiser Music.

EARLY IN THE MORNIN' (1973)
Tenor and piano. From the song cycle THE BLACK EXPERIENCE.
Published in the *Anthology of Art Songs by Black Composers,* compiled and annotated by Willis Patterson (New York: Edward B. Marks Music Corporation, 1977).

ECLIPSE (1996)
Jazz ensemble.

ELECTRIC STERE-OPTICON (1975)
Violoncello and electronic instruments. Commissioned by J. B. Floyd.

ELLINGTONES: A FANTASY FOR
SAXOPHONE AND ORCHESTRA
(1987; EXPANDED VERSION 1988)
Tenor saxophone, orchestra, jazz piano, and jazz bass. Three movements: I. Moderato; II. Waltz; III. Passacaglia. Commissioned by the New York Philharmonic. Published by Dunsinane Music.

EN ROUGE ET NOIR (1985)
Flute, piano, bass, and drums. Published by Lauren Keiser Music.

EPISCOPAL MASS FOR THE
FEAST DAYS OF BISHOP
ABSALOM JONES (2003)
Choir (SATB), boys choir, and jazz septet (trumpet, tenor saxophone, baritone saxophone, trombone, piano,

bass, and drums). I. Kyrie; II. Gloria; III. Sanctus/Benedictus; IV. Agnus Dei. Commissioned by Christ Church Cathedral; Indianapolis, Indiana.

EROS AND AGAPE (1969)
Jazz ensemble. The melody is published in Baker, *Arranging and Composing for the Small Ensemble: Jazz, R&B, Jazz-Rock.*

ESTRELLITA (2005)
Jazz ensemble.

ETC. (1972)
Jazz ensemble. Also arranged for brass quartet (trumpet, trombone, euphonium, and tuba) by Norlan Bewley. For lead sheet, see Baker, *Advanced Improvisation.*

ETHNIC VARIATIONS ON A
THEME OF PAGANINI (1976)
Violin and piano. Theme and nine variations. Based on Paganini's twenty-fourth caprice. Commissioned by Ruggiero Ricci. Published by Lauren Keiser Music.

EVENING SONG (1970)
Piano. See FIVE SHORT
PIECES FOR PIANO.

EVENING SONG (1970)
String orchestra. Published by Creative Jazz Composers.

EVENING SONG (1972)
Soprano, string quartet, and piano. See SONGS OF THE NIGHT.

AN EVENING THOUGHT (1974)
Jazz ensemble. David Baker has written two different big band arrangements on *An Evening Thought.* One is published by Lauren Keiser Music; the other is published by Sierra Music. This piece is also published in an arrangement for string orchestra by Creative Jazz Composers. It has also been arranged for brass quartet

(trumpet, trombone, euphonium, and tuba) by Norlan Bewley. Lyrics for this piece were written by Sally Champlin.

EVERYBODY'S SONG (1996)
Jazz ensemble.

THE EXODUSTERS (1971)
Television score. See THE
BLACK FRONTIER.

FACES OF THE BLUES; A FANTASY
FOR ALTO SAXOPHONE AND
SAXOPHONE QUARTET (1990)
Commissioned by Frank Bongiorno. Published by Lauren Keiser Music.

FANTASY (1954)
Soprano, brass ensemble, and harp. Text by Albert Cobine.

FANTASY (1994)
Flute, clarinet, bassoon, alto saxophone, tenor saxophone, violin, viola, guitar, and bass. Commissioned by Janis Stockhouse.

FANTASY FOR WOODWIND
QUINTET (1969); FANTASY ON
THEMES FROM *THE MASQUE
OF THE RED DEATH* BALLET
Orchestra. This piece came into being when the *Suite from "The Masque of the Red Death" Ballet* was being recorded in Prague, Czech Republic, by Paul Freeman and the Czech National Symphony Orchestra. It is the result of cuts made during the recording session by Maestro Freeman. Because this resulted in a piece which was significantly different from the original, it was given this new title by David Baker. Published by Lauren Keiser Music.

THE FELIX WALK (1973)
Jazz ensemble. For lead sheet, see Baker, *Advanced Improvisation.*

THE FIRST DAY OF SPRING (1969)
Jazz ensemble. Also published in
an arrangement for string orchestra
by Creative Jazz Composers.

5M CALYPSO (1984)
Jazz ensemble. Published by Sierra Music.

FIVE SETTINGS FOR SOPRANO
AND PIANO (1969)
Song cycle for soprano and
piano. If There Be Sorrow (text by
Mari Evans); The Smile (text by
William Blake); The Optimist (text
by Kenneth Ferling); A Song (text
by Paul Laurence Dunbar); Parades
to Hell (text by Solomon Edwards).
Commissioned by Janice Albright.

FIVE SHORT PIECES
FOR PIANO (1970)
Rêve; To Bird; Passacaglia; Evening
Song; Blues Waltz (née Terrible T).
Published by Lauren Keiser Music.

FIVE SONGS TO THE SURVIVAL
OF BLACK CHILDREN (1970)
Chorus (SATB) unaccompanied. Now
That He Is Safely Dead (text by Carl
Hines); Religion (text by Conrad Kent
Rivers); Black Children (text by Conrad
Kent Rivers); The Dream Boogie (text
by Langston Hughes); If We Must Die
(text by Claude McKay). Commissioned
by the Fisk Jubilee Singers.

FOLKLIKE (1973)
Jazz ensemble. Published by Walrus
Music. Jazz septet arrangement published
by Studio PR (trumpet, alto saxophone,
tenor saxophone, trombone, piano,
bass, and drums). Also arranged for
brass quartet (trumpet, trombone,
euphonium, and tuba) and for quartet
of trumpet, woodwinds, trombone, and
tuba by Norlan Bewley. For lead sheet,
see Baker, *Advanced Improvisation*.

FOR ALL TO SEE (2005)
Jazz ensemble.

FOR GOLD AND GLORY (2001)
Film score. PBS documentary on the life
of Charlie Wiggins, a black champion
racecar driver of the 1920s and 1930s. Todd
Gould, producer. David Baker won an
Emmy in 2003 for the music for this film.

FOREVER (1988)
See SONGS OF LIVING AND DYING
(1988). See also 2003 adaptation for
contralto, violoncello, and piano.

FOUR BIBLICAL TALES IN
SPIRITUAL STYLE (1993)
Chorus (SATB) and piano. I.
When I'm Dead; II. Golgotha; III.
Witness; IV. What a Morning.
Published by Subito Music.

438 (2005)
Jazz ensemble.

THE FROG WHO WANTED
TO SING (1989)
Theater piece for storyteller, soprano,
and chamber ensemble (flute/piccolo/
alto flute, bassoon/oboe, French horn,
bass trombone, and percussion).
Commissioned by Tales and Scales.

FUUP BLUES (1973)
Jazz ensemble. For lead sheet, see
Baker, *Advanced Improvisation*.

GENTLE TIMES (2005)
Jazz ensemble.

GEO RUS (1974)
Jazz ensemble.

THE GEORGIA PEACH (1973)
Jazz ensemble. Published by Creative
Jazz Composers. For lead sheet, see
Baker, *Advanced Improvisation*.

GIVE AND TAKE (1975)
Song cycle for soprano and chamber
ensemble (flute/alto flute, oboe/English
horn, viola, violoncello, and percussion).
Text by Terence Diggory. Six move-
ments: I. The Branch of a Green Tree; II.
The Gift; III. The Funeral Is All; IV. They
Will Not Tell; V. An Almost Death; VI.
Canonization II. Commissioned by Edith
Diggory. Published by Lauren Keiser
Music.

GOLGOTHA (1976)
Jazz ensemble.

A GOOD ASSASSINATION
SHOULD BE QUIET (1973)
Tenor and piano. From the song cycle
THE BLACK EXPERIENCE. Published
in the *Anthology of Art Songs by Black
Composers,* compiled and annotated by
Willis Patterson (New York: Edward
B. Marks Music Corporation, 1977).

GREEN MINUS YELLOW (1973)
Jazz ensemble.

THE GRIP (1973)
Jazz ensemble. For lead sheet, see
Baker, *Advanced Improvisation.*

GROOVIN' FOR DIZ (1984)
Jazz ensemble.

THE GROWTH SINGLE SEED (2003)
Chorus (SATB), string quartet,
guitar, piano, bass, and drums. Text
by John Ha. Commissioned for the
Bloomington (Indiana) Chamber
Singers by Kim Walker and the Indiana
University Office of Arts and Cultural
Outreach for Arts Week 2004 as a
part of the SPRING SONG project.

THE HARLEM PIPES (1973)
Jazz ensemble. Also arranged for brass
quartet (trumpet, trombone, euphonium,

and tuba) by Norlan Bewley. For lead
sheet, see Baker, *Advanced Improvisation.*

THE HARLEM PIPES (1973)
Orchestra and jazz trio. See
TWO IMPROVISATIONS FOR
ORCHESTRA AND JAZZ COMBO.

HELLO WORLD (1959)
Jazz ensemble.

HERITAGE: A TRIBUTE TO
GREAT CLARINETISTS (1996)
Clarinet and piano. Four move-
ments: I. Buddy and Beyond;
II. Artie; III. BBBB; IV. BG.
Commissioned by James Campbell.

HERMAN'S THEME (1976)
Jazz ensemble. Jazz septet arrangement
published by Studio PR (trumpet,
alto saxophone, tenor saxophone,
trombone, piano, bass, and drums).

HHHCCC (1975)
Jazz ensemble. Jazz septet arrangement
published by Studio PR (trumpet,
alto saxophone, tenor saxophone,
trombone, piano, bass, and drums).

HOMAGE: BARTOK, BIRD,
AND DUKE (1988)
Chamber ensemble (flute, oboe, clarinet,
bassoon, French horn, two trumpets,
trombone, tuba, two harps, violin, viola,
violoncello, contrabass, and two percussion). Published by Lauren Keiser Music.

HOMAGE A L'HISTOIRE (1994)
Clarinet, bassoon, trumpet, percussion,
violin, and contrabass. Six movements:
I. Little Parade March; II. Waltz; III.
Lindy Hop; IV. Samba; V. Little Song; VI.
Grande March. Commissioned by James
Campbell. Published by Subito Music.

HONESTY (1960)
Jazz ensemble. Published by Lauren Keiser Music. Also published in an arrangement for jazz nonet (trumpet, alto saxophone, tenor saxophone, trombone, baritone saxophone, guitar, piano, electric bass, and drums) by Three Fifteen West Fifty-Third Street Corp. in their Dave Baker Jazz Rock Series (Charles Colin Publications).

HOY HOY (1973)
Jazz ensemble. For lead sheet, see Baker, *Advanced Improvisation.*

I DREAM A WORLD (1973)
Chorus (SATB) and piano.
Text by Langston Hughes.

I HEARD MY WOMAN CALL (1969)
Incidental music for *I Heard My Woman Call,* a dramatic presentation adapted from Eldridge Cleaver's *Soul On Ice.*

THE I.U. SWING MACHINE (1968)
Jazz ensemble. Published by Sierra Music. For lead sheet, see Baker, *Arranging and Composing for the Small Ensemble: Jazz, R&B, Jazz-Rock* and *Jazz Improvisation: A Comprehensive Method of Study for All Players.*

I WILL TELL OF THY NAME (1966)
Jazz ensemble. See PEACE, MY BROTHER.

I WHO WOULD ENCOMPASS MILLIONS (1973)
Tenor and piano. See THE BLACK EXPERIENCE (1973).

IF THERE BE SORROW (1969)
Soprano and piano. See FIVE SETTINGS FOR SOPRANO AND PIANO.

IF THERE BE SORROW (1986)
Tenor, string quartet, and piano. See THROUGH THIS VALE OF TEARS.

IF THERE BE SORROW (1993)
Chorus (SATB), flute, guitar, piano, bass, and percussion. See IMAGES, SHADOWS, AND DREAMS: FIVE VIGNETTES.

IF WE MUST DIE (1970)
Chorus (SATB), unaccompanied. See FIVE SONGS TO THE SURVIVAL OF BLACK CHILDREN.

IISLY (2005)
Jazz ensemble.

ILLEGAL ENTRANCE (1996)
Jazz ensemble.

IMAGES, SHADOWS, AND DREAMS: FIVE VIGNETTES (1993)
Chorus (SATB), flute, guitar, piano, bass, and percussion. Text by Mari Evans. Five movements: I. Rent's Due Monday; II. The Nonagenarian; III. If There Be Sorrow; IV. The Rebel; V. Let Me Tell You How To Meet the Day. Tri-commission by the Plymouth Music Series, the Los Angeles Master Chorale, and the New York Ars Nova. Published by Subito Music.

IMAGES OF CHILDHOOD
Orchestra. Three movements: I. Maypole; II. Lazy Summer Days; III. Follow the Leader. Published by Lauren Keiser Music.

IMPRESSIONS FOR TWO CELLOS (1988)
Commissioned by Janos Starker. Published by Lauren Keiser Music.

IMPROVISATION #1 FOR UNACCOMPANIED VIOLIN (1975)
Commissioned by Ruggiero Ricci.

IMPROVISATION #2 FOR UNACCOMPANIED VIOLIN (1975)
Commissioned by Ruggiero Ricci.

IN MEMORIAM: FREEDOM (1971)
See JAZZ SUITE FOR SEXTET IN
MEMORY OF BOB THOMPSON.

INFINITY (1964)
Jazz ensemble.

INSPIRATION (1987)
Flute and piano. Commissioned by Carol
Wincenc. Published by Lauren Keiser
Music. Also published in the *National
Flute Association 20th Anniversary
Anthology of American Flute Music* (New
York: Oxford University Press, 1992).

THE INSURGENT (1973)
Tenor and piano. See THE BLACK
EXPERIENCE (1973).

INTROSPECTION (1968)
Soprano and piano. See ABYSS.

IT DID (2005)
Jazz ensemble.

J IS FOR LOVELINESS (1962)
Jazz ensemble. For lead sheet, see Baker,
*Arranging and Composing for the Small
Ensemble: Jazz, R&B, Jazz-Rock.*

JAM SESSION
Jazz ensemble. This arrangement of
JAM SESSION was commissioned by
the Smithsonian Jazz Masterworks
Orchestra, to be used as its theme song.

THE JAMAICAN STRUT (1970)
String orchestra. Published by
Creative Jazz Composers.

JAZZ DANCE SUITE (1988)
Piano. Four movements: I. Some
Sort of Waltz; II. Jitterbug Boogie;
III. Solo Dance; IV. Double Dance.
Commissioned by Gary Smart.
Published by Lauren Keiser Music.

JAZZ CELEBRATION (2009)
Trumpet, alto saxophone, tenor
saxophone, baritone saxophone, piano,
bass, and drums. Commissioned by
Indiana University–Purdue
University Indianapolis [IUPUI]
for the tenth anniversary celebration of the University College.

JAZZ MASS (1967)
For the Lutheran jazz mass, see
LUTHERAN MASS. For the Roman
Catholic jazz mass, see CATHOLIC MASS
FOR PEACE. For the Episcopal jazz mass,
see EPISCOPAL MASS FOR THE FEAST
DAYS OF BISHOP ABSALOM JONES.

JAZZ SUITE FOR CHAMBER
ORCHESTRA AND RHYTHM
SECTION (1987)
Four movements: I. Birdsong; II.
Jeanne Marie at the Picture Show;
III. Lerma Samba; IV. Lima Beba
Samba. Published by Subito Music.

JAZZ SUITE FOR CLARINET
AND SYMPHONY ORCHESTRA:
THREE ETHNIC DANCES (1992)
Three movements: I. Jitterbug; II. Slow
Drag; III. Calypso. Commissioned
by the Akron Symphony Orchestra.
Published by Lauren Keiser Music.

JAZZ SUITE FOR SEXTET IN
MEMORY OF BOB THOMPSON (1971)
Alternate title: IN MEMORIAM:
FREEDOM. Trumpet, tenor
saxophone, trombone, piano, bass, and
drums. One movement.

JAZZ SUITE FOR VIOLIN
AND PIANO (1979)
Published by Lauren Keiser Music.

JEANNE MARIE AT THE PICTURE SHOW (1982)

Jazz ensemble. Also arranged for five saxophones and rhythm section; this arrangement is published by Advance Music. Also arranged for brass quartet (trumpet, trombone, euphonium, and tuba) by Norlan Bewley. Also arranged for orchestra; see JAZZ SUITE FOR CHAMBER ORCHESTRA AND RHYTHM SECTION.

JUST BEFORE SEPTEMBER (1968)

Jazz ensemble. For lead sheet see Baker, *Arranging and Composing for the Small Ensemble: Jazz, R&B, Jazz-Rock.*

K.C.C. (1966)

Jazz ensemble.

KENTUCKY OYSTERS (1958)

Jazz ensemble. Also published in an arrangement for jazz nonet (trumpet, alto saxophone, tenor saxophone, trombone, baritone saxophone, guitar, piano, electric bass, and drums) by Three Fifteen West Fifty-Third Street Corp. in their Dave Baker Jazz Rock Series (Charles Colin Publications). For lead sheet, see Baker, *Arranging and Composing for the Small Ensemble: Jazz, R&B, Jazz-Rock* and *Jazz Improvisation: A Comprehensive Method of Study for All Players.* In addition, a play-along track and lead sheets (for concert key treble clef, concert key bass clef, Bb, and Eb instruments) can be found in the book and CD set *David Baker: Eight Classic Jazz Originals You Can Play*, Jamey Aebersold Play-Along volume 10.

KIRSTEN AND HER PUPPY KATIE (1996)

Jazz ensemble.

KIRSTEN'S FIRST SONG (1990)

Jazz ensemble.

KOSBRO (1973; REVISED IN 1975)

Orchestra. Commissioned by Paul Freeman. Published by Associated Music.

LACYPSO (1974)

Jazz ensemble.

LERMA SAMBA (1982)

Jazz ensemble. Scheduled for publication by Sierra Music. Also arranged for five saxophones and rhythm section; this arrangement is published by Advance Music. Also arranged for brass quartet (trumpet, trombone, euphonium, and tuba) and for quartet of trumpet, wood-winds, trombone, and tuba by Norlan Bewley. Also arranged for orchestra; see JAZZ SUITE FOR CHAMBER ORCHESTRA AND RHYTHM SECTION.

LET ME TELL YOU HOW TO MEET THE DAY (1993)

Chorus (SATB), flute, guitar, piano, bass, and percussion. See IMAGES, SHADOWS, AND DREAMS: FIVE VIGNETTES.

LET'S GET IT ON (1970)

Jazz ensemble. Also published in an arrangement for jazz nonet (trumpet, alto saxophone, tenor saxophone, trombone, baritone saxophone, guitar, piano, electric bass, and drums) by Three Fifteen West Fifty-Third Street Corp. in their Dave Baker Jazz Rock Series (Charles Colin Publications).

LEVELS: A CONCERTO FOR SOLO CONTRABASS, JAZZ BAND, FLUTE QUARTET, HORN QUARTET, AND STRING QUARTET (1973)

Three movements. Commissioned by Bertram Turetzky. This work was nominated for a Pulitzer Prize in 1973.

LIFE CYCLES (1988)
Song cycle for tenor, French horn, and string orchestra. Also scored for tenor, French horn, and piano. Text by Terence Diggory. Five movements: I. Night Song; II. Surface; III. Autumn Moral; IV. What It Means When Spring Comes; V. Saints and Hermits. Commissioned by William Brown. Published by Lauren Keiser Music.

LIFE FORCE (2008)
Jazz ensemble.

LIGHT BLUE, DARK BLUE (1962)
Jazz ensemble.

LIKE FATHER, LIKE SON (2001)
Jazz ensemble and two trumpet soloists. Written for Edmund Cord and his son Benjamin J. Cord.

LIMA BEBA SAMBA (1982)
Jazz ensemble. Published by Walrus Music. Also arranged for five saxophones and rhythm section; this arrangement is published by Advance Music. Also arranged for orchestra; see JAZZ SUITE FOR CHAMBER ORCHESTRA AND RHYTHM SECTION.

LISOIL (2005)
Jazz ensemble.

THE LITTLE PRINCESS (1959)
Jazz ensemble. For lead sheet, see Baker, *Arranging and Composing for the Small Ensemble: Jazz, R&B, Jazz-Rock*.

LITTLE PRINCESS WALTZ (1959)
String orchestra. Published by Creative Jazz Composers.

A LITTLE WALTZ (1973)
Jazz ensemble.

THE LONE RANGER AND THE GREAT HORACE SILVER (1957)
Jazz ensemble.

LOROB (1982)
Jazz ensemble.

LOUIS ARMSTRONG IN MEMORIAM (1972)
Jazz ensemble. Seven movements: I. Introduction; II. Genesis; III. Funeral March; IV. The Creoles; V. 1928; VI. Evolution; VII. Louis/Life/Love. Commissioned by Grand Valley State College.

LUMO (1973)
Jazz ensemble.

LUNACY (1959)
Original title: STONE NUTS.
    Jazz ensemble. Published by Creative Jazz Composers. Also published in an arrangement for jazz nonet (trumpet, alto saxophone, tenor saxophone, trombone, baritone saxophone, guitar, piano, electric bass, and drums) by Three Fifteen West Fifty-Third Street Corp. in their Dave Baker Jazz Rock Series (Charles Colin Publications).

LUTHERAN MASS (1967)
Chorus (SATB) and jazz septet. Text based on the liturgy of the Lutheran Church. Ten parts. I. Prelude; II. Introit; III. Kyrie; IV. Gloria; V. Gradual; VI. Credo; VII. Sanctus; VIII. Agnus Dei; IX. Nunc Dimittis; X. Postlude. Also includes the offertory "Create in Me a Clean Heart" (Biblical text). Commissioned by the National Campus Lutheran Ministry.

LYDIAN APRIL (1959)
Jazz ensemble.

MA279 BOOGALOO (1970)
Jazz ensemble. Also published in an
arrangement for jazz nonet (trumpet,
alto saxophone, tenor saxophone,
trombone, baritone saxophone, guitar,
piano, electric bass, and drums) by
Three Fifteen West Fifty-Third Street
Corp. in their Dave Baker Jazz Rock
Series (Charles Colin Publications).

MABA TILA (1973)
Jazz ensemble. Jazz septet arrangement
published by Studio PR (trumpet,
alto saxophone, tenor saxophone,
trombone, piano, bass, and drums). Also
arranged for brass quartet (trumpet,
trombone, euphonium, and tuba) by
Norlan Bewley. For lead sheet, see
Baker, *Advanced Improvisation.*

MAKE A JOYFUL NOISE (1963)
Jazz ensemble.

M'AM (1953)
Jazz ensemble.

MAMA TU (1973)
Jazz ensemble.

MARTINOVA (2005)
Jazz ensemble.

THE MASQUE OF THE
RED DEATH (1998)
Ballet (orchestra). Commissioned
by Jacques Cesbron for the Indiana
University Ballet Theatre.

MAUMA (1973)
Jazz ensemble. For lead sheet, see
Baker, *Advanced Improvisation.*

MEET THE ARTIST (1970)
Theme music for the television
show *Meet the Artist.*

MEMORIES OF MARIAN (2002)
Flute, clarinet, alto saxophone, and
piano. Written for the memorial
service of Marian (Mrs. P. A.) Mack.

MEN SHALL TELL OF
THE LORD (1966)
Soprano and piano. Arrangement of "Men
Shall Tell of the Lord" from PSALM 22.

MIAMI NIGHTS (1991)
Jazz ensemble. See MIAMI SUITE.

MIAMI SUITE (1991)
Jazz ensemble. Three movements: I.
Tippin'; II. Miami Nights; III. Sunfest.
  Published by Walrus Music. Original
version for jazz sextet had the title SUITE
FOR JAZZ SEXTET. Commissioned by
JB Dyas for the New World School of the
Arts (Miami, Florida).

MID-EVIL (1973)
Jazz ensemble.

LE MIROIR NOIR (1974)
Jazz ensemble. Jazz septet arrangement
published by Studio PR (trumpet, alto
saxophone, tenor saxophone, trombone,
piano, bass, and drums). Also arranged
for brass quartet (trumpet, trombone,
euphonium, and tuba) by Norlan
Bewley. In addition, a play-along track
and lead sheets (for concert key treble
clef, concert key bass clef, Bb, and Eb
instruments) can be found in the book
and CD set *David Baker: Eight Classic
Jazz Originals You Can Play,* Jamey
Aebersold Play-Along volume 10.

LE MIROIR NOIR (1974)
Orchestra, soprano, and jazz quartet.
See LE CHAT QUI PÊCHE.

MOD WALTZ (1970)
String orchestra. Published by
Creative Jazz Composers.

MODALITY, TONALITY,
AND FREEDOM (1962)
Alto saxophone, five trumpets,
four trombones, tuba, piano, bass,
and drums. Three movements.
Commissioned by Jamey Aebersold.

MODERN DANCE SUITE (1987)
Commissioned by Bill Evans.

MOMENTS
This is David Baker's jazz composition
"Folklike." When Sally Champlin added
lyrics to it, she retitled it "Moments."

MON (1973)
Jazz ensemble.

MONKIN' AROUND (1962)
Jazz ensemble.

MOODY'S MOUNTAIN (1999)
Jazz ensemble.

MORNING SWING (2005)
Jazz ensemble.

A MORNING THOUGHT (1973)
Jazz ensemble.

MY GOD, WHY HAST THOU
FORSAKEN ME? (1986)
Tenor, string quartet, and piano. See
THROUGH THIS VALE OF TEARS.

MY LORD, WHAT A MORNING (1990)
Baritone and contrabass. See WITNESS:
SIX ORIGINAL COMPOSITIONS
IN SPIRITUAL STYLE (1990).

MY LORD, WHAT A
MORNING (2000)
Tenor and chorus (SATB) unac-
companied. See THREE CHORAL
PIECES IN SPIRITUAL STYLE.

MY INDIANAPOLIS (1969)
Jazz ensemble and orchestra.
See REFLECTIONS.

NAPTOWN STRUT
Jazz ensemble.

THE NEW AMERICANS (1971)
Television score. See THE
BLACK FRONTIER.

NINA, EVER NEW (1966)
Jazz ensemble.

NJSO CALYPSO
Jazz ensemble.

THE NONAGENARIAN (1993)
Chorus (SATB), flute, guitar,
piano, bass, and percussion. See
IMAGES, SHADOWS, AND
DREAMS: FIVE VIGNETTES.

NONE A PLACE ME BE (1971)
Jazz ensemble. For lead sheet, see
Baker, *Advanced Improvisation.*

NOSTALGIA (2008)
Jazz ensemble.

NOW THAT HE IS SAFELY
DEAD (1970)
Chorus (SATB), unaccompanied. See
FIVE SONGS TO THE SURVIVAL
OF BLACK CHILDREN.

NOW THAT HE IS SAFELY
DEAD (1986)
Tenor, string quartet, and piano. See
THROUGH THIS VALE OF TEARS.

OBSERVATION (1968)
Soprano and piano. See ABYSS.

ODE TO STARKER (1999)
Cello orchestra. See COLLAGE.

OF OTHER TIMES (2005)
Jazz ensemble.

OFTEN (2005)
Jazz ensemble.

ON WINGS OF SONG (2001)
Bass clarinet and piano. See AND THEN.

ONE FOR J. S. (1969)
Jazz ensemble. Also published in an
arrangement for jazz nonet (trumpet,
alto saxophone, tenor saxophone,
trombone, baritone saxophone, guitar,
piano, electric bass, and drums) by
Three Fifteen West Fifty-Third Street
Corp. in their Dave Baker Jazz Rock
Series (Charles Colin Publications).

121 BANK (1960)
Jazz ensemble.

125TH STREET (1968)
Jazz ensemble, narrators, chorus
(SATB), soloists, and string
orchestra. See BLACK AMERICA.

125TH STREET (1969)
Jazz ensemble. Also published in an
arrangement for jazz nonet (trumpet,
alto saxophone, tenor saxophone,
trombone, baritone saxophone, guitar,
piano, electric bass, and drums) by
Three Fifteen West Fifty-Third Street
Corp. in their Dave Baker Jazz Rock
Series (Charles Colin Publications).

ONLY YOU (2005)
Jazz ensemble.

THE OPTIMIST (1969)
Soprano and piano. See FIVE SETTINGS
FOR SOPRANO AND PIANO.

PADOSPE (1982)
Jazz ensemble. Published by Walrus
Music. Also arranged for five saxophones

and rhythm section; this arrangement
is published by Advance Music.

PAGANINI VARIATIONS (1967)
See ETHNIC VARIATIONS ON
A THEME OF PAGANINI.

PARADES TO HELL (1969)
Soprano and piano. See FIVE SETTINGS
FOR SOPRANO AND PIANO.

PARADES TO HELL (1986)
Tenor, string quartet, and piano. See
THROUGH THIS VALE OF TEARS.

PARALLEL PLANES (1992)
Alto/soprano saxophone soloist and
chamber orchestra. Three movements:
I. Mirror, Mirror; II. A Crystal Tear; III.
Doppelganger. Commissioned by Howie
Smith. Published by Lauren Keiser Music.

PASSION (1956)
Original title: SANDRA.
    Jazz ensemble. For lead sheet see Baker,
*Arranging and Composing for the Small En-
semble: Jazz, R&B, Jazz-Rock.* In addition,
a play-along track and lead sheets (for
concert key treble clef, concert key bass
clef, B♭, and E♭ instruments) can be found
in the book and CD set *David Baker: Eight
Classic Jazz Originals You Can Play,* Jamey
Aebersold Play-Along volume 10.

PASSIONS (1966)
Brass quintet. Commissioned
by the Montreal Brass Quintet.
Published in Montreal as part of the
Montreal Brass Quintet Series.

PASTORALE (1959)
String quartet. Published by Fema
Music Publications (Interlochen
series). Also arranged for brass quartet
(trumpet, trombone, euphonium, and
tuba) by Norlan Bewley.

PEACE, MY BROTHER (1966)
Jazz ensemble. This is an arrangement
for jazz ensemble of "I Will Tell of
Thy Name" from PSALM 22.

PEACE IS THE WAY (2003)
Chorus (SATB) and soloist. Text
by Sara Stevens. Commissioned for
the 2004 Bloomington (Indiana)
community celebration in honor
of Dr. Martin Luther King, Jr.

PENETRATION (1968)
Soprano and piano. See ABYSS.

PENICK (1970)
Jazz ensemble. Published by Creative
Jazz Composers. Also published in an
arrangement for jazz nonet (trumpet,
alto saxophone, tenor saxophone,
trombone, baritone saxophone, guitar,
piano, electric bass, and drums) by
Three Fifteen West Fifty-Third Street
Corp. in their Dave Baker Jazz Rock
Series (Charles Colin Publications).

PERCEPTION (1968)
Soprano and piano. See ABYSS.

PIECE FOR BRASS QUINTET
AND ORCHESTRA (1988)
Commissioned by Top Brass.
Published by Lauren Keiser Music.

PIECE FOR VIOLONCELLO
AND PIANO (1966)

THE PLACE WHERE THE
RAINBOW ENDS (1988)
Soprano, tenor, and piano. See SONGS
OF LIVING AND DYING (2003).

THE PLACE WHERE THE
RAINBOW ENDS (2000)
Soprano, trumpet, multiple winds,
trombone, tuba, and percussion. Five
movements. I. We Wear the Mask (text

by Paul Laurence Dunbar); II. A Song
(text by Paul Laurence Dunbar); III. To
a Dead Friend (text by Paul Laurence
Dunbar); IV. Sympathy (text by Paul
Laurence Dunbar); V. The Place Where
the Rainbow Ends (text by Paul Laurence
Dunbar). Commissioned by Top Brass.

PO' NED (1956)
Jazz ensemble.

POCKET CHANGE (2005)
Jazz ensemble.

PRELUDE (1967)
Jazz ensemble. Also published in an
arrangement for jazz nonet (trumpet, alto
saxophone, tenor saxophone, trombone,
baritone saxophone, guitar, piano,
electric bass, and drums) by Three Fifteen
West Fifty-Third Street Corp. in their
Dave Baker Jazz Rock Series (Charles
Colin Publications). For lead sheet, see
Baker, *Arranging and Composing for the
Small Ensemble: Jazz, R&B, Jazz-Rock.*

THE PROFESSOR (1966)
Jazz ensemble. Also published in an
arrangement for jazz nonet (trumpet, alto
saxophone, tenor saxophone, trombone,
baritone saxophone, guitar, piano,
electric bass, and drums) by Three Fifteen
West Fifty-Third Street Corp. in their
Dave Baker Jazz Rock Series (Charles
Colin Publications). For lead sheet, see
Baker, *Arranging and Composing for the
Small Ensemble: Jazz, R&B, Jazz-Rock.*

PROMISE AND
PERFORMANCE (1974)
Music for a documentary drama.
Text by Victor Amend.

PSALM 22 (1966)
A modern jazz oratorio. Chorus (SATB),
narrators, jazz ensemble, string orchestra,
and dancers. Biblical text. Seventeen

parts: Prelude; My God, My God; Yet Thou Art Holy; But I Am a Worm; Narration; I Am Poured Out Like Water; Thou Dost Lay Me in the Dust of Death; Narration; Deliver My Soul; Pastorale; I Will Tell of Thy Name; Yea, To Him Shall All the Proud of the Earth Bow Down; All the Ends of the Earth Shall Remember; Narration; Praise Him; Men Shall Tell of the Lord; Finale. Commissioned by Christian Theological Seminary; Indianapolis, Indiana.

PSALM 23 (1968)
Chorus (SATB) and organ. Biblical text. Commissioned by the United Christian Missionaries.

PSALM 150 (1969)
See CATHOLIC MASS FOR PEACE.

RAINBOWS (2005)
Jazz ensemble.

RAMU (1972)
Jazz ensemble. Published by Creative Jazz Composers.

RANDOM THOUGHTS (2006)
Clarinet quartet. Three movements: I. Evening; II. Nostalgia; III. The Foot Is Understood. Commissioned by Howard Klug.

THE REBEL (1973)
Tenor and piano. See THE BLACK EXPERIENCE (1973).

THE REBEL (1993)
Chorus (SATB), flute, guitar, piano, bass, and percussion. See IMAGES, SHADOWS, AND DREAMS: FIVE VIGNETTES.

REFLECTIONS (1969)
Alternate title: MY INDIANAPOLIS.

Jazz ensemble and orchestra. Commissioned by the Indianapolis Arts Council for the Indianapolis Summer Symphony.

REFLECTIONS ON A SUMMER'S DAY (1986)
Cello choir. Published by Lauren Keiser Music.

REFRACTIONS FOR CELLO QUARTET (1993)
Three movements: I. Crescent; II. Crepuscule; III. Convergence. Commissioned by Janos Starker. Published by Subito Music.

REFRACTIONS (1998 ADAPTATION FOR STRING ORCHESTRA OF REFRACTIONS FOR CELLO QUARTET)
String orchestra. Commissioned by Paul Freeman. Published by Lauren Keiser Music.

RELIGION (1970)
Chorus (SATB), unaccompanied. See FIVE SONGS TO THE SURVIVAL OF BLACK CHILDREN.

RENT'S DUE MONDAY (1993)
Chorus (SATB), flute, guitar, piano, bass, and percussion. See IMAGES, SHADOWS, AND DREAMS: FIVE VIGNETTES.

REX (1973)
Jazz ensemble.

ROLY POLY (1968)
Jazz ensemble. Published by Walrus Music. Also published in an arrangement for jazz nonet (trumpet, alto saxophone, tenor saxophone, trombone, baritone saxophone, guitar, piano, electric bass, and drums) by Three Fifteen West Fifty-Third Street Corp. in their Dave Baker Jazz Rock Series (Charles Colin

Publications). For lead sheet, see Baker,
*Jazz Improvisation: A Comprehensive
Method of Study for All Players.*

ROMANZA AND MARCH (1961)
Three trombones.

ROOTS (1976)
Violin, violoncello, and piano. Five
movements: I. Walpurgisnacht; II. Blues
Waltz; III. Sorrow Song; IV. Calypso
Row; V. Finale. Commissioned by The
Beaux Arts Trio. Published by Lauren
Keiser Music. Portions of this work
were incorporated into a revision of
this work, which became ROOTS II.

ROOTS II (1992)
Violin, violoncello, and piano. Five
movements: I. Incantation; II.
Dance in Congo Square; III. Sorrow
Song; IV. Boogie Woogie; V. Jubilee.
Commissioned by the Beaux Arts Trio.
Published by Lauren Keiser Music.

EN ROUGE ET NOIR (1985)
Flute, piano, bass, and drums.
Published by Lauren Keiser Music.

R.S.V.P. MR. MOODY (1982)
Jazz ensemble. Also arranged by
David Baker for five saxophones and
rhythm section; this arrangement
is published by Advance Music.

A SALUTE TO BEETHOVEN (1970)
Piccolo, flute, oboe, clarinet, bassoon,
F horn, backstage flute choir, jazz
ensemble, and pre-recorded tape.
Commissioned by Sidney Foster.

SANDRA (1956)
Jazz ensemble. See PASSION.

SANGRE NEGRO (1974)
Jazz ensemble.

SANGRE NEGRO (1974)
Jazz ballet. Jazz ensemble, flute
choir, and percussion ensemble.
Commissioned by Marina Svetlova.

SANGRE NEGRO (1974)
Orchestra and jazz trio. See
TWO IMPROVISATIONS FOR
ORCHESTRA AND JAZZ COMBO.

SATCH (1976)
Jazz ensemble. Jazz septet arrangement
published by Studio PR (trumpet,
alto saxophone, tenor saxophone,
trombone, piano, bass, and drums).

SATURDAY EVENING (2005)
Jazz ensemble.

SAVE ME A PLACE
This is David Baker's jazz composition "Roly Poly." When Sally
Champlin added lyrics to it, she
retitled it "Save Me a Place."

THE SCREEMIN' MEEMIES (A.K.A.
SCREAMIN' MEEMIES) (1958)
Jazz ensemble. Published by
Lauren Keiser Music.

SECIL THE HAWG MAN (2005)
Jazz ensemble.

SEE HOW THEY DONE
MY LORD (2000)
Tenor and chorus (SATB) unac-
companied. See THREE CHORAL
PIECES IN SPIRITUAL STYLE.

SENTIMENTAL (2005)
Jazz ensemble.

SET (1976)
Jazz ensemble. Jazz septet arrangement
published by Studio PR (trumpet,
alto saxophone, tenor saxophone,
trombone, piano, bass, and drums).

THE SEVEN LEAGUE BOOTS (1970)
Jazz ensemble. Published in an
arrangement for jazz nonet (trumpet,
alto saxophone, tenor saxophone,
trombone, baritone saxophone, guitar,
piano, electric bass, and drums) by
Three Fifteen West Fifty-Third Street
Corp. in their Dave Baker Jazz Rock
Series (Charles Colin Publications).

SHADOWS (1966)
Jazz ensemble.

SHADES OF BLUE (1993)
Orchestra. Four movements: I. Boogie;
II. Melancholy Blues; III. Blues Waltz;
IV. Blues for a Dancer. Commissioned
by the Roanoke Symphony Orchestra.
Published by Lauren Keiser Music.

SHAPES (1977)
Percussion ensemble. Five move-
ments. I. March; II. Boogie Woogie;
III. Song; IV. Calypso; V. Bebop.
Commissioned by J. C. Combs.
Published by Lauren Keiser Music.

SHARING THE WAY
This is David Baker's jazz composition
"Walt's Barbershop." When Sally
Champlin added lyrics to it, she
retitled it "Sharing the Way."

SHIMA 13 (1973)
Jazz ensemble. Published by Walrus
Music. Jazz septet arrangement
published by Studio PR (trumpet,
alto saxophone, tenor saxophone,
trombone, piano, bass, and drums).

SINGERS OF SONGS, WEAVERS
OF DREAMS (1980)
Subtitle: Homage to My Friends.
Violoncello and solo percussion.
Seven movements: I. Rollins; II.
Miles; III. Yancey; IV. Robeson;
V. Trane; VI. Duke; VII. Dizzy.

Commissioned by Janos Starker.
Published by Lauren Keiser Music.

THE SILVER CHALICE (1966)
Jazz ensemble.

SIMPLICITY (1973)
Jazz ensemble.

SIX POEMES NOIR POUR
FLUTE ET PIANO (1974)
Rêve; Papillon; Omniscient;
Chanson; Image; Nocturne.
Published by Lauren Keiser Music.

SLEEPLESS EYES (2005)
Jazz ensemble.

SLOW GROOVE (1970)
String orchestra. Published by
Creative Jazz Composers.

SMELL THE ROSES (2005)
Jazz ensemble.

THE SMILE (1969)
Soprano and piano. See FIVE SETTINGS
FOR SOPRANO AND PIANO.

SOFT SUMMER RAIN (1968)
Jazz ensemble. Published by Lauren
Keiser Music. For lead sheet see Baker,
*Arranging and Composing for the Small
Ensemble: Jazz, R&B, Jazz-Rock.* Lyrics for
this piece were written by Sally Champlin.

SOFTLY (2005)
Jazz ensemble.

SOLEIL D'ALTAMIRA (1974)
Jazz ensemble. Also, a play-along track
and lead sheets (for concert key treble
clef, concert key bass clef, B♭, and E♭
instruments) can be found in the book
and CD set *David Baker: Eight Classic
Jazz Originals You Can Play,* Jamey
Aebersold Play-Along volume 10.

SOLEIL D'ALTAMIRA (1974)
Orchestra, soprano, and jazz quartet.
See LE CHAT QUI PÊCHE.

SOLEIL IMPROMPTU (1990)
Brass quartet (trumpet, trombone, euphonium, and tuba). This piece is Norlan
Bewley's adaptation and arrangement
of musical material from David Baker's
composition SOLEIL D'ALTAMIRA.

SOMBER TIME (1970)
String orchestra. Published by
Creative Jazz Composers.

SOME LINKS FOR BROTHER TED
Jazz ensemble. Published by Sierra Music.

SOME NOT SO PLAIN
OLD BLUES (1989)
Voice, solo violin, string quartet,
tuba, and piano. Published by
Lauren Keiser Music.

SOMETIMES I FEEL LIKE A
MOTHERLESS CHILD (1986)
Tenor, string quartet, and piano. See
THROUGH THIS VALE OF TEARS.

SON MAR (1968)
Jazz ensemble. Published by Lauren
Keiser Music. Also published in an
arrangement for jazz nonet (trumpet,
alto saxophone, tenor saxophone,
trombone, baritone saxophone, guitar,
piano, electric bass, and drums) by
Three Fifteen West Fifty-Third Street
Corp. in their Dave Baker Jazz Rock
Series (Charles Colin Publications).
Used as the theme music for the
television series The Black Experience
(WTTV; Indianapolis, Indiana).

SONATA FOR BRASS QUINTET
AND PIANO (1970)
Three movements.

SONATA FOR CLARINET
AND ORGAN
Arrangement for clarinet and organ
by Faythe Freese of SONATA FOR
CLARINET AND PIANO.

SONATA FOR CLARINET AND PIANO
Three movements. I. Blues; II.
Loneliness; III. Dance. Published*
by Lauren Keiser Music.

SONATA FOR FLUTE AND PIANO
Published by Lauren Keiser Music.

SONATA FOR JAZZ VIOLIN AND
STRING QUARTET (1987)
Four movements. Commissioned
by Joseph Kennedy, Jr. Published
by Lauren Keiser Music.

SONATA FOR PIANO (1968)
Three movements. I. Black Art;
II. A Song – After Paul Laurence
Dunbar; III. Coltrane. Commissioned
by Natalie Hinderas. Published
by Lauren Keiser Music.

SONATA FOR PIANO AND
STRING QUINTET (1971)
Piano, two violins, viola, violon-
cello, and contrabass. Four movements.
Commissioned by Helena Freire.
Published by Lauren Keiser Music.

SONATA FOR SOLO CELLO (1990)
Commissioned by Ed Laut. Published
by Lauren Keiser Music.

SONATA FOR TUBA AND
STRING QUARTET (1971)
Four movements. Commissioned
by Harvey Phillips. Published
by Lauren Keiser Music.

SONATA FOR TWO PIANOS (1971)
Four movements. Commissioned
by Ken and Frina Boldt.

SONATA FOR VIOLA
AND PIANO (1966)
Three movements. Commissioned
by Hugh Partridge.

SONATA FOR VIOLA, GUITAR,
AND CONTRABASS (1973)
Four movements. Commissioned
by Hugh Partridge.

SONATA FOR VIOLIN, CELLO,
AND FOUR FLUTES (1980)
Three movements. Commissioned
by April Baker Ayers. Published
by Lauren Keiser Music.

SONATA FOR VIOLIN
AND CELLO (1974)
One movement.

SONATA FOR VIOLIN
AND PIANO (1967)
Alternate title: SONATA IN
ONE MOVEMENT.
    Commissioned by David Collins. Pub-
lished by Lauren Keiser Music.

SONATA FOR VIOLONCELLO
AND PIANO (1973)
Three movements. Commissioned
by Janos Starker. Published
by Associated Music.

SONATA IN ONE MOVEMENT (1967)
See SONATA FOR VIOLIN AND PIANO.

A SONG (1969)
Soprano and piano. See FIVE SETTINGS
FOR SOPRANO AND PIANO.

A SONG (1976)
Violin, violoncello, and piano.
See CONTRASTS.

A SONG (2000)
Soprano, trumpet, multiple winds,
trombone, tuba, and percussion. See THE
PLACE WHERE THE RAINBOW ENDS.

A SONG – AFTER PAUL
LAURENCE DUNBAR (1968)
Piano. See SONATA FOR PIANO.

A SONG OF MANKIND (1970)
This work is a seven-part cantata, each
part of which was written by a different
composer. David Baker wrote one
part of this work. Chorus (SATB),
orchestra, jazz ensemble, rock band,
vocal soloists, lights, and sound effects.
Commissioned by Faith for a City, for the
sesquicentennial of the state of Indiana.

SONGS OF LIVING AND
DYING (1988)
Song cycle for soprano, tenor, and
piano. Six movements: I. Forever (text
by Paul Laurence Dunbar); II. The Place
Where the Rainbow Ends (text by Paul
Laurence Dunbar); III. To a Dead Friend
(text by Paul Laurence Dunbar); IV. To
Satch (text by Samuel Allen); V. Trifle
(text by Georgia Douglas Johnson); VI.
Without Benefit of Declaration (text
by Langston Hughes); Commissioned
by The Rookwood Trio [Denise
Abbott, soprano; Roald Henderson,
tenor; Robert Haigler, piano].

SONGS OF LIVING AND DYING
(ADAPTATION, 2003)
Arrangement for contralto,
violoncello, and piano. Commissioned
by Patricia Stiles.

SONGS OF THE NIGHT (1972)
Song cycle for soprano, string quartet,
and piano. Twelve movements. Rêve and
Evening Song are for solo piano; all other
parts of this work are for soprano and
string quartet. Reve; Night: Four Songs

(text by Langston Hughes); Fragments
(text by Langston Hughes); Kid Stuff (text
by Frank Horne); Poppy Flower (text
by Langston Hughes); Borderline (text
by Langston Hughes); Where Have You
Gone? (text by Mari Evans); Gethsemane
(text by Arna Bontemps); Religion (text
by Conrad Kent Rivers); Now That He
Is Safely Dead (text by Carl Hines); End
(text by Langston Hughes); Evening
Song. Commissioned by Rita Sansone.

SORROW SONG (1990)
Contrabass. See WITNESS: SIX
ORIGINAL COMPOSITIONS IN
SPIRITUAL STYLE (1990).

SOUL OF A SUMMER'S DAY (1969)
Jazz ensemble.

THE SOUL OF '76 (1975)
Jazz ensemble. Commissioned by and
published by the J. C. Penney Company
in commemoration of the Bicentennial of
the United States of America; distributed
during the Bicentennial year (1976).

SOUL ON ICE (1969)
See I HEARD MY WOMAN CALL.

SOUL SIX (1969)
Jazz ensemble. Based on music from I
HEARD MY WOMAN CALL. For lead
sheet, see Baker, *Advanced Improvisation.*

SPEPAI (1972)
Jazz ensemble.

SPLOOCH (1962)
Jazz ensemble.

STATUS SYMBOL (1973)
Tenor and piano. From the song cycle
THE BLACK EXPERIENCE. Published
in the *Anthology of Art Songs by Black
Composers,* compiled and annotated by

Willis Patterson (New York: Edward
B. Marks Music Corporation, 1977).

STEPPIN' OUT (1990)
Jazz ensemble.

STEREOPHRENIC (1959)
Jazz ensemble.

STICKIN' (1973)
Jazz ensemble. Also arranged for quartet
of trumpet, woodwinds, trombone, and
tuba by Norlan Bewley. For lead sheet,
see Baker, *Advanced Improvisation.*

STONE NUTS (1959)
Jazz ensemble. See LUNACY.

STORIES OF THE UNDERGROUND
RAILROAD (2008)
Narrator and orchestra. Commissioned
by the Bloomington (Indiana)
Symphony Orchestra.

STRING QUARTET NO. 1 (1962)
One movement. Commissioned by
the Meredian String Quartet.

SUITE FOR CELLO AND JAZZ TRIO
Violoncello, piano, bass, and drums.
Four movements: I. Swagger; II.
Meditation; III. Slow Blues; IV.
Calypso. Commissioned by Ed
Laut. Published by Subito Music.

SUITE FOR JAZZ SEXTET (1991)
Commissioned by the New World
School of the Arts (Miami, Florida).

SUITE FOR FRENCH HORN,
STRING QUARTET, AND
CONTRABASS (1986)
Published by Lauren Keiser Music
under the title SUITE FOR HORN
AND STRING QUINTET.

SUITE FOR FRENCH HORN
AND JAZZ COMBO (1986)
Published by Lauren Keiser
Music under the title SUITE FOR
HORN AND JAZZ COMBO.

SUITE FOR UNACCOMPANIED
VIOLIN (1975)
Five movements. Commissioned
by Ruggiero Ricci. Published
by Lauren Keiser Music.

SUITE FROM *BLACK AMERICA* (1970)
Jazz ensemble. Based on music from
BLACK AMERICA (1968). This
composition won the *DownBeat*
award as best composition of the 1970
National Collegiate Jazz Festival.

SUITE FROM *THE MASQUE OF
THE RED DEATH BALLET*
Orchestra. Published by
Lauren Keiser Music.

SUITE IN FOLK STYLE (1990)
Brass quartet (trumpet, trombone,
euphonium, and tuba). SUITE IN FOLK
STYLE is the title given by the ensemble
Top Brass to a group of seven David
Baker compositions which Top Brass
performed and recorded in arrange-
ments by Norlan Bewley. These pieces
are "The Harlem Pipes," "Pastorale,"
"To Dizzy With Love," "Jeanne Marie
at the Picture Show," "Folklike,"
"Stickin'," and "Walt's Barbershop."

SUITE OF LITTLE ETHNIC
PIECES (1983)
String orchestra and jazz quartet.

SUITE FOR JAZZ SEXTET (1991)
See MIAMI SUITE.

SUITE (SWEET) LOUIS: A TRIBUTE
TO LOUIS ARMSTRONG (1971)
Percussion ensemble. One movement.
Commissioned by the American
Conservatory Percussion Ensemble.

SUMMER 1945 (1968)
See A SUMMER'S DAY IN 1945.

A SUMMER'S DAY IN 1945 (1968)
Alternate title: SUMMER 1945.
   Jazz ensemble and prerecorded tape.

SUMMER MEMORIES (1988)
String quartet. Three movements: I.
Playground; II. A Summer's Eve; III.
Clouds and Hills and Fishing Ponds.
Commissioned by the Audubon Quartet.
Published by Lauren Keiser Music.

THE SUN AND THE MOON (1989)
Theater piece for storyteller, soprano,
and chamber ensemble (flute/piccolo/
alto flute, bassoon/oboe, French horn,
bass trombone, and percussion).
Commissioned by Tales and Scales.

SUNFEST (1991)
Jazz ensemble. See MIAMI SUITE.

THE SUNSHINE BOOGALOO (1970)
String orchestra. Published by
Creative Jazz Composers.

SYMPATHY (2000)
Soprano, trumpet, multiple winds,
trombone, tuba, and percussion. See THE
PLACE WHERE THE RAINBOW ENDS.

10/21/17 (1996)
Jazz ensemble.

TEOALA (2005)
Jazz ensemble.

TERRIBLE T (1962)

Jazz ensemble. Also published in an arrangement for jazz nonet (trumpet, alto saxophone, tenor saxophone, trombone, baritone saxophone, guitar, piano, electric bass, and drums) by Three Fifteen West Fifty-Third Street Corp. in their Dave Baker Jazz Rock Series (Charles Colin Publications). For lead sheet, see Baker, *Arranging and Composing for the Small Ensemble: Jazz, R&B, Jazz-Rock.*

THADDEUS

Jazz ensemble.

THAT'S THE WAY, LORD
NELSON (1968)

Trumpet, tenor saxophone, bass, and percussion. Commissioned by James Nelson. Also arranged for jazz ensemble.

THEME AND VARIATIONS (1970)

Woodwind quintet. Theme and four variations. Published by Lauren Keiser Music.

THEME AND VARIATIONS
FOR PIANO AND STRING
QUINTET (1971)

From SONATA FOR PIANO AND STRING QUINTET. Published by Lauren Keiser Music.

THING (1959)

Jazz ensemble.

THIS ONE'S FOR TRANE (1980)

Jazz ensemble.

THOU DOST LAY ME IN THE
DUST OF DEATH (1966)

From PSALM 22. Chorus (SATB) unaccompanied. Published by Associated Music. Also arranged for brass quartet (trumpet, trombone, euphonium, and tuba) by Norlan Bewley.

THOU DOST LAY ME IN THE
DUST OF DEATH (1986)

From PSALM 22. Arrangement for tenor, string quartet, and piano. See THROUGH THIS VALE OF TEARS.

THREE CHORAL PIECES IN
SPIRITUAL STYLE (2000)

Tenor and Chorus (SATB) unaccompanied. I. When I'm Dead; II. See How They Done My Lord; III. My Lord, What a Morning. Traditional texts adapted by David Baker. Commissioned for William Brown and the Fisk Jubilee Singers by Fisk University for the installation of Dr. John Smith as twelfth president of Fisk University.

THREE FOR MALCOLM (1970)

Jazz ensemble.

THREE JAZZ MOODS (1963)

Brass ensemble. Three movements. Commissioned by Howard Liva for the Purdue University Brass Choir.

THREE VIGNETTES (1968)

Jazz ensemble and four French horns. For lead sheet, see Baker, *Arranging and Composing for the Small Ensemble: Jazz, R&B, Jazz-Rock.*

THROUGH THIS VALE
OF TEARS (1986)

Song cycle for tenor, string quartet, and piano. Eight movements: I. Thou Dost Lay Me in the Dust of Death (text from Psalm 22); II. If There Be Sorrow (text by Mari Evans); III. My God, Why Hast Thou Forsaken Me? (text from Psalm 22); IV. Parades to Hell (text by Solomon Edwards); V. Deliver My Soul (text from Psalm 22); VI. Sometimes I Feel Like a Motherless Child (traditional text); VII. Now That He Is Safely Dead (text by Carl Hines); VIII. Thou Dost Lay Me in the Dust of Death (text from Psalm

22). Commissioned by William Brown. Published by Lauren Keiser Music.

TIME LANDSCAPES (2000)
Percussion ensemble and brass. Commissioned by Jacques Cesbron for the Indiana University Ballet Theatre.

TIPPIN' (1991)
Jazz ensemble. See MIAMI SUITE.

TO A DEAD FRIEND (1988)
Song cycle for soprano, tenor, and piano. See SONGS OF LIVING AND DYING (1988). See also 2003 adaptation for contralto, violoncello, and piano.

TO A DEAD FRIEND (2000)
Soprano, trumpet, multiple winds, trombone, tuba, and percussion. See THE PLACE WHERE THE RAINBOW ENDS.

TO DIZZY WITH LOVE (1988)
Jazz ensemble.

TO SATCH (1988)
See SONGS OF LIVING AND DYING (1988). See also 2003 adaptation for contralto, violoncello, and piano.

TO THE FORE (1996)
Jazz ensemble.

TO THE POINT (2005)
Jazz ensemble.

TONIGHT'S LOOK (2005)
Jazz ensemble.

THE TRIAL OF CAPTAIN HENRY FLIPPER (1972)
Incidental music for the National Educational Television [NET] television program *The Trial of Captain Henry Flipper.*

A TRIBUTE TO WES (1972)
Jazz ensemble.

TRIFLE (1988)
See SONGS OF LIVING AND DYING (1988). See also 2003 adaptation for contralto, violoncello, and piano.

TRILOGY (1998)
Bassoon, string orchestra, electric bass, and percussion. Three movements: I. Once Upon a Time; II. Blues Kaleidoscope; III. Dénouement. Commissioned by Kim Walker.

TRIPLET BLUES (1970)
String orchestra. Published by Creative Jazz Composers.

TRITONE (2005)
Jazz ensemble.

TRUCKIN' (1992)
Jazz ensemble. Published by Walrus Music.

TUFFY (1973)
Jazz ensemble.

25TH AND MARTINDALE (1973)
Jazz ensemble. Published by Walrus Music. Jazz septet arrangement published by Studio PR (trumpet, alto saxophone, tenor saxophone, trombone, piano, bass, and drums).

TWILIGHT (2005)
Jazz ensemble.

TWO CELLO QUINTET (1987)
Violoncello and string quartet. Commissioned by Janos Starker. Published by Lauren Keiser Music.

TWO FACES OF THE BLACK FRONTIER (1971)
Jazz ensemble. Based on music from the television series *The Black Frontier.*

TWO IMPROVISATIONS
FOR ORCHESTRA AND
JAZZ COMBO (1974)
Orchestra and jazz trio (piano, bass, and drums). Two movements: I. The Harlem Pipes; II. Sangre Negro. Commissioned by the Louisville Orchestra. Published by Associated Music.

TWO SONG SIX (2005)
Jazz ensemble.

UNCLA (1973)
Jazz ensemble.

UNCLEE (1973)
Jazz ensemble.

VARIATIONS AND
PASSACAGLIA (1997)
Contrabass and piano. Commissioned by Gary Karr for the American String Teachers Association as the model composition for their double bass competitions.

VELVET ROSE (1996)
Jazz ensemble.

VERISM (1959)
Jazz ensemble.

VIBRATIONS (1972)
Jazz ensemble.

VORTEX (1962)
Jazz ensemble.

VOTIVE MASS FOR PEACE (1969)
See CATHOLIC MASS FOR PEACE.

W830007K (1975)
Jazz ensemble. Jazz septet arrangement published by Studio PR (trumpet, alto saxophone, tenor saxophone, trombone, piano, bass, and drums).

A WALK WITH A CHILD (1968)
Voice and guitar. Text by Andrew Jacobs, Jr. Music for use in Andrew Jacobs's 1968 congressional campaign.

WALPURGISNACHT (1975)
Jazz ensemble.

WALPURGISNACHT (1976)
Violin, violoncello, and piano. See ROOTS.

WALT'S BARBERSHOP (1974)
Jazz ensemble. Published by Creative Jazz Composers. Also arranged for brass quartet (trumpet, trombone, euphonium, and tuba) and for quartet of trumpet, woodwinds, trombone, and tuba by Norlan Bewley.

THE WALTZ (1957)
Jazz ensemble.

WAR GEWESEN (1959)
Jazz ensemble.

WE HAS A HARD TIME (1990)
Baritone and contrabass. See WITNESS: SIX ORIGINAL COMPOSITIONS IN SPIRITUAL STYLE (1990). See also 2003 adaptation for soprano and string orchestra.

WE WEAR THE MASK (2000)
Soprano, trumpet, multiple winds, trombone, tuba, and percussion. See THE PLACE WHERE THE RAINBOW ENDS.

WELLSPRING (1995)
Jazz ensemble. Three movements: I. The Wells Touch; II. A Gentle-man; III. Favorite Son of Old I.U./Citizen of the World. Commissioned by Indiana University in honor of the 175th anniversary of the founding of Indiana University and dedicated to chancellor Herman B Wells.

WESTERN SONG (1966)
Jazz ensemble.

WHEN? (1972)
Jazz ensemble. For lead sheet, see
Baker, *Advanced Improvisation.*

WHEN I'M DEAD (2000)
Tenor and chorus (SATB) unac-
companied. See THREE CHORAL
PIECES IN SPIRITUAL STYLE.

WHEW!! (1972)
Jazz ensemble. For lead sheet, see
Baker, *Advanced Improvisation.*

WITHOUT BENEFIT OF
DECLARATION (1988)
See SONGS OF LIVING AND DYING
(1988). See also 2003 adaptation for
contralto, violoncello, and piano.

A WIND IN SUMMER (1971)
Jazz ensemble.

WITNESS: SIX ORIGINAL
COMPOSITIONS IN
SPIRITUAL STYLE (1990)
Baritone and contrabass. Traditional texts
adapted by David Baker. Six movements.

Sorrow Song is for solo contrabass. All
other movements are for baritone and
contrabass. I. We Has a Hard Time; II.
Didn't My Lord Deliver Daniel; III. Death
Is Riding; IV. Sorrow Song; V. And He
Never Said a Mumbalin' Word; VI. My
Lord, What a Morning. Commissioned
by the Plymouth Music Society.
Published by Lauren Keiser Music.

WITNESS: SIX ORIGINAL
COMPOSITIONS IN SPIRITUAL
STYLE (ADAPTATION, 2005).
Arrangement for soprano and
string orchestra. Commissioned
by Louise Toppin.

WOODWIND QUINTET FROM
THE BLACK FRONTIER (1971)
From the music for the television
series *The Black Frontier.* Published
by Lauren Keiser Music.

WOODWIND QUINTET NO. 1
Published by Lauren Keiser Music.

APPENDIX B

Awards and Honors

- Hall of Fame, Crispus Attucks High School (Indianapolis, Indiana)
- Indiana University Scholastic Achievement Award, 1954
- Indiana University Philharmonic Gold Award, 1954
- Indiana Music Promoters Merit Award, 1959
- *DownBeat Magazine* Hall of Fame Scholarship Award, 1959
- Best Big Band, Notre Dame Collegiate Jazz Festival, 1959
- Indiana University Cream and Crimson Award
- *DownBeat Magazine* New Star Award: Trombone, 1962
- Cellist with Best Jazz Group, Notre Dame Collegiate Jazz Festival, 1964
- Outstanding Musician Award, National Association of Negro Musicians, 1968
- *DownBeat Magazine* Award for the Best Composition of the 1970 National Collegiate Jazz Festival
- Pulitzer Prize nomination for *Levels: A Concerto for Solo Contrabass, Jazz Band, Flute Quartet, Horn Quartet, and String Quartet,* 1973
- Indiana Distinguished Citizen Award, 1976
- National Association of Negro Musicians Special Award, 1976
- Key to the City of Indianapolis, Indiana
- Member, Indianapolis Jazz Hall of Fame
- Grammy Award Nomination for the liner notes to New World Record
- N W-228: *Jazz and Black Elements in Art Music*
- National Endowment for the Arts grant, 1972 and 1979
- National Association of Jazz Educators Hall of Fame Award, 1981
- Dr. Martin Luther King Drum Major Award, 1982
- Outstanding Achievement in Business and the Professions Award: Arts/Music/Theatre. Leadership Development Center, 1983
- Phi Beta Kappa Visiting Scholar, 1985–86
- President's Award for Distinguished Teaching, Indiana University, 1986
- Jazz Educators Poll Winner, *Jazz Educators Journal,* 1986
- *DownBeat Magazine* Lifetime Achievement Award, 1987
- Artistic Achievement Award, Indianapolis Musicians (Local 3) and the American Federation of Musicians, 1988
- Resolutions in honor of David N. Baker, Jr., by the Indiana General Assembly, 1989
- Arts Midwest Jazz Masters Award, 1990
- Governor's Arts Award, State of Indiana, 1991

- Honoree, New York Brass Conference for Scholarships, 1991
- Sigma Delta Chi Leather Medal Award, Indiana University School of Journalism, 1991
- Honorary doctorate, Doctor of Humane Letters, Wabash College, 1993
- *DownBeat Magazine* Jazz Education Hall of Fame, 1994
- Letter of Distinction, American Music Center, 1994
- Chevalier du violoncelle, Eva Janzer Cello Center, Indiana University School of Music, 1995
- Citation for outstanding contributions to the field of music in the United States and worldwide, National Federation of Music Clubs, 1995
- Named an Ambassador to the Arts, National Endowment for the Arts, 1995
- Honoree, "Salute to Indiana's African American Jazz Artists." Indianapolis chapter of LINKS, Inc. (philanthropic organization), 1996
- Honoree, "Stars in the Sidewalk." Star bearing David Baker's name placed in the sidewalk outside the historic Walker Theatre in Indianapolis as a part of the Indiana Avenue Walk of Fame project, 1996
- National Jazz Scholarship Award, International Jazz Hall of Fame, 1997
- Honoree, mural entitled "Indiana Avenue Jazz: The Street of Dreams," Indianapolis, Indiana (David Baker's portrait appears in this mural of famous jazz musicians from Indianapolis), 1998
- Teaching Excellence Recognition Award, Indiana University School of Music, 1998
- Grammy Award nomination in the category "Best New Work by a Contemporary Composer" for the recording of his Sonata for Clarinet and Piano from the compact disc *Welcome Home: A Collection of*

American Works for Clarinet and Piano (Arabesque Recordings z6703), 1998
- American Jazz Masters Award, National Endowment for the Arts, 2000
- Brown Derby Award, Indiana University Society of Professional Journalists (given annually to a faculty member who has been deemed outstanding and popular with his or her students and who merits their highest respect), 2000
- "Spirit of the Prairie" Award, Conner Prairie Living History Museum, Indianapolis, Indiana, 2000
- First Annual Paul Laurence Dunbar Award, Brass Chamber Music Foundation, Dayton, Ohio, 2001
- Indiana Living Legend Award, Indiana Historical Society, Indianapolis, Indiana, 2001
- Al Cobine Award, Jazz from Bloomington, Bloomington, Indiana, 2002
- James Smithson Bicentennial Medal, Smithsonian Institution, Washington, D.C., 2002
- Inductee, Hall of Fame, Indianapolis Jazz Foundation, Indianapolis, Indiana, 2002
- Outstanding Hoosier Musician Award, Indiana Music Educators Association; 2003
- Maria Fisher Founder's Award, the Thelonious Monk Institute, Washington, D.C., 2003
- P. A. Mack Award, FACET [Faculty Colloquium on Excellence in Teaching], Indiana University–Bloomington, 2003
- Emmy Award for the music for the television documentary *For Gold and Glory,* produced by WFYI-TV/ PBS Indianapolis, Indiana, 2003
- Honorary doctorate, Doctor of Music, Oberlin College, 2004
- Living Treasure Award, Bloomington (Indiana) Arts Council, 2004

- Lowell Mason Award, Music Educators National Conference, 2005
- Honorary doctorate, Doctor of Music, New England Conservatory of Music, 2006
- Tracy M. Sonneborn Award, Indiana University, 2006
- Fall 2006–2007 (volume 3, no. 1) issue of the *International Jazz Archives Journal* dedicated to David Baker, in recognition of his contributions to the profession
- Lawrence Berk Leadership Award, International Association for Jazz Education, 2007
- John F. Kennedy Center for the Performing Arts Living Jazz Legend Award, 2007
- Honorary doctorate, Doctor of World Music, Martin University, 2007
- Inductee, Indianapolis (Indiana) Public Schools Hall of Fame, 2007
- Baker Building Dedication (115 South Walnut Street in Bloomington, Indiana, was dedicated as "The Baker Building," in his honor. The first floor houses retail space; the second floor is an upscale residential apartment unit and art gallery of 2800 square feet, named "Baker Place"), 2007
- *Basically Baker,* Buselli-Wallarab Jazz Orchestra CD of David Baker's jazz ensemble music, selected by *DownBeat Magazine* as one of the "Best CDs of 2007," January 2008
- *Billy Strayhorn: Lush Life* won Best Television Documentary at the Sixtieth Annual Writers Guild of America Awards Ceremony (David Baker was an interviewee and consultant on this film, and appeared on camera several times, giving commentary on Billy Strayhorn's work), 2008
- National Guild of Community Schools of the Arts National Leadership Award, 2008
- Jazz Journalists Association "A Team" Award, 2009
- Ralph Adams Lifetime Achievement Award, 2009
- Who's Who in Black Indianapolis: Honoree for Lifetime Achievement in Creative Activity, Teaching, and Service, 2009
- *Basically Baker,* the Buselli-Wallarab Jazz Orchestra CD of David Baker's jazz ensemble music, selected by *DownBeat Magazine* as one of the 100 best jazz albums of the 2000s, January 2010

APPENDIX C

Service

NATIONAL AND INTERNATIONAL

· Afro-American Music
Bicentennial, Hall of Fame and
Museum – Member, advisory board
· American Music Center – Member,
board of directors
· American Music Conference – Judge,
National Music Awards
· American Pianists Association – Judge,
American Jazz Piano Competition
· American Recording Orchestra of
Duke University – Board member
· American Symphony Orchestra
League – Member, board of directors;
member, directors council
· Arts Midwest – Member,
board of directors
· Atlantic Center for the Arts [New
Smyrna Beach, Florida] – Member,
national council
· Broadcast Music, Inc. – Member; Judge,
BMI Young Composers Competition
· The Brubeck Institute [University
of the Pacific; Stockton,
California] – Member, honorary board
· Center for Black Music Research,
Columbia College Chicago
[Chicago] – Consultant
· Chamber Music America – Member,
board of directors
· Contemporary Music Project – Member
· The Copland House [The
Copland Heritage Association

of Cortlandt; Cortlandt Manor,
New York] – Charter member
· *DownBeat Magazine* – Judge,
dee bee Awards/Student Music
Awards; editor, Jazz Styles and
Analysis Series, *DownBeat* Music
Workshop Publications
· Golden Press/Charles Hansen
Publications – Jazz editor
· The Harvey Phillips
Foundation – Member,
board of directors
· The Henry Mancini Institute – Member,
national advisory board
· Hoagy Carmichael Competition – Judge
· Institute for Advanced Study – Member
· Institute of Black Music – Consultant
· Interlochen Arts Academy – Member,
advisory board
· International Association for Jazz
Education – President; vice president;
member, Past Presidents Council;
Member, executive board; Member,
advisory council; Tri-chair with
Dr. Billy Taylor (Jazz at Kennedy
Center) and Bruce Lundvall
(president and CEO, EMI Music)
of the Ten Million Dollar Capital
Campaign for the International
Association for Jazz Education
· International Bass Competition – Judge
and jazz panel chairman

- *International Jazz Archives
  Journal* – Member, editorial
  review board
- International Trombone
  Association – Member, pedagogy
  council; Member, advisory
  council on pedagogy
- James Moody Scholarship
  Fund – Member, honoree
  benefit committee
- Jazz Action Coalition – President
- Jazz Artists in the Schools
  Program – Consultant to the director
- Jazz at Lincoln Center – Judge,
  Essentially Ellington Competition;
  member, international voting panel,
  Nesuhi Ertegun Jazz Hall of Fame;
  editor, Essential Jazz Editions – a
  joint project of the Smithsonian
  Institution, the Library of Congress,
  and Jazz at Lincoln Center
- John F. Kennedy Center for the
  Performing Arts – Chairman,
  jazz advisory panel
- *Journal of Jazz Studies,* Rutgers
  University – Associate editor
- Kentucky Jazz Foundation – Member,
  distinguished board of directors
- Lost Jazz Shrines Project – Consultant
- Minnesota Composers
  Forum – Member
- Mu Phi Epsilon – Honorary
  Sterling Patron
- National Endowment for the
  Arts – Member, Jazz/Folk/Ethnic
  panel; chairman, Jazz/Folk/
  Ethnic panel; member, National
  Council on the Arts [presidential
  appointment by Ronald Reagan];
  member, selection committee,
  American Jazz Masters Awards
- National Jazz Foundation – Member
- National Jazz Service
  Organization – President
- National Music Council – Member,
  board of directors
- National Public Radio – Consultant,
  Jazz Profiles series, produced by Tim
  Owens; consultant, *Making the Music*
  series, hosted by Wynton Marsalis
- New England Jazz Alliance Hall of
  Fame – Member, selection committee
- New South Wales Conservatory
  and Secondary School System
  [Sydney] – Consultant, jazz curriculum
- Oberlin College – Consultant
- Philadelphia Jazz Institute – Member,
  honorary advisory board
- The Pulitzer Prizes – Member,
  Nominating Jury in Music; Member,
  Music Prize Study Committee
- Quincy Jones Musiq
  Consortium – Member,
  board of directors
- Rockefeller Foundation – Member,
  Recorded Anthology of
  American Music, Inc.
- Royal Danish
  Conservatory – Consultant
- Secondary Schools of
  Sweden – Consultant in jazz
- Smithsonian Institution – Senior
  consultant to the music programs;
  member, executive board, Jazz
  Masterworks Editions; member,
  board of directors, Jazz Masterworks
  Editions; editor, Essential Jazz
  Editions [a joint project of the
  Smithsonian Institution, the Library
  of Congress, and Jazz at Lincoln
  Center]; member, advisory committee,
  *Smithsonian Collection of Classic
  Jazz;* member, executive committee,
  Jazz: The Smithsonian Anthology
- The Sphinx Competition – Judge
- Super-Sensitive Musical
  String Company – Endorser,
  Super-Sensitive strings
- Thelonious Monk Institute of
  Jazz – Consultant; member,
  advisory board
- Top Brass – Member, board of directors

- US State Department – Member, State Department Folk Music and Jazz Advisory Panel
- USA International Harp Competition – Member, honorary advisory board
- Young American Symphony Orchestra – Member, artistic advisory board

STATE OF INDIANA

- Bloomington Area Arts Council – Member, Leadership Awards selection committee; member, Living Treasure Award selection committee
- Bloomington Jazz Festival – Adjudicator
- Camerata Chamber Orchestra [Bloomington] – Member, executive council
- Indiana Arts Commission – Member
- Indiana Civil Rights Commission – Judge, "Spirit of Justice" Awards
- Indiana Historical Society – Member, honorary committee/Musical Heritage Committee
- Indianapolis Jazz Club – Honorary lifetime member
- Indy JazzFest – Consultant; member, advisory board; member, board of directors; honorary co-chairman [with Indianapolis mayor Stephen Goldsmith and Indiana lieutenant governor Joseph Kernan]; tri-chairman of Indy JazzFest [with Indianapolis mayor Bart Peterson and Indiana lieutenant governor Joseph Kernan]
- Indianapolis Public Television – Consultant on the program *Indianapolis in the 1950s*
- National Black Colloquium and Competition – Indiana state chairman
- Purdue University Jazz Festival – Adjudicator
- The Stardust Road Project [Bloomington] – Musical and historical advisor

- Starr-Gennett Foundation [Richmond] – Member, national advisory board
- Starr-Gennett Museum Project [Richmond] – Consultant
- WFHB Community Radio Station [Bloomington] – Member, advisory board

INDIANA UNIVERSITY

- African American and African Diaspora Studies Department – Adjunct faculty member
- American Studies Program – Member of the faculty
- Art Museum – Member, advisory board
- Athletic Committee – Member
- Auditorium Committee – Member
- Commitment to Excellence Review Committee – Member
- Distinguished Ranks Committee – Member
- Gender Equity/Salary Equity Committee – Member
- Honorary Doctorate Committee – Member
- Indiana University American Association of University Professors – Member-at-large
- Jacobs School of Music – Chairman, Jazz Studies Department; member, School of Music Council; member, Dean's Advisory Committee; member, Distinguished Ranks Committee; board member, Eva Janzer Cello Center; member, Academic Fairness Committee; member, Affirmative Action Advisory Committee; member, Artist Diploma Committee; member, Instrumental and Choral Operations Committee; member, Martin Luther King, Jr., Celebration Committee; member, Ensemble Committee; member, DeLone Undergraduate Essay Prize Committee; associate director, Black Music Center

- President's Task Force/Strategic Planning Committee – Member
- Search and Screen Committees – Member of numerous search and screen committees [chancellor, provost, deans, department chairs, and other faculty], both for the University and for the Jacobs School of Music
- Sonneborn Awards/Chancellor Professor Committee – Member
- WFIU-FM [Public radio station] – Member, advisory board

APPENDIX D

Performing Experience

JAZZ GROUPS
- Various All-Star groups, including those at the Jamey Aebersold Summer Jazz Workshops
- Association for the Advancement of Creative Musicians (AACM)
- Various Australian jazz groups
- David Baker & Friends
- The David Baker Quintet
- The David Baker Septet
- The David Baker Sextet
- The David Baker String Ensemble
- David Baker's 21st Century Bebop Band
- Composition (David Baker–Richard Dunbar–Charles Tyler Trio)
- The Curtiss Counce Orchestra
- Fred Dale
- Nathan Davis
- The Ted Dunbar Quartet
- Maynard Ferguson
- Lionel Hampton
- Slide Hampton
- The Barry Harris Ensemble
- Indiana University Jazz Faculty
- Indy Jazz All-Stars
- Jazz Fables
- Buddy Johnson
- Quincy Jones
- Stan Kenton
- Harold Land
- The Livingston College/Rutgers University Jazz Professors
- Wes Montgomery
- The George Russell Sextet
- Composer/Performer at the Spoleto Festival [South Carolina]
- The Swedish Radio Orchestra
- The Charles Tyler Ensemble
- *Various additional groups, including the following:*
  - Richie Beirach
  - Bill Evans
  - Frank Foster
  - Curtis Fuller
  - Eddie Gomez
  - Freddie Hubbard
  - Paul Jeffrey
  - Philly Joe Jones
  - Virgil Jones
  - David Liebman
  - Monk Montgomery
  - Larry Ridley
  - Art Taylor
  - Leroy Vinnegar
  - Freddie Waits
- Guest appearance as jazz soloist on Garrison Keillor's *American Radio Company* show (NPR), 1992
- Currently conductor and musical and artistic director, Smithsonian Jazz Masterworks Orchestra [performances in the United States and throughout the world]

NON-JAZZ GROUPS
· Bloomington Symphony
  (Bloomington, Indiana)
· Butler University Band
  (Indianapolis, Indiana)
· Butler University Orchestra
· Indiana Central College String Quartet
· Indiana University Brass Ensemble
· Indiana University Opera Orchestra
· Indiana University
  Philharmonic Orchestra
· Indiana University Wind Ensemble
· Indianapolis Civic Orchestra
· Jefferson City Symphony
  (Jefferson City, Missouri)

· *Soloist with*
  · Boston Symphony Orchestra
  · Evansville Philharmonic Orchestra
  · Indianapolis Symphony Orchestra
· *Guest conductor with*
  · Akron Symphony Orchestra
  · Diablo Valley College Orchestra
  · Evansville Youth Orchestra
  · Indiana University Concert
    Symphony Orchestra
  · Indianapolis Civic Orchestra
  · Indianapolis Philharmonic Orchestra
  · Indianapolis Symphony Orchestra
  · New Tokyo Philharmonic
    Orchestra (Tokyo)

APPENDIX E

Teaching

CURRENT ACADEMIC APPOINTMENT

Indiana University School
of Music, 1966–present
   Distinguished Professor of Music and
chairman of the Jazz Department

PREVIOUS ACADEMIC APPOINTMENTS

· Indiana Central College, 1963–64
· Indianapolis Public Schools, 1958–59
· Lincoln University (Jefferson
   City, Missouri), 1956–57

PRIVATE TEACHING

Private teaching full time, 1960–66.
   However, since receiving a fulltime
academic appointment in the Indiana
University School of Music in 1966, David
Baker has done very little private teaching, working only with selected outstanding students not affiliated with Indiana
University and with professional players.
Some of these musicians took only a few
lessons with him, just to fix problems or
work on new concepts they wanted to
explore with him, such as Wynton and
Delfeayo Marsalis. Others have come
on a more regular basis for lessons over
a period of time, such as Ralph Bowen,
who is now chair of jazz studies at Rutgers
University.

David Baker does not teach privately as
part of his assigned duties in the School
of Music and as such has no students
officially assigned to him for private
teaching. When time permits, he
coaches individual students and
groups in the Jazz Department.

STEANS INSTITUTE, RAVINIA FESTIVAL

In summer 2000 David Baker designed,
directed, and taught at the inaugural
program for jazz which was a part of the
Steans Institute for Young Artists at
the Ravinia Festival in Chicago. He has
continued to do that every summer since
that time and also continues to serve as
Founding Chair of the Jazz Faculty. Each
year approximately fifteen exceptional
young jazz musicians identified as having
the potential for major careers are
handpicked for this study program.

SUMMER JAZZ WORKSHOPS

David Baker has been a member of the
faculty of the Summer Jazz Workshops
[started by Stan Kenton in the late
1950s and now run by Jamey Aebersold]
from 1959 to the present day.

SELECTED ADDITIONAL TEACHING

This list represents some of the universities, colleges, institutions, festivals, and cities in which David Baker has conducted master classes and residencies.

USA

· Alcorn State University
· Atlanta University
· Bellarmine College
· Berea College
· Berklee College of Music (Boston)
· Brigham Young University
· California Polytechnic State University, San Luis Obispo
· Carleton College
· Chicago State University
· Christian Theological Seminary
· Cleveland State University
· The Charles Colin Studios (New York City)
· Diablo Valley College
· Duke University
· Eastern Illinois University
· Elmhurst College
· The Festival at Sandpointe (Sandpointe, Idaho)
· Florida Atlantic University
· Great Lakes Chamber Music Festival
· Illinois Central College
· Indiana State University
· Indianapolis Public Schools
· Interlochen Arts Academy
· Ithaca College
· Kentucky State University
· Langston University
· Livingston College/Rutgers University
· Long Beach City College
· Louisiana State University (Baton Rouge)
· Marycrest College
· Miami University (Ohio)
· Miami-Dade Community College
· Montana State University
· Morehouse College

· Morris Brown College
· The Nashville [Tennessee] Jazz Workshop
· New England Conservatory of Music
· New World School of the Arts (Miami, Florida)
· New York University (Brockport)
· New York University (Binghamton)
· North Carolina School of the Arts
· Oberlin College
· Omaha [Nebraska] Public Schools
· Prairie State College
· Rock Valley College
· San Diego State College
· Simpson College [Iowa]
· Smithsonian Institution
· Spelman College
· Tanglewood (summers)
· Temple University
· Tennessee Performing Arts Center
· Thelonious Monk Institute
· Wartburg College
· Wichita State University
· United States Military Academy at West Point
· University of Connecticut
· University of Illinois
· University of Louisville
· University of Maryland
· University of Massachusetts (Amherst)
· University of Minnesota
· University of Nebraska
· University of Nebraska (Omaha)
· University of Nevada at Las Vegas
· University of New Hampshire
· University of Northern Colorado
· University of Oklahoma
· University of Pittsburgh
· University of South Florida
· University of Wisconsin (Eau Claire)
· University of Wisconsin (Superior)
· Valparaiso University
· Vigo County [Indiana] Public Schools

The National Stage Band Camps/Jamey Aebersold Summer Jazz Workshops at numerous colleges and conservatories, including those in the following states, provinces, and countries:

- California
- Colorado
- Connecticut
- Florida
- Illinois
- Kansas
- Kentucky
- Nevada
- Rhode Island
- South Dakota
- Texas
- Utah
- Australia
- Canada
- Denmark
- England
- Germany
- New Zealand
- Nova Scotia
- Sweden

OUTSIDE THE USA
(other than the National Stage Band Camps/Jamey Aebersold Summer Jazz Workshops)

Australia
- Narrabundah College (Canberra)
- Victoria School of the Arts (Melbourne)
- New South Wales Conservatory (Sydney)

Canada
- Orford Arts Centre (Québec)
- University of Alberta

Denmark
- Copenhagen

Egypt
- Cairo

England
- London

Germany
- Rottenburg

Mexico

Monaco
- Monte Carlo

New Zealand
- The Entrance High School (Entrance)
- Wellington (Auckland)

Sweden
- Stockholm

APPENDIX F

Professional Societies and Organizations, Past and Present

- Alliance of Distinguished and Titled Professors, Indiana University
- Broadcast Music, Inc.
- International Association for Jazz Education
- Jazz Education Network
- Minnesota Composers Forum
- Mu Phi Epsilon [Honorary Sterling Patron]
- National Association of Jazz Educators
- National Jazz Service Organization
- Phi Mu Alpha Sinfonia
- Local 3, American Federation of Musicians (Indianapolis, Indiana)
- Local 161-710, American Federation of Musicians (Washington, D.C.)
- Local 802, American Federation of Musicians (New York City)

Bibliography of Written
Works by David Baker

BOOKS AND ARTICLES

Abrams, Richard, David N. Baker, and Charles Ellison. "The Social Role of Jazz." In *Reflections on Afro-American Music,* edited by Dominique-René De Lerma, 99–110. Kent, Ohio: Kent State University Press, 1973.

Advanced Ear Training for Jazz Musicians. Lebanon, Ind.: Studio PR, 1977. Revised ed., Van Nuys, Calif.: Alfred, 1996.

Advanced Improvisation. Chicago: Maher Publications, 1979.

Advanced Improvisation, volume 1: Improvisational Concepts. Van Nuys, Calif.: Alfred, 1990.

Advanced Improvisation, volume 2: Rhythmic and Melodic Concepts. Van Nuys, Calif.: Alfred, 1990.

"An Approach to Acquiring Facility with the Bebop Vocabulary through the Practice and Study of Bebop Compositions." *Jazz Player* 2, no. 2 (February/March 1995): 59–61.

Anderson, T. J., David N. Baker, John Carter, and John E. Price. "The Black Composer Discusses His Music." In *Reflections on Afro-American Music,* edited by Dominique-René De Lerma, 90–98. Kent, Ohio: Kent State University Press, 1973.

Anderson, T. J., David N. Baker, John Carter, John E. Price, and Herndon Spillman. "The Composer and His Relationship to Society." In *Reflections on Afro-American Music,* edited by Dominique-René De Lerma, 76–89. Kent, Ohio: Kent State University Press, 1973.

Arranging and Composing for the Small Ensemble: Jazz, R&B, Jazz-Rock. Revised ed. Van Nuys, Calif.: Alfred, 1988.

"The Battle for Legitimacy: 'Jazz' Versus Academia." *Black World* 23, no. 1 (November 1973): 20–27.

Bebop Jazz Solos: Correlated with Volumes 10 and 13 of Jamey Aebersold's Play-A-Long Book and Record Series. B♭ ed. New Albany, Ind.: Jamey Aebersold, 1981.

Bebop Jazz Solos: Correlated with Volumes 10 and 13 of Jamey Aebersold's Play-A-Long Book and Record Series. Bass clef ed. New Albany, Ind.: Jamey Aebersold, 1981.

Bebop Jazz Solos: Correlated with Volumes 10 and 13 of Jamey Aebersold's Play-A-Long Book and Record Series. E♭ ed. New Albany, Ind.: Jamey Aebersold, 1981.

Bebop Jazz Solos: Correlated with Volumes 10 and 13 of Jamey Aebersold's Play-A-Long Book and Record Series. Treble clef ed. New Albany, Ind.: Jamey Aebersold, 1981.

"The Bebop Major Scale." *Jazz Player* 1, no. 3 (April/May 1994): 40–41.

"The Bebop Scales (Dominant and Major)." *Jazz Educators Journal* 17, no. 3 (February/March 1985): 8–11.

"Bebop-Era Standards." In *Jazz: The First Century*, edited by John Edward Hasse, 102. New York: William Morrow, 2000.

"Bill Harris." *DownBeat* 36, no. 1 (January 9, 1969): 39–41.

"Bobby Bryant's 'Good Morning Starshine' Solo." *DownBeat* 36, no. 20 (October 2, 1969): 31–32.

"Breaks and Fours." In *Jazz: The First Century*, edited by John Edward Hasse, 120. New York: William Morrow, 2000.

Charlie Parker: Alto Saxophone. David Baker Jazz Monographs. New York: Shattinger International, 1978.

"Charlie Parker's 'Now's the Time' Solo." *DownBeat* 38, no. 19 (November 11, 1971): 32–33.

"Chord Substitutions and Bitonals, Part 1: Non-Contextual Substitutions." *Jazz Player* 3 , no. 1 (December 1995/January 1996): 63, 79.

"Chord Substitutions and Bitonals, Part 2: Contextual Substitutions." *Jazz Player* 3, no. 2 (February/March 1996): 48–49.

"Clark Terry's 'Feedin' the Bean.'" *DownBeat* 37, no. 8 (April 16, 1970): 32–34.

"Communicating Human Emotion through Improvisation: A Psychological Approach." *DownBeat* 63, no. 10 (October 1996): 70.

Contemporary Patterns. Bass clef ed. New York: Charles Colin, 1979.

Contemporary Patterns. Treble clef ed. New York: Charles Colin, 1979.

Contemporary Techniques for the Trombone. 2 vols. New York: Charles Colin, 1974.

A Creative Approach to Practicing Jazz: New and Exciting Strategies for Unlocking Your Creative Potential. New Albany, Ind.: Jamey Aebersold Jazz, 1994.

"Creative Scale Practicing." *Jazz Player* 1, no. 4 (June/July 1994): 20–21.

"Creating Contrafacts and Using Them in Imaginative and Challenging Ways." *Jazz Player* 3, no. 3 (April/May 1996): 17–19.

"Creating Contrafacts and Using Them in Imaginative and Challenging Ways, Part 2." *Jazz Player* 3, no. 5 (August/September 1996): 25–27.

"Curtis Fuller." *DownBeat* 36, no. 4 (February 20, 1969): 33.

"Curtis Fuller's 'Bongo Bop' Solo." *DownBeat* 40, no. 1 (January 18, 1973): 40–41.

"The Cycle and the Turnback in Jazz." *DownBeat* 61, no. 10 (October 1994): 62.

"Developing Skill with Quotation Techniques." *DownBeat* 62, no. 3 (March 1995): 54.

"Dizzy Gillespie's 'One Bass Hit.'" *DownBeat* 37, no. 4 (February 19, 1970): 34–x38.

"Double Brass: J. J. Johnson and Freddy Hubbard." *DownBeat* 38, no. 3 (February 4, 1971): 34–38.

Ear Training for Jazz Musicians, volume 1: Intervals. Lebanon, Ind.: Studio PR; Miami, Fla.: Columbia Pictures Publications/Belwin Mills, 1981.

Ear Training for Jazz Musicians, volume 2: Triads/Three Note Sets/Four and Five Note Sets. Lebanon, Ind.: Studio PR; Miami, Fla.: Columbia Pictures Publications/Belwin Mills, 1981.

Ear Training for Jazz Musicians, volume 3: Seventh Chords/Scales. Lebanon, Ind.: Studio PR; Miami, Fla.: Columbia Pictures Publications/Belwin Mills, 1981.

Ear Training for Jazz Musicians, volume 4: Major Melodies/Turnarounds/I VI7 Formulae. Lebanon, Ind.: Studio PR; Miami, Fla.: Columbia Pictures Publications/Belwin Mills, 1981.

Ear Training for Jazz Musicians, volume 5: II V7 Patterns. Lebanon, Ind.: Studio PR; Miami, Fla.: Columbia Pictures Publications/Belwin Mills, 1981.

"Exercising Options in Improvisation." *DownBeat* 64, no. 3 (March 1997): 62–63.

"Extending the Coltrane Changes." *DownBeat* 61, no. 3 (March 1994): 63.

Foreword, in Nathan Davis, *African American Music*, v. Needham Heights, Mass.: Simon and Schuster Custom Publishing, 1996.

Foreword, in Aaron Horne, *Brass Music of Black Composers*, xvii–xviii. Westport, Conn.: Greenwood Press, 1996.

"Gary Bartz's 'Rise' Solo." *DownBeat* 38, no. 13 (June 24, 1971): 32–33.

"Herbie Mann's 'Memphis Underground' Solo." *DownBeat* 37, no. 25 (December 10, 1970): 34–36.

How to Learn Tunes: A Jazz Musician's Survival Guide. Includes play-along book and CD. New Albany, Ind.: Jamey Aebersold Jazz, 1997.

How to Play Bebop, volume 1: The Bebop Scale and Other Scales in Common Use. Bloomington, Ind.: Frangipani Press, 1985. Reprint, Van Nuys, Calif.: Alfred, 2006.

How to Play Bebop, volume 2: Learning the Bebop Language: Patterns, Formulae and Other Linking Materials. Bloomington, Ind.: Frangipani Press, 1985. Reprint, Van Nuys, Calif.: Alfred, 2006.

How to Play Bebop, volume 3: Techniques for Learning and Utilizing Bebop Tunes. Bloomington, Ind.: Frangipani Press, 1985. Reprint, Van Nuys, Calif.: Alfred, 2006.

"How to Use Strings in Jazz: Part 11." *DownBeat* 41, no. 8 (April 25, 1974): 38, 40. (This is the same as "How to Use Strings in Jazz," *Orchestra News*. The "Part 11" appearing in the title of this article is erroneous. It has been included in the citation because it appears in the title as printed in *DownBeat*. "How to Use Strings in Jazz" was published in its entirety in the April 25, 1974, issue.)

"How to Use Strings in Jazz." *Orchestra News* 14, no. 3 (July 1974): 11.

"Hubert Laws' 'Gula Matari' Solo." *DownBeat* 38, no. 8 (April 15, 1971): 32–34.

"Improvisation: A Tool for Musical Learning." *Music Educators Journal* 66, no. 1 (January 1980): 42–51.

Improvisational Patterns: The Bebop Era. 3 vols. Bass clef ed. New York: Charles Colin, 1979.

Improvisational Patterns: The Bebop Era. 3 vols. Treble clef ed. New York: Charles Colin, 1979.

Improvisational Patterns: The Blues. Bass clef ed. New York: Charles Colin, 1980.

Improvisational Patterns: The Blues. Treble clef ed. New York: Charles Colin, 1980.

"Improvisational Techniques and Performance Practices Related to the Various Jazz Styles." Paper commissioned for and published in the 100 Years of Jazz and Blues Festival program. Brooklyn, N.Y.: 651/Kings Majestic Corporation, 1992.

"Indianapolis, Indiana." In *Lost Jazz Shrines*, edited by Willard Jenkins, 29–33. N.p.: Lost Jazz Shrines Project, 1998.

"Internalizing the Sound of the Changes." *DownBeat* 61, no. 5 (May 1994): 62–63.

Introduction, in Nathan T. Davis, *Writings in Jazz*, ix–x. 6th ed. Dubuque, Iowa: Kendall/Hunt, 2002.

J. J. Johnson, interview by Lida Baker and David Baker, February 26–27, 1994, transcript, Smithsonian Jazz Oral History Project, http://www.smithsonianjazz.org/oral_histories/pdf/joh_JJJohnson_transcript.pdf.

"J. J. Johnson: Part 2." *DownBeat* 35, no. 22 (October, 1968): 38–39.

J. J. Johnson: Trombone. David Baker Jazz Monographs. New York: Shattinger International, 1978.

"J. J. Johnson: Trombone Giant." *DownBeat* 35, no. 17 (August 22, 1968): 47–49.

"Jazz: The Academy's Neglected Stepchild." *DownBeat* 32, no. 9 (September 23, 1965): 29–32.

Jazz Bass Clef Expressions and Explorations: A New and Innovative System for Learning to Improvise for Bass Clef Instruments and Jazz Cello. New Albany, Ind.: Jamey Aebersold Jazz, 1995.

Jazz Etudes: Correlated with Volumes 5 and 6 of Jamey Aebersold's Play-A-Long Book and Record Series. B♭ ed. New Albany, Ind.: Jamey Aebersold, 1979.

Jazz Etudes: Correlated with Volumes 5 and 6 of Jamey Aebersold's Play-A-Long Book and Record Series. Bass clef ed. New Albany, Ind.: Jamey Aebersold, 1979.

Jazz Etudes: Correlated with Volumes 5 and 6 of Jamey Aebersold's Play-A-Long Book and Record Series. E♭ ed. New Albany, Ind.: Jamey Aebersold, 1979.

Jazz Etudes: Correlated with Volumes 5 and 6 of Jamey Aebersold's Play-A-Long Book and Record Series. Treble clef ed. New Albany, Ind.: Jamey Aebersold, 1979.

Jazz Improvisation: A Comprehensive Method of Study for All Players. Revised ed. Van Nuys, Calif.: Alfred, 1988.

Jazz Improvisation: Eine umfassende Methode für alle Instrumente. Rottenburg, Germany: Advance Music, 1990.

"Jazz Improvisation – The Weak Link." *The Instrumentalist* 26, no. 11 (November 1971): 21–24.

Jazz Improvisation Method: Strings, volume 1: Violin and Viola. Chicago: Maher; Van Nuys, Calif.: Alfred, 1976.

Jazz Improvisation Method: Strings, volume 2: Cello and Bass Viol. Chicago: Maher; Van Nuys, Calif.: Alfred, 1976.

Jazz Pedagogy: A Comprehensive Method of Jazz Education for Teacher and Student. Chicago: Maher Publications, 1979. Reprint, Van Nuys, Calif.: Alfred, 1989. Revised and enlarged ed. forthcoming.

The Jazz Style of Clifford Brown: A Musical and Historical Perspective. Lebanon, Ind.: Studio PR; Van Nuys, Calif.: Alfred, 1982.

The Jazz Style of Fats Navarro: A Musical and Historical Perspective. Lebanon, Ind.: Studio PR; Miami, Fla.: Columbia Pictures Publications/Belwin Mills, 1982.

The Jazz Style of John Coltrane: A Musical and Historical Perspective. Lebanon, Ind.: Studio PR; Van Nuys, Calif.: Alfred, 1980.

The Jazz Style of Julian "Cannonball" Adderley: A Musical and Historical Perspective. Lebanon, Ind.: Studio PR; Miami, Fla.: Columbia Pictures Publications/Belwin Mills, 1980.

The Jazz Style of Miles Davis: A Musical and Historical Perspective. Lebanon, Ind.: Studio PR; Van Nuys, Calif.: Alfred, 1980.

The Jazz Style of Sonny Rollins: A Musical and Historical Perspective. Lebanon, Ind.: Studio PR; Van Nuys, Calif.: Alfred, 1980.

Jazz Styles and Analysis, Trombone: A History of the Jazz Trombone via Recorded Solos; Transcribed and Annotated. Chicago: Maher; Van Nuys, Calif.: Alfred, 1973.

Jazz Treble Clef Expressions and Explorations: A New and Innovative System for Learning to Improvise for Treble Clef Instruments and Jazz Violin. New Albany, Ind.: Jamey Aebersold Jazz, 1995.

"Jean-Luc Ponty." *DownBeat* 36, no. 17 (August 21, 1969): 51–52.

"Jeremy Steig's 'Superbaby' Solo." *DownBeat* 37, no. 10 (May 14, 1970): 42–45.

"John Coltrane's 'Giant Steps' Solo and Composition." *DownBeat* 38, no. 14 (July 22, 1971): 35–38.

"Johnny Hodges' 'Passion Flower' Solo." *DownBeat* 37, no. 16 (August 20, 1970): 37–38.

"Kennedy, Jelly Roll, Bix, and Hoagy." *Indiana Magazine of History* 91, no. 3 (March 1995): 109–11.

"Kid Ory." *DownBeat* 40, no. 4 (March 1, 1973): 32–33.

"Lew Soloff's 'Lucretia's Reprise' Solo." *DownBeat* 37, no. 18 (September 17, 1970): 33–37.

"Mainstream Jazz Standards." In *Jazz: The First Century*, edited by John Edward Hasse, 119. New York: William Morrow, 2000.

"Miles Davis' 'Petits Machins' Solo." *DownBeat* 36, no. 26 (December 25, 1969): 44–47.

"Milt Jackson's 'Theme from *the Anderson Tapes*.'" *DownBeat* 39, no. 4 (March 2, 1972): 31–32.

Modern Concepts in Jazz Improvisation: A Comprehensive Method for All Musicians; A New Approach to Fourths, Pentatonics and Bitonals. Van Nuys, Calif.: Alfred, 1990.

Modern Jazz Duets for All Bass Clef Instruments, volume 1: Cookin'. New York: Charles Colin, 1979.

Modern Jazz Duets for All Bass Clef Instruments, volume 2: Smokin'. New York: Charles Colin, 1979.

Modern Jazz Duets for All Treble Clef Instruments, volume 1: Cookin'. New York: Charles Colin, 1980.

Modern Jazz Duets for All Treble Clef Instruments, volume 2: Smokin'. New York: Charles Colin, 1979.

A New Approach to Ear Training for the Jazz Musician. Lebanon, Ind.: Studio PR, 1976. Revised ed., Miami, Fla.: Warner Brothers, 1995.

"Pentatonics & Fourths." *DownBeat* 62, no. 12 (December 1995): 79.

"A Periodization of Black Music History." In *Reflections on Afro-American Music*, edited by Dominique-René De Lerma, 143–60. Kent, Ohio: Kent State University Press, 1973.

"Perspectives of John Coltrane 1926–1967: Profile of a Giant." NAJE *Educator* 11, no. 2 (February/March 1979): 10+.

"Pharaoh Sanders' Solo 'Sun in Aquarius: Part 2.'" *DownBeat* 39, no. 12 (June 22, 1972): 34–36.

"Playing on *I Got Rhythm* Changes, Part 1: Rhythm Changes for the Novice." *Jazz Player* 2, no. 3 (April/May 1995): 39–40.

"Playing on *I Got Rhythm* Changes, Part 2: Traditional Approaches to Rhythm Changes." *Jazz Player* 2, no. 4 (June/July 1995): 24–25.

"Playing on *I Got Rhythm* Changes, Part 3: Using Bebop Compositions as an Approach to Learning to Play Rhythm Changes." *Jazz Player* 2, no. 5 (August/September 1995): 60–61.

"Playing on *I Got Rhythm* Changes, Part 4: Expanding the Horizons of Playing 'I Got Rhythm' Changes." *Jazz Player* 2, no. 6 (October/November 1995): 20–21.

"President's Message." *Jazz Education Journal* 35, no. 2 (September/October 2002): 4.

"President's Message." *Jazz Education Journal* 35, no. 3 (November/December 2002): 4.

"President's Message." *Jazz Education Journal* 35, no. 4 (January/February 2003): A10.

"President's Message." *Jazz Education Journal* 35, no. 5 (March/April 2003): 4.

"President's Message." *Jazz Education Journal* 35, no. 6 (May/June 2003): 4.

"President's Message." *Jazz Education Journal* 36, no. 1 (July/August 2003): 4.

"President's Message." *Jazz Education Journal* 36, no. 2 (September/October 2003): 4.

"President's Message." *Jazz Education Journal* 36, no. 3 (November/December 2003).

"President's Message." *Jazz Education Journal* 36, no. 4 (January/February 2004): A10.

"President's Message." *Jazz Education Journal* 36, no. 5 (March/April 2004): 4.

"President's Message." *Jazz Education Journal* 36, no. 6 (May/June 2004): 4.

Quincy Jones, interview by David Baker and Ken Kimery, September 7, 2008, transcript, Smithsonian Jazz Oral History Project, http://www.smithsonianjazz.org/oral_histories/pdf/Jones.pdf.

Review of *Black Composers Series* (Columbia Records). *DownBeat* 41, no. 16 (October 10, 1974): 26–29.

Review of *Charles Ives: The 100th Anniversary* (Columbia Masterworks M4-32504). *DownBeat* 42, no. 2 (January 16, 1975): 32.

Review of *The Evolving Bassist* by Rufus Reid. *DownBeat* 42, no. 6 (March 27, 1975): 33.

"The Rhetorical Dimensions of Black Music: Past and Present." In *Black Communication: Dimensions of Research and Instruction,* edited by Jack L. Daniel, 3–27. New York: Speech Communication Association, 1974.

"Richard Davis' 'Shiny Stockings' Solo." *DownBeat* 38, no. 22 (December 23, 1971): 39–40.

"Roswell Rudd's 'Wherever June Bugs Go.'" *DownBeat* 39, no. 2 (February 3, 1972): 30–32.

"'Round Midnight." In *Jazz: The First Century,* edited by John Edward Hasse, 101. New York: William Morrow, 2000.

"Some Thoughts on Problems and Solutions of a Third Stream Composer." *International Jazz Archives Journal* 3, no. 1 (Fall 2006–07): 7–21.

"Stan Getz's 'Con Alma' Solo." *DownBeat* 37, no. 26 (December 24, 1970): 40–42.

"The String Approach in Jazz" (part 1 of a series). *Orchestra News* 9, no. 2 (March 1970): 5–6. (This is the same as "The String Player in Jazz, Part 1," *DownBeat*.)

"The String Approach in Jazz" (part 2 of a series). *Orchestra News* 9, no. 3 (May 1970): 8–9. (This is the same

as "The String Player in Jazz, Part 2," *DownBeat*.)

"The String Approach in Jazz" (part 3 of a series). *Orchestra News* 9, no. 3 (September 1970): 10–11. (This is the same as "The String Player in Jazz, Part 3," *DownBeat*.)

"The String Player in Jazz, Part 1." *DownBeat* 37, no. 5 (March 5, 1970): 37–38. (This is the same as "The String Approach in Jazz" [part 1 of a series], *Orchestra News*.)

"The String Player in Jazz, Part 2." *DownBeat* 37, no. 9 (April 30, 1970): 37–39. (This is the same as "The String Approach in Jazz" [part 2 of a series], *Orchestra News*.)

"The String Player in Jazz, Part 3." *DownBeat* 37, no. 11 (May 28, 1970): 34–37. (This is the same as "The String Approach in Jazz" [part 3 of a series], *Orchestra News*.)

"Studying with the Jazz Masters via Recordings, Part 1." *Jazz Player* 4, no. 2 (February/March 1997): 16–17.

"Studying with the Jazz Masters via Recordings, Part 2." *Jazz Player* 5, no. 1 (December 1996/January 1997): 41–42.

"Teaching Jazz." *Jazz Player* 1, no. 1 (December 1993): 6–7.

"Teaching Jazz." *Jazz Player* 1, no. 2 (February/March 1994): 44–45.

"A Technique for Learning Tunes: Melody and Changes." *Jazz Player* 1, no. 5 (August/September 1994): 58–59.

"A Technique for Learning Tunes: Melody and Changes, Part 2." *Jazz Player* 1, no. 6 (October/November 1994): 42–43.

"A Technique for Learning Tunes: Melody and Changes, Part 3." *Jazz Player* 3, no. 1 (December 1994/January 1995): 55–56.

Techniques of Improvisation, volume 1: A Method for Developing Improvisational Technique (Based on the Lydian Chromatic Concept by George Russell).

Chicago: Maher, 1971. Revised ed., Van Nuys, Calif.: Alfred, 1987.

Techniques of Improvisation, volume 2: The II V7 Progression. Chicago: Maher, 1971. Revised ed., Van Nuys, Calif.: Alfred, 1987.

Techniques of Improvisation, volume 3: Turnbacks. Chicago: Maher Publications, 1971; Revised ed., Van Nuys, Calif.: Alfred, 1987.

Techniques of Improvisation, volume 4: Cycles. Chicago: Maher Publications, 1971; Revised ed., Van Nuys, Calif.: Alfred, 1987.

"Ted Dunbar's 'There Is No Greater Love' Solo." *DownBeat* 41, no. 2 (January 31, 1974): 32–33.

"Thad Jones' 'H and T Blues' Solo." *DownBeat* 40, no. 2 (February 1, 1973): 32–33.

"Thad Jones' Solo on 'Oh! Karen O.'" *DownBeat* 40, no. 21 (December 20, 1973): 41–42.

"Two B. B. King Solos." *DownBeat* 38, no. 12 (June 10, 1971): 31–32.

"Two Classic Louis Armstrong Solos." *DownBeat* 38, no. 16 (September 16, 1971): 44–45.

"Two Electronic Solos: 1. Jean-Luc Ponty's 'Sunday Walk'; 2. Monk Montgomery's 'Big Boy.'" *DownBeat* 37, no. 14 (July 23, 1970): 32–34.

"Urbie's 'Slats' transcribed and annotated by David Baker." *DownBeat* 43, no. 6 (June 3, 1976): 43.

"Vic Dickensen's 'Bourbon Street Parade' Solo." *DownBeat* 39, no. 14 (August 17, 1972): 42.

"Wes Montgomery's 'Naptown Blues' Solo." *DownBeat* 39, no. 15 (September 14, 1972): 43–45.

"What Makes a Truly Good Jazz Solo: Chops *and* Vision." *DownBeat* 62, no. 6 (June 1995): 63.

"When an Improvisor Thinks Like a Composer, Part 1." *Jazz Player* 4, no. 4 (June/July 1997): 16, 38–39.

"When an Improvisor Thinks Like a Composer, Part 2." *Jazz Player* 4, no. 5 (August/September 1997): 3–5.

"Writing for Three Horns Plus Rhythm Section." *DownBeat* 63, no. 3 (March 1996): 62.

Baker, David N., ed. *New Perspectives in Jazz.* Washington, D.C., and London: Smithsonian Institution Press, 1990.

Baker, David N., ed. *Jazz Styles and Analysis: Alto Sax,* by Harry Miedema. Chicago: *DownBeat* Music Workshop Publications, 1975.

Baker, David N., ed. and comp. *The Monk Montgomery Electric Bass Method: With Supplementary Information Regarding the Upright Bass,* by Monk Montgomery. Lebanon, Ind.: Studio PR, 1978.

Baker, David N., and Jeanne Baker. *The Jazz Quiz Book.* Bloomington, Ind.: Frangipani Press; Van Nuys, Calif.: Alfred, 1984.

Baker, David N., and William Banfield. *American Popular Music Curriculum, Quincy Jones Musiq Consortium.* Los Angeles: Quincy Jones Foundation, forthcoming.

Baker, David N., and Patty Coker. *Vocal Improvisation: An Instrumental Approach.* Lebanon, Ind.: Studio PR; Miami, Fla.: Columbia Pictures Publications/Belwin Mills, 1981.

Baker, David N., Lida M. Belt, and Herman Hudson. *The Black Composer Speaks.* Metuchen, N.J.: Scarecrow Press, 1978.

Baker, David N., Leon Breeden, William Fowler, M. E. Hall, and Jerry Coker. "A Consortium of Opinion on Jazz Education." N.p.: Creative Jazz Composers, n.d.

Baker, David N., Marian Tally Brown, Phyllis Rauch Klotman, Robert Howard Klotman, Roslyn Adele Walker, and Jimmy L. Williams. *The Humanities Through the Black Experience.* Dubuque, Iowa: Kendall/Hunt, 1976.

Wahlum, Wendell, David N. Baker, and
Richard A. Long. "Afro-American
Music." In *The Black American Refer-
ence Book,* edited by Mabel M. Smythe,
791–826. Englewood Cliffs, N.J.: Pren-
tice Hall, 1976.
Morgenstern, Dan, David Baker, Stephen
Bernstein, and Branford Marsalis.
"Why Jazz Endures." *DownBeat* 76, no.
10 (October 2009): 46–47.

LINER NOTES

Afro Blue, Cynthia Felton (compact disc
recording, 2008).
Amy Stephens Group, Amy Stephens (compact disc recording, 1998).
Bass, Buddies, and Blues, Keter Betts
(compact disc recording, 1998).
Circles, Michael Hackett (compact disc
recording, 2005).
Coming Home, Graham Breedlove (com-
pact disc recording, 2001).
Crossroads, Tim Coffman (compact disc
recording, 2004).
Dominic Spera Big Band (compact disc
recording, 1998).
Falcon's Quest, Ted Falcon (compact disc
recording, 1995).
First Song, Sara Caswell (compact disc
recording, 2000).
First Step, The New World School of the
Arts Jazz Septet (compact disc record-
ing, 1990).
Flying Home. Kentucky Jazz Repertory
Orchestra (compact disc recording,
2009).
"Giant Steps," John Coltrane Quartet.
Notes to track 4, disc 4, of *Jazz: The
Smithsonian Anthology,* 124–25.
*Gil Evans: The Complete Pacific Jazz Ses-
sions.* (2006 compact disc reissue by
Blue Note on their Connoisseur CD
series. The liner notes written by Da-
vid Baker for an earlier reissue of this

recording were reprinted in the book-
let accompanying this compact disc
recording.)
Happenstance, The Buselli-Wallarab Jazz
Orchestra [Mid Coast Jazz Orchestra]
(compact disc recording, 2001).
Heart's Desire, Janiece Jaffe (compact disc
recording, 2003).
Heart and Soul, Buselli-Wallarab Jazz Orchestra (compact disc recording, 2003).
In Black and White, Gary Smart (compact
disc recording, 1998).
It's About Time, Hank Marr (compact disc
recording, 1995).
Jazz: The Smithsonian Anthology (boxed
set of compact disc recordings, 2011).
Jazz in Clear Water (In Transit), The Uni-
versity of Wisconsin–Eau Claire Jazz
Ensemble (compact disc recording,
1994).
"King of the Road," Jimmy Smith and
Wes Montgomery. Notes to track 6,
disc 5 of *Jazz: The Smithsonian Anthol-
ogy,* 146–47.
Moments in Time, Jim Donica (compact
disc recording, 1995).
Right There, Steve Turre (compact disc
recording, 1991).
Some Other Time, Rachel Caswell (com-
pact disc recording, 2003).
Remembrance: African-American Songs,
Dina Foy (compact disc recording,
1996).
The Scheme of Things, Scott Wendholt
(compact disc recording, 1993).
Simple Complexity, Rick Simerly (compact
disc recording, 1998).
Smack Dab in the Middle, John Clayton/
Hal Leonard Orchestra (compact disc
recording, 2009).
*Through the Prism of the Black Experience:
Chamber Music by David N. Baker*
(compact disc recording, 1997).
Travelin' Light, Sam Pilafian (compact
disc recording, 1991).

"23 Degrees North, 82 Degrees West,"
Stan Kenton. Notes to track 5, disc 3
of *Jazz: The Smithsonian Anthology*,
100–101.
"Work Song," Cannonball Adderley.
Notes to track 8, disc 4 of *Jazz: The
Smithsonian Anthology*, 130–31.

EDITED MUSIC PUBLICATIONS

These are the publications edited by
David Baker in his position as editor
for Essential Jazz Editions [EJE], a
joint project of the Smithsonian
Institution, the Library of Congress,
and Jazz at Lincoln Center.

Set #2: Louis Armstrong, 1926–1929
  "Cornet Chop Suey"
  "Hotter Than That"
  "Mahogany Hall Stomp"
  "Tight Like This"
  "West End Blues"
Set #3: Music of the 1930s, Part 1
  "Big Jim Blues"
  "For Dancers Only"
  "From A-flat to C"
  "Lonesome Road"
  "Symphony in Riffs"

Set #4: Music of the 1930s, Part 2
  "Avalon"
  "King Porter Stomp"
  "South Rampart Street Parade"
  "Sweet Sue, Just You"
  "Swingtime in the Rockies"
Set #5: Music of the 1940s, Part 1
  "Cupid's Nightmare"
  "The Hour of Parting"
  "Yard Dog Mazurka"
  "Loose Lid Special"
  "Flying Home"
Set #6: Music of the 1940s, Part 2
  "Sidewalks of Cuba"
  "Second Line"
  "C Jam Blues"
  "Sophisticated Lady"
  "Robbin's Nest"
  "Mango Mangüé"
  "Cool Breeze"
  "Liberian Suite"

Discography

Art of the Trumpet, New York Trumpet
Ensemble, Edward Carroll, trumpet;
Edward Brewer organ. Vox/Turnabout,
PVT 7183, 1982. (Recorded at the
Madeira Festival, June 1–2, 1981.)

BAKER AS COMPOSER

An After Hours Lament (Jazz ensemble), *Wood*, David Eyges, violoncello.
MidLantic Records USA, MR2002-102, 2002.

Alabama Landscape (Bass-baritone and orchestra), *Paul Freeman Introduces . . . David N. Baker*, William Brown, tenor soloist, Czech National Symphony Orchestra, Paul Freeman, conductor. Albany Records, Troy CD 377, 2000.

Alto (Three movement concerto for saxophone and jazz ensemble), *Water Music*, Bruce Jordan, saxophone soloist, the Sinclair Community College Jazz Ensemble. Mark 4324-MCD, 2002.

April B (Jazz ensemble), *Basically Baker*, the Buselli-Wallarab Jazz Orchestra, GM Recordings GM 3049CD, 2007. Licensed to Owl Studios 2011; reissue forthcoming.

Aspects of Andy (clarinet, bass, piano, and string quartet), *David Baker at Bay Chamber Concerts*, James Campbell, clarinet; Bruce Bransby, bass; Luke Gillespie, piano; Corey Cerovsek, violin; Sara Caswell, violin; Kirsten Johnson, viola; Marc Johnson, violoncello. Cala CACD 77010, 2002.

The Black Experience (Song cycle for tenor and piano), *Through the Prism of the Black Experience: Chamber Music by David N. Baker*, William Brown, tenor; Toni-Marie Montgomery, piano. Liscio Artist Series LAS-11972, 1997.

Blues (Violin and piano)
1. *Anne Akiko Meyers: The American Album*, Anne Akiko Meyers, violin; André-Michel Schub, piano. RCA Victor Red Seal CD 09026-68114-2, 1996.
2. *American Diversions*, Rene Gailly International Productions, Jenny Spanoghe, violin; Jacqueline Herbein, piano. Jewels CD 87042, 1989.

Blues Odyssey (Tuba ensemble), *Legacy*, Tennessee Tech Tuba Ensemble 40th Anniversary with All-Star Alumni Ensemble, Winston Morris, conductor. Mark CD 6960-MCD, 2007.

Borderline (Soprano, string quartet, and piano), *Calvary*, The Samuel Coleridge-Taylor String Quartet, John M. Williams, violin; Hillary Cumming, violin; Paul Goldberg, viola; William Thomas, violoncello. No soprano listed; no pianist listed. Videmus Recordings 104, 2002.

Le chat qui pêche (Orchestra, soprano, and jazz quartet), *Louisville Symphony Orchestra,* Louisville Symphony Orchestra, Jorge Mester, conductor. Soloists: Linda Anderson, soprano; Jamey Aebersold, alto saxophone, Dan Haerle, piano; John Clayton, bass; and Charlie Craig, drums. First Edition Records LS-751, 1970.

Concerto for Alto Saxophone and Orchestra, *Paul Freeman Introduces . . . David Baker, volume 12,* Thomas Walsh, alto saxophone soloist, Czech National Symphony Orchestra, Paul Freeman, conductor. Albany Records, Troy CD 843, 2006.

Concerto for Cello and Chamber Orchestra

1. *Paul Freeman Introduces . . . String Concertos,* Albany Records, Milos Jahoda, violoncello soloist, Czech National Symphony Orchestra, Paul Freeman, conductor. Troy CD 559, 2003.
2. *African Heritage Symphonic Series, volume 3,* Katinka Kleijn, violoncello soloist, The Chicago Sinfonietta, Paul Freeman, conductor. Cedille Records CDR 90000 066, 2002.

Concerto for Tuba and Orchestra, *Paul Freeman Introduces . . . David N. Baker,* Daniel Perantoni, tuba soloist, Czech National Symphony Orchestra, Paul Freeman, conductor. Albany Records, Troy CD 377, 2000.

Concerto for Violin and Jazz Band, James Getzoff, violin soloist, The Hollywood All-Star Jazz Band, Carmen Dragon, conductor. Laurel Records LR-125; 1986, reissued on CD by Laurel Records, LR 825, 2010.

Concertpiece for Trombone and String Orchestra

1. *Paul Freeman Introduces . . . David Baker, volume 12,* Jiri Novotny, trombone soloist, Czech National Symphony Orchestra, Paul Freeman,

conductor. Albany Records, Troy CD 843, 2006.
2. Recorded in a piano reduction arrangement for future release. Dee Stewart, trombone; Ashley Toms, piano.

Concertpiece for Viola and Orchestra, *Paul Freeman Introduces . . . String Concertos,* Paul Silverthorne, viola soloist, Czech National Symphony Orchestra, Paul Freeman, conductor. Albany Records, Troy CD 559, 2003.

Contrasts (Violin, violoncello, and piano), *The Western Arts Trio, vol. 2,* The Western Arts Trio, Brian Hanly, violin; David Tomatz, violoncello; Werner Rose, piano. Laurel Records LR 106, 1977.

Dance (Clarinet, piano, and rhythm section), *After Hours,* James Campbell, clarinet, Stephane Lemelin, piano, The Gene DiNovi Trio [Gene DiNovi, piano; Dave Young, bass; Terry, Clark, drums]. Marquis Records CD ERAD 153, 1993. (This piece is an adaptation by David Baker of the last movement of his Sonata for Clarinet and Piano. James Campbell is accompanied by the Gene DiNovi Trio for the Latin jazz–flavored middle part of the piece and accompanied by Stephane Lemelin in the more classical outer sections.)

Dance of the Jitterbugs (Jazz ensemble), *Basically Baker,* the Buselli-Wallarab Jazz Orchestra. GM Recordings GM 3049CD, 2007. Licensed to Owl Studios 2011; reissue forthcoming.

Duet for Alto Saxophones, *After the Rain: Takashi Yonekura Plays the Saxophone,* Jiroh Akamatsu, alto saxophone I; Takashi Yonekura, alto saxophone II. Soundfix Laboratory SL-5042, 2007.

Duo for Clarinet and Cello, David Bellman, clarinet; Ingrid Fischer-Bellman, violoncello. Forthcoming release.

Early in the Mornin' (Tenor and piano), *Art Songs by Black Composers,* the University of Michigan School of Music, Richard Taylor, baritone. University of Michigan Records SM0015, 1981.

Ethnic Variations on a Theme of Paganini (Violin and piano)

1. Ruggiero Ricci, violin. Forthcoming release on Vox.
2. *Degrees of Mastery,* Aaron Dworkin, violin, 1998.
3. *Pavel Sporcl & Paganini,* Pavel Sporcl, violin; Petr Jirikovsky, piano. Supraphon SU 3772-2 (Czech Republic), 2004.
4. *In My Own Voice,* Kelly Hall-Tompkins, violin; Craig Ketter, piano. MSR Classics MS 1278, 2008.

An Evening Thought (Jazz ensemble)

1. *Basically Baker,* the Buselli-Wallarab Jazz Orchestra. GM Recordings GM 3049CD, 2007. Licensed to Owl Studios 2011; reissue forthcoming.
2. *Portrait of the Artist,* Rita DiCarlo, singer [lyrics written by Sally Champlin]. MANNA NR-16819, 1986.
3. Jerry Coker, tenor saxophone, 1984.

Faces of the Blues: A Fantasy for Alto Saxophone and Saxophone Quartet, *Classic Saxophone, vol. 2: Musica da camera,* Liscio, Frank Bongiorno, alto saxophone soloist. Recordings LCD-09193, 1993.

Fantasy on Themes from *The Masque of the Red Death* Ballet (Orchestra), *Paul Freeman Introduces . . . David Baker, volume 12,* Czech National Symphony Orchestra, Paul Freeman, conductor. Albany Records, Troy CD 843, 2006. (This recording presents a considerably shortened version of the **Suite from *The Masque of the Red Death* Ballet**. The cuts made to create this piece were made by Maestro Paul Freeman at the recording session. Because this resulted in a piece that was significantly different from the original, it was given this new title by David Baker.)

The 5M Calypso (Jazz ensemble), *Basically Baker,* the Buselli-Wallarab Jazz Orchestra, GM Recordings GM 3049CD, 2007. Licensed to Owl Studios 2011; reissue forthcoming.

Five Settings for Soprano and Piano

1. Recorded by Jennifer Poffenberger under the title **Song Cycle,** *Mostly American,* Jennifer Poffenberger, soprano; Lori Piitz, piano. Enharmonic Records ENCD 93-012, 1993.
2. Recorded by Dina Caneryn Foy under the title **Song Cycle,** *Remembrance: African-American Songs,* Dina Caneryn Foy, soprano; Polly Brecht, piano. DCF Records (compact disc), 1996.
3. Two songs from this work, "The Smile" and "A Song," were recorded on the compact disc recording *Dimensions,* Thomas King, tenor; Vicki King, piano. Aeolian Digital Recordings ADR60003D, 1997.

Folklike (Jazz ensemble)

1. *Top Brass – Distinctly American,* Top Brass [David Coleman, trumpet; Darin Cochran, euphonium; Ted Hale, trombone; Norlan Bewley, tuba]. TB 001 [DIDX 0006510], 1989. (This is a recording of Norlan Bewley's arrangement of this composition for the ensemble Top Brass [trumpet, euphonium, trombone, and tuba].)
2. *Top Brass Quartet – Artistic Growth,* Top Brass [David Coleman, trumpet; Miles Osland, woodwinds; Dale Warren, trombone; Norlan Bewley, tuba], TBQ-001, 1992. (This is a recording of Norlan Bewley's arrangement of this composition for the ensemble Top Brass [trumpet, woodwinds, trombone, and tuba].)

Give and Take (Soprano and chamber ensemble), Edith Anne Diggory, soprano soloist; Michelle Milter, flute and alto flute; Emily Agnew, oboe and

English horn; Glenn Mellow, viola; Patrick Binford, violoncello; Ric Dimond, percussion and wind machine. Laurel Records L R 115; reissued on C D by Laurel Records, L R 815, 2010.

A Good Assassination Should Be Quiet (Tenor and piano)
1. *Art Songs by Black Composers,* the University of Michigan School of Music, Laura English-Robinson, soprano. University of Michigan Records S M0015, 1981.
2. *Black Art Song,* Kevin Maynor, voice; Eric Olsens, piano. Fleur de Son 57942, 1999.

The Harlem Pipes (Jazz ensemble), *Top Brass – Distinctly American,* Top Brass [David Coleman, trumpet; Darin Cochran, euphonium; Ted Hale, trombone; Norlan Bewley, tuba]. T B 001 [D I DX 0006510], 1989. (This is a recording of Norlan Bewley's arrangement of this composition for the ensemble Top Brass.)

Heritage: A Tribute to Great Clarinetists (clarinet, violin, bass, and piano), *David Baker at Bay Chamber Concerts,* James Campbell, clarinet; Corey Cerovsek, violin; Bruce Bransby, bass; and Gene DiNovi, piano. Cala C A C D 77010, 2002.

Homage a L'Histoire (Chamber ensemble), *David Baker at Bay Chamber Concerts,* Paul Biss, violin; Bruce Bransby, bass; James Campbell, clarinet; Kim Walker, bassoon; John Rommel, trumpet; Dee Stewart, trombone; Craig Hetrick, percussion, Geoffrey Simon, conductor. Cala C A C D 77010, 2002.

Honesty (Jazz ensemble)
1. Jamey Aebersold. Isis I-608, c. 1965.
2. Clark Terry. For future release.

The I.U. Swing Machine (Jazz ensemble), *Basically Baker,* the Buselli-Wallarab Jazz Orchestra. G M Recordings G M 3049C D, 2007. Licensed to Owl Studios 2011; reissue forthcoming.

Images, Shadows and Dreams: Five Vignettes (Chorus [S A T B] and chamber ensemble [flute, guitar, piano, bass, and drums]), *Witness, volume 3: Towards the Future,* Ensemble, Chorus, and Orchestra of the Plymouth Music Series of Minnesota, Philip Brunelle, conductor. Collins Classics 14762, 1996.

Images of Childhood (Orchestra), *Paul Freeman Presents, volume 8,* Czech National Symphony Orchestra, Paul Freeman, conductor. Albany Records, Troy C D 499, 2002.

Inspiration (Flute and piano), *Flute Impressions,* Nina Assimakopoulos, flute; George Boespflug, piano. Euterpe Recordings 201, 2002.

J Is For Loveliness (Jazz ensemble), Jamey Aebersold. Isis I-608, c. 1965.

Jazz Dance Suite (Piano), *Double Dance – Classical and Jazz Connections II,* Willis Delony, piano. Centaur C R C 2914, 2008.

Jazz Suite for Violin and Piano, Ruggerio Ricci, violin; Mitchell Andrews, piano. Grenadilla Records GS-1056, 1985.

Jeanne Marie at the Picture Show (Jazz ensemble), *Top Brass – Distinctly American,* Top Brass [David Coleman, trumpet; Darin Cochran, euphonium; Ted Hale, trombone; Norlan Bewley, tuba]. T B 001 [D I DX 0006510], 1989. (This is a recording of Norlan Bewley's arrangement of this composition for the ensemble Top Brass.)

Kosbro (Orchestra)
1. *Symphonic Brotherhood,* Bohuslav Martinu Philharmonic Orchestra of Zlin Czech Republic, Julius Williams, conductor. Albany Records, Troy 104, 1993.
2. *Paul Freeman Introduces . . . David Baker, volume 12,* Czech National Symphony Orchestra, Paul Freeman, conductor. Albany Records, Troy C D 843, 2006.

Le roi (Jazz ensemble)
1. *Together,* Philly Joe Jones and Elvin Jones. Atlantic 1428, 1961.
2. *Together: Philly Joe Jones and Elvin Jones.* Collectables COL-CD-6264, 1999; reissue on CD of Atlantic Records 1428, 1961.
3. *Impacto,* the Hector Costita Sexteto. Fermata FB-97, 1965.

Lerma Samba (Jazz ensemble), *Top Brass Quartet – Artistic Growth,* Top Brass [David Coleman, trumpet; Miles Osland, woodwinds; Dale Warren, trombone; Norlan Bewley, tuba]. TBQ-001, 1992. (This is a recording of Norlan Bewley's arrangement of this composition for the ensemble Top Brass.)

Life Cycles (Song cycle for tenor, French horn, and string orchestra), *Paul Freeman Introduces ... David N. Baker,* William Brown, tenor soloist, Zdenek Tylsar, French horn soloist, Czech National Symphony Orchestra, Paul Freeman, conductor. Albany Records, Troy CD 377, 2000.

Miami Suite (Jazz ensemble), *Miami Sweet,* New World School of the Arts (Miami, Fla.) Big Band. NWSA-002, 1992.

Moments (Jazz ensemble), *Portrait of the Artist,* Rita DiCarlo, singer. MANNA NR-16819, 1986. (This is David Baker's jazz composition "Folklike." When Sally Champlin added lyrics to it, she retitled it "Moments.")

The Optimist (Soprano and piano), *Black Art Song,* Kevin Maynor, voice; Eric Olsens, piano. Fleur de Son 57942, 1999.

Parallel Planes (Chamber orchestra and saxophone soloist), *The New American Scene II,* Howie Smith, saxophone soloist, Cleveland Chamber Symphony, Edwin London, conductor. Albany Records, Troy 303, 1999.

Pastorale (string quartet), *Top Brass – Distinctly American,* Top Brass [David Coleman, trumpet; Darin Cochran, euphonium; Ted Hale, trombone; Norlan Bewley, tuba]. TB 001 [DIDX 0006510], 1989. (This is a recording of Norlan Bewley's arrangement of this composition for the ensemble Top Brass.)

Refractions (String orchestra), *Paul Freeman Introduces ... David N. Baker,* Czech National Symphony Orchestra, Paul Freeman, conductor. Albany Records, Troy CD 377, 2000.

Roots II (Violin, violoncello, and piano)
1. *Spring Music,* the Beaux Arts Trio, Menahem Pressler, piano; Ida Kavafian, violin; Peter Wiley, violoncello. Philips 438 866-2, 1994, available from ArkivMusic.
2. *Café Music,* the Samaris Piano Trio, Newport Classic, 1999.
3. Sara Caswell, violin; Mark Kosower, violoncello; and Marianne Ackerson, piano. Recorded for future release.

Save Me a Place (Jazz ensemble), *Portrait of the Artist,* Rita DiCarlo, singer. MANNA NR-16819, 1986. (This is David Baker's jazz composition "Roly Poly." When Sally Champlin added lyrics to it, she retitled it "Save Me a Place.")

The Screemin' Meemies [a.k.a. Screamin' Meemies] (Jazz ensemble), *Basically Baker,* the Buselli-Wallarab Jazz Orchestra. GM Recordings GM 3049CD, 2007. Licensed to Owl Studios 2011; reissue forthcoming.

Shades of Blue (Orchestra)
1. *Shades of Blue: Symphonic Works by African American Composers,* Prague Radio Symphony, Julius Williams, conductor. Albany Records, Troy CD 431, 2000.
2. Czech National Symphony Orchestra, Paul Freeman, conductor. Forthcoming release on Albany Records.

Shapes (Percussion orchestra and amplified cello), *World Influences: Wichita State University Percussion Department.* University of Wichita recording, 1996.

Sharing the Way (Jazz ensemble), *Portrait of the Artist,* Rita DiCarlo, singer. MANNA NR-16819, 1986. (This is David Baker's jazz composition "Walt's Barbershop." When Sally Champlin added lyrics to it, she retitled it "Sharing the Way.")

Singers of Songs, Weavers of Dreams (Violoncello and solo percussion)
1. *Starker Plays Baker,* Janos Starker, violoncello; George Gaber, percussion. Laurel Records LR 117, 1980; reissued on CD by Laurel Records, LR 817, 2000.
2. *Music for Cello and Percussion,* Anthony Cooke, violoncello; Steven Brown, percussion. Golden Crest CRDG 4223, 1983.
3. *Cello Matters,* Dennis Parker, violoncello; Michael Kingan, percussion. Centaur CRC 2589, 2004.
4. *Musicorda Festival Series 2002,* Matt Haimovitz, violoncello; Eduardo Leandro, percussion. legrandice audio CD, 2002.

The Smile (Soprano and piano), *Dimensions,* Thomas King, tenor; Vicki King, piano. Aeolian Digital Recording ADR6003D, 1997.

Soft Summer Rain (Jazz ensemble)
1. *Song for My Daughter,* Jack Wilson. Blue Note BST 84328, 1968.
2. *Portrait of the Artist,* Rita DiCarlo, singer [lyrics written by Sally Champlin]. MANNA NR-16819, 1986.

Soleil Impromptu (Trumpet, euphonium, trombone, tuba), *Top Brass – Distinctly American,* Top Brass [David Coleman, trumpet; Darin Cochran, euphonium; Ted Hale, trombone; Norlan Bewley, tuba]. TB 001 [DIDX 0006510], 1989. (This piece is Norlan Bewley's adaptation and arrangement of material from David Baker's composition "Soleil d'Altamira.")

Some Links for Brother Ted (Jazz ensemble), *Basically Baker,* the Buselli-Wallarab Jazz Orchestra. GM Recordings GM 3049 CD, 2007. Licensed to Owl Studios 2011; reissue forthcoming.

Sonata for Clarinet and Piano
1. *Welcome Home: A Collection of American Works for Clarinet and Piano,* Marcus Eley, clarinet; Lucerne DeSa, piano. Arabesque Recordings Z6703, 2009.
2. *David Baker at Bay Chamber Concerts,* James Campbell, clarinet; Leonard Hokanson, piano. Cala CACD 77010, 2002.

Sonata for Jazz Violin and String Quartet
1. *Through the Prism of the Black Experience: Chamber Music by David N. Baker,* Joseph Kennedy, Jr., jazz violin; the Audubon Quartet [David Ehrlich, violin; David Salness, violin; Doris Lederer, viola; C. Thomas Shaw, violoncello]. Liscio Artist Series LAS 11972, 1997.
2. *The Oregon String Quartet and All That Jazz,* Diane Monroe, jazz violin; the Oregon String Quartet, [Kathryn Lucktenberg, violin; Fritz Gearhart, violin; Leslie Straka, viola; Steven Pologe, violoncello]. Koch International Classics KIC-CD-7672, 2006.

Sonata for Piano
1. Carol Stone, piano. Forthcoming release.
2. *Dark Fires, volume 2,* Karen Walwyn, piano. Albany Records, Troy CD 384, 2000.

Sonata for Piano and String Quintet, Helena Freire, piano; Stephen Shipps, violin; Vickie Sylvester Gosa, violin; James Van Valkenberg, viola; Eugene Bondi, violoncello; James Rapport, double bass, Michael Nowak, conductor. AAMOA Records [LP] NS-7401, 1974.

Sonata for Piano and String Quintet, Movement 3 (Excerpt), *Afro-American Music and Its Roots,* Helena Freire, piano; Stephen Shipps, violin; Vickie Sylvester Gosa, violin; James Van Valkenberg, viola; Eugene Bondi, violoncello; James Rapport, double bass, Michael Nowak, conductor. Silver Burdette Records 74-187-47, 1976.

Sonata for Solo Cello, *Cellofire,* Ed Laut, cello. Liscio Recordings LAS 21793, 1993.

Sonata for Tuba and String Quartet, Harvey Phillips, tuba; the Composers String Quartet [Matthew Raimondi, violin; Anahid Ajemian, violin; Jan Dupouy, viola; Michael Rudiakov, violoncello]. Golden Crest Records CRS 4122, 1959.

Sonata for Tuba and String Quartet, Movement II, *ITEA Legacy Series – featuring Harvey Phillips, Tuba,* Harvey Phillips, tuba. Mark CD 6069-MCD, 2005.

Sonata for Violoncello and Piano
1. *Starker Plays Baker,* Janos Starker, violoncello; Alain Planes, piano. Laurel Records LR 117, 1980; reissued on CD by Laurel Records, LR 817, 2000.
2. *Volume 6, Black Composers Series,* Janos Starker, violoncello; Alain Planes, piano. Columbia Records M-33432, 1974.
3. *Music for Cello and Piano by African American Composers,* Anthony Elliott, violoncello; Toni-Marie Montgomery, piano. Independent release, 2003.

A Song (Soprano and piano), *Dimensions,* Thomas King, tenor; Vicki King, piano. Aeolian Digital Recording ADR6003D, 1997.

Song Cycle (High voice and piano). See also **Five Settings for Soprano and Piano**
1. *Mostly Americana,* Jennifer Poffenberger, soprano; Lori Piitz, piano. Enharmonic Records ENCD 93-012, 1993.
2. *Remembrance: African-American Songs,* Dina Foy, soprano; Polly Brecht, piano. DCF Recordings, 1996.
3. Two songs from this song cycle, "The Smile" and "A Song," were recorded on the compact disc recording *Dimensions,* Thomas King, tenor; Vicki King, piano. Aeolian Digital Recordings ADR60003D, 1997.

Songs of Living and Dying (Soprano, tenor and piano)
1. The Rookwood Trio [Denise Abbott, soprano; Roald Henderson, tenor; Robert Haigler, piano]. Forthcoming release.
2. *Song Tapestry,* Jacobs School of Music, Indiana University, Patricia Stiles, contralto; Emilio Colon, violoncello; Davis Hart, piano. IUMUSIC CD 09-001, 2009. (This is a recording of an adaptation of this work done by David Baker for contralto Patricia Stiles.)

Status Symbol (Tenor and piano), *Art Songs by Black Composers,* the University of Michigan School of Music, Charsie Randolph, soprano. University of Michigan Records SM0015, 1977.

Stickin' (Jazz ensemble)
1. *Top Brass – Distinctly American,* Top Brass [David Coleman, trumpet; Darin Cochran, euphonium; Ted Hale, trombone; Norlan Bewley, tuba]. TB 001 [DIDX 0006510], 1989. (This is a recording of Norlan Bewley's arrangement of this composition for the ensemble Top Brass.)

2. *Top Brass Quartet – Artistic Growth,*
Top Brass [David Coleman, trumpet; Miles Osland, woodwinds;
Dale Warren, trombone; Norlan
Bewley, tuba]. TBQ-001, 1992. (This
is a recording of Norlan Bewley's
arrangement of this composition for
the ensemble Top Brass.)

Suite for Cello and Jazz Trio (Violoncello, piano, bass and drums), *Cellofire,* Ed
Laut, cello soloist, Komei Harasawa,
piano; Charles Hoag, bass; George
Boberg, drums. Liscio Recordings LAS
21793, 1993.

Suite for Jazz Sextet, *First Step,* the New
World School of the Arts (Miami, Fla.)
Jazz Septet [David Siegel, piano; Gregg
Fine, guitar; Andy Cohen, trumpet
and flugelhorn / Vince Beard, trum-
pet; Luis Hernandez, alto saxophone;
Howard Karp, drums; Jeff Rose, bass;
Glenn Williams, percussion]. NWSA-
001, 1990.

Suite in Folk Style (Trumpet, eupho-
nium, trombone, and tuba), *Top
Brass – Distinctly American,* Top Brass
[David Coleman, trumpet; Darin
Cochran, euphonium; Ted Hale, trom-
bone; Norlan Bewley, tuba]. TB 001
[DIDX 0006510], 1989. (*Suite in Folk
Style* is the title given by the ensemble
Top Brass to a group of seven David
Baker compositions that Top Brass
performed and recorded in arrange-
ments by Norlan Bewley. These pieces
are "Harlem Pipes," "Pastorale," "To
Dizzy with Love," "Jeanne Marie at the
Picture Show," "Folklike," "Stickin',"
and "Walt's Barbershop.")

Summer Memories (String quartet), the
Audubon Quartet [David Ehrlich, violin; David Salness, violin; Doris Lederer, viola; C. Thomas Shaw, violoncello].
Forthcoming release.

Through This Vale of Tears (Tenor,
string quartet and piano)

1. *Videmus: Work,* William Brown,
tenor; Vivian Taylor, piano, Lynn
Chang, violin; Marylou Speaker
Churchill, violin; Marcus Thompson, viola; Mark Churchill, violoncello. New World Records CD
80423-2, 1992.

2. *Through the Prism of the Black Ex-
perience: Chamber Music by David
N. Baker,* William Brown, tenor;
Toni-Marie Montgomery, piano, the
Audubon Quartet [David Ehrlich,
violin; David Salness, violin; Doris
Lederer, viola; C. Thomas Shaw,
violoncello]. Liscio Artist Series
LAS 11972, 1997.

3. *A La Par,* William Brown, tenor;
Brandt Fredrickson, piano; Anne
Shih, violin; Janet Bond-Sutter, vio-
lin; Matthew Michelic, viola; Janet
Anthony, violoncello. Composers
Recordings, Inc., CRI CD-823, 1999.

To Dizzy with Love (Jazz ensemble)

1. *Basically Baker,* the Buselli-Wallarab
Jazz Orchestra. GM Recordings GM
3049CD, 2007. Licensed to Owl Studios 2011; reissue forthcoming.

2. *Top Brass – Distinctly American,* Top
Brass [David Coleman, trumpet;
Darin Cochran, euphonium; Ted
Hale, trombone; Norlan Bewley,
tuba]. TB 001 [DIDX 0006510], 1989.
(This is a recording of Norlan Bew-
ley's arrangement of this composi-
tion for the ensemble Top Brass.)

Two Cello String Quintet, Janos Starker,
violoncello. Forthcoming release.

Walt's Barbershop (Jazz ensemble)

1. *Top Brass – Distinctly American,* Top
Brass [David Coleman, trumpet;
Darin Cochran, euphonium; Ted
Hale, trombone; Norlan Bewley,
tuba]. TB 001 [DIDX 0006510], 1989.
(This is a recording of Norlan Bew-
ley's arrangement of this composi-
tion for the ensemble Top Brass.)

2. *Top Brass Quartet – Artistic Growth,*
Top Brass [David Coleman, trumpet; Miles Osland, woodwinds;
Dale Warren, trombone; Norlan
Bewley, tuba]. TBQ-001, 1992. (This
is a recording of Norlan Bewley's
arrangement of this composition for
the ensemble Top Brass.)

War Gewesen (Jazz ensemble), *So What,*
George Russell and the Living Time
Orchestra. Blue Note CDP 7 46391 2,
1983.

**Witness: Six Original Compositions
in Spiritual Style** (Baritone and solo
contrabass), *Witness,* Louise Toppin,
soprano, Czech National Symphony
Orchestra, Paul Freeman, conductor.
Albany Records, Troy CD 868, 2006.
(This is a recording of an adaptation of
this work done by David Baker for soprano and string orchestra. Five of the
original six movements appear on this
recording.)

BAKER PERFORMANCES

Trombone/Bass trombone

*Don Jacoby and his College All Star Dance
Band.* MGM E3881, 1960.

A Dedication in Music. Thomas Beversdorf. Martinique HB 2579, 1958.

*The Golden Striker: John Lewis Conducts
Music for Brass.* Atlantic 1334, 1960.

Jazz in the Space Age. George Russell.
Decca DL 79219, 1973.

Living Time. George Russell and Bill Evans. Columbia KC 31490, 1972.

New York, N.Y./Jazz in the Space Age.
George Russell. MCA 2-4017, 1973/
Leonard Feather Series, 1973.

Cello

Basically Baker, The David Baker String
Ensemble with the Paul McNamara
Trio, David Baker, cello; Tom Fitzger-
ald, violin; Marcus Holden, violin;
Christine Jarczewsky, viola; Paul

McNamara, piano; Craig Scott, bass;
Barry Woods, drums. Larrikin Records
LRJ 066, 1981 (Includes David Baker's
compositions "Walt's Barbershop,"
"Mon," "Le miroir noir," and "Naptown
Strut.")

David Baker's 21st Century Bebop Band,
David Baker, cello; Harvey Phillips,
tuba; Hunt Butler, tenor saxophone;
Jim Beard, piano; Kurt Bahn, bass;
Keith Cronin, drums. Laurel Records
LR 503, 1983. (Includes David Baker's
compositions "Bebop Revisited," "An
Evening Thought," and "This One's for
'Trane.")

David Baker's 21st Century Bebop Band.
Laurel Records LR 8503, 2010. (This is
a reissue compilation CD that includes
tracks from the Laurel Records albums
David Baker's 21st Century Bebop Band
["An Evening Thought"], *R.S.V.P.:
David Baker's 21st Century Bebop Band*
["Cahaphi," "Lima Beba Samba,"
"Jeanne Marie at the Picture Show,"
and RSVP Mr. Moody"], and *Struttin':
David Baker's 21st Century Bebop Band*
["Almaco" and "Padospe"].)

Eastern Man Alone, Charles Tyler, alto
saxophone; Dave Baker, cello; Brent
McKesson, bass; Kent Brinkley, bass.
ESP 1059, 1967. Also on CD ESP 1059-2,
2002. (Includes David Baker's composition "Le roi.")

Ezz-thetics, The George Russell Sextet,
Don Ellis, trumpet; Dave Baker, trombone; Eric Dolphy, alto saxophone and
bass clarinet; George Russell, piano;
Stephen Swallow, bass; Joe Hunt,
drums. Riverside 375/RLP-9375, 1961.
Also on CD Riverside OJCCD-070-2,
2007. (Includes David Baker's composition "Honesty.")

Folk and Mystery Stories, Charles Tyler,
alto and baritone saxophones; Richard
Dunbar, French horn; David Baker, cello; Wilbur Morris, bass; John Ore, bass;
Steve Reid, drums. Sonet SNTF-849,

1980. (Includes David Baker's composition "Folklike.")

The George Russell Sextet at the Five Spot, David Young, tenor saxophone [this corrects the record jacket, which lists him as playing alto]; Alan Kiger, trumpet; David Baker, trombone; George Russell, piano; Charles Israels, bass; Joseph Gayle Hunt, drums. Decca DL 9220, 1960; reissued on Verve CD 088-112-287-2, 2000. (Includes David Baker's composition "121 Bank.")

The George Russell Sextet in Kansas City, Don Ellis, trumpet; Dave Baker, trombone; Dave Young, tenor saxophone; George Russell, piano; Chuck Israels, bass; Joe Hunt, drums. Decca DL 4183, 1961. (Includes David Baker's compositions "War Gewesen" and "Lunacy.")

The Harlem Pipes: David Baker's 21st Century Bebop Band, David Baker, cello; Harvey Phillips, tuba; Lida Baker, flute; Tom Gullion, tenor and soprano saxophones; Luke Gillespie, piano; Charles Ledvina, bass; Scott Latzky, drums. Liscio Records LCD 02032, 2003. (Includes David Baker's compositions "Groovin' for Diz," "The Harlem Pipes," "Birdsong," and "The 5M Calypso.")

Jazz from Bloomington 1997. IN-19-22, 1997. (David Baker's 21st Century Bebop Band is one of the groups on this album, performing David Baker's composition "Groovin' for Diz" [Benefit recording project, Bloomington Area Arts Council].)

Live from Bloomington, IN-286, 1986. (The David Baker Quintet is one of the groups on this album, performing David Baker's composition "Bourne" [Benefit recording project for world and local hunger relief].)

Nica's Dream: Small Jazz Groups of the 50s and Early 60s, New World Records NW 242, 1977. (Compiled by Recorded Anthology of American Music, Inc. In-

cludes David Baker's composition "War Gewesen" from the album *The George Russell Sextet in Kansas City* [Decca DL 4183, 1961]).

Outer Thoughts, Milestone M-47027, 1975. Includes David Baker's composition "Honesty" from the album *Ezz-thetics* [Riverside 375/RLP-9375, 1961. CD reissue on Riverside OJCCD-070-2, 2007.] Also includes selected tracks from four previously issued George Russell Sextet/Septet albums: *Stratusphunk, Ezz-thetics, The Stratus Seekers,* and *The Outer View.* Personnel include four versions of the George Russell Sextet, three of which include David Baker: [1] Al Kiger, trumpet; Dave Baker, trombone; Dave Young, tenor saxophone; George Russell, piano; Chuck Israels, bass; Joe Hunt, drums. [2] Don Ellis, trumpet; Dave Baker, trombone; Eric Dolphy, alto saxophone and bass clarinet; George Russell, piano; Steve Swallow, bass; Joe Hunt, drums. [3] Don Ellis, trumpet; Dave Baker, trombone; John Pierce, alto saxophone; Paul Plummer, tenor saxophone; George Russell, piano; Steve Swallow, bass; Joe Hunt, drums. [4] Don Ellis, trumpet; Garnett Brown, trombone [David Baker missed this date because of jaw problems]; Paul Plummer, tenor saxophone; George Russell, piano; Steve Swallow, bass; Pete LaRoca, drums.)

The Other Side of Morning. All-star jazz group led by saxophonist Nathan Davis. Tomorrow International, Inc. 2004.

Parisian Hoedown. All-star jazz group led by saxophonist Nathan Davis. David Baker performs on "Mind Yo' Business" and "Calyspo Lady." Tomorrow International, Inc., 2010.

R.S.V.P.: David Baker's 21st Century Bebop Band, David Baker, cello; Harvey Phillips, tuba; Pat Harbison, trumpet; David Kay, tenor saxophone; Jim

Beard, piano; Bob Hurst, bass; Shawn Pelton, drums. Laurel Records LR 504, 1984. (Includes David Baker's compositions "Cahaphi," "Lima Beba Samba," "Jeanne Marie at the Picture Show," "R.S.V.P. Mr. Moody," and "Lerma Samba.")

Steppin' Out: The David Baker Sextet, David Baker, cello; Lida Baker, flute; David Hammer, piano; Michael DiLiddo, guitar; JB Dyas, electric bass; Jean Bolduc, drums. Liscio Recordings CD LAS 31591, 1982. (Includes David Baker's compositions "Steppin' Out," "An After Hours Lament," "To Dizzy With Love," "Autumn's Dreams," "Birdsong," and "NJSO Calypso.")

The Stratus Seekers, the George Russell Septet, Don Ellis, trumpet; Dave Baker, trombone; John Pierce, alto saxophone; Paul Plummer, tenor saxophone; George Russell, piano; Stephen Swallow, bass; Joe Hunt, drums. Riverside 412/RLP-9412, 1962. Also on CD: Riverside OJCCD-365-2, 1989. (Includes David Baker's composition "Stereophrenic.")

Stratusphunk, the George Russell Sextet, Al Kiger, trumpet; Dave Baker, trombone; Dave Young, tenor saxophone; George Russell, piano; Chuck Israels, bass; Joe Hunt, drums. Riverside 341, 1960. Also on CD: Riverside OJCCD-232-2, 1995. (Includes David Baker's composition "Kentucky Oysters.")

Struttin': David Baker's 21st Century Bebop Band, David Baker, cello; Harvey Phillips, tuba; Pat Harbison, trumpet; David Kay, tenor saxophone; Jim Beard, piano; Bob Hurst, bass; Shawn Pelton, drums. Laurel Records LR 505, 1986. (Includes David Baker's compositions "Almaco," "The Aebersold Strut," "Padospe," and "Lorob.")

BAKER AS COMPOSER/CONDUCTOR

Black America: To the Memory of Martin Luther King, Jr. (cantata for jazz ensemble, narrators, chorus (SATB), soloists, and string orchestra), Indiana University Jazz Ensemble, David N. Baker, conductor. Soloists: Linda Anderson, Janice Albright, Bob Ingram, Pablo Elvira, and Julie Smith. Narrators: John Joyner and Solomon Edwards. University of Illinois Press, for future release. (For many years this recording was broadcast annually by Voice of America on the anniversary of Dr. King's death.)

Le chat qui pêche (Jazz ensemble), *1969. 15th National Conference. College Band Directors National Association,* Indiana University Jazz Ensemble, David N. Baker, conductor. Silver Crest CBD-69-6B, 1969.

Check It Out (Jazz ensemble), *Jazz at Canterbury,* Indiana University Jazz Ensemble, David N. Baker, conductor. Canterbury Records, n.d.

Concerto for Cello and Jazz Band, *Cellofire,* Ed Laut, cello soloist, Indiana University Jazz Ensemble, David N. Baker, conductor. Liscio Recordings LAS-21793, 1993.

Concerto for Flute and Jazz Band, James Pellerite, flute soloist, Indiana University Jazz Ensemble, David N. Baker, conductor. Laurel Records LR-125, 1971; reissued on CD by Laurel Records, LR 825, 2010.

Concerto for Two Pianos, Jazz Band, Strings, and Percussion, Charles Webb and Wallace Hornibrook, piano soloists, Indiana University Jazz Ensemble, David N. Baker, conductor. Laurel Records LR-115, 1982; reissued on CD by Laurel Records, LR 815, 2010.

Ellingtones (Tenor saxophone, orchestra, jazz piano, and jazz bass), Dexter

Gordon, tenor saxophone soloist, Tokyo Philharmonic Orchestra, David N. Baker, conductor. Forthcoming release on Blue Note Records.

An Evening Thought (Jazz ensemble), *Sheryl Shay: Sophisticated Lady,* the David Baker Big Band featuring vocalist Sheryl Shay, David N. Baker, conductor. Laurel Records LR 506, 1985.

Honesty (Jazz ensemble), *Jazz At Canterbury,* Indiana University Jazz Ensemble, David N. Baker, conductor. Canterbury Records, n.d.

The I.U. Swing Machine (Jazz ensemble), *1969 15th National Conference: College Band Directors National Association,* Indiana University Jazz Ensemble, David N. Baker, conductor. Silver Crest CBD-69-6A, 1969.

Jazz Suite for Clarinet and Symphony Orchestra: Three Ethnic Dances, *American Voices,* Alan Balter, clarinet soloist, Akron Symphony Orchestra, David N. Baker, conductor. Telarc CD-80409, 1995.

Penick (Jazz ensemble), *Jazz at Canterbury,* Indiana University Jazz Ensemble, David N. Baker, conductor. Canterbury Records, n.d.

Screemin' Meemies [a.k.a. Screamin' Meemies] (Jazz ensemble)
1. *1969 15th National Conference: College Band Directors National Association,* Indiana University Jazz Ensemble, David N. Baker, conductor. Silver Crest CBD-69-6B, 1969.
2. *Highlights from the Indiana University School of Music,* Indiana University Jazz Ensemble, David N. Baker, conductor. Compact disc recording issued by the Trustees of Indiana University, 1997.

The Silver Chalice (Jazz ensemble), *1969 15th National Conference: College Band Directors National Association,* Indiana University Jazz Ensemble, David N.

Baker, conductor. Silver Crest CBD-69-6A, 1969.

Soft Summer Rain (Jazz ensemble), *1969 15th National Conference: College Band Directors National Association,* Indiana University Jazz Ensemble, David N. Baker, conductor. Silver Crest CBD-69-6B, 1969.

Son Mar (Jazz ensemble), *1969 15th National Conference: College Band Directors National Association,* Indiana University Jazz Ensemble, David N. Baker, conductor. Silver Crest CBD-69-6A, 1969.

Two Faces of "The Black Frontier" (Jazz ensemble), *Jazz at Canterbury,* Indiana University Jazz Ensemble, David N. Baker, conductor. Canterbury Records, n.d.

ARRANGER-CONDUCTOR

With David Liebman: *Dedication.* CMP 9 ST, 1980.
With Eugene Rousseau: *Mr. Mellow.* Liscio Artist Series LAS-01188, 2000.
With Sheryl Shay: *Sheryl Shay: Sophisticated Lady.* Laurel Records LR 506, 1985.
With Wanda Stafford: *Wanda Stafford: Let's Face the Music.* W., Inc., Records 8817-2, 1998.

CONDUCTOR ONLY

Big Band Treasures, Live, Smithsonian Jazz Masterworks Orchestra, David N. Baker, conductor. Smithsonian RJ0044, 1997.
The National Museum of American History Presents the Smithsonian Jazz Masterworks Orchestra "In Performance," David N. Baker, conductor. Videocassette recording, Smithsonian Jazz Masterworks Orchestra, 1997.
The Smithsonian Jazz Masterworks Orchestra: Live at MCG, Smithsonian Jazz

Masterworks Orchestra, David N. Baker, conductor. MCGJ 3004, 2008. (DVD of a live performance at the Manchester Craftsmens Guild [MCG], Pittsburgh, Pa.)

USAir in the Air, Indiana University Jazz Ensemble, David N. Baker, conductor. (USAir In-Flight Jazz Program featuring the music of Duke Ellington. In use in March and April 1995.)

Imagine: Indiana in Words and Music, poems by Norbert Krapf, music by Monika Herzig. Acme Records CD P56605-41962, 2008. (David Baker did a recitation of "On the Road with the Hampton Sisters," a tribute to the Hampton Sisters, longtime performers of jazz and popular music on the Indianapolis entertainment scene.)

OTHER

David Baker: Eight Classic Jazz Originals You Can Play. Jamey Aebersold Play-Along Series 10. New Albany, Ind.: Jamey Aebersold Jazz, 1976. (Book and CD set.)

Selected List of Books, Articles, and Other Publications about David Baker

Anderson, E. Ruth, comp. *Contemporary American Composers: A Biographical Dictionary*. 2nd ed. Boston: G. K. Hall, 1982.

Arnove, Robert. *Talent Abounds: Profiles of Master Teachers and Peak Performers*. Boulder, Colo.: Paradigm Publishers, 2009. See the chapter "Jazz in the Halls of Academe: David Baker and Dominic Spera."

"Baker . . . Jazz and the Liturgy." *Indiana Alumni Magazine* 34, no. 2 (December 1970–January 1971): 14–16.

Baker, David N., Lida M. Belt, and Herman Hudson. *The Black Composer Speaks*. Metuchen, N.J.: Scarecrow Press, 1978. One chapter is devoted to the life and work of David Baker.

Barman, Greg. "Dave Baker – Jazzman." *WIUS TipSheet* (WIUS Radio/Indiana University Student Broadcast Association) 33 (1975): 4–6.

Bourne, Michael. "Defining Black Music: An Interview with David Baker." *DownBeat* 38, no. 19 (September 18, 1969): 14–15.

Brooke, K. Rebecca. "All That Jazz." *Indiana Alumni Magazine* 54, no. 1 (September/October 1991): 24–27.

Brubeck, Darius. "David Baker and the Lenox School of Jazz." *Jazz Education Journal* 35, no. 2 (September/October 2002): 42–55.

Caswell, Austin. "David Baker: A Wise and Powerful Voice." *DownBeat* 38, no. 17 (October 14, 1971): 18, 41.

Claghorn, Charles E. *Biographical Dictionary of American Music*. West Nyack, N.Y.: Parker, 1973.

Claghorn, Charles Eugene. *Biographical Dictionary of Jazz*. Englewood Cliffs, N.J.: Prentice Hall, 1982.

"Dave Baker's Sonata for Tuba and String Quartet for Harvey Phillips." *DownBeat* 43, no. 16 (October 7, 1976): 43.

"David Baker." *Musart* 21, no. 2 (February/March 1969): 44.

David Baker, interview by Lida Baker, June 19–21, 2000, transcript, Smithsonian Jazz Oral History Project, www.smithsonianjazz.org/oral_histories/pdf/joh_DavidNBaker_transcript.pdf.

"David Baker – Those Who Can Do, Teach." *JazzEd* 5, no. 1 (January 2010): cover and 24–30.

De Lerma, Dominique-René, ed. *Black Music in Our Culture: Curricular Ideas on the Subjects, Materials, and Problems*. Kent, Ohio: Kent State University Press, 1970.

———. *Reflections on Afro-American Music*. Kent, Ohio: Kent State University Press, 1973.

DeMichael, Don. "Vortex: The Dave Baker Story." *DownBeat* 31, no. x24 (December 17, 1964): 16.

Derkacy, David. *On the Downbeat: A Jazz Heritage.* Videocassette, 1982; DVD, 2009. Self-released video documentary by David Derkacy on the history of jazz in Indiana. David Baker is among the artists featured.

Devens, Jeff. "Hoosier in Profile: Dave Baker." Sunday Magazine, *Indianapolis Star,* March 7, 1971, 12–18.

Dyer, Max. "David Baker." *Cello City Ink* 6, no. 1 (Spring/Summer 1999): n.p.

Elaine, Karen. "The Cadenzas to David Baker's Concert Piece for Viola." *Journal of the American Viola Society* 7, no. 1 (Spring 1991): 21–32.

Everett, Thomas. "Five Questions, Fifty Answers." *The Composer* 5, no. 2 (Spring–Summer 1974): 71–79.

Feather, Leonard. *The Encyclopedia of Jazz in the Sixties.* New York: Horizon Press, 1966.

———. *The New Edition of the Encyclopedia of Jazz.* New York: Horizon Press, 1960.

Feather, Leonard, and Ira Gitler. *The Encyclopedia of Jazz in the Seventies.* New York: Horizon Press, 1976.

"Governor's Arts Award, 1991." WISH-TV (Indianapolis, Ind., CBS affiliate station), n.d. David Baker was the subject of this feature.

Hasse, John Edward. "The Insider: Jazz on the Nile; The Smithsonian Takes the Nation's Jazz Band to Egypt." *DownBeat* 75, no. 9 (September 2008): 20–21.

Herrema, Robert D. "Choral Music by Black Composers." *The Choral Journal* 10, no. 4 (1970): 15–17.

"He's a Black Man." Series of sixty-second nationwide radio spots on prominent blacks, one of whom was David Baker, sponsored by Sears and produced by Laubhan-Moran-Noyes, 1969.

Hildreth, John. "The Keyboard Works of Selected Black Composers." PHD diss., Northwestern University, 1978.

Hitchcock, H. Wiley, and Stanley Sadie, eds. *The New Grove Dictionary of American Music.* London: Macmillan Press, 1986.

Indiana's Own. WISH-TV (Indianapolis, Ind., CBS affiliate station), n.d. David Baker was the subject of this episode.

Johnson, David Brent. "Jazzman Extraordinaire: 20 Questions for David Baker." *Bloom Magazine* 1, no. 2 (August/September 2007): cover and 56–66.

Johnson, John Andrew. *International Dictionary of Black Composers.* Chicago and London: Fitzroy Dearborn, 1999.

Jones, Eve. "Jazz Goes Classical." Sunday Magazine, *Indianapolis Star,* August 18, 1968, 42–45.

Keating, Sister Marie Thomas. "Jazz – A Tanglewood Conversation." *Music Educators Journal* 57, no. 2 (March 1971): 55–56.

Kernfeld, Barry, ed. *The New Grove Dictionary of Jazz, volume 1.* London: Macmillan Press, 1988.

Kessel, Rick. "Publisher's Letter: Among the Greats." *JazzEd* 5, no. 1 (January 2010): 4.

Koransky, Jason. "Blindfold Test: Dr. David Baker and Jamey Aebersold." *DownBeat* 75, no. 6 (June 2008): 130.

Kuzmich, John. "An Interview with the A, B, C's of Improvisation." *Jazz Educators Journal* 16, no. 5 (February/March 1984): 22–25, 81–82.

Leonard, Michael. "Jazz Man." *Indiana Alumni Magazine* 73, no. 3 (November/December 2010): cover and 28–33.

———. "Music/All His Jazz." *Indianapolis Monthly* 23, no. 11 (June 2000): 56–60.

Lockhart-Moss, Eunice, and Elaine Guregian. "David Baker: Jazz Advocate." *The Instrumentalist* 41, no. 5 (December 1986): 10–14.

Maurer, Michael S. *Nineteen Stars of Indiana: Exceptional Hoosier Men.* Indianapolis: Indiana Historical Society and IBJ Book Publishing, 2010.

Press, Jaques Cattell, ed. *Who's Who in American Music: Classical.* 2nd ed. New York and London: R. R. Bowker, 1985.

"The Professor Plays Jazz." *Ebony* 25, no. 7 (May 1970): 104–111.

Putney, Michael. "Jazz Thrives – and Expands – on the Campus." *National Observer,* May 24, 1971), n.p.

Roach, Hildred. *Black American Music: Past and Present.* Boston: Crescendo, 1973.

Schuller, Gunther. "Indiana Renaissance." *Jazz Review* 2, no. 8 (September 1959): 48–50.

Solothurnmann, Jurg. "The Diverse David Baker." *Jazz Forum* 25 (1973): 46–50.

Southern, Eileen. *Biographical Dictionary of Afro-American and African Musicians.* Westport, Conn., and London: Greenwood Press, 1982.

———. *The Music of Black Americans.* New York: W. W. Norton, 1971.

Spilka, Bill. "Interview with David Baker." *Journal of the New York Brass Conference for Scholarships* 9 (1981): 76–84.

Smith, Whitney. "Professor of Rhythm." Sunday Magazine, *Indianapolis Star,* April 6 2008, cover and multiple interior pages.

Sturm, Paul. "David Baker: The Symphonic Side." *Arts Indiana* 10, no. 2 (February 1988): 14–15.

Svoboda, Elizabeth. "Profiles in Creativity." *Saturday Evening Post* 281, no. 5 (September/October 2009): 40–43.

Tinder, Clifford. "Dave Baker: An Interview with Clifford Tinder." *Coda* 176 (December 1, 1980): 4–7.

Wilkerson, Michael. "'In This for Love': Jazzman David Baker's Extraordinary Career." *Journal of the New York Brass Conference for Scholarships* 19 (1991): 16–20.

Winne, Heather. "Jazz Man." *Home and Lifestyles of South-Central Indiana* 2 (Summer 2006): 24–29.

Listed in *Community Leaders in America*

Listed in *Who's Who among Black Americans*

Listed in *Who's Who in America*

Worldwide newspaper, radio, and television coverage via Reuters, Associated Press, and other media services about David Baker's composition *Concertino for Cellular Phones and Symphony Orchestra,* 2006. This included feature stories, interviews, and reviews, among them a segment on CBS television's *The Early Show* and a lengthy feature story in the October 3, 2006, arts section of *New York Times,* which also posted a story with audio on their website.

About the Contributors

NATHAN DAVIS is currently director of the University of Pittsburgh Jazz Studies Program. He is founder of Pitt's annual jazz seminar and concert, which marked its fortieth anniversary this fall. It is the longest-running jazz event of its kind in the country and is considered one of the most successful university jazz programs in the world. Nathan received his bachelor's degree in music education from the University of Kansas in 1960. In 1974, Nathan earned his PHD in ethnomusicology from Wesleyan University. After college, Nathan served in the US Army's 298th Army Band in Berlin, Germany and obtained a European discharge to remain in Europe, working mainly with Pittsburgh-born drummer Kenny Clark. While in Paris, Nathan taught, performed, and recorded with some of the era's most elite jazz stars – including Donald Byrd, Eric Dolphy, Woody Shaw, Art Blakey's Jazz Messengers, Bud Powell, Ray Charles, and Johnny Griffin. He enrolled at the Sorbonne in 1967 to study ethnomusicology. He studied composition with French composer Andre Hodeir in 1968, and has composed over two hundred original compositions – including film scores, four symphonies. In 2004, he premiered his opera, *Just above My Head,* based on the book by James Baldwin. He has published four books, including a scholarly text on the history of jazz. Nathan has recorded over twenty albums and several videos, with such groups as Roots and the Paris Reunion Band. He is founder and editor of the prestigious *University of Pittsburgh International Jazz Archive Journal.* With a grant from Gulf Oil Corporation, he recorded and produced an LP entitled *Nathan Davis: A Tribute to Dr. Martin Luther King, Jr.,* for the annual "Hand in Hand" celebration of Martin Luther King Week.

His recording *I'm a Fool to Want You* – with Grover Washington, Jr., as a special guest – can be found on the Tomorrow International, Inc. label. In 2005, Davis released *The Other Side of Morning* and most recently released *Parisian Hoedown*, also on the Tomorrow International, Inc. label.

JB DYAS has been a leader in jazz education for the past two decades. Formerly director of jazz studies at New World School of the Arts and executive director of the Brubeck Institute, Dyas currently serves as vice president for education and curriculum development for the Thelonious Monk Institute of Jazz in Los Angeles. He received his MM in Jazz Pedagogy from the University of Miami and PHD in Music Education from Indiana University, and is a recipient of the prestigious *DownBeat Magazine* Achievement Award for Jazz Education.

JOHN EDWARD HASSE is a music historian, pianist, author, and record producer. He serves as curator of American Music at the Smithsonian Institution's National Museum of American History, where he founded the Smithsonian Jazz Masterworks Orchestra, the acclaimed big band, and Jazz Appreciation Month, celebrated each April in over forty countries. Hasse is the author of *Beyond Category: The Life and Genius of Duke Ellington*; editor of *Jazz: The First Century*; co-editor of *Jazz Changes*; and co-producer and co-author of *Discover Jazz*. A contributor to the *Wall Street Journal,* Hasse has lectured on leadership and music on six continents.

WILLARD JENKINS is an independent arts consultant and producer, writer, and broadcaster under his Open Sky banner. Willard Jenkins's current activity includes concert, festival, and concert series planning and development, artistic direction, consulting, music journalism, teaching, and broadcast work.

LISSA MAY is associate professor at the Indiana University Jacobs School of Music and holds DME, MS, and BME degrees from Indiana University. Noted for her work in music education and jazz, her publications include compositions for concert and jazz bands and articles in JRME, JHRME, and the IAJE Research Proceedings.

BRENT WALLARAB is a faculty member at Indiana University's Jacobs School of music where he teaches in the jazz studies program. Wallarab has worked professionally as trombonist and arranger for Wynton Marsalis, Count Basie, Bobby Short, Ray Charles, and Jack Sheldon, among others. Appointed specialist in jazz to the Smithsonian Institution, Wallarab has transcribed and edited hundreds of important jazz scores and served as lead trombonist for the Smithsonian Jazz Masterworks Orchestra for nearly twenty years. He co-leads the Indianapolis-based Buselli-Wallarab Jazz Orchestra.

DAVID WARD-STEINMAN is a composer, pianist, adjunct professor at the Indiana University Jacobs School of Music, and distinguished professor emeritus from San Diego State University where he chaired the composition division, founded and directed the Comprehensive Musicianship Program and also the New Music Ensembles. A winner of major composition prizes, his commissions and premiers include those from the Chicago Symphony Orchestra, Joffrey Ballet, San Diego Ballet, California Ballet, Japan Philharmonic, Seattle Symphony, New Orleans Philharmonic, and the San Diego Symphony. Ward-Steinman is featured on numerous recordings as a composer, pianist, and polystylistic improviser.

CD Track Listing

1. "Kentucky Oysters" – *Stratus-phunk*, George Russell Sextet, featuring George Russell (piano), Al Kiger (trumpet), David Baker (trombone), David Young (tenor saxophone), Chuck Israels (bass), Joe Hunt (drums); recorded October 18, 1960, Plaza Sound Studios, New York City; Riverside OJCCD-232-2, 1995 (8:21)

2. "Sandu" – featuring Killer Ray Appleton (drums), David Baker (trombone), Harold Gooch (bass), David Young (tenor saxophone); live recording from the Topper (Indianapolis), c. 1959 (10:13)

3. "Le miroir noir" – Le chat qui pêche: *For Orchestra, Soprano, and Jazz Quartet*, featuring the Louisville Orchestra, Jorge Mester (conductor), Linda Anderson (soprano), Jamey Aebersold (alto and tenor saxophone), Dan Haerle (piano and electric piano), John Clayton (bass and electric bass), Charlie Craig (drums); recorded October 10, 1974; Louisville First Edition Records, 1975 (5:11)

4. "Dizzy," from *Singers of Songs, Weavers of Dreams – Through the Prism of the Black Experience*, the Audubon Quartet, Janos Starker (cello), George Gaber (percussion); recorded 1980 at Indiana University, Bloomington; released in 1981 on LP; Laurel Records, DAD 1032, 2000 (2:40)

5. "Now That He Is Safely Dead," from *Through This Vale of Tears – Through the Prism of the Black Experience*, William Brown (tenor), Toni-Marie Montgomery (piano); Liscio LAS 11972, 1997 (3:52)

6. "Concerto for Cello and Jazz Band" – *Fast, Cellofire*, featuring the Indiana University Jazz Ensemble, Edward Laut (cello soloist); recorded February 7, 1993 at the Indiana University Musical Arts Center in Bloomington; Liscio LAS-21793 (9:50)

7. "Groovin' for Diz" – *The Harlem Pipes*, 21st Century Bebop Band, featuring David Baker (cello, composition), Lida Baker (flute), Harvey Phillips (tuba), Luke Gillespie (piano), Charles Ledvina (bass), Scott Latzky (drums); recorded May 19 and 20, 1987, Homegrown Studios, Bloomington, Indiana; Liscio LCD 02032, 2003 (10:26)

8. "Jubilee," from *Roots II* – previously unreleased recording with Marianne Ackerson, piano; Sarah Caswell, violin; Mark Kosower, cello (5:11)

9. Concerto for Alto Saxophone and Orchestra, movement 3 in *Paul Freeman introduces . . . David Baker*, volume 12 – featuring the Czech National Symphony Orchestra, under the direction of Paul Freeman, soloist Tom Walsh (alto saxophone); Albany, Troy 843, 2006 (7:38)

10. "Dance of the Jitterbugs" – *Basically Baker,* featuring the Buselli/Wallarab Jazz Orchestra, soloists Mike Stricklin (tenor sax), Peter Kienle (guitar), Brent Wallarab (trombone), Tom Walsh (alto sax), Mark Buselli (flugelhorn); recorded September 4–5, 2004, Echo Park Studios, Bloomington, Indiana; GM3049, 1997 (9:46); rerelease on Owl Studios forthcoming

11. "On the Road with the Hampton Sisters" – *Imagine: Indiana in Music and Words* featuring David Baker (reader), Monika Herzig (piano), Frank Smith (bass), Jamey Reid (drums); with "Route 66" (Bob Troup) and "God Bless the Child" (Arthur Herzog/Billie Holliday); ACME P 56605-49162, 2008 (5:04)

Index

Page numbers in italics refer to figures and musical examples. The letter t after page numbers refers to tables.

a cappella, 206–208
A New Approach to Ear Training for Jazz Musicians (Baker), 69–70
ABCs of jazz education, 55, 57
Abrams, Muhal Richard, 297
acoustic set, 148–149
action, without vision, 324
active learning, 118n112
Adderley, Cannonball, 25, 291
Adkins, Jessie, 286n52
Aebersold Summer Jazz Workshops, 32, 118n108, 118n111, 127
Aebersold, Jamey, xv, 23, 122, 313–314; ABCs of jazz education, 55, 57; *Combo Rehearsal Guidelines*, 103; *Kosbro* solo, 212, 213; play-along recordings, 81
"The Aebersold Strut," 144
affirmative action, 296
African American aesthetic, 87–88
African American classical composers, 187
African American community, 1–2, 3, 11–12
African American roots, 227
against-the-grain playing, 41–42
"Agnus Dei," 210
"Ain't Nobody Here but Us Chickens," 195
Akiyoshi, Toshiko, 138
Akron Symphony Orchestra, 221

Alabama Landscape, 198–199, 215
Allen, Geri, 253
"Almaco," 144
altered blues, 79, 115n28, 117n86
altered four-bar turnaround, 155
Alvarez, Nelson, 9
ambassador for jazz, 312–313
American Jazz Masters, 56–58, 174, 321
American Jazz Orchestra, 285n26
American Music Curriculum, 235t
American Symphony Orchestra League, 297
America's Jazz Heritage (AJH), 232t–233t, 276, 285n33
America's music, 47, 150–151, 301
Ammons, Gene, 9
analysis, course in, 90–92
"And He Never Said a Mumbalin' Word," 205
And Then . . . , 191–192
Anderson, Linda, 213
Angelou, Maya, 202
Annual Jazz Education Guide (*Jazz Times*), 54
Apollo Theater, 8, 233t
Appleton, Killer Ray, Links Tribute to Indiana African-American Jazz Artists, *131*
"The Apprentice's Sources," 192
appurtenances, necessary, 98, 117n94
"April B," 171
Armstrong, Louis, 204, 234t, 261, 265, 312
Army Blues, 321

arranging, 92–96; vs. composing, 150
Arranging and Composing for the Small Ensemble (Baker), 92–93, 97, 150
Arsenal Technical High School, 3
Arthur Jordan Conservatory of Music, 17–18
"Artie," 195
arts funding, for jazz, 290–292
ascending melodic passages, 168
A-sections, 158–159
Ash, Steve, 142
Aspects of Andy, 196
audience survey, 292, 298
augmented triad pattern, 40
"Autumn Moral," 200
Ayers, April (daughter), 21, 22, 132, 318–319
Ayers, Brad (son-in-law), 132
Ayers, Kirsten (granddaughter), 132

"B's," 223–224
Bach, J. S., 153, 154
bachelor's degree in jazz studies, 53
"Back Home Again in Indiana," 144
"backup plan," 101
Bahn, Kurt, 142, 143
Bailey, Buster, 195
Bain, Wilfred C., 52, 290, 312
Baker, Archie (stepbrother), 4
Baker, Cleela (half-sister), 4
Baker, David: birth, 4; car accident, 48–49; doctoral work, 21; family life, 319; injury, 17, 48–49; jobs, 12; master teacher, 58–63; masters, learning from, 289, 301; Master's degree, 20; marriage, 21; medical treatment, 48–49; money, not about, 311; most important things, 318, 325n38; prom, performing at, 142; puns, 38, 106, 317; swimming, 12, 317; word games, 317–318; word play, 38; work ethic, 12. *See also* pedagogy
Baker, David, photographs: 25, 26, 124, 125, 126; ABCs of jazz education, 57; with A. B. Spellman and Billy Taylor, 294; with Chris Botti, 147; in the classroom, 61; *Dancing Shadows*, 134; David Baker Sextet, 149; with David Liebman, 135; with Dizzy Gillespie, 140; at French

Lick Jazz Festival, 121; high school reunion, 133; Indiana Living Legends Award, 132; with James Moody, 145; with J. J. Johnson, 277; Johnnie & Jazz festival billboard, 128; with Joseph Gingold, 218; at Lenox School of Jazz, 28; Links Tribute to Indiana African-American Jazz Artists, 131; Living Jazz Legends photograph, 138; Monaco, 128, 129, 130; National Jazz Service Organization, 299; at Notre Dame Jazz Festival, 122; publicity shots, 124, 137, 176; *Singers of Songs, Weavers of Dreams*, 183; Smithsonian Jazz Masterworks Orchestra, 134; 21st Century Bebop Band; 143; at White House, 136; at WTIU, 123
Baker, Edwin "Buddy," 52
Baker, Eugenia "Jeannie" (first wife), 21, 133, 318–319
Baker, Lida (wife), 58, 67, 128, 132, 144, 146, 148, 149, 234t, 278, 311–312, 314
Baldwin, Don, 122
Balliet, Whitney, 233t
Balter, Alan, 221
bandstand, conventions on, 310
Baraka, Amiri, 298
Barber, Stephanie and Philip, 29–30
Baroque counterpoints, 153, 154
Bartók, Béla, 220, 223
Basically Baker, 149, 154, 170–171, 174
Basie, Count, 86, 242; mutes, 167; "Splanky," 167
bass, doubling on, 117n93
bass motif, 155
Battle of Swing (Ellington), 153
"BBBB" (Baker), 195
Beard, Jim, 142, 143, 144 145, 146
Beaux Arts Trio, 185, 186
bebop, 75, 82; defined, 141; history of, 82–84; theory, 105–106
bebop mannerisms, 115n20
"Bebop Revisited," 144
bebop scale, 141
bebop style ii–V pattern, 40
Bebop: The Music and the Players, 84
Bell, Oliver, 20
Bellson, Louie, 138, 250, 253

Bennett-Gordon Hall, 112
Benny Carter Orchestra, 8
"Berceuse," 223
Berendt, Joachim, 91
Berg, Alban, 223
Berg Violin Concerto, 189
Berklee School of Music, 30, 54
Bernstein, Leonard, 187
"Better Git It in Your Soul" (Mingus), 152
Beversdorf, Thomas, 18
Beyond Category: The Life and Genius of Duke Ellington (Hasse), 85
"Beyond Category: The Musical Genius of Duke Ellington," 233t, 249
"BG" (Baker), 196
Big Apple Lindy Hoppers, 233t, 245
"Big Band Extravaganza: When Swing Was King," 99–100
Big Band Renaissance, 246
Big Band Treasures, Live, 233t, 248–249
big bands, 121; arrangements, 94; directing, 103; "Honesty," 153; members in SJMO, 252, 274t
Bigard, Barney, 195
Billy Taylor Trio, 250
bi-meter tension, 152
"Birdsong" (Baker), 76, 115n18, 146
Birth of the Cool, 172n32, 201
bitonal, 161, 163; defined, 114n16
bitonal changes in "Birdsong," 115n18
bitonal substitutions, 164–165
Black America: To the Memory of Martin Luther King, 196, 206
"Black Art," 178
The Black Frontier, 194
Black Music Center, 206
Black World, 47
Blagman, Diane, 240
Blakey, Art, 170
Bley, Paul, 33
Bloomington High School North, 194
Blue Note jazz club, 59
"Blue Rondo à la Turk" (Brubeck), 152
blues: American music, 150–151; categorization, 79; origin of jazz, 157; rhythmic exploration, 151–152; styles defined,

115n28, 117n86; twelve-bar structure, 150, 151
"Blues" (Concerto for Tuba and Orchestra), 223–224
"Blues" (Sonata for Clarinet and Piano), 184–185
Blues Alley, 321
blues form, extension of, 151–152, 153, 154, 156
blues music, 37–38
blues progressions, 40
"Blues Waltz" (Roach), 152
"Blues Waltz (née Terrible T)," 178
"Body and Soul," 10
body language, 310
Boghdady, Magdy, 264
Bolduc, Jean, 148, *149*
boogie, 179–180, 185
"Boogie Woogie" (Baker), 186
boogie-woogie bass pattern, 155
Botti, Chris, 144, 146, *147*
Boulanger, Nadia, xiii, 36, 59
boundaries, 289
"Bourne," 163, *165*
Bowden, David, 199
Bowen, Otis, 132
Bowen, Ralph, 144, *146*
Boyd, Bill, 20
Brahms, Johannes, 223
brass ensemble, 153
Brecker, Randy, 21, 23, 316
Bright, George, 5, 13
Britten, Benjamin, 199
Broder, David S., 232t, 242
Brown, Anthony, 278, 286n52
Brown, Russell W., 6, 7, 11, 12, 14n21; choice of cello, 50
Brown, William, 196, 198, 199
Brubeck, Darius, 312
Brubeck, Dave, *129*, *138*, 152
"Buddy and Beyond" (Baker), 195
Buggs, Tillman, 7, 8, 9–10, 12, 178, 317; on Baker writing a book, 55
Burns, George, xiv
Buselli, Mark, 154, 155
Buselli-Wallarab Jazz Orchestra, 154
business side of jazz, 324

Butler University, 17
Butler, George, 298
Butler, Hunt, 142, 143
Byard, Jaki, 231
Byrd, Donald, *138*, 297

"Cahaphi," 144, 168
Cairo Opera House, 261, 264
call-and-response exercises, 70
"Calypso" (*Jazz Suite for Clarinet and Symphony Orchestra: Three Ethnic Dances*), 223
"Calypso" (Suite for Cello and Jazz Trio), 195
Campbell, Gary, 24, 313–314
Campbell, James, 184, 192
Capitol Records, 9
Carmichael, Leonard, 285n19
Carr, Bob (Congressman), 240, 241, 284n11
Carter, Benny, 152, 309; orchestration devices, 166
Carter, Chuck, 50
Carter, Warrick, 300
cell phones, 225–226
cello, new instrument, 50
Chamber Music America, 297
chamber works: four or more performers, 192–194; with jazz rhythm section, 195–196; larger works, 192–194; small groups, 180–192; two to three performers, 180–192
changes, altered, 79
changes, conventional, 79
Charles, Ray, 9
"China Doll" (Goodman), 196
Chicago Sinfonietta, 225
choral music, 206–211
chord progression, 97, 114n14; "Bourne," 164; challenging, 148; conventional rhythm changes, 115n29
chord sequences, 79, 80
chord substitutions, 115n29
chord superposition, 114n16
chord/scale relationships in improvisation, 31, 33

chords, 33–34, 114n16; V–IV–I chord structure, 37; identification, 69–70; singing, 69; traditional blues, 117n86; unplayable as written, *181*
choruses, and solo breaks, 39
chromaticism, defined, 114n16
Churchman, Ray, 48
civil rights movement, 296
civilizing students, 90
Clarke, Kenny, 59–60, 63, 141
classroom visitations, 102
Clayton, John, 213
Cleveland Chamber Symphony, 224
Clinton, Hillary, *136*
Clinton, President Bill, *136*
cluster chord, 155
Coe, Jimmy, 8, 9, 11
Coker, Jerry, xv, 19, 290, 312; ABCs of jazz education, 55, 57; on Baker's accident, 49; on Baker's appointment at IU, 52; *How to Listen to Jazz*, 92; *Improvising Jazz*, 55
Cole, Nat "King," 9
Coleman, Ornette, 30, *138*, 156, 157, 306
College Music Society (CMS), 232t, 240
college programs, 54
college-educated jazz musicians, 304–305
colleges as feeder systems, 307
"Coltrane," 179
Coltrane, John, 31
"Coltrane Matrix," 75
Coltrane substitutions, 75
Columbus (Indiana) Pro Musica, 198
Columbus Jazz Orchestra, 285n25
Combo Rehearsal Guidelines (Aebersold), 103
combos: directing, 103; instrumentation, 167–168; Jamey Aebersold Summer Jazz Workshops, 106–108; small, 141–142, 143; Steans Institute for Young Artists, 110–112
commercial pressures, 308–309
community, role in jazz, 86
composing, vs. arranging, 150
composition: 96–98, cantata, 51; melodic fragments, 117n84
compound meter, 152

compromises, 297
Concertino for Cellular Phones and Symphony Orchestra, 225–226
Concerto for Alto Saxophone and Symphony Orchestra, 224
Concerto for Cello and Chamber Orchestra, 219
Concerto for Flute, String Quartet, and Jazz Band, 216–217
Concerto for Saxophone and Chamber Orchestra, 225
Concerto for Tuba and Orchestra – The B's, 223–224
Concerto for Two Pianos, Jazz Band, Strings, and Percussion, 220
Concerto for Violin and Jazz Band, 217–219
concerto grosso, 153, 167–168
concertos, 216–224, paired, 227; saxophone concertos, 224–226
Concertpiece for Viola and Orchestra, 221
"Confirmation" (Parker), 74
Congolese Mass, 208
Congressional Black Caucus Foundation, 235t
contrafacts, 74, 97, 114n14; "Back Home Again in Indiana," 144; bebop, 106
contrasting material, use of, 153–154
conventions, on bandstand, 310
"Convergence," 215
Conyers, John, Jr. (Congressman), 235t, 240, 241, 297, 298, 299
Cook Music Library, 194
Copland, Aaron, 187, 193
Corea, Chick, *138*
corporate angels, 299
Cotton Club, 2, 10
"Cotton Club Revue," 233t, 251
Count Basie Band, 307; use of mutes, 167
courses, sequencing, 87
Craig, Charlie, 213
Crawford, Shirley (sister), 4, 21, 132
creative energy, 311–312
creativity vs. technical skills, 309–310
credibility, 81
"Crepuscule," 215
"Crescent," 215

Crew, Spencer, 245
Crispus Attucks High School, 5–8, 11, 12; opening of, 3; reunion, *133*
Cronin, Keith, 142, 143
Crouch, Stanley, 298
Csikszentmihalyi, Mihaly, 311
Cultural Olympiad, 233t, 250
Cunliffe, Bill, 308
curriculum, 62
Czech National Symphony Orchestra, 199, 212, 219, 225

daily learning, 78
Dale, Fred, 19
Dameron, Tadd, 144, 161
Dance/USA, 297
"Dance" (Baker), 185
"Dance in Congo Square" (Baker), 186
"Dance of the Jitterbugs," 154–158, *155*, 171
Dancing Shadows, 134
dancing, 18, 245
Dankworth, John, *138*
"David Baker Bebop," 141
David Baker Sextet, *149*
David Baker's 21st Century Bebop Band, 143
Davis, Jim, *132*
Davis, Miles, 31, 156, 172n32, 195, 201
Davis, Nathan, 46–47, 58–63, 112
Davis, Ursula, 60
day jobs, 308–309
Daybreak Express (Ellington), 233t, 238
"Death Is Riding," 205
DeFranco, Buddy, *138*, 195
"Deliver My Soul," 196, 198
Delony, Willis, 179
DeMichael, Don, 50
descending melodic passages, 168
developmental techniques, 116n62
"The Devil's Song" (Stravinsky), 193
Dial Records, 9
diatonic melodies, 164
"Didn't My Lord Deliver Daniel," 205
Dies Irae, 216
Diggory, Terrence, 199
digital patterns, *40*
DiLiddo, Michael, 148, *149*

diminished scale, 165–166, 168, 169
diplomacy, 312
discipline, 317
Dobbins, Bill, 307
dodecaphonic, 175
Dolphy, Eric, 31, 153
"doodle-tonguing," 41
Dorian minor scale, 23
"Double Dance" (Baker), 180
"double Q" school notebooks, 10
doubles (instruments), 98, 117n93
DownBeat Magazine: article on jazz cur-
    riculum, 53; Established Talent award,
    50; "Guide to College Jazz Programs
    1965–1969," 47; Hall of Fame in Jazz
    Education, 174; "Jazz on the Nile: The
    Smithsonian Takes the Nation's Jazz
    Band to Egypt," 235t; Lifetime Achieve-
    ment Award, 173–174; New Star award,
    17, 34–36, 49–50, 173
dramatic devices, 116n61
dress code, Musical Arts Center students,
    117n96
Drexler, Michael, 225
D'Rivera, Paquito, 138
drop-the-needle identification, 231
"Duke Ellington: A Retrospective," 240
Duke Ellington Collection, 232t, 239, 240,
    284n4, 285n32
Dunbar, Paul Laurence, 178–179, 201, 202
"dump truck method," 30–31
Dutton, Denny, 12, 17
Dyas, JB, 148, 149

Eastman School of Music, 307
"Easy Gwyn," 9
eclecticism, 174, 175, 177
Egypt, 235t, 261–265; tour documentary,
    286n48
Einhorn, Lawrence, 132
Elaine, Karen, 221
Eldridge Morrison Big Band, 11
Ellington Collection, 232t, 239, 240,
    284n4, 285n32
Ellington, Duke, 225, 313; Battle of Swing,
    153; course on, 84–86; hundredth birth-
    day, 233t, 250; Jazz Masterworks Edi-

tions, 235; mutes, 167; National Council
    on the Arts, 293; orchestration devices,
    166; Sacred Concerts, 233t, 250, 251;
    SJMO performances of, 242; on stagna-
    tion, 289; Symphony in Black, 284n10;
    transcriptions of, 248; urtexts, 235
Ellington, Mercedes, 285n34
Ellingtones: A Fantasy for Saxophone and
    Orchestra, 225
Ellis, Don, 153
embouchure, 41, 48
endings, 310
energy, creative, 311–312
Enright, Ed, 154
ensembles, top combo, 106–108
Episcopal Mass for the Feast Days of Bishop
    Absalom Jones, 208–210
Essential Jazz Editions, 234t
ethnic jazz, 116n53
Eubanks, Ray, 285n25
Evans, Bill, 33, 117n71, 156
Evans, Gil, 166, 172n32
Evans, Mari, 3, 13, 197, 198
"Evening Song," 178
"An Evening Thought," 144, 171
experiential opportunities, value of, 323
Ezz-thetics, 49, 151

fake cluster (black keys), 192
Fantasy, 194
Fantasy on Themes from Masque of the Red
    Death Ballet, 216
Fender Rhodes keyboard, 213
Ferguson, Maynard, group, 24
Fields, Dorothy, 51
"52nd Street" (Baker), 190–191
First Step, 148–149
firsts, list of, 116n65
Fischer, Clare, 308
Fischer, Lou, 319
Fischer, Nancy, 278
"5M Calypso," 146, 158–160, 169, 171
Five Short Pieces, 177–178
Five Spot, 34
Florida Memorial University, 62
flow, state of, 311
flugelhorns, doubling on, 117n93

focus, lack of, 298
follow the leader, 80
"Follow the Leader," 214
Folk-Ethnic panel of NEA, 290–291
"Forever," 203
form, 158–160; post facto, 177
Foster, Frank, *138*, 253
Four Lives in the Bebop Business (Spell-man), 291
four-bar turnaround, 154
1444 North Pennsylvania Avenue (India-napolis Jazz Club series), 24
Francis Parker Elementary School, 4–5
Fred Dale band, 48, 49
freedom, 153–154, 161–163, 164; *Alabama Landscape*, 199; modal jazz, 156
Freeman, Paul, 199, 212, 214, 216, 225
Freese, Faythe, 185
French Lick Jazz Festival, *121*
"French Six" neoclassicism, 193
fretting, 42; string players, 109, 118n119
Fuller, Curtis, *138*

Gaber, George, *183*, 184
Gardner, DeVonne, 250
George, Luvenia, 234t
George Russell Sextet, 32, 33–36, 49, 50, 143; original blues, 151
Gershwin, George, 187, 220
"ghost" bands, 244
GI Bill, 21
Giddins, Gary, 285n26, 298
Gilbert, Herschel Burke, 143
Gillespie, Dizzy, 9, *140*, 141, 146, 310–311; trumpet to Smithsonian, 231, 232t, 235
Gillespie, Luke, 144, 148, 315; on American Jazz Masters Award, 56–58
Gingold, Josef, 217–218, *218*
Gioia, Dana, 313
"Gloria," 209
The Golden Striker, 142
Golson, Benny, *138*
Goodman, Benny, 196
Google, 95
Gordon, Dexter, 224, 225
Gordon, Edwin, 139
Gordon, Michael, 198

gospel music, 37–38
grades, performance and, 81, 82–83, 100
"Grande March" (Baker), 193
Great Depression, 5, 11
Green, Bunky, 300
Green, Dottie, 249
Greenlee, Sam, 296–297
griots, 289
Grofsorean, Michael, 301n6
"Groovin' for Diz," 146
"Groovin' High" (Gillespie), 9, 106
The Growth Single Seed, 210–211
"Guadeloupe calypso," 213
guitar, substituted for drums, 117n70
Gullion, Tom, 146, 148

Haerle, Dan, 213, 307
"Half Nelson" (Davis), 106, 195
Hall of Fame in Jazz Education, 174
Hamilton, Chico, *138*
Hammer, David, 148, *149*
Hampton, Deacon, 10
Hampton, Locksley "Slide," 10, 17, 36, 50
Hampton, Maceo, 11
Hampton, Slide, 146
Hampton Band, 11, 24
Hampton Institute, 4
Hancock, Herbie, 296
Handy, Antoinette, 291, 293, 297
Handy, W. C., 6
Hanks, Nancy, 290
Hanna, Roland, 231
Harbison, Pat, 139–140, 142–143, *143*, 144, 304
Hardiman, David, Links Tribute to Indiana African-American Jazz Artists, *131*
The Harlem Pipes, 144, 146
"The Harlem Pipes," 146
"Harlem, Saturday Night" (Baker), 188–189
harmonic rhythm, 79
harmonic style, summarized, 175
harmonization, diminished scale, *169*
harmony, 160–166; parallel, 169
Harris, Barry, *138*
Harris, Roy, 187
Hasse, John, 85, 115n44, 234t

Heath, Jimmy, *138*
Hefti, Neal, 167
Hegazy, Ibrahim, 261, 263
Hellmer, Jeff, 308
Hemphill, Julius, 21
Henderson, Fletcher, 166, 235
Henderson, Joe, 59
Hendricks, Cedric, 235t, 240
Hendricks, Jon, *138*
Henri's, 2
Hensley, Tom, *122*
Heritage: A Tribute to Great Clarinetists, 195–196
Herman, Woody, 307
Herzig, Monika, 308
Hesburgh, Theodore, *132*
Hibbert, Mr., 11
Hill, Willie, 234t
Hinderas, Natalie, 178
Hines, Carl, 198, 206
Hinton, Milt, 33
Histoire du soldat (Stravinsky), 192–193
historical context, 323
historical presence, 313–314
history, 81–90; bebop era, 82–84; Duke Ellington, 84–86; general history, 86–90
Hodeir, André, 59
Hodges, Johnny, 240
Hoffman, Ernst, 18, 20
Hoffman, Everett, *122*
Hollywood, not a temptation, xiii
Homage à l'Histoire, 192–193
"Honesty," 151, 153–154
honors, 173–174
Horne, Lena, 233t, 248
Hornibrook, Wallace, 220
Horowitz, Harold, 292, 298, *299*
"Hosanna," 210
"Hot House" (Dameron), 144, 161–162; original, *163*; reharmonization, *162*
Houston, Jim, 20
How to Learn Tunes (Baker), 97
How to Listen to Jazz (Coker), 92
How to Play Bebop, 105, 141
Hubbard, Freddie, *138*
Hudgins, Shannon, 240, 307

Hudson, Gene, 20
Hughes, Langston, 202, 206
humor, 89, 106, 226
Hunt, Joe, 32, 33
Hurst, Bob, 144, 146
Hyman, Dick, 253

"I Got Rhythm" (Gershwin), 106, 220; chord progression, 114n14, 115n29
IAJE. *See* International Association for Jazz Education
"If There Be Sorrow," 197
illegal music downloads, 322
Images of Childhood, 213–214
imagination, 97–98
Imagine: Indiana in Music and Words, xvi
imitation, 94, 97, 98; historical strategy, 139; private lessons, 113
implied half-time duple meter, 152
improvisation, 33–34, 38–40; chord/scale relationships in, 31, 33; classes, 55; "Dance of the Jitterbugs," 155; "Honesty," 153; teaching, 72–77, 102; three levels of, 67–68
Improvising Jazz (Coker), 55
"Incantation" (Baker), 185, 186
independence, 95, 101, 315
Indiana Living Legends Award, *132*
"Indiana Renaissance" (article in *Jazz Review*), 26
Indiana University, 18, 20, 21; Jacobs School of Music, 36, 52, *125*; Jazz Department, job placement, 306–307; Jazz Ensemble, 232t; Distinguished Professor of Music, 174
Indianapolis Jazz Club, 24
Indianapolis Philharmonic, 18
Indianapolis School Board, 3
Indianapolis Symphony Orchestra, 19, *134*
individual artist grants (NEA), 295–296
individuality, 315–316
institutions, 320–321
instrument choice, 172n32
instruments: doubling on, 117n93; learning new, 174
"Integrating Ellington into the College Music Curriculum," 240

integration, in jazz scene, 19
International Association for Jazz Education (IAJE), 56, *149*, 232t, 300–301, 312, 319–320; David Baker Sextet, 149; 21st Century Bebop Band, 149
International Association of Jazz Educators, 300
interracial marriage, 21
interval recognition, 68–69
interval singing, 68–69
intervals: in "Follow the leader," 80; and tune organization, 79
Israels, Chuck, 32, 284n10
"I.U. Swing Machine," *166*, 171
Ives, Charles, 187

Jacobs School of Music, 36
Jacquet, Illinois, 246
jam sessions, xiii, 9, 25, 146; learning cello, 50; on train, 35, 36
"Jamaican Jam" (Baker), 190
Jamal, Ahmad, *138*
James Smithson Founder's Medal, 283
Jamey Aebersold Play-Along Series, 118n108
Jamey Aebersold Summer Jazz Workshops, xv, 32, 55–56, 66, 104–110; David Baker Sextet, 149; strings master class, 108–110; top combo, 106–108; 21st Century Bebop Band, 149
Jarreau, Al, *138*
Jarrett, Keith, 117n71
The Jay Arnold Swing Method, 8, 11
Jay Jay Johnson and the Beboppers, 8
jazz: acceptance of, 47; business of, 324; as fine art form, 293–295, 296; input from other continents, 300; living art form, 304–305; opinions on teaching, 308; origins, 157, 312; styles defined, 116n53
"Jazz – A Reflection of Democracy" (speech), *136*
Jazz Appreciation Month (JAM), 234t, 282–283
Jazz Arts Group, 285n25
Jazz at Lincoln Center Orchestra, 234t, 239, 285n27
jazz audience survey, 292, 298

The Jazz Book (Berendt), 91
jazz camps, Lenox School as prototype, 32
jazz curriculum, 53
Jazz Dance Suite, 179–180
Jazz Education Network, 300; keynote address, 319–324
jazz ensemble, 98–100, 102, 103
Jazz Gallery, 34
jazz history, 81–90; bebop era, 82–84; Duke Ellington, 84–86; general history, 86–90
Jazz Improvisation (Baker), 40, 55, 75
Jazz in Our Time Celebration (Kennedy Center), *138*
Jazz in the Space Age, 33
Jazz In ¾ Time, 152
jazz Mass, 208–210
Jazz Masters in the Schools, 321
Jazz Masterworks Editions (JME), 233t, 235–238, 241
"Jazz on the Nile," 235t
Jazz Oral History Project (Smithsonian Institution), 54, 233t–235t, 276–279, 286n52
Jazz Pedagogy (Baker), 103
jazz pedagogy course, 101–104
Jazz Smithsonian radio series, 233t, 248
jazz standards, 79
jazz styles, 88, 296
Jazz Suite for Clarinet and Symphony Orchestra: Three Ethnic Dances, 221–223
Jazz Suite for Violin and Piano, 187–191, 195
Jazz: The Smithsonian Anthology, 234t–235t, 280, 282
jazz theory, 71, 72–73; arranging, 93, 94
Jazz Times: Annual Jazz Education Guide, 54; conventions, 301
The Jazz Workshop, 33
JazzEd, 320, 322
"Jeanne Marie at the Picture Show," 144
Jenkins, Willard, 302n8
"Jitterbug," 222
"The Jitterbug Boogie" (Baker), 179–180
"Jitterbug Waltz" (Waller), 152
John D. Harza Building, 112
John Gingrich Management, 233t
Johnnie & Jazz festival billboard, *128*

Johnson, Alonzo "Pookie," 7, 8, 51; Links Tribute to Indiana African-American Jazz Artists, *131*

Johnson, David Brent, xviii

Johnson, Dick, 52

Johnson, J. J., 8, 9, 11, 233t, 277, 278–279; *DownBeat Magazine* Established Talent award, 50; influence of, 41; Links Tribute to Indiana African-American Jazz Artists, *131*; play-along albums, 55

Johnson, Osie, 33

Johnson, Sonny, 8, 26

Johnson Foundation, 297

Jones, Elvin, 50

Jones, Eugenia Marie, 21

Jones, Quincy, 36, 322; on American music, 292; conducting SJMO, 253; mutes, 167; Quincy Jones Musiq Consortium, xiv; Smithsonian Jazz Oral History Program, 235t, 278

Jones, Roger, 9

Jones, Thad, 167

Jones, Virgil, Links Tribute to Indiana African-American Jazz Artists, *131*

Jordan, James, 297

Jordan, Louis, 195

Joyce, Mike, 244

Joyner, John, *123*

"Jubilee" (Baker), 186–187, 192

"Jumpin' at the Woodside," 8

"Kaleidoscope," 206

Karr, Gary, 205

Kay, David, *143*, 144

"Keep on Steppin', Brothers," 212

Keepnews, Orrin, 25–26

Kennedy, Roger, 235, 238, 240, 241

Kennedy Center for the Performing Arts, 174

Kenton, Stan, 166, 300

"Kentucky Oysters," 36–39, *37, 39, 40, 42–43,* 151–153

Kienle, Peter, xv

Kiger, Al, 27, 32, 33, 50

Kimery, Ken, 233t, 234t, 239, 249, 253, 286n52, 313; on Baker's communication skills, 265; director of Oral History

Program, 278; sole manager of SJMO, 261

Kind of Blue (Davis), 31

King, Martin Luther, Jr., 196, 206, 296; on facts, 84; song cycle, 196

Kirk, Clara Reese, 4–5

Kirk, Willis, 50, 51

Knight, Bobby, 146

Konitz, Lee, 224

Kosbro – A Piece for Orchestra, 212, 222

Krapf, Norbert, xvi

Krivd, Ernie, 224

Ku Klux Klan, 3, 6

"Kyrie," 209

"Lady Bird" (Dameron), 163, *165*

Lahm, David, 50, 51

Laine, Cleo, *138*

Lake Hamilton Resort, 48, 49

Lane, Russell, 5–6

language, bebop, 106; contemporary, 75–76; loss of, 51; similarity to improvisation, 73, 75

LaRue's Supper Club, 12, 16–17, 18

Lasocki, David, 317

Latzky, Scott, 148

Laurel Records, 143

Laurel releases, 171n10

Laut, Ed, 195

Lawson, Janet, 51, 316

laziness, 97

"Lazy Summer Days," 214

Le chat qui pêche, 212–213

"Le miroir noir," 213

leadership and life lessons, 282–283

"Leadership Lessons from the Jazz Masters," 283

learning through immersion, 30–31

LeClaire, Shannon Hudgins, 240, 307

Ledvina, Charles, 148

Legrand, Michel, *138*

Lenox School of Jazz, 26–27, 27–32, 51; faculty, 28–29

"Lerma Samba," 144

Lewis, John, 27, 30, 142

Library of Congress, 234t, 239, 322

licks, 42; bebop, 115n20

Liebman, David, 135
Life Cycles, 199–201
Lila Wallace – Reader's Digest Fund, 232t, 248, 285n33, 299
"Lima Beba Samba," 144
Lincoln Center Jazz Orchestra, 285n27
Lincoln University, 20–21, 320
"Lindy Hop" (Baker), 193
Links Tribute to Indiana African-American Jazz Artists, 131
Lipman, Samuel, 294–295
listening, to music, 322–323
listening quizzes, 81, 84, 89
listening to people, 297
"Little Parade March" (Baker), 193
"Little Song" (Baker), 193
liturgical jazz, 116n53
Live at MCG, 235t
live performance, 243
Living Jazz Legends, 138, 174
"L'odeur du blues," 213
"Loneliness" (Baker), 185
"Lorob," 144
loss of language, 51
Louis Armstrong Education Kit, 234t, 280
Louisville Orchestra, 212
loyalty, 86
"Lullaby of the Leaves," 12, 17
Lundvall, Bruce, 297
Lydian Chromatic Concept, 31–32, 33–34, 48
Lydian Chromatic Concept of Tonal Organization and Improvisation (Russell), 141
Lydian hybrid scale, 182
Lyons, Jimmy, 298
Lyric Record Shop, 9

Madame Walker Theatre, 2
Mahogany, Kevin, 250
major scales, 31
"The Man I Love," 8
Manchester Craftmen's Guild, 235t
Manning, Frankie, 233t, 245
Mapplethorpe, Robert, 295
marriage, interracial, 21
Marrow, Queen Esther, 250

Marsalis, Wynton, 138, 239, 246
"Martyrs: Malcolm, Medgar, Martin," 206
Mason, Jack, 20
Masque of the Red Death Ballet, 216
Mass, 208–210
Masters, Joe, 208
May, Billy, 167
"Maypole," 213–214
McCurdy, Ron, 300
McDonald, Brian, 262
MCG Jazz, 235t
McKay, Claude, 206
McKinley, Dan, 199
McPartland, Marian, 136, 138
McShann, Jay, 8
McShann Band, 8
McWhorter, Charles, 294
"Meditation" (Baker), 195
melodic fragments, 96–97, 117n84
melodic material, 40
memorization, 77–81
Menotti, Gian Carlo, 294
Mercury Records, 36
Merrifield, Norman, 3, 6, 11–12, 317
meters, and tension, 152
metric modulation, 38–39
Metronome Magazine collegiate contest, 19
"Miami Nights," 148
Miami String Quartet, 148
Miami Suite, 148
military bands, 253, 275t, 307, 321
Miller, David, 144
Miller, Norma, 233t, 245
Mingus, Charles, 152
Mingus Ah Um, 152
minor scales, 23, 31
"Minton's" (Baker), 187–188
Minton's Playhouse, 141
Missile Room, 2
modal jazz, 31, 33, 155–156
modal sections, "5M Calypso," 160
modal tunes, 74, 76
modeling, 94, 97, 98, 317; historical strategy, 139; private lessons, 113
Modern Concepts in Jazz Improvisation (Baker), 75

Modern Jazz Septet, 20
Monk, Thelonious, 34, 141
Montgomery, Buddy, 8, 11
Montgomery, Monk, 8, 11
Montgomery, Wes, 2, 8, 11, 24, 25, 26;
    signed with Riverside Records, 25–26
Montgomery-Johnson Quintet, 8
Moody, James, 112, 138, 145, 253, 316–317
Morgan State University Choir, 250, 251
Morgenstern, Dan, 298
Morton-Finney, Dr., 12, 17
Mubarak, Suzanne, 261
Mulligan, Gerry, orchestration devices,
    166
Murray, Pauli, 206
music and dancing, 245
Music Educators National Conference
    (MENC), 234t
Music Inn, 29–30
music minus one recordings, 55
Music of Fats Waller and James P. Johnson,
    284n10
Music of Louis Armstrong, 236t
Music of the 1930s, Part 1, 234t, 236t
Music of the 1930s, Part 2, 234t, 236t
Music of the 1940s, Part 1, 234t, 237t
Music of the 1940s, Part 2, 234t, 237t
Musicians' Union, 20
mutes, 95, 167; straight mutes, 168
"My God, Why Hast Thou Forsaken
    Me?," 198
"My Lord, What a Morning," 205, 207

NAACP. See National Association for the
    Advancement of Colored People
NAJE. See National Association of Jazz
    Educators
Nancy Hanks Center, 290
Nat King Cole Trio, 117n70
Nathan, Davis, 313
National Association for the Advance-
    ment of Colored People (NAACP), 3
National Association of Jazz Educators
    (NAJE), 56, 300
National Association of Negro Musicians,
    18
National Council on the Arts, 292–297

National Endowment for the Arts (NEA),
    290–292, 313, 321; American Jazz Mas-
    ters Award, 56–58, 174; Survey of Public
    Participation in the Arts, 305–306
National Jazz Ensemble, 284n10
National Jazz Service Organization
    (NJSO), 279, 297–299, 302n8
National Museum of American History,
    284n4, 322
National Music Chairman of the Federa-
    tion of Women's Clubs, 47
natural overtone series, 31
NEA. See National Endowment for the
    Artsneglected music, 309
Nelson, Oliver, 309
Nesaule, Agate, 16–17
New England Foundation for the Arts,
    298
New Perspectives on Jazz, 232t, 298
New World School of the Arts Jazz Sextet,
    148
New York Jazz Repertory Company,
    284n10
New York Philharmonic, 224
New York Times, article about teaching of
    jazz, 308
Newsome, LaVerne, 6, 12
Nicholson, Stuart, 304–305
"Night Song," 200
"Night Train," 182–184
Nikisch-Furtwangler school of conduct-
    ing, 20
Nissan, 233t
NJSO. See National Jazz Service
    Organization
Nolcox, Matthius, 5
North Central High School, 112
North Texas State College, 54
nostalgia bands, 167
Notre Dame Jazz Festival, 26, 122
"Now That He Is Safely Dead," 196, 198
NPR Jazz, 234t

Oberlin College, 235
Ohio Chamber Orchestra, 224
Oliver, Sy, 242
Olympic Games, 233t, 250

"On Wings of Song" (Baker), 192
"125th Street," 206
opportunity, value of, 12–13
oral histories, 54, 233t–235t, 276–279, 286n52
oral tradition, 289, 301, 304
orchestra, 212–216
orchestration, 166–171
organization of tunes, 79
"Over the Rainbow," 10, 75, 80
Owen, Jane, 132
Owens, Jimmy, 291
Owens, Tim, 234t, 248

"Padospe," 144
Paige, Satchel, 204
Papich, Mary Jo, 312, 319
parable of the talents, 310
"Parades to Hell," 198
Paris, jazz performers and, 46–47; 58–60
Paris American Academy of Music, 59–60
Parker, Charlie 8, 9, 141, 312
Parker, Paul, 2
passacaglia, 188–189
"Passacaglia," 177
patterns and sequences, 40
Peck, Gregory, 297
pedagogy, 62; active learning, 118n112; analysis, 90–92; approach to, 315–316; arranging, 92–96; commitment to teaching, 312–313; composition, 96–98; course in, 101–104; ear learning, 80; ear training, 67–72; essays, 84, 85, 89; experiential, 94–95; ideal teachers, 53; immersion, 96; improvisation, 72–77, 102; in-class concerts, 77; instructional materials, availability, 321–322; jazz ensemble, 98–100, 102, 103; jazz history, 81–90; jazz styles, 90–92; listening quizzes, 81, 84; private lessons, 112–114, 315, 316; sequencing courses, 87; teaching jazz, 308; tune learning, 77–81; "you can't teach jazz," 60, 101
Pelton, Shawn, 144, 145–146, 315
Pemberton, Roger, 52
Penn, Marshall, 20–21
pentatonics, defined, 114n16

Perantoni, Daniel, 223
performance and grades, 81, 82–83, 100
performance circuit vs. stationary position, 291
performance etiquette, 39, 310
performances practices, 116n63, 323
"Perfume/Perspiration" (Baker), 189–190
Perkinson, Coleridge-Taylor, 309
Phillips, Harvey, 142, 143, 144, 146, 172n32
phrase transcription, 114n6
Piano Concerto in G Major (Ravel), 185
piano, attempts to learn, 50
piano solos, 177–180
Pierce, Billy, 307
"Piss Christ" (Serrano), 295
The Place Where the Rainbow Ends, 201–202
"The Place Where the Rainbow Ends," 202, 203
play-along albums, 55, 81
playback speed, 72, 114n6
Plummer, Paul, 50
Plymouth Music Society, 205
Poe, Edgar Allen, 216
Polin, Roscoe, 18
polyrhythm, 38–39
Porter, Cole, 161
post-bop, 75–76, 82
Potts, Noble, 250
practice privileges, 20, 320
practice sessions, 318
practice time, 50, 63n7
pre-bebop, 82
Pressler, Menahem, 185
professional touring ensembles, 307
profile in creativity, 311
Program for Jazz for the Steans Institute for Young Artists, 110–112, 118n126, 118n127
Program in African American Culture, 231
Public School 26 (Indianapolis), 5
pyramids, 168–169
Pyramids, 262, 263

quartal playing, 114n16
Quincy Jones Big Band, 35, 36

Quincy Jones Musiq Consortium, xiv
quotas, 296
quotes, 115n20, 318

racism: in hiring, 52; interracial mar-
    riage, 21; and NEA grants, 296. *See also*
    segregation
"Ragtime" (Stravinsky), 193
Randy's Record Shop, 9
Ravel, Maurice, 185
Ravinia Festival, 110
Reagan, Bernice Johnson, 231
"Recreating Ellington's Masterworks"
    240
Red Death, 216
reel-to-reel tape, 114n6
Reeve, Al, 51
Reeves, Dianne, 250
Refractions, 214–215
Regula, Ralph (Congressman), 241
reharmonization, 76, 162
Reid, Rufus, 112
repertoire, for improvisation, 73, 76; for
    teaching, 103; top combo, 106–108;
    tune learning, 77–81
Requiem Mass, 216
respect, 313
"Rêve," 177
Rhyne, Melvin, 2, 26; Links Tribute to
    Indiana African-American Jazz Art-
    ists, 131
rhythm changes, altered vs. convention-
    al, 79, 115n29
rhythm 'n' blues, 116n48
Rhythm Rockets, 8
rhythm section, 108; arrangements, 93;
    chamber works, 195–196
Ridley, Larry, 26, 27, 297, 312; on Ornette
    Coleman, 30; Links Tribute to Indiana
    African-American Jazz Artists, 131
riff blues, 79, 115n28, 117n86
ritornello, 153, 168
Riverside Records, 25–26
Roach, Max, 152
"Robert Mapplethorpe: The Perfect Mo-
    ment," 295
Rockefeller Foundation, 238

rock 'n' roll, birth of, 30
"Roly Poly," harmonization, 169
rondo, 215
root scale, 31
roots, 151, 227
Roots II (for violin, cello, and piano),
    185–187, 205
ROTC (Reserve Officer Training Corps)
    marching band, 7
Roy, Richard, 59–60
R.S.V.P., 144
"R.S.V.P. Mr. Moody," 144
Rugulo, Pete, orchestration devices, 166
Russell, George, 138, 291, 319; George
    Russell Sextet, 32, 33–36, 143; Lydian
    Chromatic Concept, 31–32, 33–34, 141;
    on Ornette Coleman, 30
Russo, William, 30–31, 166
Rutgers University jazz archives, 322

Sacred Concerts (Ellington), 233t, 250, 251
"St. Louis Blues" (Handy), 6
"Saints and Hermits," 201
Salman, Randy, 313, 315–316
"Samba" (Baker), 193
"Sanctus/Benedictus," 209–210
Sandke, Randy, 253
Saturday night music, 292
saxophone concertos, 224–226
saxophones, doubling, 117n93; "Roly Poly"
    harmonization, 169
scales, bebop, 141; blues scale, 37; dimin-
    ished, 165–166; F-major, 39, 40; major,
    31; minor, 23, 31; recognition, 69–70;
    symmetrical, 165
Schiedt, Duncan, 134
Schifrin, Lalo, 208
Schoenberg, Arnold, 96
Schola Cantorum, 59
Schuller, Gunther, 26, 233t, 240, 284n10,
    298; on Baker's teaching, 72; conduct-
    ing style, 246; National Council on the
    Arts, 293, 294; Oberlin, 235, 238; Third
    Stream jazz, 116n53, 175
Schuman, William, 187
Scofield, John, 305
Scott, Jimmy, 138

"Screamin' Meemies," xiii, 36, 171
Scriabin, Alexander, 31
"See How They Done My Lord," 207–208
segregation, 2, 3; dancing, 18; hospitals, 49; labor unions, 4; restaurants, 18, 49; symphony, 19. *See also* racism
self-sufficiency, 95, 101, 315
selling out, 60, 313
Sepia Panorama (Ellington), 233t, 238
Serenade (Britten), 199
Serrano, Andrew, 295
service bands, 253, 275t, 307, 321
service organization, 297–299
"set asides," 296
Sevitzky, Fabien, 19
Shaw, Artie, 195
sight-reading, 100
Silbert, Scott, 265, 275
simplicity, 169–170
Singers of Songs, Weavers of Dreams, 183, 184
skiing, xiii
skills, technical, vs. creativity, 309–310
skill mastery, time needed for, 50, 63n7
sleep, 311–312
"Slow Blues" (Baker), 195
"Slow Drag," 222
Smart, Gary, 179
Smith, Howie, 224
Smithsonian Collection of Classic Jazz (Williams), 240, 280, 282, 284n13
Smithsonian Collection of Recordings, 284n10
Smithsonian Folkways Recordings, 234t, 235t
Smithsonian Institute: chronology, 232t–235t
Smithsonian Jazz Masterworks Orchestra (SJMO), 117n92, 134, 169–170, 232t–235t, 241, 247, 252; accomplishments summarized, 276; concert history, 254t–260t, 266t–273t; *Congressional Record, 281;* *Demo Disc,* 233t; differences from other bands, 243–245; members, 251–253, 274t, 275t; pyramids, 263; touring, 249–250; "world tour," 233t

Smithsonian Jazz Oral History Program, 54, 233t–235t, 276–279
Smithsonian Jazz Repertory Ensemble, 284n10
Smithsonian magazine, 233t
Smithsonian, National Museum of American History, 231, 239, 240, 322
Snow, Robert, 47, 60
social commentary, 157
"The Soldier's March" (Stravinsky), 193
"Soleil d'Altamira," 212
Solo Dance, 179
soloists, 38–39
solos, "Bourne," 164
solos: break placement, 39; challenging, 148; complementary, 159; learning, 77; patterns and sequences, 40; piano solos, 177–180; private lessons, 113; solo forms, *159, 160;* transcription, 77, 90, 113; "Warm Valley" (Ellington), 240–241
"Some Links for Brother Ted," 170, 171
"Some Sort of Waltz" (Baker), 179
"Sometimes I Feel Like a Motherless Child," 197, 198
Sonata for Cello and Piano, 180–184
Sonata for Clarinet and Organ, 185
Sonata for Clarinet and Piano, 184–185
Sonata for Piano, 178–179
Sonata for Two Pianos and Percussion (Bartok), 220
sonata, *Kosbro,* 212
"A Song," 202
"A Song – After Paul Lawrence Dunbar," 178–179
"The Song Also Rises" (Baker), 192
song cycles, 196–205
Songs of Living and Dying, 201, 202–204
"Sons voilés," 213
"Sorrow Song" (Baker), 185, 186, 187, 205
soul food, 170
sousaphones, 6
South African musicians, 312
Spellman, A. B., 291, 292, 294, 312–313; National Council on the Arts, 293, 294–295
Spera, Dominic, *125, 130*
Sphinx, 261, 262

"Splanky" (Basie), 167

Spoleto Festival, 294, 301n6

The Spook Who Sat by the Door (Greenlee), 296–297

SRO Artists, 233t

Stack, Robert, 297

stage arrangements, 100

stage left, defined, 117n95

staggered entrances, 168–169

stagnation, 289

Stan Kenton National Stage Band Camps,
24, 32, 300

standards, 79

Starker, Janos, 181, *183*, 184, 214, 219

Starr, S. Frederick, 235, 238

starting tunes, 310

stationary position vs. performance circuit, 291

Steans Institute for Young Artists, 62,
110–112, 118n126, 118n27

Stearns, Marshall, 27

Steppin' Out, 148

Stewart, Lisa, 286n52

Still, William Grant, 187

Stitt, Katea, 286n52

Stockhouse, Janis, 194

"Stompin' at the Smithsonian," 233t, 245

straight mutes, 167, *168*

"Straight No Chaser," 20

The Stratus Seekers, 49

Stratusphunk, 151; "Kentucky Oysters,"
36–39, *37, 39, 40, 42*–43

Stravinsky, Igor, 192–193

Strayhorn, Billy, 85, 238, 248

string players, fretting for, 109, 118n119

strings master class, 108–110

Stripling, Byron, 253

Struttin', 144

students, 23–24

styles, 90–92; principles of, 62

Suite for Cello and Jazz Trio, 195

*Suite from the Masque of the Red Death
Ballet*, 216

Suite Thursday, 234t

summer jazz camps, 55–56

"Sunfest," 148

Sunset Terrace, 2, 8, 10

"Surface," 200

Survey of Public Participation in the Arts,
305–306

Suzuki, Shin'ichi, 139

"Swagger" (Baker), 195

Swallow, Steve, 153

Sykes, Jubilant, 205

"Sympathy," 202

Symphony in Black (Ellington), 284n10

"Take Me Out to the Ball Game," 204

Take the "A" Train (Ellington), 233t, 238

"Tango" (Stravinsky), 193

Tartell, Joey, 262

Taylor, Billy, *138*, 291, 293, 294, 297, 298,
299, 312

teaching. *See* pedagody

technical skills vs. creativity, 309–310

Teller, Betty, 278

"Terrible T," 13

Terry, Clark, *138*, 250, 253; on stagnation,
289

Thelonious Monk Institute of Jazz, 66

thematic development, 34

*Theme and Variations for Woodwind Quin-
tet*, 194

theory: bebop, 105–106; Jamey Aebersold
Summer Jazz Workshops, 105–106;
teaching, 72–73, 76

Third Stream, 116n53; Concerto for Alto
Saxophone and Symphony Orchestra,
224; Concerto for Flute, String Quartet, and Jazz Band, 216–217; concertos,
227; defined, 175; *Jazz Suite for Clarinet
and Symphony Orchestra: Three Ethnic
Dances*, 221–223; *Jazz Suite for Violin
and Piano*, 187–191

thirty-two-bar song form, 158

"This One's for 'Trane," 144

Thomson, Virgil, 187

"Thou Dost Lay Me in the Dust of Death,"
196

Three Choral Pieces in Spiritual Style,
206–208

Through This Vale of Tears, 196–198

through-composed blues, 79, 115n28

time implications, 152

Time Out, 152

Timmons, Bobby, 170

"Tippin'," 148

"To a Dead Friend," 202, 203

"To Bird," 177

"To Dizzy with Love," 171

"To Satch," 204

Tokyo Philharmonic, 225

tonal relationships, 31

tone, 43

tonguing techniques, 41

top combo, Jamey Aebersold Summer
    Jazz Workshops, 106–108

touring ensembles, 307

traditional blues, 117n86

traditional standards, 79

transcription, 71–72, 75, 77; and arrang-
    ing, 93; choices, 117n71; for copyright,
    307; of Ellington's music, 248; private
    lessons, 113; solos, 90; "Trifle," 204

transposed instruments, 191, 200

Traverse City, Michigan, 20

triad singing, 69

*Tribute to a Generation: Salute to the Big
    Bands,* 234t, 249

trio arrangements, and transcriptions, 93,
    117n71

trios, 146, 117n71; transcription of, 117n71

triple-meter tune, 152

"Triumphal March of the Devil" (Stravin-
    sky), 193

trombone, 17; influence of J. J. Johnson,
    41; loss of ability to play, 48–49; tech-
    nique, 41–43

trumpets, doubling on, 117n93; "5M Ca-
    lypso," *169*; staggered entrance, *169*

tubas, 5, 6

tune detectors, 307

tune learning, 77–81

tunes: categorization, 79, 116n60; diffi-
    culty of, 73–74, 76, 115n17; starting and
    ending, 310

Turf Bar, 8

turnaround, altered four-bar, *155*

turnaround, four-bar, 154

twelve keys, work in, 40

twelve-bar structure, 150, 151

twelve-tone technique, 96

"25th and Martindale," 13

21st Century Bebop Band, *143*, 317; first
    incarnation, 142; frequent rotation of
    players, 144; influence on orchestra-
    tion, 167–168; instrument choice,
    172n32

University of Miami, 52

University of Natal, 312

University of North Texas, 52, 54, 307

University of Pittsburgh, 46–47, 60–61;
    Seminar on Jazz, 62

Upper, Andrew Mayne, 196

urtext, 235, 285n32

U.S. Census Bureau, jazz audience survey,
    292, 298

Vandermeer, Aaron, 226

"Variations and Passacaglia" (Baker), 192

venues, 142, 306, 307–308

Venzago, Mario, *134*

versatility, 307–308

vibrato, 109–110

Vinnegar, Leroy, 11

vision without action, 298, 324

vocabulary, bebop, 106

voice, 157

voicing techniques: three part; 93–94;
    two-part, 93

Walker, C. J., 2

Wallarab, Brent, 174, 242; on trombone
    technique, 41–42

Waller, Fats, 152

Walsh, Tom, 155, 224, 304; on the "dump
    truck method," 31

"Waltz" (Baker), 193

"Waltz" (Stravinsky), 193

"Waltzing the Blues" (Carter), 152

"Warm Valley" (Ellington), 240–241

Warner Brothers Publications, 234t, 239

Warren, Stanley, 206

Washburn, Dick, *122*

Washington National Cathedral, 233t,
    250, *251*

Watrous, Peter, 241–242

Watson, Matt, 286n52
"We Has a Hard Time," 204–205
"We Wear the Mask," 202
Weather Report, 213
Weaver, James, 245
Webb, Charles, 220, 242
Webb-Hornibrook Duo, 220
Webster, Ben, 4
Wein, George, 284n10
Weiss, Michael, 144
Wes Montgomery Trio, 2
Wess, Frank, *138*, 250
WFIU, xviii, 217
"What Is This Thing Called Love?" (Porter), 161
"What It Means When Spring Comes," 200–201
"When I'm Dead," 208
White House, *136*, 323
White House Jazz Festival, 233t, 246
Whitmore, Chester, *252*
WIBC, 9
Wilber, Bob, 284n10
Wilder, Joe, *134*
Wilkins, Jack, 144
Williams, James, 253
Williams, Martin, 232t, 238, 240, 298; *Smithsonian Collection of Classic Jazz,* 284n13

Wilson, Gerald, *138*
Wilson, Nancy, *138*
Wilson, Olly, 298
Wilson, Steve, 242
Wingspread Conference Center, 232t, 297–299
"Without Benefit of Declaration," 204
Witness – Six Original Compositions in Spiritual Style, 204–205
Woman in Amber (Nesaule), 17
Woods, Phil, *138*
Woodwind Quintet No. 1, 194
Woody Herman Band, 307
"The Wretched of the Earth (Machinations, Missionaries, Money, Marines)," 206
WTIU, *123*

Yardley, Jonathan, 249
Yates, Sidney (Congressman), 241
Yianilos, Peter, 148
YMCA band, 9
Young, David, 20, 26, 32, 33; Links Tribute to Indiana African-American Jazz Artists, *131*

Zale, Toni, 20
Zale, Tony, 20
Zimmerman, James, 234t, 249, 261

MONIKA HERZIG holds a doctorate in music education from Indiana University, where she teaches as a member of the Arts Administration faculty. As a recording artist for Owl Studios and touring jazz pianist, she has performed at many prestigious jazz clubs and festivals worldwide. Groups under her leadership have toured Europe and Japan, and opened for acts such as Tower of Power, Sting, the Dixie Dregs, Yes, and more. Her music has received awards from *DownBeat Magazine,* ASCAP, and *Billboard.*

This book was designed by Jamison Cockerham and set in type by Tony Brewer at Indiana University Press, and printed by Sheridan Books, Inc.

The typefaces are Arno, designed by Robert Slimbach in 2007, Clarendon, designed by Robert Besley in 1845, and Avenir, designed by Adrian Frutiger in 1988. All were issued by Adobe Systems.